LANGUAGES OF THE
WEST INDIES

❖

JOHNS HOPKINS STUDIES

IN ATLANTIC HISTORY AND CULTURE

General Editors

RICHARD PRICE   FRANKLIN W. KNIGHT

LANGUAGES
OF THE WEST
INDIES

❀

DOUGLAS
TAYLOR

❀

THE
JOHNS HOPKINS UNIVERSITY PRESS
BALTIMORE AND LONDON

The Johns Hopkins University Press,
Baltimore, Maryland 21218
The Johns Hopkins Press Ltd., London

Library of Congress Catalog Card Number 76-47382
ISBN 0-8018-1729-3
Library of Congress Cataloging in Publication data will be
found on the last printed page of this book.

TO MARTINE AND JACQUES
IN TOKEN OF GRATITUDE FOR THEIR HELP
AND ENCOURAGEMENT

CONTENTS

�✥

TABLES

❖

FOREWORD

❖

THE CARIBBEAN REGION, within which the languages Douglas Taylor treats in this book took on their present forms, was the first part of the Western Hemisphere to fall under the European yoke. An archipelago of more than fifty inhabited islands today—and scores more if one includes the Bahamas and numerous outliers—the Caribbean region is now usually defined so as to comprise substantial coastal portions of the surrounding mainland as well.[1]

The pre-Columbian peoples of this vast area were culturally and linguistically very diverse. By the close of the fifteenth century, when the Europeans first "discovered" the New World, these populations represented very ancient, indigenous demographic spread and cultural differentiation. The New World, so called, had been populated by migrants from Asia for perhaps thirty millennia, their descendants expanding throughout the hemisphere. Still, those Amerindian pioneers who moved out of South America to populate successively Caribbean islands began to do so no earlier than about 5000 B.C., and probably reached the Greater Antilles— the termini of these northward movements—no earlier than about 2000 B.C. (Rouse 1964). During the final phases of such movement from the South American mainland through the islands, apparently only a few centuries before Columbus, Karina (Cariban) speakers conquered their Arawakan-speaking and culturally different predecessors and, in the process, acquired the language of their defeated enemies in modified form. In that part of his study dealing with the so-called Island-Carib (Igneri)

[1] There is, of course, no unanimity on the limits of the Caribbean region, since such boundary-drawing properly depends on different geographical, political, sociological, and other viewpoints, and on the problem under review. For some variety of perspectives, see Cahnman 1943, Wagley 1960, Augelli 1962, Smith 1965, Mintz 1966 and 1974, and Lowenthal 1972.

inhabitants of the Lesser Antilles,[2] the author must take all this into account.

The advent of the Europeans was followed by that of enslaved Africans, whose descendants were soon to become demographically dominant in many islands (and numerically significant in all of them), as well as along the rimland of *tierra firme*, from northeast Brazil to Atlantic coastal Mexico, and the southern region of what was to become the United States. The diffusion of peoples, languages, and cultures of substantially African origin has made the Caribbean region a major component of Afro-America, and many of the languages now spoken here reveal richly one aspect of the immense contribution African civilizations have made to the contemporary New World.

The subject that Douglas Taylor addresses in the present book is highly complex, in terms of the span of time with which he must deal, the range of cultures to which he must refer, and the vast geographical spread within which his analyses apply. The Caribbean region was not only the first part of the New World "discovered" by Columbus but also the first within which long-term European interest and intent would be demonstrated. Within four decades of Columbus's first sighting on Guanahaní (San Salvador) in the Bahamas (Morison and Obregón 1964), the entire Caribbean insular area had been circumnavigated, its component islands renamed, and its indigenous populations identified (and, in the Greater Antilles, substantially conquered). Before too long, Caribbean wealth—at first, mainly in the form of gold—had begun to flow into Spanish coffers. The Arawakan peoples of the Greater Antilles were subjected to the ravages of conquest, enslavement and disease. Their cultures were put under enormous pressures and began to lose their character as parts of coherent, functioning social systems. The flow of European migrants and forced laborers, and of African slaves, to the region, which had begun as a mere trickle, soon swelled into a flood. In the Lesser Antilles, however, the impact of European power was slowed to some extent, both because of the lesser availability of mineral wealth and because of the spirited and highly mobile military resistance of the Island-Carib inhabitants against the Europeans.

This contrast in post-Columbian historical experience between the

---

[2] Taylor would prefer to refer to the Native American occupants of the Lesser Antilles at the time of the Discovery as "Ygneri" or "Iñeri," but this name (which we have written here as Igneri) has been preempted by archeological usage. The term "Island-Carib" is somewhat confusing, only in part because these people had already become Arawakan-speaking before Columbus. The so-called Black Carib of St. Vincent, who were deported to Central America by the English at the close of the eighteenth century, spoke then (and still speak) the Arawakan dialect current among the so-called Yellow and Black Carib in St. Vincent at the time, which differed somewhat from that spoken by the Island-Carib in Dominica.

greater and lesser islands persisted for more than a century after the Discovery. Still, certain general historical processes gradually came to typify the region as a whole: imperial conquest and international conflict over territories and spoils; the establishment of European colonial settlements; the creation of a large-scale plantation system to implement the economic, social, and political objectives of the European entrepreneurs, and the development of agricultural commodity production aimed at satisfying expanding European consumer markets; the institutionalization of a labor system based on slavery and forced labor, mainly of Africans, firmly tied to the plantation economy; and the gradual emergence of much-modified local cultures, drawing their character from the Amerindian, European, and African pasts of those who populated the islands under these new conditions. The original cultural complexity and diversity of the Caribbean region before the coming of the Europeans, then, was transfigured by five centuries of rapid—and often catastrophic—change, during which the aboriginal cultures were extirpated or vastly modified; the character of the local populations was radically altered; European colonial economies and forms of government were imposed; and new cultures, synthesized from a complex set of different pasts, took shape.

The linguistic phenomena that took shape under these conditions were at least as complicated as those marking the social, economic, political, and other institutional changes in Caribbean life. Out of this complexity, the author has chosen two principal subjects or problems with which to deal substantively and at length.

First, he concentrates on the language of the Island-Carib inhabitants of the Lesser Antilles—who were present at the time the European conquerors arrived—and provides the fullest account ever given of their linguistic situation and of the history of their language.

Second, he turns to the so-called creole languages of the region, languages commonly associated with the enslaved Africans whose descendants now make up the majority of the Caribbean population. Today, as Taylor demonstrates, these languages vie with standard dialects of European tongues in much of the Caribbean. In Haiti alone, probably more than five million persons speak a creole as their first language today.[3]

By choosing these two important and radically contrastive dimensions of Caribbean language for description and analysis, Taylor provides the reader with a broad, yet remarkably particular, overview of the phenomena

[3] Hancock (1971) provides a world map of pidgin and creole languages. Stewart, omitting those lexically English-based languages in the anglophone West Indies (e.g., Jamaica and Guyana), estimated 4,778,000 creole speakers in the Caribbean region more than a decade ago (Stewart 1962). If present population figures and estimates are used, and if all lexically English-based languages were included, the figure today would easily be double that.

of language and language change. Creole languages are spoken by millions of contemporary speakers; but the language of the Island-Carib has disappeared from the insular Caribbean. Thus, the idiom which once provided all of the inhabitants of the lesser islands with their principal medium of communication has now been utterly supplanted. The principal languages of much of the region today are the outgrowth of lengthy and complex encounters among speakers of many different tongues, who were themselves descended from newcomers whose own native languages were not or are no longer spoken in the region.[4] As Taylor points out in his introductory comments, language, as the primary means of perpetuating culture, profoundly reflects and informs the culture itself. Its presence is a living representation of the way of life of a people; its disappearance or destruction usually signals the replacement of one cultural system by another.

While the processes with which the author deals here are to some extent universal—in that the gradual replacement of one language by another in a speech community, the disappearance of particular languages, the emergence of pidgin languages and their transformation into creole languages, are all processes that may be documented elsewhere[5]—Taylor's treatment reveals the particularity of the Caribbean materials in all of their variegated richness. In the case of Cariban and Arawakan, he is dealing with problems rooted in social contact and in change beginning long before the arrival of the Europeans. Analysis of these problems required both very keen attention to detail and a wide grasp of the nature of linguistic differentiation within the Caribbean region. Indeed, some portion of his analysis rests on the use of comparative materials collected among contemporary Island-Carib speakers outside the islands, whose speech throws useful inferential light on the Island-Carib case.[6] That the Island-Cariban language—Karina, or "True Carib," which was gradually supplanted by an Arawakan language—is documented by the author, who

---

[4] Taylor does not deal with *dialects* of English, French, Spanish, etc., now employed in the Caribbean region, nor with the somewhat unusual cases of persisting non-European languages that are not creoles (e.g., Hindi, Lucumí [Yoruba], etc.) that have survived here and there.

[5] For a useful overview, see Hymes's preface to Hymes 1971.

[6] The Black Carib of Belize (British Honduras), among whom Taylor has worked (e.g., Taylor 1951), are the descendants of deportees transported to the Bay of Honduras in early 1797. Their language is as much Island-Carib as that spoken by the Island-Carib of Dominica and St. Vincent at the time of their deportation, and may be referred to, using Taylor's own terminology, as Central American Island-Carib (CAIC). In much the same way, Taylor points out, Breton is classified as Insular Celtic rather than as Gaulish, because it was brought to France by emigrés from Britain. The Black Carib deportees were St. Vincent islanders, who brought their language with them when they were exiled to the continent, and as Taylor points out, they have not strayed from their new homes on the Atlantic seaboard of Central America.

provides here the clearest and most complete treatment to date of the unusual circumstances under which this replacement must have occurred. The intrinsic interest of this case is enhanced by the fact that the Island-Carib were the conquerors of those whose language they came finally to speak and who did not—so far as can be told—outnumber them, and by the fact that the survival of something of the conquerors' language became linked with the division between men and women.

In the case of the Caribbean creole languages, Taylor sets forth a view that respects the historical and cultural complexity of the region. His years of work on the subject are more relevant today than ever before. When he began his studies, little attention was given to pidgin and creole languages. A leading theorist might discuss them incidentally, but sustained concern with the subject had little place in the mainstream of linguistic work. The subject and its serious students, like the languages themselves, were usually regarded as marginal. Now the intrinsic scientific and social importance of the languages is recognized by ever-widening circles.

Lively controversy concerning the origins of Caribbean pidgin and creole languages, and of the nature of such languages generally, persists, and this book will not end it. Taylor's contributions to such debate, indeed, are well known,[7] but it is worth considering here their special character. They reflect a deep sense of the complex cultural history of the region and a command of an immense amount of detailed linguistic data from a variety of the languages concerned. Scholars approaching a single language or a group of languages all dominantly influenced by the same modern European language can readily see the extent to which particular creoles might be considered descendants of particular European languages; yet the extraordinary rapidity with which the languages have been re-structured belies any claim that the process involved can have been one of normal linguistic change. Scholars concerned with what is common to all languages may be excited by the similarities among creoles, insofar as these suggest that similar processes were at work in the formation of all of them—elementary mental processes that normal linguistic change may less readily show. Yet the debate about the origin and character of the Caribbean creoles persists in part just because their history has been checkered and complex, subject to processes that are social and specific. As against the adequacy of either view, it has been Taylor's unique merit to demonstrate significant similarities of grammar among the Caribbean creoles that are yet specific to them, not universal; similarities that cannot be ascribed to normal linguistic change because they cut across division into creoles of French or English or another European lexical base;

[7] It was unfortunately not possible to republish in this volume some of Taylor's pathbreaking papers, which include Taylor 1956, Taylor 1958, Taylor 1961, and Taylor 1963.

similarities that imply a common West African source. Adapting a method for the reconstruction of grammatical structure with a language family, Taylor showed that in the Caribbean this method produced results for diverse language families.[8]

In sum, Taylor has provided original and crucial evidence that the origin and character of the Caribbean creoles must be sought in the cultural history of the Caribbean creole-speaking peoples. He adopts the view that the early stage of the languages reflected a lexicon, largely of Portuguese origin, that had been shaped in West Africa and subsequently reshaped in other regions under the influence of other languages. To this "relexification" hypothesis, as it is called, he joins a necessary grammatical hypothesis.

In the exactitude and comprehensiveness of his treatment of the languages analyzed herein, Taylor provides an example of the kind of scholarship that will be necessary if the continuing controversies over pidgin and creole languages are to produce new knowledge and insight.

That Douglas Taylor should welcome an introduction by his colleagues is a source of considerable gratification to us. This book is a culmination of a sort to more than forty years of linguistic and ethnographic research by its author, while constituting at the same time the honoring of a kind of pledge made to one of the writers more than a decade ago.[9] It may not be inappropriate, in concluding this foreword, to take note briefly of the experience and skill the author has brought to his task. While he visited the West Indies as early as 1930, Douglas Taylor has been a resident of the island of Dominica, in the anglophone West Indies, since 1938. Although not having received lengthy professional training in either anthropology or linguistics—when he studied at Cambridge, no degree was awarded there in anthropology, and no courses in linguistics were offered—he early became interested in the Island-Carib inhabitants of his new home. From that interest arose a determination to carry out linguistic and anthropological research among the Dominican and other Caribbean peoples, research that is represented by a substantial series of early publica-

[8] See in particular Taylor 1963.

[9] In 1961, one of the present writers (Mintz) was provided a grant by the Humanities Division of the Rockefeller Foundation to underwrite a year's visit to Yale University by Mr. Douglas Taylor and Dr. Mervyn Alleyne. During that period, Taylor taught courses on Caribbean linguistics in the Department of Anthropology, and this is an appropriate time to record public appreciation for the Rockefeller Foundation's support, and for the sympathetic assistance of Dr. John Harrison, then of the Foundation. During his visit, I invited Taylor to submit a book-length manuscript on Caribbean languages for consideration for the Caribbean Series of Yale University Press, which I was then editing. The manuscript was submitted in 1973, but because I resigned from Yale soon thereafter and Yale University Press subsequently suspended the Caribbean Series, the volume is being published in the Johns Hopkins Studies in Atlantic History and Culture, thanks to the help of the Press and of the series editors, Professors Franklin W. Knight and Richard Price.

tions. That the author, who was never examined in either linguistics or anthropology and does not hold a doctoral degree in either discipline,[10] is one of the world's most distinguished authorities in the fields of his specialization, and doubtless the single most knowledgeable authority alive on the Island-Carib, is of greater interest, perhaps, precisely because such mastery is, in a manner rare in the scientific world today, very much the product of individual skill, intelligence, and will. Readers of this volume will be able to share in the wealth of insights which the author's lifelong devotion to his subject has produced.

Sidney W. Mintz
The Johns Hopkins University

Dell Hymes
University of Pennsylvania

References

Augelli, John
1962   The rimland-mainland concept of culture areas in Middle America.
           Annals of the Association of American Geographers 52, 2: 119–29.
Cahnman, Werner
1943–44   The Mediterranean and Caribbean regions: a comparison in race
           and culture contacts. *Social Forces* 22: 209–14.
Hancock, Ian
1971   A map and list of pidgin and creole languages. In *Pidginization
           and creolization of languages*, ed. Dell Hymes, pp. 509–23.
           Cambridge: Cambridge University Press.
Hymes, Dell
1971   Preface. In *Pidginization and creolization of languages*, ed. Dell
           Hymes, pp. 3–11. Cambridge: Cambridge University Press.
Lowenthal, David
1972   *West Indian societies*. New York: Oxford University Press.
Mintz, Sidney
1966   The Caribbean as a socio-cultural area. *Cahiers d'Histoire
           Mondiale* 9, 4: 912–37. Reprinted in *Peoples and cultures of the
           Caribbean*, ed. Michael Horowitz, pp. 17–46. Garden City:
           Natural History Press.
1974   *Caribbean transformations*. Chicago: Aldine.

[10] The author read Modern Languages (French and German), holds B.A. and M.A. degrees (Cantab.), and is a *diplomé* of the Ecole des Sciences Politiques (Paris). During his student years, he followed courses with A. C. Haddon at Cambridge; with Marcel Mauss, Marcel Cohen, Paul Rivet, and André Siegfried in Paris; and spent a semester at Heidelberg studying philosophy. Mr. Taylor has carried out fieldwork, in addition to that in Dominica, in Belize (British Honduras) and in Suriname, and he has carried on research at York University in the United Kingdom and at the Netherlands Institute for Advanced Study in the Humanities and Social Sciences.

Morison, Samuel, and Obregón, Mauricio
1974   *The Caribbean as Columbus saw it*. Boston: Atlantic-Little, Brown.
Rouse, Irving
1964   Prehistory of the West Indies. *Science* 144: 499–513.
Smith, Michael
1965   A framework for Caribbean studies. In *The plural society in the British West Indies*, ed. Michael Smith, pp. 18–74. Berkeley and Los Angeles: University of California Press.
Stewart, William
1962   Creole languages in the Caribbean. In *Study of the role of second languages*, ed. Frank Rice, pp. 34–53. Washington: Center for Applied Linguistics.
Taylor, Douglas
1951   *The Black Carib of British Honduras*. Viking Fund Publications in Anthropology 17.
1956   Language contacts in the West Indies. *Word* 12, 3: 399–414.
1958   Use and disuse of languages in the West Indies. *Caribbean Quarterly* 5, 2: 67–77.
1961   New languages for old in the West Indies. *Comparative Studies in Society and History* 3, 3: 277–88. Reprinted in *Peoples and cultures of the Caribbean*, ed. Michael Horowitz, pp. 77–91. Garden City: Natural History Press.
1963   The origin of West Indian creole languages: evidence from grammatical categories. *American Anthropologist* 65, 4: 800–814.
Wagley, Charles
1960   Plantation America. In *Caribbean studies*, ed. Vera Rubin, pp. 3–13. Seattle: University of Washington Press.

ACKNOWLEDGMENTS

❊

IN THE FIRST PLACE I wish to express my gratitude to Professor Sidney W. Mintz, at whose instigation the writing of this book was first undertaken, and to the Netherlands Institute for Advanced Study in the Humanities and Social Sciences, for a year's fellowship, which enabled me to complete the book.

The results of my field work among the Black Carib of Central America have been published elsewhere; those of my linguistic work with Coastal Arawak of Suriname are, owing to ill health, still largely unwritten. For means to carry out the latter investigation I am endebted to WOSUNA (later WOTRO), the National Science Foundation (grant 1909), the Research Institute for the Study of Man, and the Philosophic Society of America.

Last but by no means least I wish to thank my friends and my informants (who are also my friends): Professor Jan Voorhoeve and Dr. Berend Hoff, whose field work in Suriname, on Sranan and on Carib respectively, preceded my own by several years; Mr. and Mrs. Ferdie Sabajo and Mr. Michel Sabajo, who not only initiated us into their language but also built a fine house for us to live in; and all those, Arawaks and others, who contributed to our insight, welfare, and comfort during our three sojourns (one of them lasting a year) in Sawarieweg, Suriname.

LANGUAGES OF THE
WEST INDIES

❈

LANGUAGE
ABBREVIATIONS

❀

A	Arawak	LA-G	Lesser Antillean-Guadeloupean
AB	Anobom Creole	LA-M	Lesser Antillean-Martinican
BD	Berbice Dutch		
BH	British Honduran	LA-S	Lesser Antillean-Saintlucian (St. Lucia)
CAIC	Central American Island-Carib		
CC	Cayenne Creole	LC	Louisiana Creole
DA	Djuka and Aluku	MC	Mauritian Creole
DIC	Dominican Island-Carib	ND	Negro Dutch
Du.	Dutch	OEng.	Old English
Eng.	English	PGC	Portuguese Guinea Creole
ED	Essequibo Dutch	PK	Papia Kristang (Malaya)
Fr.	French	PP	Papiamentu
G	Guajiro	PQ	Palenquero
Ger.	German	Ptg.	Portuguese
HC	Haitian Creole	S	Shebayo
IC	Island-Carib	SM	Saramaccan and Matuari
Ital.	Italian	SN	Sranan
JC	Jamaican Creole	Sp.	Spanish
K	Karina (Carib)	ST	Sãotomense
KR	Krio	T	Taino
LA	Lesser Antillean	VIC	Vincentian Island-Carib
LA-D	Lesser Antillean-Dominican	Y	Yoruba

INTRODUCTION

❉

IN THE FOLLOWING pages I try to pass on to others something of the interest I have long felt in two very different types of West Indian language and culture—the Amerindian and the Creole. Languages of either type occupy or occupied much the same geographical territory, are largely unwritten and unstandardized, and perhaps for that reason are often accorded very little thought and consideration by "pure" linguists.

Yet they are—or should be—important to both the native speaker and to the linguistic anthropologist; for as Professor Maurice Freedman has stated (1973, p. 101), "A language is at once a partial index of a culture to an outsider and a selective meta-language in which a community can express some but not all of their social and cultural life." It follows that a culture is most adequately expressed and best understood in the everyday language of its bearers; and we cannot be surprised if loss of an indigenous tongue usually entails loss of much of the culture that went with it.

Today, throughout the multiracial and primarily multilingual Caribbean, from French Guiana in the southeast to British Honduras in the northwest, many among those of the younger generation suffer from an even greater feeling of insecurity than is common to those of their age group elsewhere because they cannot find their own identity. They are not and will not be second-class Dutchmen, Englishmen, or Frenchmen, though they must and do master the Europeans' languages in order to get on in modern life. The old cultural values are fading, and new ones have yet to be found. Here it would seem that salvation might still be sought in the small but growing literary output of poets, dramatists, and other writers employing the Amerindian or creole vernacular to express and communicate the cultural outlook and social problems held and encountered as members of their own communities. (See the tale *Basha Pataka*, a modern Surinamean Creole story of old times, in Chapter 12 of this volume.)

3

These languages' importance for the nonnative—whether anthropologist or another—is rather different; in trying to understand a people's past and present culture, he or she invokes the help of the language—partly by establishing its structures, their nature, diversity, and uses, and partly by comparing its vocabulary with those of other, related and unrelated idioms. Similarities in form and meaning may be due, if few and sporadic, to chance; if many and regular, to genetic relationship; or, in either case, to linguistic borrowing or adoption by one speech community from another. And since such borrowing can occur only where and while there is some social and/or commercial intercourse between members of the two speech communities concerned, loanforms can often supplement or replace historical knowledge of cultural contacts which no longer subsist.

Island-Carib, as the Arawakan language of the Iñeri (Ignéri, Eyeri) has come to be called, presents an unusual amount of borrowing from Karina (True Carib, Galibi), details of which will be discussed in Chapter 5. The tradition of the Lesser Antilles' conquest by the Karina was still alive three hundred years ago; and in his *Relation* (Paris, 1655), Pierre Pelleprat says: "Il y a plusieurs siècles que les Galibis conquirent les Caraïbes [Iñeri]."

In his book *The Carib Language* (The Hague, 1968), Dr. B. J. Hoff lists some seventy words with similar form and meaning found in both Karina (Carib, Galibi) and in unrelated (so far as is known) Tupí. Most of them name plants and animals; and it seems safe to infer that the two tribes in question were once much closer to one another geographically than they are today, or are historically known to have been.

There are some words that Karina and Arawak (Lokono) must have borrowed from one another or from an unknown third source: K(arina) *mi*, A(rawak) *-mi* 'the late' (K *ya:wo mi* 'my late uncle', A *daiómi* 'my late mother'); K *para:na*, A *baráa*, I(sland) C(arib) *baráua* and *barána* 'sea'; K *kana:wa*, A *kanóa/-kanán* 'war canoe'; K *kuri:yara*, A *koriára* 'dugout canoe, corial'; K *sima:ri*, A *samári* '(manioc) greater'; K *mana:ri*, A *manári* '(manioc) sifter'; K *kuma:ka*, A *komáka* 'silk-cotton tree (Ceiba pentandra L.)'.

The early period of contact with Europeans left a considerable number of loanwords for innovations ('gun', 'needle', 'cloth', 'paper', 'sail', 'flag', 'cow', 'horse', etc.) in all the West-Indian Amerindian languages. These were for the most part taken from Spanish, but occasionally from Portuguese (cf. K. *piiru:ku*, but A *póroko*, 'pig', from, respectively, Sp. *puerco* and Ptg. *porco*). Later borrowing has been mainly from the local creoles, with which contact has been much greater than with the European tongues upon which they are "based." (Thus, Island-Carib has borrowed extensively from "French-based" Lesser Antillean Creole; Karina and Arawak, from "English-based" Sranan [Surinamean Creole].) And these "loans," unlike those of Amerindian origin found in the creoles (most of which name local animals, plants, implements, and utensils), include many functional or grammatical words—such as those meaning 'because', 'but', 'each', 'first', 'if', 'that' (conj.), 'then', 'time(s)', 'until' or 'as far as' or 'even' (adv.). And for the Central American dialect of Island-Carib, they also include at least one loan construction, the demonstrative adjective having been displaced from position before to that after the noun it determines: Dominican IC *thukúra hįaru*, Central American IC *hįáru tugúra* 'that woman', to accord with Lesser Antillean Creole *fãm sa-a* 'that woman' ("woman that").

With regard to the creoles themselves, it may well be asked, What is inherited and what borrowed; and what is the meaning of *X-based*? These are new languages whose earliest recordings date from the eighteenth century, and little is known of their short history. It is true that we learn something about the linguistic situation among the African slaves in Martinique around the middle of the seventeenth century from two French priests who were there at that time. Thus, Pelleprat (1655b, p. 53) says: "Nous attendons qu'ils ayent appris le françois pour les instruire," and "Nous nous accommodons à leur façon de parler qui est ordinairement par l'infinitif du verbe"; and Chevillard (1659): "Les nègres ... se familiarisent rapidement avec le langage de l'européen, langage volontairement corrompu pour faciliter sa compréhension." But the samples of this willfully corrupted language that they have left us show little or no resemblance to any of the French creoles as recorded in the following century; while their inclusion of such non-French words as *capitou* 'captain' and *pequins* 'little ones' to facilitate its understanding suggests that these slaves already knew something of a Portuguese pidgin (cf. Ptg. *capitão, pequenos*) before their arrival in Martinique.

On the other hand, in Surinam, "a Dutch traveller reported in 1693 that the slaves spoke English. He did not even mention the deviating variety of English (Alphen 1693)" (Voorhoeve 1973, p. 140). Yet in Herlein (1718), only twenty-five years later, Sranan (Surinam Creole) appears to be very much the same as it is today. And the same is true of the first recorded sample of French (Cayenne) Creole, dated 1744: *Anglai pran Yapok, yé méné mon père allé, toute blang foulkan maron dans bois* 'The English have taken Oyapock; they have carried off the priest; all the Whites have cleared out and taken refuge in the woods'.

These creoles will be called French-based and English-based because the greater or more basic part of their vocabularies is derived, respectively, from French and from English; and the same goes for Dutch-based, Portuguese-based, and other creoles. Words derived from a language other than that upon which the creole is based will be classed as borrowed, even when they may well be retentions from some African language, as is probable in the case of Sranan (SN) *unu* and Ibo *unu* 'you' (pl.), SN *i* and Ibo *i* 'you' (sg.), SN *djokoto* 'squat' and Yoruba *djôkô* 'sit'.

Such loanwords may be many or few; and their relative abundance or scarcity may depend upon which part of the lexicon is considered. Thus, Voorhoeve (1970, p. 57) made a study of all the verbs in the *Woordenlijst van het Sranan-Tongo* (Anonymous 1961) and, in a later article (1973, p. 138), one of all the words whose origin he could ascertain belonging to the Swadesh 200-item list[1] and contained in Huttar's "Comparative word list for Djuka" (1972, pp. 12–21). Table 1 summarizes Voorhoeve's findings. SN1 refers to 434 verbs from the *Woordenlijst* of Sranan; SN2, SM, and DA to items of the Swadesh list in, respectively, Sranan, Saramaccan Creole, and Djuka. As the number of items included differs with each of the last three lists, I have reduced Voorhoeve's findings to percentages.

TABLE 1.   Derivation of Loanwords in Selected Creoles

Creole	Origin			
	African	Portuguese	English	Dutch
DA	2%	4%	80%	14%
SN1	2	5	49	44
SN2	3	5	76	16
SM	5	37	53	5

SOURCE: Based on data in Voorhoeve 1970, p. 57, and Voorhoeve 1973, p. 138.

Excluded from the count are not only words of unknown or doubtful origin, but also pairs of synonyms whose members are of different origin. I count nineteen of these pairs in the same Swadesh list for Saramaccan; and fifteen of them show Portuguese/Sranan origin, as, e.g., *tánapé* (Ptg. *estar a pé*) / *taámpu* (SN *tanápu*, Eng. *stand up*) 'stand'; *komé* (Ptg. *comer*) / *nján* (SN *njan*, Wolof *njam*) 'eat'; *bebé* (Ptg. *beber*) / *diíngi* (SN *dringi*, Eng. *drink*) 'drink'. Now according to Schumann, this last word meant, in 1778, 'all strong drink' ("alles starke Getränke"), so that its present synonymity with *bebé* is a later development; and if other members of these now synonymous pairs should have developed in the same way, Saramaccan Creole of two hundred years ago had a significantly higher proportion of Portuguese-derived words than at present.

[1] Morris (or Mauricio) Swadesh, 1909–67, one of Edward Sapir's foremost pupils and himself a linguist of the first order, is perhaps most widely remembered today for his theory of glotto-chronology, which he explains very simply in *El lenguaje y la vida humana* (Swadesh 1966, pp. 370–75). Of the theory no use whatever is made in the present volume; but I have employed Swadesh's diagnostic and supplementary lists of basic notions, insofar as I have been able to find their equivalents in the Amerindian and Creole languages considered, with the hope that they, like the texts that precede them, may serve as specimens of the languages concerned.

Synonymity followed by the obsolescence of one member is one way in which words are lost. Another is through remodeling and homonymity, which results in false identification. Saramaccan (SM) *sindá* (Ptg. *sentar*) 'sit' of 1778 has now changed its last vowel to become *sindô*—probably under the influence of its Sranan equivalent, *sidón* (Eng. *sit down*) 'sit'. For the same date, Schumann gives both *luntu* and *luluntu* (Ptg. *redondo*?) for what is now *lóntu* (Du. *rond*?) 'round' in both Sranan and Saramaccan. SM *ningá* (Ptg. *negar*) 'to deny, refuse' of 1778 has unaccountably been confused with the same language's *tínga* (Eng. *think*), of which it is now a variant, *nínga* 'think'. And likewise SN *tapá* (Ptg. *tapar*) 'to cover; to stop up' of 1783 has now become, without change of meaning, *tápu*, which may well be identified with its homonym, SN *tápu* (Eng. *top*) 'on top of, top'. SN *doro* 'door; through(out); to arrive' appears to have three etyma: Eng. *door*, Eng. *through*, and Twi *dru* 'arrive'.

Dutch, the official language of Surinam, exerts pressure on Sranan; and Sranan, which is employed by nonnative speakers throughout the country as a lingua franca, exerts pressure on Saramaccan and on most of the other languages spoken there (Arawak, Carib, Hindi, Javanese, etc.). This influence results in such synonyms or near synonyms as SN *dóti* (Eng. *dirty*) | *mórsu* (Du. *mors(ig)*) 'dirty'; SN *pió* (Eng. *puke*) | *brak* (Du. *braken*) 'to vomit'; SN *síbi* (Eng. *sweep*) | *fígi* (Du. *vegen*) 'sweep; wipe'; SM *gíin* (Eng. *green*) | *gúún* (Du. and SN *grun*) 'green'; SM *baí* (Ptg. *varrer*) | *féki* (Du. *vegen*) 'sweep'.

While African loanwords are relatively few in most West Indian creoles (at least in their more basic vocabularies), African loan constructions are both common and striking; and it seems worthwhile to mention here some specific instances of such resemblances as I find between Lesser Antillean French-based Creole (LA) and Yoruba (Y), whose linguistic contacts have been mainly with English. I select these two languages only for the sake of convenience, taking the Yoruba data from E. C. Rowlands's *Yoruba* (London, 1969), and the Lesser Antillean from my own firsthand knowledge of the language. Word order is the same in both languages except where otherwise indicated by superscript numerals.

In both languages the pronominal and demonstrative determinants are postposed to their referents, the former preceding the latter where both are present: LA *kay mwẽ*, Y *ilé mi* "house my" = 'my house'; LA *kay sa*, Y *ilé yî* "house this" = 'this house'; LA *kay mwẽ sa*, Y *ilé mi yî* "house my this" = 'this house of mine'.

In both languages 'self' is expressed by a word also meaning 'body': LA *kɔ mwẽ*, Y *ara mi* "body/self my" = 'my body/myself'.

In both languages the verb meaning 'give' is employed where English would require a dative preposition, 'to' or 'for': LA *i ba mwẽ*, Y *ó fún mi* "he/she/it gave me" = 'he gave me (it)'; but as a secondary verb:

LA *gãye-y ba mwé*, Y *rà-ãfún mi* "buy it give me" = 'buy it for me'; LA *i vãn-li ba mwé* Y *ó tà-áfún mi* "she sold it gave me" = 'she sold it to me'.

In both languages verbs meaning '(sur)pass' are employed in comparison of superiority where we would have '-er than': LA *i gwã pase mwé*, Y *ó tóbi jù mi* "he is-tall pass me" = 'he is taller than I'.

In both languages verbs meaning 'come' and 'go' are employed as secondary verbs to indicate direction: LA *yo mẽnẽ-y vini*, Y *wón mú u wá* "they took him/her/it come" = 'they brought her'; LA *yo mẽnẽ-y ale*, Y *wón mú-u lɔ*" they took him/her/it go" = 'they took her away'.

In both languages 'when?' and 'where?' are expressed by forms meaning 'which/what time?' and 'which/what place?'. So LA *ki tã/lɛ?* "what time?", Y *ìgbàwo?* "time which?", both = 'when?'. And LA *ki kote?* "which place?", Y *ibo?* (< *ibi wò*) "place which?" = 'where?'.

Of the Yoruba preposition *ní* ~ *n-* ~ *l-* ~ *m-* Rowlands (1969, p. 21) says: "This word may be regarded as equivalent to 'in, at' in English and is actually the only word in Yoruba we can properly call a preposition." And further (p. 141): "Forms with *ní* are regularly used after verbs which denote movement away from a position." These remarks apply equally well to the "general locative" preposition of Lesser Antillean Creole, *na* ~ *la* ~ *ã*: LA *mwẽ tiwe-y ã didã bwet-la*, Y *mo mú-u n-ínú àpóti* "I took it at inside box" = 'I took it out of the box' (as well as LA *mwẽ jwẽn-li ã didã bwet-la*, Y *mo rí i n-ínú àpóti* 'I found it in the box'); LA *mwẽ twape liv mwẽ ã lamẽ-y*, Y *mo gbà ìwé mi l-ɔ́wɔ́ rè* "I got book my at hand his" = 'I got my book from him'.

The simple-stem form of the verb denotes, in both languages, completed action, process, or achieved state: LA *mãje sa fwet*, Y *ouńdjɛ yî tutù* 'this food ("food this") is-cold'; LA *i asid*, Y *ó djókô* 'he sat down' or 'he is sitting' (state); LA *i mɔ*, Y *ó kú* 'he (/she/it) died' or 'he (/she/it) is dead'. As opposed to this aspect, the *ka*-form of the Lesser Antillean verb and the *ń* form of the Yoruba verb denote habitual or progressive action or process, as in LA *mãje sa ka fwet*, Y *oúndjɛ yî ń-tutù* 'this food gets cold' or 'this food is getting cold'; LA *i ka asid*, Y *ó ń-djókô* 'he sits (habitually) or 'he is (in the act of) sitting down'; LA *i ka mɔ*, Y *ó ń-kú* 'he is dying'. When a secondary verb is present, the two aspects may be combined, as with LA *poze*, Y *simi* 'to rest': LA *i asid ka poze*, Y *ó djókô ńsìmi* 'he sat resting'.

In Yoruba, as in most of the creoles, we find an emphasizing construction of a type that I have called double predication, in which a finite verb is preceded by a word meaning 'it is' and the same verb in its nominal form and function. So, from LA *mwẽ ka poze* and Y *mo ń-simi* 'I am resting' we get LA *se¹ poze² mwẽ³ ka⁴ poze⁵* and Y *sísimi² ni¹ mo³ ń⁴simi⁵* "it's resting (Y "resting it-is") I'm resting" = 'I'm resting'. And similarly LA *se¹ bat² mwẽ³ ke⁴ bat⁵-li⁶*, Y *nínà² ni¹ ŋ³' ó⁴ nà⁵-á⁶* "it's beating (Y "beating it is") I shall beat him" = 'I shall give him a good beating'; LA se^1 $kase^2$ i^3 $kase^4$-y^5, Y $fif\acute{o}^2$ $l^{1\prime}\acute{o}^3$ $f\acute{o}^4$-o^5 "it's[1] breaking[2] (Y "breaking[2] it-is[1]") he[3] broke[4] it[5]" = 'he *broke* it' or 'he actually broke it'. Note that, if the direct object (LA -y, Y -o) is omitted from this last example, the verb is then understood as denoting a state rather than an action: Y $fif\acute{o}^1$ $l^{2\prime}\acute{o}^3$ $f\acute{o}^4$ "broken[1] it-is[2] it[3]-is- broken[4]" = 'it's *broken*', and so also LA *se kase i kase* 'it's really broken'.

Examples of such resemblances between Lesser Antillean French-based Creole and Yoruba could be multiplied, or comparison with another creole or another West African language made; but the evidence cited above is, I think, sufficient to show that Lesser Antillean in its formative period was in close contact with a language or languages very like Yoruba; and as French-based Haitian and Cayenne creoles, English-based Sranan and Saramaccan, and Iberian-based Papiamentu and Sãotomense (Gulf of Guinea) show very much the same and other resemblances to Yoruba (see Table 2), we conclude that these creoles have diverged from what may well have been a common pidgin by lexical replacement from the languages

TABLE 2. Resemblances between Yoruba and Selected Creoles

Loan construction*	Fr.-based		Eng.-based		Sp./Ptg.-based	
	HC	CC	SN	SM	PP	ST
I	+	−	−	−	−	+
2	+	−	+	+	+	+
3	+	+	+	+	+	+
4	+	+	+	+	−	+
5	+	+	+	+	+	+
6	+	+	+	+	+	?
7	+	+	+	+	+	+
8	+	+	+	+	+	+
9	±	+	+	+	+	±
10	+	+	+	+	+	+

NOTE: HC = Haitian Creole, CC = Cayenne Creole, SN = Sranan, SM = Saramaccan, PP = Papiamentu, ST = Sãotomense.
*Explained and discussed in the text.

of the slaves' European masters and overseers. The ten loan constructions shown in Table 2 are as follows: (1) postposed pronominal determinant, (2) postposed demonstrative, (3) same word for 'body' and 'self', (4) the verb meaning 'give' in place of our dative prepositions 'to, for', (5) the verb meaning '(sur)pass' in place of our comparative '(bigg)er than', (6) direction expressed by secondary verbs meaning 'come' and 'go', (7) phrasal 'which time?' and 'which place?' replacing our 'when?' and 'where?', (8) occurrence of a general locative preposition, (9) aspectual opposition of marked versus unmarked verb stem denoting continuity (progressive-habitual) versus completion (in HC the former denotes only the progressive, the latter both completive and the habitual; in ST the habitual is marked, the progressive is doubly marked), and (10) double predication. All ten features, as we have seen, belong to Lesser Antillean Creole and Yoruba. Moreover, the languages shown in Table 2 and all other West Indian creoles except Lesser Antillean form the nominal plural, like Yoruba, by means of their personal pronoun of third plural.

How are such resemblances to be explained? Hancock (1969) and some other creolists believe that the differently based creoles stem from different African pidgins, which evolved and were creolized, typological resemblances being due to similar linguistic background and circumstances. But there is no conclusive evidence for a pidgin other than Portuguese-based being current in Africa before the eighteenth century, nor of more than one creole being spoken in Surinam before 1779. The relationship between Sranan and Saramaccan, today both English-based according to the criterion we have chosen, is of prime importance to the problem of other creoles' origin, as Voorhoeve (1973) points out. For if these two creoles, despite a common grammar and a partially common lexicon (which, as we have seen, is increasing under Sranan influence on Saramaccan), should be of different origin, why did the latter remain so long unmentioned, and why did its spreakers show a greater propensity than the other slaves to escape to the bush? But if they had a common origin, this must have been in a Portuguese pidgin which was partly relexified by English in the case of the fugitives (among whom, to judge by the greater proportion of African-derived words in Saramaccan, were many new arrivals from Africa), and almost completely so in that of the slaves who remained on the plantations, although Sranan has retained a few Portuguese-derived words for very common concepts (*bun* 'good', *pikin* 'small', *sabi* 'know', *pasá* 'pass', *kabá* 'finish', *tra* 'other', *te* 'until; as far as; even [adv,]', etc.).

If accepted, this interpretation would mean that a creole may change its base (as defined here) by lexical replacement. If English-based Sranan and Saramaccan originated in a Portuguese-based pidgin, so most probably (as we shall see) did Spanish-based Papiamentu; and it seems at least possible that Sranan might one day become Dutch-based! On the other hand, Voorhoeve finds that Djuka Creole is a newcomer which derives from an eighteenth-century English-based pidgin. As for the origin of this or that French- or other-based creole, I shall leave the reader to form his own opinion after having taken cognizance of the relevant chapters of this little book. The evidence that I can produce is not conclusive one way or the other; but I think it is sufficient to show that, in most cases at any rate, more than two languages were involved in the pidginizing process that led to the birth of these creoles.

I
AMERINDIAN
LANGUAGES

❖

ONE

AMERINDIAN
LANGUAGES OF THE
WEST INDIES

❧

This Iland is called by the people therof *Cairi*, and in it are diuers nations: those about *Parico* are called *Iaio*, those at *Punto Carao* are of the *Arwacas*, and betweene *Carao* and *Curiapan* they are called *Saluaios*, betweene *Carao* and *punto Galera* are the *Nepoios*, and those about the Spanish Citie tearme themselues *Carinepagotos.*—W. RALEIGH, 1596

FOR THE PAST 1,750 years at least, the West Indies have been a meeting place of different cultures and languages. And it was here, at the dawn of their history, that the first significant contacts between men of Old and New World cultures took place, resulting in European knowledge of such things—and the words to denote them—as barbecue, cacique, canoe, cassava, guava, hammock, hurricane, iguana, maize, papaya, tobacco, tomally. Research on the prehistory of these islands seeks to learn when and whence came the various groups of Indians who, at different times, discovered and peopled them. Yet the languages of this area, like the cultures of those who spoke them, are known at best very imperfectly, and often not at all; while even those that are still in use seem to be losing native speakers, though the ethnic groups to which they belong are increasing.

This chapter will be mainly concerned with listing and locating the languages, and with assigning them, insofar as possible, to a linguistic family or stock. Apart from Warao (for which, see below), only two such groupings—Arawakan and Cariban—can be considered. It must be remembered that whereas Arawak = Lokono and Carib = Karina are single languages, Arawakan and Cariban are extensive families of languages whose more and less divergent members are alike presumed to have had a common origin, however remote. According to J. Alden Mason, the former is "probably the largest and most important linguistic family in South America, both in number of component languages and dialects," while the latter "is one of the great linguistic families of South America, both in number of component languages and dialects and in extent." But if we are to learn something of prehistoric human migrations and contacts and ethnography within our area, these linguistic families and stocks must be broken down so as to distinguish, by subgrouping, closer and more remote relationships—just as Indo-European has been subdivided into Germanic, Slavic, Greek, Romance, etc. For as Chaucer told us long ago, language changes both in time and space:

> Ye knowe eek in form of speche is chaunge
> With-inne a thousand yeer, and wordes tho
> That hadden prys, now wonder nyce and straunge
> Us thinketh hem; and yet they spake hem so,
> And spedde as wel in love as men now do;
> Eek for to winne love in sondry ages,
> In sondry londes, sondry been usages.   Chaucer, T.II.4.

How many distinct (mutually unintelligible) Amerindian languages were spoken in the Antilles and Bahamas at the time of the Spanish conquest or subsequent to it is uncertain: none is found there today. For some we have little or nothing except their names: *Caquetio* (Aruba and Curaçao), *Carinepagoto* (Trinidad), *Ciboney* (Cuba and Haiti), *Ciguayo* (Santo Domingo), *Guaccaierima* (Haiti), *Guaiqueri* or *Waikeri* (Margarita), *Macorixe* (Cuba), and *Maisi* (Cuba); although *Caquetio* and *Ciguayo* (the latter equated by some with *Macorixe*, and of which only two words are recorded: *tuob* 'gold' and *baeza* 'a negation') have been assigned to Arawakan, *Carinepagoto* to Cariban, and it has been suggested that *Guaiqueri* was related to *Warao*.

For others we have at least short wordlists which permit more or less plausible inferences as to the languages' genetic affiliation: *Nepuyo* (Trinidad and parts of the neighboring mainland), *Shebayo* or *Salvaio* (Trinidad; cf. *Sabayo*, the name of a modern Arawak clan which had, according to tradition, an independent origin), *Yao* or *Iaio* (Trinidad and the Guianese coastal region from the Orinoco eastward to the Mayacare), and *Taino* (including *Sub-Taino* and *Lucayo*; Greater Antilles and Bahamas).

Three more languages formerly recorded in the West Indian islands are still spoken on the American continent and can be known in some detail. They are *Arawak* or *Lokono* (Trinidad and the Guianese coastal region from the Orinoco as far east as the Oyapock), *Carib* or *Karina* or *Galibi* or *Cariñaco* (Tobago, Grenada, and probably other of the Lesser Antilles, the Guianas from north of the Orinoco eastward to the Amazon), and *Island-Carib* or *Iñeri* or *Igneri* (the Lesser Antilles except Trinidad and Tobago, and from Stann Creek in British Honduras, south and east around the Gulf of Honduras to the Black River).

A fourth living language, *Warao*, may or may not have been spoken in Trinidad during historical times, since some toponyms of that island suggest that it once was current there. Today, Warao is spoken in several mutually intelligible dialects by some ten thousand Indians, most of whom live in the delta of the Orinoco river. It is not known to be related to any other language; and lexical similarities to neighboring Carib (Karina) and Arawak (Lokono) may probably be attributed to borrowing. As we have a good modern description of this language by H. A. Osborn (1962), it need concern us no further here.

I select one of these living languages, Island-Carib, for detailed presentation, not only because I am most familiar with it, but also because it best exemplifies the results of prehistoric and historic contacts and conquests. Despite the name, Island-Carib is an Arawakan language not too far removed from Arawak proper (Lokono), which has come under the influence of and borrowed freely from Carib (Karina), Spanish, French, and English, in that order of succession and importance. I adopt a discursive mode of presentation because I have previously given a linguistic description of this language elsewhere; and this book is not addressed primarily to linguists.

DEAD LANGUAGES ATTESTED BY WORDLISTS

Nepuyo

A. Vazquez de Espinosa, in chapter 16 of his *Compendium* (first published in 1629), gives scraps of various languages, among which we find (p. 95): "La nacion de los Indios de la isla Trinidad, llamada Nepuya, y los de la Provincia de Guayana, hablan casi una misma lengua, para dezir, 'a ti digo', *amuere*, 'dame de comer', *chare yerepare*, 'aguarda', *tamacare*, 'no lo ai', *ipura mana*, 'mientes', *acayaremate*, 'digo verdad', *quanane*, 'yo me muero de hambre', *corpiase*, 'date priessa', *yomeyomese*, 'yo me doi la que puedo', *tamacaresea pone*, 'lumbre', *guapot*." Most of these words and phrases appear to belong to a Cariban language; compare, for example, K *amo:ro* 'thou', *saro:ya* 'I take it', *ye:repa:ri* 'my cassava-bread', Wayana *wapot*, Cumanagoto and Yao *oapoto*, and K *waxto*.

Shebayo

The Shebayo list, taken from De Laet's *Novus Orbis*, is as follows (divergent spellings found in different editions are shown in parentheses): *heia* (*heja*) 'pater', *hamma* 'mater', *wackewijrrij* 'caput', *wackenoely* (*wackenoey*) 'auris', *noeyerri* (*noeyerii*) 'oculus', *wassibaly* (*wassi*) 'nasus', *darrymaily* 'ōs', *wadacoely* 'dentes', *watabaye* 'crura', *wackehyrry* 'pedes', *ataly* 'arbor', *hoerapallii* 'arcus', *hewerry* 'sagittae', *kyrtzyrre* 'luna', and *wecoelije* 'sol'.

Such meager material justifies no more than a plausible guess at the genetic relationship of this language. If we assume that most of the words contain, as they do in other of De Laet's lists, unrecognized (or at any rate untranslated) grammatical affixes (such as, perhaps, *wa-* 'our', *da-* 'my', *-rrij*, *-rii*, *-ly*, etc., a dependent suffix), what remains may sometimes be compared to similar equivalents or near equivalents in Arawakan languages. So, compare S(hebayo) *-ckewij-* with G(uajiro) *ekiwi* 'head', S *-eckenoe-* 'ear' with I(sland) C(arib) *-kuniu-* '(sense of) hearing', S *-si(ba)-* with A(rawak) *-siri* 'nose' or A *-sibaroko* 'forehead', S *-rryma-* with Wirina *-luma* 'mouth', S *-dacoe-* with Atorai and Wapishana *-dako* 'teeth, mouth', S *-tabaye* with Wapishana *-tabai* 'leg', S *-ckehy-* with Atorai *-kheti* 'foot, feet', S *ata-* with A *áda* 'tree; wood', and S *kyrtzy-* with Mapidian *kirsu* and Mehinacu *kerzi* 'moon'. On the other hand, the Shebayo word given for 'bow' is clearly Cariban (cf. K *ira:pari* 'bow'), as probably is also that for 'arrow', while that for 'sun' (cf. K *we:yu*) may be.

Yao

Like some other writers on the subject, Sven Lovén (1933, p. 40) considers the language of the Yaos (or Jaos) to have been Arawakan, though "mixed with Carib words"—perhaps because they "seem to have maintained close relations with the True Arawaks" and "appear to have followed them in their migration from Trinidad to the coast of Guiana." But the Yao wordlist, collected near Parico in southwestern Trinidad toward the end of the sixteenth century and published by Jan De Laet, points to a closer relationship between that language and Karina (True Carib) than the latter has with Wayana, a living Guianese language whose Cariban affiliation has never been questioned. And none of the Yao forms shows any resemblance to its Arawak equivalent, as given either in contemporary or in modern wordlists.

In order that the reader may form his own opinion in this matter, the Yao forms are given below as published by De Laet (1640), together with their modern Karina and Wayana equivalents as recorded by B. J. Hoff (personal communication) and C. H. de Goeje (1946), respectively. It should be noted that many of the Yao words contain untranslated, possessive, or other affixes. So, for example, "Pyelapo 'La Poitrine'" is probably contained in "Hoppelabolle 'Le Coeur'," which latter word may have meant 'thy heart' (with prefixed *ho-* and suffixed *-le*).

Yao	Karina	Wayana	Gloss
ouate	wa:ti	ua-, uwa	not
tewyn	o:win	pekenatpē	one
tage	o:ko	hakēnē	two
terrewaw	o:ruwa		three
tagyne	o:kopaime		four
mepatoen	aiyato:ne		five

Yao	Karina	Wayana	Gloss
pemoene	kari?na		twenty
nomone	po:to	yunme, pepta	big
enchique	a:sito	apsik	a little
wewe, ueüe	we:we	wewe	tree
boppe	upu:po	uputpē	head
pannaëe	pa:na	pana	ear
uoere	o:nu	eu	eye
hoenaly	onaxta	emna	nose
hopataly	po:ta	upota	mouth
hoieely	ye-	ye	tooth
poepe	pu:pu	-pta	foot
goenaly	oku:na	ēhemu	knee
holopotaly	uwembo	wakton	belly
boppomery	pɨ:mɨ	puimu	neck
mannatii	mana:tɨ	manati	breast
hoppelabolle	turu:po	ewani	heart
iapelly	apo:rɨ		(fore)arm
hoomotaly	-mota-		shoulder
pollelii	po:rirɨ		shin, leg
ieene	-ene:sa-		throat
pape	pa:pa		father
immer	ta:ta		mother
waryee	enauxtɨ	wolisi	sister
comi	emɨirɨ	kami	daughter
euenike	enɨ:rɨ	telihe	drink
ouaoninne	ena:pɨ	tēkhe	eat
uniguené	onɨ:kɨ, o:no	uwenkat-	sleep
pogue	wo-; po:ka	-woyai	kill
tase	wo:pɨ	tumokhe	come
weyo	we:yu	šiši	sun
noene, nonna	nu:no	nunuē	moon
chirika	siri:ko	sirikē	star
kenape	kono:po	kopē	rain
tapou	to:pu	tēpu	stone
soye	no:no	lo	earth
oapoto	waxto	wapot	fire
capou	ka:pu	kapu	sky
tonimerou			thunder
pepeïte	pepeito		wind
parona	para:na		sea
oussari	kusa:ri		stag
ouamonu	a:mo		weep
coure	iru:pa; yu:pa	ipok	good
icone	ya?wa:me	ipokela	bad
carecouri	karu:kuri		gold
ia; iasay	a:ha	ɨhɨ; ēhē	yes

Taino

Writing of the Bahamas and Greater Antilles, Bartolomé de las Casas tells us that "en todas estas islas eran una lengua y mismas costumbres";

and Andrés Bernáldez (1856) enlarges upon the same theme as follows: "Todos parecían que se entendían y eran de una misma lengua, que es maravillosa en tantas islas no haber diversidad de lengua, y podíale causar el navegar, que eran señores de la mar, y por eso las Islas Canarias no se entendían, porque no tenían con qué navegar y cada isla había una lengua." Unfortunately, the only extant record of this long extinct language, which has since been called Taino (meaning, according to Travesan, *nobili* 'nobles'), after the name of a social or political class, consists of "deux cents mots environ et quelques phrases qui se trouvent éparpillés dans les écrits espagnols et italiens des 15ᵉ et 16ᵉ siècles" (C. H. de Goeje 1939, p. 1); and many of these few recorded forms designate unidentified flora and fauna, while yet others are proper names.

Nevertheless, some threescore Taino forms appear to have likely cognates in one or more better-known Arawakan languages. So, for example, compare T(aino) *aon*, I(sland) C(arib) *ánli* (modern *áɥli*), Adzaneni, Maipure, and Piapoco *auri*, Paraujano *ieri*, and Wapisiana *anir*, all meaning 'dog'; T *hage* (also recorded as *haje, age, aje, axe*, and *ase*), G(uajiro) *haiši*, A(rawak) *haliti* or *halti* (modern /hálithi/), Yavitero *kaliti*, Adzaneni *kaliri*, and Saravecca *kače*, all meaning 'sweet potato'; T *nahe*, IC *-néhene*, A *-nahàlle* (modern /náhele/), Baré *neheu*, Yavitero *nehu*, and Maipure *nau*, all meaning 'paddle' (n.).

Such lexical concordances do not suffice to demonstrate a genetic relationship between the languages concerned, for any but the most sporadic type of contact between members of different speech communities necessitates some degree of bilingualism on one side or the other, and the fact that bilinguals are very apt to employ certain words of their second language while speaking their mother tongue leads to the adoption of so-called loanwords by unilingual members of the same community. Moreover, while loanwords may alone bear witness to unrecorded contacts long since broken off and forgotten, it is not always possible to determine the source of a linguistic borrowing. For example, one can hardly doubt the common ancestry of T *bagua, bahaua* 'sea' and its equivalents in the following languages, of which the first six are Arawakan, the following six Cariban, and the last Tupían: IC *balánna* or *balaoua*, A *baráa*, G *palaa*, Palicur *palawa*, Maipure *parana*, Wapisiana *paranabauk*, Chayma and Cumanagoto *paraua*, Tamanaco *paráva*, Akawaio *paráho*, Yao *parona*, K *para:na* and Tupinambá *parana*. (Cf. also Mayan Quiché *paló* 'sea', Quechua *para* 'rain', and Arauá *paha* 'water'.) Yet no evidence of a relationship between Arawakan, Cariban, and Tupían has been published; and if such a relationship should exist, it is so remote as to render improbable the inheritance of almost identical forms of the same meaning in Arawakan Maipure, Cariban Karina, and Tupían Tupinambá. It therefore seems likely that most of these forms were borrowed at a comparatively recent date—possibly, though undemonstrably, from an Arawakan language in the first place (see Taylor 1957).

Luckily, we are not entirely dependent upon lexical comparison, even in the case of Taino. Thus we are told that T *guarocoel* meant 'our grandfather'; and this word seems to be at least partly cognate with IC *ouárgouti* (modern /uáruguti/), A *wadukuntti* (modern /oadokónthi/), and G *watú?usi*, which contain a prefix *u(a)-*, *o(a)-* or *w(a)-* 'our; us; we' and have the same meaning. And although T *guatiao* and *datiao* are alike glossed 'amigo, compañero' without any possessive, the former appears to be cognate with IC *ouatíaon* 'our friend' (a formalized relationship), and the latter to contain a prefix cognate with A *d(a)-* 'my; me; I', as in A *dadukutti* (modern /dadokóthi/) 'my grandfather'. And this is the more likely since T *daca* or *dacha* 'yo' has as its apparently cognate equivalent A *dákia* and *dái* 'I; me'.

From T *buti-caco* 'zarco de los ojos' and *xeyti-caco* 'negro de los ojos', we extract *caco*, which appears to be cognate with IC *kácou-* and A *kakússi* 'having eyes; (blue/black)-eyed', both of the latter containing, together with a stem, IC *ácou* or A *akússi* 'eye(s)', an attributive prefix *k(a)-*.

If T *mahiz* or *máhici* 'maize' is cognate with equivalent IC *márichi* and A *márissi*, we may probably assume that T *mahite* 'desdentado' contains a stem *-ahi-* that is cognate with IC *-ári* and A *-ári*, both 'tooth, teeth', together with a prefix equivalent to IC *m(a)-* and A *m(a)-*, both of which are privative, as in *mári* 'toothless' of the latter languages. Moreover, the possessed, attributive, and privative derivatives of some (but not all) Island-Carib and Arawak nouns include a dependent suffix *-te*, as in IC *maioúlite* (modern /maiúrite/) and A *majúlite* (modern /maiórithe/) 'without tobacco', from IC *ioúli* and A *júli* 'tobacco'; and it seems reasonable to recognize a cognate of this suffix in the last syllable of T *mahite* 'without teeth/tooth'.

Finally, Arawak has a pluralizing suffix *-no*, as in *mathinín-no* 'fatherless, plural human', from *mathinín* 'fatherless, singular', and in *lokóno* 'people; Indians' from *lóko* 'person; Indian'; and it is at least possible that its cognate equivalent should be contained in T *Matininó*, said to have been the name of an island where only women and their small children were allowed to remain (men being admitted on short visits), and in the word *taino* or *tayno* itself.

The following list of likely cognates—which reproduces (as do also the preceding paragraphs) the spellings of early Spanish chroniclers for Taino, of the seventeenth-century French missionary Father Raymond Breton for Island-Carib, and of the anonymous eighteenth-century German compiler of the *Arawakisch-Deutsches Wörterbuch* for Arawak—offers a few phonological hints or indications, meager though they are. It seems likely that Taino, like Island-Carib and Arawak, had only one sibilant, variously written *s*, *x*, *j* or $g^{i,e}$, *z* or $c^{i,e}$ by the chroniclers (though these last two symbols may have represented an assibilant phoneme distinct from that indicated by the others), and that the *g* of sequences in *gua* and *güe* was at least often a dummy. It will be noticed that Taino shows initial *d-* and intervocalic *-r-* corresponding to *d* (in both positions) of Arawak, while Island-Carib has always and only *r* in this correspondence (see also Taylor 1960b). This suggests that the sounds [d] and [r] may well have been allophones of one phoneme in Taino, as they are at the present time in Warao. Taino agrees with Arawak and Guajiro in marking the first person singular by forms in an apical stop, T *d(a)-*, A *d(a)-*, and G *t(a)-*, as against the nasal *n-* of the equivalent morpheme in Island-Carib and in perhaps most other Arawakan languages. On the other hand, Taino appears to have more lexical cognates with Island-Carib than with Arawak, although here, borrowing cannot be excluded.

Taino	Island-Carib	Arawak (G = Guajiro)	Gloss
-aco	ácou	akússi	eye(s)
-ahi-	-ári	-ári	tooth/teeth
anaqui	ácani	(G ainíi)	enemy
aon	ánli	—	dog
arcabuco	arábou	(cf. adda 'tree')	woodland
-arima	árima, áriouma	—	anus
-ariquen	arícae	-adikke	ear
-arocoel	árgouti	adukutti	grandfather
bagua, bahaua	balánna, balaoua	baráa	sea
batea	batáya	—	trough
bixa, bija	bíchet	—	Bixa orellana L.
buh(u)iti	bóye	—	shaman
burén	boúrrêlet	búddali	griddle
cabuya	cáboya	(G apí)	cord, mooring
caniba, canima	callíponam	kallipina	Carib
canoa	canáoa	kanóa, -kanan	canoe
canocum	—	kabbuhin	three
caona	caouánam	—	gold; yellow metal
caya, cayo	acáera	kaíri	island
cocuyo	cógouyou	kokkui	Pyrophorus spp.
conuco 'garden'	—	kúnnuku 'forest' (G unú?u 'tree')	
cori	coúli	kúri	mouse
daca, dacha	—	dákia, dái	I; me
dita	rita	—	calabash cup, dish, or dipper
duhu	—	(G tulú)	Indian bench
guaiba	ouáiba	waiiba	let us leave
guanábana	ouallápana	oarafana	Annona muricata L.
guayaba	coyábou	máliaba	guava
haba	hába	hábba	(kind of) basket

Taino	Island-Carib	Arawak (G = Guajiro)	Gloss
hage, axe, etc.	—	háliti, halti	sweet potato
hequeti 'one'	lígueti	ikini-, -ikin	single
hibiz	hébechet, íbichet	—	basketry sifter
hicaco	icácou	(G kaáko)	coco plum
higüera	huira	iwida	calabash (Crescentia cujete)
hobo	oúbou	hóbo	Spondias mombin L
hupia	ópoyem	—	specter
hyen	ínhali	kehélli	manioc juice
iguana	-youhána-, -yoána	jóana, ioána	iguana
macaná	—	sappakanne	wooden sword
máhici, mahiz	márichi	márissi	maize
manati	manáttoui	—	manatee
manaya 'stone knife'	-mana	-mana-	sharp edge
maní	mánli	—	peanut
Matininó	—	mattinnînno	(see text)
mayani	maní-	mani-	be quiet; not do/say
nacan	ánac, ánackê	ánnakē	middle (of a place)
nagua	—	(G naáwa)	woman's loincloth
nahe	néhene	-nahàlle	paddle (n.)
nigua	—	(G niíwa)	chigoe (pulex penetrans)
papaya	abábai	papáia	papaya
cemí, zemí	chemíin, çeméen	sémehe	spirit-helper, god
ciba, ziba	(ichíbani 'anchor stone')	síba	stone
cigua	chíoua	—	sea snail (Fr. burgau)
simu, zimu	ichíbou	íssibu	face
-tiao	-tíaon	—	(formal) friend
xagua, jagua	cháoua	—	genipa
xagüeye	chaouái	—	cave; grotto
yagua	iaouálla	awára	spp. of palm
yamoca	biama	biama	two
yamoncobre	biánbouri	biábite, bíbiti	four
yari	íari, ínhari	-iédi	necklace, jewelry

A few Taino words have been omitted from the list because their form or their meaning appears to be doubtful. Such are T *behique* 'medico', which seems to be related to IC *ibíę* and A *ibihi* 'medicine' and to A *ibihikin* 'to treat with medicine'. T *hatty*—also recorded as *hatsi, haxi, hagi*, etc.—is clearly cognate with CAIC *áti*, DIC *áthi*, A *háthi*, and G *haší*, all meaning 'capsicum (cayenne pepper)'. T *manicato* is said to mean "esforzada é fuerte é de grande ánimo," although it is suspiciously like A *manikatho* 'she is silent; she says/does nothing' (which might, of course, have been employed in the sense of 'forbearing, patient'). Finally

T *nacan*, which is listed above, should be compared with modern A *nakán* 'middle (of night)' and *nakín* 'middle (of forest or other place)'.

It has been claimed that T *manaya* 'stone knife' is a loan from Italian *mannaia* 'kind of ax', itself a reflex of Lat. *manuarias* 'used by hand'. Such a model chosen to name such an implement would be surprising, although the occurrence of similar words for 'knife', not only in other Arawakan but also in Cariban languages, suggests that borrowing took place somewhere. (Cf. Arawakan Baniva *marlía*, Guinao *maria*, Maipure *manuri*, Tariana *marliá*, and Cariban Karina *mari:ya*, Chayma *mereya*, Crichana *mariai*, Hishkaryana *mareya*, all glossed 'knife'.)

LIVING LANGUAGES

Arawak

In 1594–95, three years before Jan de Laet's wordlists were collected in Trinidad, Robert Dudley and Captain Wyatt recorded near Punta Carao in the southwest of the same island lists containing, respectively, sixty-seven and twenty-seven items of a language which Wyatt called "Aroaca, *sermo Indianus*." There can be little doubt that this language is to be identified with that now called Arawak or Lokono, still spoken by several thousand Indians in Surinam and British Guiana (Guyana). Forty of these words are given below, together with a few recorded about the same time "near the mouths of the river Orinoco" by Vazquez de Espinosa, and opposite them are listed their equivalents (and a few only near equivalents) as recorded in 1968 by me in Surinam. (The complete list may be found in Taylor 1957, and, for Dudley and Wyatt, in Warner 1899.) It should be noted that Arawak forms beginning in *d(a)*- are possessed by first person singular 'my', and those beginning in *w(a)*- or *o(a)*-, by the first person plural 'our'. (For the phonemes of modern Arawak, see below, p. 134, and Taylor 1969, 1970, 1976.)

Trinidad, 1594–98 (D = Dudley, W = Wyatt, L = de Laet, V = Vazquez de Espinosa)	Surinam, 1968	Gloss
dadena (D)	dadína	arm
semaro (D), symare (L)	simára	arrow
marrahabo (D), semarape (L)	simarábo	bow
haculle (D)	híkili	bowstring
callit (D)	kháli	cassava
dudica (D), dadica (W), wadycke (L)	dadíke, oadíke	ear
dacosi (D), dacasi (W), wackosije (L)	dakósi, oakósi	eye
daciboh (W)	dasíbo	face
hicket (D), iquigî (V)	híkihi	fire
dacutti (D), dackosye (L)	dakóti	foot
viauite (V)	bíbithi	four
dabarra (D), dabarah (W)	dabára	hair
dacan, dacabbo (D), dacabo (W)	dakhábo	hand

Trinidad, 1594–98	Surinam, 1968	Gloss
dacy (W), wassijehe (L)	dasí, oasí	head
dacurle (D)	dakóro	knee
yeddola (D), eduóla (W)	iadóala	knife
daddano (D), dadane (L)	dadána	leg
maurisse	márisi	maize
cattie (D), cattehee (L)	káthi	moon
saeckee (L)	sáke 'uterus; eggshell'	mother
dalacoak (D), dalarócoh (W), dalerocke (L)	daléroko	mouth
dabodda (D), dabádoh (W)	dabáda	nail, claw
dacirey (W), wassyerii (L)	dasíiri, oasíiri	nose
abarùa (V)	abá(ro)	one
heldaro (D)	haararo	pot spoon
arguecona, arkeano (D), arkekano (W)	arikikoána	scissors
weeuah (D), weeuah (W)	oíoa 'star'	sky
dadite (V)	dáithi (< dádithi)	son
addehegaeno (D)	adikhikoána	spyglass
sibath (D)	síba	stone
haddalle (D), hadaley (W), adaly (L)	hádali	sun
halete (D)	hálithi	sweet potato
cabuin (V)	kábiin	three
ureit (D), uree (W)	ióri	tobacco
dill (= diee?)	daiée	tongue
areheh (D), dary (W), darii (L)	aríhi, dári	tooth
addoth (D), adda (W), hada (L)	áda	tree
viama (V)	bíama, bían	two
güine (V), oronuie (D)	óni 'rain', oniábo 'water'	water
sakel (D)	sákili 'he is well/good'[1]	it is well

Most probably printer's errors, in Dudley's list, are "dill' for "diee" (the spelling Dudley might well have used for /daiée/ 'my tongue') and "dalacoak' for "dalaroka" (/daléroko/ 'my mouth'). Clearly innovations are the words for 'scissors' and 'spyglass', made up of the verb stems meaning, respectively, 'cut' and 'see' together with an instrumental suffix -koána (cf. Island-Carib, which, for 'scissors', borrowed Sp. tijeras as IC sírasi). The word given in De Laet's publication for 'mother' is a compound of A sa- 'child, offspring; egg' and -ke (éke) 'container'. Cognate with this latter is IC ácae (modern /ágai/) 'container', which served and serves to designate the physiological as distinct from the sociological mother (Mo, MoSi, MoFaBrDa, etc.). Finally, Dudley's, Wyatt's, and De Laet's lists include—besides d(a)- 'my; me; I' (common to Arawak and Taino)—words for 'mouth' and 'sun', cognate equivalents of which are attested for no other language but Arawak.

[1] The Arawak word has male-human gender (-li) and cannot therefore refer to 'it', although Dudley's gloss has 'it is well'.

Island-Carib

At the time of first contact with the Europeans, Island-Carib was spoken throughout the Lesser Antilles (excluding Trinidad); but the native Indians were exterminated or chased away from one island after another till it became virtually confined to Dominica and St. Vincent. In 1797 it was carried by some five thousand deportees from the latter island to Central America, where it is now the home language of more than thirty thousand of their descendants, the so-called Black Caribs or (in Spanish) Morenos. This people originated in the mixture of Indian women with escaped Negro slaves who had taken refuge in St. Vincent; and although nearly all adults belonging to it today speak English or Spanish as a second language, they are proud of their mother tongue and show no inclination to abandon it (Taylor 1951).

In Dominica and St. Vincent, on the other hand, the language was gradually replaced during the course of the nineteenth century, by a French creole in the former and by an English dialect in the latter; and the last native speakers of Island-Carib on either island died about 1920.

In 1853, just two hundred years after Breton's departure, the Caribs of Dominica were tackled by another French priest, Father de Lettré, who finally accomplished their conversion. In his two-volume manuscript diary (in the presbytery of Vieille Case, Dominica), he tells us (pp. 405-9) that they were then reduced to some 125 shy and timorous individuals and says of their language: "Ils ont à peu près oublié leur ancienne langue, dont ils ne se servent entre eux que comme en cachette des autres personnes. . . . Ils parlent le créole comme les autres naturels du pays" (cited from Léon Thomas 1953). Twenty-five years later an American ornithologist, Frederick Ober, said of them: "A few old men and women only can speak the ancient Carib tongue" (Ober 1879, p. 447). Nevertheless, after yet another twenty years, Dr. Rat, a physician, was able to record short texts in the language (Rat 1898).

In 1930, when I first came to Dominica, the language was extinct; but the last native speaker, a woman called Ma Gustave, had died not more than twelve years previously, according to my informants; and it was still possible to find upwards of half a dozen older individuals who claimed to have spoken or understood the language as children, and who could with some difficulty recall sizeable bits of it.

This differential viability may seem surprising. But the relative isolation of the deportees in a sparsely inhabited area undoubtedly favored their increase and expansion; while in each of the two islands, which are some 150 miles apart, there remained only a few hundred Caribs, "Red" and "Black" together; and these were progressively crowded out of such bits of land as they had hitherto managed to retain. At last, in 1904, the few remaining Caribs of Dominica were given a reserve of some 3,700 mountainous acres on the windward side of the island; but Negro squatters were never expelled, and together with their mixed progeny, they now outnumber the Caribs there by more than ten to one.

The earliest mention of the Island-Carib is that made by Columbus, who, on November 26 1492, wrote in his diary: "Toda la gente que hasta hoy he hallado diz que tiene grandissimo temor de los de Caniba ó Canima" (Navarrete 1825–37). Modified to *caníbal* (perhaps by addition of the Romance suffix *-al*), this name was partly replaced in subsequent Spanish writings by *caribi* or *caribe*, borrowed from an unknown model. But Columbus probably came very close to this people's tribal name in its Taino form, which may have been **kanibna* (cf. Cariban Chayma *karibna* 'Carib', *mereya* 'knife', with Arawakan Taino *manaya* 'stone knife').

A hundred and fifty years later in Dominica, Raymond Breton recorded the Island-Caribs' own name for themselves as *Callíponam* in the women's speech, *Callínago* in that of the men, the latter form showing syncope (cf. modern Cariban Karina /kari?na/ 'person; Carib') and the addition of an honorific suffix *-go*.

What appears to be a correspondence of T *n* to Breton's IC *l* or *ll* is seen also in T *burén* : IC *boúrrêlet* 'griddle' and T *guanábana* : IC *ouallápana* (modern /ouaráfana/) 'soursop (Annona muricata L.)'. In some other instances, however, the Island-Carib form shows what is today a nasalized vowel, as in T *aon* : IC *ánli* (modern /áu̯li/) 'dog', T *hyen* : IC *ínhali* (modern /i̯ali/) 'manioc juice', T *maní* : IC *mánli* (modern /máli/) 'peanut'; and since Taino *n* elsewhere corresponds to IC *n* (see above; also in T *canoa* : IC *canáoua* 'canoe'), it seems possible that the apparent correspondence of nasal to lateral resulted from vowel syncope followed by consonantal assimilation—with or without simplification of geminates.

If this hypothesis should be correct, the various but similar words referring to 'Carib' may go back to an ancestral **kaniriphuna*, meaningful in Arawakan but not, I think, in Cariban. The suffix *-na* is a collectivizer or pluralizer of Island-Carib and of Arawak; the suffix *-phu* (modern A /-fo/) is employed in the latter language to derive clan names from the names of plants (so, A /haiaoáfona/ 'incense-tree clan', from A /háiaoa/ 'incense tree'); while the stem of this tentatively reconstructed word may be compared to such Arawakan words for 'bitter manioc' as Campa *kániri*, A *kálli* (modern /kháli/), and IC *cánhim* (modern /gái̯/).

During the course of the sixteenth century the Island-Carib were on several occasions attacked by the Spaniards and visited by ships of other European nations; and in 1597 Dr. Layfield, chaplain to the Duke of Cumberland, noted that those of Dominica seemed anxious to learn English:

For some of them, pointing to the limbs of their body one after the other, told us the names in their language and desired to know what they were called in English. This they then kept repeating till they were able to pronounce it well, or what to them seemed well enough and was fairly well indeed. Only that to every word that ended in a consonant they had to add a vowel, thus making of every monosyllabic word a polysyllabic one. (Hakluyt 1903–5, vol. 3)

But these early travelers apparently anticipated no such curiosity on the part of their readers, for not until half a century later do we begin to get any record of the Island-Carib language.

Father Raymond Breton was one of the first Europeans to settle in Guadeloupe, where he helped to establish a house for missionaries of his Dominican order. But five of his eighteen years in the West Indies (1635–54) were spent in various "field trips" among the Indians of Dominica, then that island's only inhabitants. And there he was told "que les insulaires étaient des Galibis de terre ferme qui s'étaient détachés du continent pour conquêter les Iles, que le Capitaine qui les avait conduits était petit de corps, mais grand en courage, qu'il mangeait peu et buvait encore moins, qu'il avait exterminé tous les naturels du pays à la réserve des femmes, qui ont toujours gardé quelque chose de leur langue" (Breton 1665, p. 229).

There is neither reason to doubt that these islands had indeed been conquered by Galibi (i.e., Karina or True Carib) warriors, nor, as yet, any way of dating that event. But it is quite clear that the language described by Breton was Arawakan, not Cariban (though containing many Carib elements), and that it was the men of Breton's time who had kept only "something" of the invaders' tongue. Somewhat similarly, Mozarabic—a Romance and not an Arabic dialect—survived eight hundred years of Arab rule, and the following remarks concerning it apply, *mutatis mutandis*, to the Island-Carib situation:

It was the language of all women. . . . The caliphs and the entire upper classes were bilingual, with Spanish for their mother tongue. . . . Arabic was an official speech, but those who were not officials did not trouble to acquire it. (Entwistle 1936, p. 115)

Thus from the first there was produced a mixed stock from Muslim Arabic-speaking males and Christian Romance-speaking females. . . . To the feminine element in the racial melting-pot may be attributed the persistence both of Christian religion and of Romance speech. (Elcock 1960, p. 276)

Perhaps the first to point out that words of the Island-Carib women's speech were, for the most part, related to Arawak, and those of the men's speech, to Karina, was Lucien Adam (1878). Still later, C. H. de Goeje (1939, pp. 4, 22) summed up the situation by showing that Breton's work contains "several expressions" that are purely Karina; "a much greater number" in which a Karina word—sometimes containing Karina affixes whose sense had been lost—is incorporated into an Arawakan grammatical construction; and "numerous forms" whose lexical and grammatical components alike are purely Arawakan. And he concludes (my translation): "Although the Karina were the victors and their descendants still considered themselves as belonging to the Karina nation, the mothers' Iñeri language, while absorbing a considerable number of Karina words, was maintained. In modern Island-Carib and in Honduranian Carib, we encounter only a few remnants of Karina grammar, which there have the appearance of irregularities in a grammatical whole that is fundamentally Arawak-Maipure, and therefore of Iñeri origin."

Breton himself was not concerned with linguistic comparison; and although he often indicated by an "f." forms of the women's speech, following others ascribed to that of the men, it is evident that he regarded both as constituting but one language, which he called "la langue caraïbe." So, in the French-Carib volume of his dictionary (1666, pp. 230, 299, 365, 378), we find "*lune*, nónum; f. cáti," "*pluye*, conóboui; f. óya," "*soleil*, huéyou; f. cáchi," "*terre*, nónum; f. mónha"; and in the Carib-French volume (1665, pp. 92, 228, 420), "boúpou, iboúpoulou, *pied, mon pied*," "eyepoue; f. lapourcou, *l'autre*," and (Arawakan) "ougoútti, nougoútti, *pied, mon pied*." Yet under the Arawakan word for 'foot, feet' which we have just noted, he also enters the mixed forms "lougoútti huéyou, *le rayon du soleil*" and "tougoútti conóboui, *sont nuées pleines de vent & de pluye, qui font comme de longs traits, ou rayes*."

Less than one-fifth of the entries in the French-Carib volume of his dictionary (much fewer in the Carib-French volume) are distinguished in this way; while men's and women's forms are treated together in his *Grammaire*. So, for example, we find (1667, p. 18) "*nembouiàtina tibónam, ou chileàtina tóne*, je suis venu à elle," whose stems, meaning respectively 'come' and 'to', are Cariban in the first instance (*nemboui-, -ibónam*) and Arawakan in the second (*chile-, -óne*), but whose common grammatical affixes *-a-ti-na* (perfective aspect, 1st sg.) and *t-* (3rd sg. f.) are Arawakan.

It is true that Breton mentions a very few affixes of Karina ancestry as belonging to the men's speech; so, "*ichánum*, ma mère," "*achánum*, ta mère," and "*kichánum*, notre mère." But affixes belonging to the women's speech were employed for other persons (*lichánum* 'his mother', *tichánum* 'her mother'), and might, it would seem, be employed for all persons, even with stems of Karina ancestry belonging to the men's speech; for "*uhèmbou*, ventre" (elsewhere "*ventre*, huémbou; f. oullácae"); cf. K *uwembo* with the same meaning) is inflected as "*nuhémbou*, mon ventre, *buhémbou*, ton ventre," etc., for all persons, with the same Arawakan prefixes as are taken by forms of the women's speech (*noullácae, boullácae*, etc.).

Moreover, most of the words listed as common to both sexes are clearly Arawakan (e.g., those for 'claw', 'dog', 'ear', 'feather', 'to fly', 'four', 'hand', 'he', 'leaf', 'nose', 'one', 'root', 'round', 'she', 'sit', 'small', 'smoke', 'stand', 'tail', 'that', 'they', 'this', 'tongue', 'two', 'walk', 'we', 'what', 'who', 'yellow', 'you'), although others are just as clearly Cariban (e.g., those for 'fire', 'fish', 'good', 'long', 'mountain', 'new', 'sand', 'stone', 'three', 'tree', 'water').

I conclude that bilingualism among the Island-Carib had given way by Breton's time to what may be called partial bilexicalism or "diglossia"—a state that has not yet, three hundred years later, been entirely outgrown.

As time went by, new forms were added to the lexicon (Breton's dictionary already contained some six dozen loans from Spanish; and at least several hundred stems were subsequently borrowed from French), while former "equivalents" were much reduced in number—sometimes by loss of the Arawakan or, more often, of the Cariban term, and especially by semantic differentiation. Thus, of the forms cited above, Breton's *cáchi* 'sun' (of the women's speech), and *boúpou, eyépoue, -ibónam,* and *nónum* (of the men's speech) have been lost; *conóboui* (modern /gunúbu/) is now obsolescent, /húia/ 'rain' being normally employed today by men as well as women; and the reflexes of Breton's *nemboui-* and *chile-* have been differentiated as 'come' vs. 'arrive'.

That such differentiation was not altogether unknown in Breton's day may be gathered from the fact that words given as men's and women's equivalents in the French-Carib volume of the dictionary are often defined somewhat differently in the Carib-French volume. For example, under *habitation, place d'un Sauvage,* we find "autê; f. obogne"; but the former, now meaning 'town', is defined as "*habitation de Sauvage, ville,*" and the latter, now meaning 'home', as "*une place, une habitation.*" And similarly, under *coeur, courage,* we find "iouánni; f. nanichi" (with *n-* 'my'); but the former—now meaning 'soul; vital principle; courage'—is defined as "coeur, âme, vie, courage," and the latter—now meaning 'my heart (as an organ); my mind, my inclination'—is defined as "coeur, âme, envie, volonté, désir." Nevertheless, some forms were and remain synonyms affected to the speech of men and to that of women, respectively. Thus, "*femme (sans restriction),* ouélle; f. ínharou," "*homme,* ouekélli; f. eyéri," "*moy,* áo; f. noúcouya," and "*toy,* ámanle; f. boúcouya" have become, without any change of meaning, /uóri/ or /hįáru/, /uogóri/ or /eiéri/, /áu/ or /nugúia/, and /amóro/ or /bugúia/ of the modern Central American dialect of Island-Carib.

TWO

THE PHONOLOGY OF
ISLAND-CARIB

❀

CLEARLY, Breton strove in the face of certain material and conceptual difficulties to render his spelling of Island-Carib quasi-phonetic; and he complains that a printer's shortage of the letter *k* has obliged him to represent this sound by *c* before *a*, *o*, or (*o*)*u*, and occasionally by *qu* before *i* or *e* (and see below for what he says concerning *ê*). He seems to come near to the phonological principle in one place, where he writes: "La consonnante *s* se prononce quelquefois comme the sygma des Grecs ou le *ç* François, qui a une virgule sous soy, comme *sanyánti*, je ne puis, mais plus souvent comme *ch*, *chanyánti*." But though he may have recognized the irrelevance to the language he was describing of some familiar distinctions, he continued to indicate them nevertheless ("*chibíba* ou *cibíba*," "*poupouli* ou *pfoupfouli*," "*oúpoyem* ou *ópoyem*," "*lo* ou *lou*," etc.); and apparently he failed, as we shall see, to recognize some others which, while unknown to French, were pertinent to Island-Carib of his day.

VOWELS AND ACCENTS

Breton employs the following symbols to represent simple vowel sounds: *a* "n'a point d'autre son que celuy du latin," *i* "est toujours voyelle chez les Caraïbes," *ou* "se prononce toujours comme l'*u* voyelle des Italiens," *e* "comme l'*é* masculin au françois; ... comme au latin," *eu* "se prononce comme le mot françois, *peu*," *ê* "tel que l'*e* féminin au françois; par ce qu'il ne se prononce qu'à demy," and again, *ê* "tire sur nostre diphtongue, *eu*. On le distingue aisément ... quand un François dit ces particules, *de, ne, me, te, se*." Of these last two sounds, both represented by *ê*, Breton says that the one is pronounced "quelque peu autrement" than the other; but that, having found nothing by which to distinguish them, he has marked both with a circumflex. He also employs, without any comment, *o* (*ouébo* 'mountain'), *y* (*huéyou* 'sun; day'), and *u*—this last always followed by *e* or *i*, never accented, and usually preceded by *h* (*huíra* 'calabash')—presumably with the values that they have in Fr. *yoyo*, *huer*, and *huit*, respectively.

Of the digraph *ei* he says that it sometimes has "le son d'un *e* ouvert, comme on le voit en ce mot françois, *peine*, & en ce mot caraïbe, *netéignon*"; but that at other times "il se prononce séparé en deux, comme *bebéite*, vent, *kéili*, encores"; while "par fois les deux lettres se prononcent, & si elles ne font qu'une syllabe, comme on le voit en ces deux mots, *Ichéiri*, Dieu, *aleiba*, cassave."

His *au* and *ay* are falling diphthongs; his *ia*, *ie*, and *io* are rising diphthongs except when the first element, *i*, is accented, in which case they are disyllabic sequences. And analogously, his unaccented *oi*, as in *manàttoi* (elsewhere written *manáttoui*) 'manatee', is monosyllabic (presumably [wɛ] or [we]), while *ói*, as in *hói* 'prairie, savane', is disyllabic. Disyllabic also are his *àe*, *ài*, and *ào*—irrespective, it would seem, of accentuation, for he gives as examples *aétera*, *àcai*, and *aócàba*. The negation *oúa* 'no' has two syllables ([úa]); *toualéba*, *éleboue*, *kíoua*, and *iouíne* are said to have three each.

Breton stresses the importance of "l'accent, ou quantité," but adds that general rules concerning it could hardly be made until a thorough knowledge of the language (which he did not claim to possess) should be acquired. He describes three sorts of accent. "L'un est bref, dont le son est aigu"; and this occurred on final syllables ending in consonants (*atálimac*) or in *eu* (*cayheù*, *haggueú*, *hatequeú*), being "plutôt grave qu'aigu" in the latter position. Of the other two, the second

est aigu et long, comme celuy qui est sur l'*a* des dictions terminées en *áim*, comme *nàim*, *nyàim*: sur l'*a* des impératifs terminés en *àe*, comme *àricabàe*, regarde le, *bàoua*, *bàyem*, &c., sur l'*e* metoyen de *nehuégne*, sur l'*e* final du vocatif, comme *bibioué*, sur l'*i* de *chíkea*, sur le premier *o* de *nócobou*, sur la diphtongue d'*àuthê*, &c. L'*e* féminin final renvoye quelquefois cet accent sur la première syllabe du nom, si long qu'il puisse être: . . . *láourgoutonê*, *lábourracatonê*. Le troisième accent est encore plus long, c'est celuy qui dénote les superlatifs, comme *nàneguaiti*. Pour le bien prononcer, il faut peser sur l'*a* autant que sur trois syllabes, & le terminer par une aspiration, comme *naahàneguaiti*, il est très malade.

I have cited Breton verbatim in the four preceding paragraphs because his sometimes ambiguous statements undoubtedly have some bearing on the subsequent evolution of this language's phonology. Apparently, affixation might then involve not only displacement of the accent but also replacement of one or more stem vowels by others: cf. his *aguétte* 'grandmother' vs. *náguettêni* 'my grandmother', and *illíguini* (elsewhere *íliguini*) 'tame animal; nursling; grandchild' vs. *kalleguênnêtina* 'I have (a) tame animal'. In the modern Central American dialect of this language (abbreviated here as CAIC), affixation may or may not involve displacement of stress; but only allophonic variation of stem vowels and not their identity is normally affected in this way: CAIC /sabádu/ 'shoes' vs. /nisábadu̧/ 'my shoes', /agóto/ 'grandmother' vs. /nagóto/ 'my grandmother', /ilógoni/ 'tame animal' vs. /galógo̧tina/ 'I have (a) tame animal' (CAIC /o/ is a back *unrounded* vowel, varying from mid to high).

That at least one of Breton's accents was free (as is stress in the modern CAIC dialect) seems to be borne out by his *álloucouraba ouátou* (CAIC /álugura bà uátu/) 'warm thyself at the fire!' vs. his *alloùcourába* (CAIC /alúgura bà/) 'sell!; give!' (2nd sg. imperative).

Divergent spellings of the same form—such as Breton's *noúcouya, noúcoya*, and *nócoya* (CAIC /nugúia/) 'I; me'—lead one to the conclusion that his *ou* and *o* were nondistinctive (as are [u] and [o] in the modern dialect and in Arawak); and this view is supported by the shape, in his record, of such early borrowings from Spanish as *bácachou* (as well as *bácacho*) 'cow', *bouírocou* 'pig', *boúrbrê* 'gunpowder', *cabáyo* 'horse', *cáyou* 'hen', *crábou* 'iron', *méchou* 'cat', *sabátto* 'shoes', and *nichabáttoni* 'my shoes' (CAIC /bágasu, buíruhu, búroburo, gabáiu, gáiu, grábu, mésu, sabádu, nisábadu̧/), whose models presumably were Sp. *vacazo, puerco, pólvora, caballo, gallo, clavo, micho*, and *zapato*.

Divergent spellings also indicate that Breton's *eu* and at least one variety of his *ê* represent allophones of one and the same phoneme—if not, indeed, homophones. His *ê* is most commonly employed in positions where no prosodic accent was required; but typographical difficulties probably explain why it never bears a second diacritic, even in what was almost certainly an accented syllable: cf. his *arrêna* as well as *areúnna* (CAIC /-aróna/, A /adína/) 'arm; wing'. His other variety of *ê*, which "ne se prononce qu'à demy," probably represents a reduced or partly devoiced vowel, as when he writes *tónê* (but elsewhere *tóna*; cf. CAIC /dúna/) 'water; river', a word borrowed from Karina, which today has /tu:na/ with the same reference.

A comparison of such forms as Breton's *huíouma* 'our mouths' and *huerébe* 'our foreheads' with his *ouácou* 'our eyes' and *ouaрícae* 'our ears' (cf. his *níouma* 'my mouth', *nerébe* 'my forehead', *nácou* 'my eyes', and *narícae* 'my ears') leads to the conclusion that his (*h*)*u*(*i*/*e*)- represents a nonsyllabic, palatalized variant of /u/ (Breton's *ou*), of about the same phonetic value as *hu* in Fr. *huit* and *huer*. This is at any rate true of the modern Central American dialect, in which, for example, /uerébe/ 'our foreheads' = [y̑e'rebe], but /uarígai/ 'our ears' = [y̑a'rigɛi].

But what then shall we say of such forms as Breton's *ouébo* 'mountain', *ouécou* 'cassava beer', *ouekélli* 'man; male', *ouélle* 'woman; female', and *houéhoue* 'ax', the last of which appears to be in minimal opposition with his *huéhue* 'wood; tree'? Either his (*h*)*ou* and (*h*)*u* represent different phonemes after all, or else his *e* does not represent a front vowel when it is preceded by *ou*! The second alternative seems the more plausible if we may judge by the phonological shape of these words' modern reflexes in the Central American dialect of Island-Carib (in which the back unrounded vowel is written /o/) and in Karina, the language from which they were borrowed (whose back unrounded vowel is written /ɨ/ and whose /o/ = [o]). Thus, CAIC /uóbu, uógu, uogóri, uóri, -áuori (with no absolute form)/, but /uéue/; and /wɨ:pɨ, wo:ku, wokɨ:rɨ, wo:rɨi, wɨ:wɨ ~ -wɨ:rɨ, we:we/. What appears to have been a retraction of front to back unrounded vowel is not confined to the position after IC /u/; for Breton's *éleoua* or *éloua* 'three', *kéoue* 'fishhook', and *tébou* 'stone' have given modern CAIC /óroua/ or /órua/, /góui/, and /dóbu/, and were borrowed from models that have given modern K /o:ruwa/, /ko:wei/, /to:pu/. Nor is this change, if it be one, confined to words borrowed from Karina; cf. Breton's *ék(ê)rik(ê)* 'flesh' and -*ék(ê)ra* 'hammock' with their modern reflexes, CAIC /ógorogo/ and /-ógora/ (G /iʔirúku/ 'flesh' and /-ʔuula/ 'hammock', A /-síroko/ 'flesh' and /-kóra/ 'hammock').

Two different solutions to the problem outlined above suggest themselves, and it may be that both of them contain something of the truth. Since it is elsewhere clear that Breton's *ê* or *eu* (cf. his alternative spellings of *arrêna, areúnna*) and *e* were in opposition—as in his "*chéba*, verse" vs. "*cheúba*, rostis" (CAIC /sé-ba/ 'pour out!' vs. /só-ba/ 'roast!' or 'sting!' (2d sg. imperative)—it seems not unlikely that where he had written an acute or a grave accent over the circumflex, his printer always eliminated one or the other diacritic (this happens today!). This would still leave the apparent change in several vowels which bear no diacritic unaccounted for except by assimilation. On the other hand, there is some evidence of the retraction (with or without rounding) of high and especially of mid front vowels in contact with a dorsovelar stop or with a bilabial sound not only in Island-Carib but also in Arawak, Guajiro, and Karina. This may have begun as conditioned variation, until the phonemicization of the back unrounded vowels (IC /o/, A, G, and K /ɨ/) led to such alternation as appears in Breton's *aguétte* 'grandmother' but *náguettêni* 'my grandmother'.

In his *Grammaire*, Breton tells us that "on prononce la consonante à la fin du mot, lors qu'il s'en rencontre une autre au commencement de celuy qui suit, comme *nítem loária*, il s'en est allé sans luy: on la fait couler par fois plus doucement." Nevertheless, he writes syllable-final *m* and *n* with seeming indifference (*bíem* and *bíen* 'tu dis', *biámbouri* and *biánbouri* 'quatre'); and his intervocalic -*nh*- (not to be confused with his initial *nh*-, an aspirated nasal) almost certainly represents only nasalization of the preceding vowel, as in his *ínharou* 'woman', with which compare recent Dominican /hįaru/, CAIC /hįáru/, and A /híaro/, which have the same meaning.

Breton sometimes replaces intervocalic *-nh-* by *-gn-*, by *-ny-*, or by zero—"*ínhouti* élevé," "*ignouráali* il est bien haut élevé," "*línhem* or *línyem* son pissat," "*ínhari* or *íari* bijoux"—and elsewhere replaces *-gn-* by *-y-*, by zero, or by syllable-final *m* or *n* following a disyllabic vowel sequence—"*ágnaca* or *áyaca* faire de la cassave," "*itígne* joues," "*nitíem* mes joues" (cf. CAIC /nidíę/ [ni'dĩẽ] 'my cheeks', in which the stressed vowel receives the stronger nasalization), "*itígnaom* compère," "*nitígnaon* mon compère," but "*áo katiaónbou* que je sois ton compère & ton amis," and *matíaon* 'without (a) comrade (formal friend)'.

I conclude that Breton's *y* belonged to the same phoneme as his *i* (nonsyllabic when unaccented in vowel sequences) and that his intervocalic *-nh-* and *-gn-* were merely devices employed to indicate nasalization followed by a *y*-like glide in such vowel sequences as *įV* and *V̨iV̨*. So, for example, his *netéignon* or *nétegnon* (and cf. identically glossed *nitígnon* and *nítignon*) 'my progenitor; my husband's mother; my husband's father' probably was, if we omit the erratic accent, /netęių/ [netɛ̃ĩjõ].

The dialect described by Breton seems, therefore, to have had five simple vowels (which he wrote as shown here in parentheses): /a/ (*a*, *ê*), /i/ (*i*, *y*) /u/ (*ou*, *o*, *hu*), /e/ (*e*, *ei*) and /o/ (*eu*, *ê*, and perhaps, through elimination of the circumflex in printing, *e*). These are also the vowel phonemes of the modern Central American dialect. Whether /o/ was front rounded, as Breton described it, or back unrounded as it is today cannot be directly determined, although from what has been said concerning palatalization of /u/ before front vowels, we might infer that it was back unrounded. Prosodic features almost certainly included nasalization of vowels and vowel sequences (as in the modern dialect) and free "accentuation"; though whether the latter was a matter of stress (as I believe it to be in the modern dialect) or one of tone and/or length (as Breton's remarks suggest) remains uncertain.

CONSONANTS

Although *b* of Breton's record occurred much more frequently than his *p* and *pf* (thirty as against eight pages of the dictionary, so far as initial position is concerned), there are enough minimal pairs like *boutoúba* 'gather!' vs. *poutoúba* 'pierce!', and *aboúcacha* 'to chase away' vs. *apoúcacha* 'to lay (eggs)', to show that there were two bilabial stops, one of which was sometimes affricated (*pf* in Breton's spelling). But while the personal prefix of second singular is said to be *b-*, and so appears in the vast majority of Breton's examples (*biráiti* 'thy husband', *bíouma* 'thy mouth', *boúcabo* 'thy hands', etc.), it is occasionally represented by *p*-(though never by *pf*-), as in *piáni* 'thy wife', *pitíouma* 'thy beard', and *pougoútti* 'thy feet', although *p* never replaces *b* in the personal *suffix* of second singular, *-bou*. I conclude that the two bilabial stops of this dialect were distinguished as unaspirated and aspirated rather than as voiced and voiceless.

Breton wrote the letter *d* in only three Island-Carib morphemes: *dimíttira*, the name of a kind of grass, *Oualádli*, the name of the island now called Antigua, and *dleu-* 'absent, not there'. Of the first two he says that he may have mistaken *t* for *d*; and of the last, "Pour *dleuti*, la plus part disent *leuti*, mais cet *l* se forme par le bout de la langue engagée entre les dents." In his *Grammaire* he discards *d* altogether, as representing "a sound too rare in the language to rank in the Carib alphabet." Elsewhere we find only *t*, *tt*, or, in two or three instances only, *th* (*áuthê*, as well as *áutê*); but he nowhere considers the possibility of a distinction based on aspiration of an apical stop.

Of *g* he says: "Le *g* n'est pas fréquent dans l'idiome caraïbe, au moins trouve-t-on peu de mots qui se commencent par cette consonnante"; and even medially, voicing of the dorsovelar stop or stops appears to have been nondistinctive: *inoúcoura* as well as *inoúgoura* 'there (yonder) she is', *abáichacoua* as well as *abáichagoua* 'to whip'.

Clearly, there were at least two nasals, *m* and *n* (*míri* 'nameless' vs. *níri* 'my name'), one sibilant (indifferently hissing or hushing, as exemplified by Breton's *sanyánti* or *chanyánti* 'it is impossible, it cannot be'), and one aspirate (cf., from *ácou* 'eye, eyes': *nácou, bácou, lácou, tácou, oácou, hácou, nhácou* 'my, thy, his, her, our, your, their eyes'). Whether the aspirated nasal, initial *nh-*, was a unit phoneme or a sequence may be questioned on account of its very limited distribution. Finally, the lateral *l* and the trill (or flap) *r* were distinct: *líli* 'his tail' vs. *líri* 'his name', *lóali* 'it has split' vs. *róali* 'he has given', *lála* 'his seat' vs. *lára* 'its dry heat'. That Breton's intervocalic *-ll-*, *-nn-*, *-tt-*, etc., should represent true geminates, or unit phonemes distinct from his *l*, *n*, *t*, etc., is improbable because of inconsistency in their use (*ouátou* as well as *ouáttou* 'fire', etc.).

Thus, from his own record, we can deduce the occurrence of only ten or—with *nh*—eleven consonant phonemes in the dialect Breton described. From other and more recent records, however, there is evidence which suggests that he missed two or possibly three consonantal oppositions: aspirated vs. unaspirated apical and dorsovelar stops (*th* ≠ *t*, *kh* ≠ *k*), and, doubtfully, aspirated vs. unaspirated laterals (*lh/l*).

Vincentian Island-Carib records (VIC) show both *d* and *t* as corresponding to *t* of Dominican (DIC) records: VIC *dúna*: DIC *túna* 'water', VIC *túri* : DIC *túri* 'her breasts', VIC *bádi* : DIC *báti* 'hut', but VIC *báti* : DIC *báti* 'thy brother', VIC *bídiuma* : DIC *bítiuma* 'thy moustache',

VIC *bíta* : DIC *bíta* 'thy blood', VIC *údu* : DIC *útu* 'fish', VIC *uátu* or *wat'ho* : DIC *uátu* 'fire'. Yet I can find only one instance of *d* recorded in recent Dominican: VIC *ugúdi* : DIC *ukúdi* or *ukúti* 'foot, feet'.

VIC *ch* [tš] and *s* are both shown as corresponding to DIC *s* : thus, VIC *nugúchuru* : DIC *nukúsuru* 'my mother', VIC *súgubai* : DIC *súgubai* 'all', VIC *bíchiri* : DIC *bísiri* 'thy nose', VIC *díseti* : DIC *tíseti* 'far', VIC *naníchi* : DIC *nanísi* 'my heart', VIC *hísanti* : DIC *hisanti* or *chisenti* 'he is loved', VIC *íchiga* : DIC *ísika* 'to give', VIC *sísira* : DIC *sísira* 'rattle' (n.), VIC *bachárua* : DIC *basárua* 'drunk' (pred. adj.), and borrowed VIC *gusínyu* : DIC *kusíyu* 'knife' (from Sp. *cuchillo*).

VIC *g* and *k* are both shown as corresponding to DIC *k* : VIC *gíbeti* : DIC *kíbeti* 'many', VIC *káti* : DIC *káti* 'moon', VIC *núgubu* : DIC *núkubu* 'my body', VIC *núkabu* : DIC *núkabu* 'my hand', etc. But VIC *k* is also shown as corresponding to DIC [x]—written *h*, but likened by Rat (1898) to the *ch* of Scottish *loch*, to a sound written sometimes *h* and at others *sh* which I take to have been the 'ich-Laut' [ç], and to velar and palatal affricates containing these sounds as their second element. So, we find VIC *yáka* : DIC *yáha* 'here', VIC *abínaka* : DIC *abínaha* and *abínakha* 'to dance', VIC *naríki* : DIC *naríhi* and *naríshi* 'my seeing', VIC *hísanti* : DIC *hisanti* and *chísenti* 'he is loved'. The last two examples represent reflexes of Breton's *naríkini* and *kínchenti* respectively.

We may probably conclude that the recent Vincentian dialect had two apical stops, a hushing assibilant (affricate), and a hissing sibilant, neither of which oppositions is attested for the Dominican dialect of any period. It also apparently had two dorsovelar stops; and there is some indication that this opposition was present also in recent Dominican and based on aspiration or its absence. It is easy to understand how an inexperienced recorder could confuse aspirated /kh/ and unaspirated /k/ so long as both remained voiceless and completely occlusive—as in recent DIC *núkabu* (with /kh/) 'my hand' and *núkubu* (with /k/) 'my body'—and yet distinguish them when their allophones betokened different phonemes of his own language—as in recent DIC *aríha* (with [x] as an allophone of /kh/) 'to see, to look' vs. *atíka* (with [k] = /k/) 'to catch (fish)'. So also, such divergent spellings as recent DIC *naríshi* and *naríhi* (with [ç] = /kh/), *chísenti* and *hísanti* (with /kh/ heard as [tš] in one case and as [ç] or [h] in another), rather dimly reflect what in all probability were nondistinctive palatalization and affrication or spirantization of an aspirated stop, /kh/. But since Breton did not distinguish the dorsovelar stop of his *aríca* 'to see' (*naríkini* 'my seeing', *kínchenti* 'he is loved') from that of his *atíca* 'to catch' or *kíbeti* 'many', we must assume that affricated allophones of the aspirated dorsovelar stop, unlike those of the aspirated bilabial stop (Breton's *p* ~ *pf*), were a recent development.

We have seen how the distinction between aspirated and unaspirated bilabial stops of the early Dominican dialect was in most cases correctly recorded for the wrong reason: because the latter was usually though nondistinctively voiced. And the distinction between aspirated and unaspirated apical and dorsovelar stops of recent Vincentian appears to have been correctly recorded, in most cases, for the same wrong reason. For, as in the case of Breton's *b* and *p*, so in that of recent VIC *g* and *k*, *k* and *h* (though not, or very rarely, in that of *d* and *t*), there seems to be occasional confusion of a sort that forbids us to regard voicing as the distinctive feature. So, besides Ober's (1877) *guríera* 'canoe', *karábali* 'wind', and *káti* 'moon', we also have *kuríera*, *garábali*, and *háti* from later recorders on the same island. Moreover, had voicing rather than aspiration been distinctive in the Vincentian correlation, such models as Fr. *table* and *cullier* (modern *cuiller*) would not have given, as they did, borrowed VIC *dábula* 'table' and *gulíeru* 'spoon'; nor is it likely that an earlier *p* would have passed to *f*. The shapes of VIC *fúdu* and DIC *pútu* 'pot, jug' suggest that *b* of both dialects had become distinctively voiced by the time that the borrowing was made; but it is at least as likely that here the model was English (in which the *p* of *pot* is aspirated) rather than French, as it surely was in the case of VIC *fáifa* and DIC *páipa* 'pipe'.

COMPARISON

The question then arises, What phonological differences, if any, existed between the early and recent Dominican dialects, or between the recent Dominican and recent Vincentian? In no record of Dominican is there evidence of an opposition between two apical stops, nor of one between two sibilants or between sibilant and assibilant; while the only evidence of two dorsovelar stops in the early Dominican dialect is the fact that Breton consistently wrote medial -*k*- (or -*c*- or -*qu*-) in some morphemes and medial -*g*- in others. But yet others show, without change of environment, now -*k*- and now -*g*- (*inoúcoura* as well as *inoúgoura*); and only *k*- (or *c*-) appears in word-initial. And since Breton did distinguish initial *nh*- (attested also for recent Dominican, and described as an aspirated nasal) from *n*- and *h*-, his failure to recognize analogous oppositions, such as *th* ≠ *t* and *kh* ≠ *k* (if they occurred in the dialect described by him), is surprising.

On the other hand, assuming that the Dominican and Vincentian dialects of c. 1650 had a common phonological system, it would be remarkable, though not of course impossible, for a single dorsovelar stop to have split in both dialects, and a single apical stop and a single sibilant to have split only in Vincentian—all within some two hundred years; and evidence that the two dialects remained mutually intelligible to the end militates against such a conclusion.

Moreover, recent investigation in Surinam (Renselaar and Voorhoeve 1962; Taylor 1969*a*, 1969*b*) has shown that Arawak, which is rather closely related to Island-Carib, has at least two hitherto unrecognized consonantal oppositions based on aspiration: /th/ as well as /t/ and /d/, /kh/ as well as /k/; while the *p* (probably /ph/) of earlier Arawak records having passed to /f/, a new, voiceless, and unaspirated /p/, apparently found only in recent loanwords, is now opposed to voiced /b/. Renselaar and Voorhoeve believed that there was also an opposition between a sound that they write as *lh* and both /l/ and /r/; but I am convinced that this sound (an apical vibrant with unilateral release) is, in the dialect of my informants, but an allophone of their *r*-phoneme (otherwise a flapped or mildly trilled apical [r]), although it may well be or may once have been distinctive for other native speakers of Arawak.

My own analysis shows Arawak to have the following phonemes:

m	n	–		i	[u]
b	d	–		ɨ	
p	t	k		e	[o]
–	th	kh		a	
f	s	h		Plus long or double	
–	l, r	–		vowels (VV) and	
				free stress (V́)	

[u] and [o] are both heard as allophones of a single back rounded vowel which will be written /o/. All vowels may be either oral or nasalized, but nasalized vowels are almost always preconsonantal or word-final and in the latter position often represent the addition of a suffix. Here they will be written as *V* + *n*.

Examples of minimal pairs showing the oppositions of *d* ≠ *t* ≠ *th*, and of *k* ≠ *kh*, are *thididá dadiáko* 'it-jumped upon-me', *thitidá dáoria* 'it-got-away from-me', and *thithidá dakhábo* 'it-stung my-hand' (or *tórodon* 'to lie down' vs. *thórodon* 'to open'), and *kídin* 'to bathe' vs. *khídin* 'to chase away' (both v.t.).

Most (perhaps all) of the apical consonants undergo some palatalization when followed by /i/. This is most pronounced in the cases of /d, t, th, s/, which in this position are heard as [dj] ~ [ǧ], [tj] ~ [č], [č] and [š], respectively. /n/ before /i/ is frequently but not regularly palatalized to [ñ], but I never heard any palatalization in the cases of /li/ and /ri/. In all other positions, /d/, /t/, and /th/ are, respectively, unaspirated voiced, unaspirated voiceless, and aspirated voiceless apical stops, /s/ a hissing sibilant, and /n/ an apical gingival nasal. /k/ and /kh/ are, respectively, unaspirated and aspirated velar occlusives [k] and [kʰ], the latter being occasionally heard as an affricate, [kx].

A comparison of some Central American Island-Carib forms with likely cognates in Arawak and/or in Guajiro (the latter taken for the most part from Holmer 1949 and from Hildebrandt 1963) tends to support this analysis.

CAIC	Arawak	Guajiro	Gloss
tugúdi	thokóti	si ʔuli	her foot
líta	lithina	niša	his blood
áta	-ithi- ~ -itha-	asá(a)	drink (v.)
lídiuma	litíima	niliíma	his moustache
abuídaha	—	epítahaa	sweep (v.)
bagóto	bakíthi	poúšuu	thy grandmother
áruguti	-dokothi	atúuši	grandfather
-óho	-íkhi	ahí	sap; pus; extract (n.)
-ógo	—	á ʔi	kernel; core
hóro-	khídi-	—	heavy
túhabo	thíkhabo	sahápi	her hand
aríha	dikha- ~ dikhi-	atíha(a) ~ atíha(a)	see (CAIC & A); know (G)
háti	káthi	kaší	moon
—	dáthi	tašíi	my father
dábu-	tabú(sia)	—	sleepy
daga-	taka- ~ taki-	—	close(d) up, obstruct(ed)
adóro-	—	atíri-	thunder
barígai	badíke	pacé ʔe	thy ear
agába	kanaba- ~ kanabo-	aápa(a)	hear
arúmuga	-donka- ~ -donko-	atúka	sleep

It is improbable that distinctions such as those seen in the correspondences exemplified above should result from new and parallel developments in three related languages. And it is impossible that a distinction lost in borrowing could be restored out of all contact with the model. So that if we compare CAIC [uátu/ 'fire', /átiri/ 'how many?' or 'how much?', /dúna/ 'water', and /údu/ 'fish', all borrowed from Karina (True Carib) in prehistoric times, with their models' modern reflexes in the source language, K /waxto, oxtoro, tu:na, wo:to/ (Hoff 1968), we must, I think, conclude that the Island-Carib dialect described by Breton also had two apical stops, confused by him as in his *ouátou* or *ouáttou*, *átêli*, *tóna* or *tônê*, and *óto* or *áoto*, with the same meanings as above. These two stops most probably were unaspirated /t/ and aspirated /th/, both usually voiceless (cf. William Young's "*wat'ho* 'fire'", dated St. Vincent, 1795).

Further evidence of the correspondences discussed above is not wanting, although there is one counter example in the CAIC word for 'moon' (CAIC *h* : A *k* : G *k*, instead of *g* : *k* : *k*, or *h* : *kh* : *h*), and it is not certain that the Guajiro word for 'know' is a cognate of the Central American Island-Carib and Arawak words for 'see'. (It could be, rather, a cognate of *aitha-* ~ *aithi-* 'know', from earlier (attested) A *aditha-*, with which compare CAIC *aríta* 'be of the opinion; think'. For although A

/th/ regularly corresponds to G /s/ or /š/, there appears to be considerable dialectal confusion in Guajiro between these latter phonemes and /h/.)

Nevertheless, I think we must conclude that Dominican Island-Carib also inherited two dorsovelar stops: aspirated /kh/, as in Breton's *noúcabo* > CAIC /núhabu/ 'my hand(s)', and unaspirated /k/, as in his *nócobou* > CAIC /núgubu/ 'my body'. For just as Breton failed to distinguish aspirated /th/ and unaspirated /t/ in his "*cáti* la lune" and "*ítiouma* barbe," aspirated /kh/ and unaspirated /k/ in his "*oúcabo* main" and "*arónca* dormir," so the anonymous eighteenth-century compiler of the *Arawakisch-Deutsches Wörterbuch* failed to make the same distinction for Arawak: "*kátti* der Mond; ein Monat," "*ittímahü* der Bart," "*úekkabbu* die Hand," and "*adumkin* schlafen."

Cognates showing the correspondence of CAIC *d* : A *t* : G *t* or *l*—the latter (*d* : *t* : *l*) found only and apparently always before an immediately following /i/—are scarce and merit further investigation, especially so far as Guajiro is concerned.

Those showing CAIC *r* : A *d* : G *t*—as in CAIC *-aróna* : A *-adína* : G *atína* 'arm'—are, on the other hand, well attested, as are those of CAIC *r* : A *r* : G *l* (*-ágoro* : *-ákiri* : *-a?ilíi* 'husband's mother', *-ári* : *-ári* : *a(l)íi* 'tooth', *-áru* : *-aróma* : *olú* 'edge; border', *baráua* : *baráa* : *paláa* 'sea', *háburi* : *háburi* : *hapílee* 'shame', *-ógora* : *-kóra* : *-(?)ulá* 'hammock'). Yet we also find CAIC *r* : A *r* : G *r* (*ógorogò* : *síroko* : *e(?)irúku* 'flesh', *euéra* : *ioéra* : *eéra* 'penis', *-íra* : *-íra* : *-erá* 'juice; sauce; gravy', *hįáru* : *híaro* : *hiéri* 'woman; female') and CAIC *l* : A *l* : G *l* (*balígi* : *bálisi* : *palí?i* 'ashes', *-lógǫ-* : *-líkin-* : *alįí* 'tame animal; grandchild', *amúlę* : — : *emíle* 'younger brother'), without there appearing to be any conditioning factor that could explain these differences.

Breton's distributionally restricted, aspirated nasal *nh-* persisted in recent Dominican but (assuming it to have been a unit phoneme) has fallen together with CAIC /h/ (the meager Vincentian data contain no correspondence). This phoneme (or sequence?) corresponds to /n/ of both Arawak and Guajiro, as in DIC *nháku* : CAIC *hágu* : A *nakósi* : G *na?ú* 'their eyes'.

That the hissing and hushing sibilants of the early Dominican dialect of Island-Carib were nondistinctive is evident both from Breton's remarks on the subject and from his alternative spellings with *ch-* or *s-*, *-ch-* or *-ss-*. And while the hushing variety was, we are told, the more common in his time, only the hissing variety is recorded in recent Dominican, in which it corresponds both to *s* [s] and to *c* [tš] of contemporary Vincentian (the latter written *ch* by Ober 1877, *tch* by Ballantyne 1893). So, Breton's *aoáchi* > recent DIC *auási* and VIC *auási* 'maize', but Breton's *aníchi* > recent DIC *anísi* and VIC *aníci* 'heart'.

In early borrowings from Spanish, orthographic *s*, *x*, *j*, *z*, and *ch* of the model are alike replaced by Breton's IC *ch* [š], becoming *s* [s] of all later dialects. Examples: Breton's *acoúcha* (Sp. *aguja*) > CAIC *agúsa* 'needle', his *racaboúchou* (Sp. *arcabuz*) > CAIC *arágabusu* 'gun', his *camícha* (Sp. *camisa*) > CAIC *gamísa* 'cloth', his *couchígno* (Sp. *cuchillo*) > CAIC *gusíu* 'knife', his *(i)chiboúchi* (Sp. *espejo*) > CAIC *isíbuse* 'mirror' (perhaps by way of *esibésu through contamination with inherited *isíbu* 'face'), and his *méchou* (Sp. *micho*) > CAIC *mésu* 'cat'. Moreover, the single sibilant phoneme of Arawak, which is hushing before a high front vowel and hissing elsewhere, corresponds both to *s* and to *c* of the Vincentian and Central American dialects of Island-Carib, as in A *semée-* : VIC and CAIC *semée-* 'good tasting' (Breton's *cheménhen-* and *cheméen-*), A *-sika-* : VIC and CAIC *íciga* 'give; put' (Breton's *íchiga*), and A *simára* 'arrow' : VIC *cimára* : CAIC *cimára* > *gimára* 'bow' (Breton's *chimála*).

I think we must conclude that Breton made no mistake in finding only one sibilant in the Dominican dialect of his day, and that this was later split in St. Vincent (though not in Dominica) into *s* and *c*. But since these new phonemes are found in exactly the same positions, it does not seem possible to recover the factors of the presumed split:

Dominica	St. Vincent	Central America	
1650–1900	*1870–1900*	*1947–48*	*Gloss*
sísira	sísira	sísira	(shaman's) rattle
ísika	ícika	íciga	to give; to put
ísira	ícira	ígira	to leave

Thus, where only one form (or two homonyms) existed in Breton's day, we may now have two quite distinct forms, as in the case of Breton's "*chába nitibouri* 'tond, rase moy'" (*nitibouri* 'my hair'), and "*chába noucoúnni* 'estoupe les fentes de mon canot, . . . calfate-le'" ("*noucoúnni* 'mon canot'") being distinguished today as CAIC *sá-ba nídiburi*, containing *sa* 'shear; shave', and *cá-ba nugúne*, containing *ca* 'thrust into; stuff up'.

In the Central American dialect, though not in Vincentian, a still more remarkable development took place about one hundred years ago: $c^{i,e}$ was largely though not entirely replaced by $g^{i,e}$ or, more rarely, by $c^{u,o}$. Thus, we now find, for example, modern CAIC *ígira* 'leave', *-igína* 'neck', *anígi* 'heart', *igíbu* 'face', and *ígiri* 'nose', but *íciga* 'give; put', *anícigu* 'wisdom', *núguci* 'my father', and *sísira* 'rattle', *sígai* 'porpoise', corresponding to VIC (and earlier CAIC) *ícira*, *-iciena*, *aníci*, *icíbu*, *íciri*, *íciga*, *anícigu*, *nugúcili*, *sísira*, *sígai*, and to recent DIC *ísira*, *-isíuna*, *anísi*, *isíbu*, *ísiri*, *ísika*, *anísiku*, *nukúsili*, *sísira*, and *síkai* (cf. A *-sika-* 'give; put', *-sibo* 'face', *-siri* 'nose', etc.).

There is some slight evidence that this replacement of $c^{i,e}$ in the Central American dialect was still in a state of flux as recently as 1872, when

Henderson recorded *cimára* 'bow' for what is now *gimára* and *-giba-* 'wash (v.; used of clothes)' for what had been and is again today *-ciba-* (DIC *-siba-*). And since a following front vowel clearly was requisite for the replacement to be made, analogic leveling seems to offer the most likely explanation for the change. Progressive palatalization of the dorsovelar stop (there appears to have been only one at that time; see below) before /i/ or /e/ could have led to its confusion in these positions with /c/ and, as a result, some anomalous morphophonematic alternations. So, for example, the attributive prefix /g(a)-/ (then indifferently [k(a)-] or [g(a)-]), as in *gála-* 'having contents' (contrast *mála-* 'empty', both from *-íla* 'contents') would have occurred as *c-* in **cibe-* instead of *gibe-* 'much; many' (contrast *míbe-* 'little; few'); and such a verb as *áiga* 'to eat' would have given *áicini instead of *áigini* 'eating', although another like *arúmuga* 'to sleep' would still have formed *arúmuguni* 'sleeping' quite regularly. If we were to assume this hypothesis to be correct, it would be easy to understand why analogic leveling should have taken place and how it could have overshot its mark. It might be thought that the substitution of $g^{i,e}$ for $c^{i,e}$ in cases where no analogy existed would have created as many morpho-phonematic alternations as it removed elsewhere; but /c/ being a much less frequent phoneme than /g/, extremely few such anomalies have in fact resulted; and *anícigu* 'wisdom; intelligence', which is still felt to contain a variant of *anígi* 'heart; mind', is in this respect exceptional.

The consonantal correspondences and patterns of the three Island-Carib dialects and of modern Surinam Arawak are shown tentatively in Table 3; Vincentian is especially doubtful. Aspirated consonants are written as digraphs; others are shown by symbols representing their commonest allophones. The apparent correspondence of CAIC /g/ to VIC /c/, DIC /s/, and A /s/ is not shown in the table, as this does not result from sound change.

TABLE 3. Consonantal Correspondences and Patterns of Island-Carib Dialects and Modern Surinam Arawak

DIC	m	b	b	ph	n	nh	t	th	r	r	l	l	s	s	k	k	kh	h
VIC	m	b	b	f	n	–	d	th	r	r	l	–	s	c	g	g	kh	h
CAIC	m	b	p	f	n	h	d	t	r	r	l	l	s	c	g	k	h	h
A	m	b	p	f	n	n	t	th	d	r	l	h	s	s	k	k	kh	h

DIC			VIC				CAIC				Surinam A		
m	n	–	m	n	–	–	m	n	–	–	m	n	–
–	nh	–											
b			b	d	–	g	b	d	–	g	b	d	–
	t	k			c		p	t	c	k	p	t	k
ph	th	kh	–		th	kh					–		th	kh
	s	h	f		s	h	f		s	–	h	f	s	h
–	l, r	–	–		l, r	–		–	l, r	–	–	–	l, r	–

Since there is reason to believe that both Dominican and Vincentian dialects had two series of stops, distinguished by the presence or absence of aspiration rather than of voicing, my representation of the former's unaspirated series as *b*, *t*, *k* may seem odd. But phonetic change does not always affect every order in the same way at the same time, and distinguishing features are often complex. Both early and recent records of Dominican Island-Carib indicate that of its three unaspirated stops, only the bilabial was usually voiced in all positions, the apical stop being regularly voiceless and the dorsovelar voiced only—though by no means always (rarely in the recent dialect)—in medial positions (cf. Warao, whose /p/ is usually voiced, but whose other stops, /t/, /k/, and /kʷ/, are always voiceless). And of the Dominican dialect's three aspirated stops only the bilabial seems to have been sometimes affricated in Breton's time, although in that dialect's recent stage, /kh/ was also often affricated and sometimes spirantized.

The one remaining bilabial stop of recent Vincentian is consistently shown as voiced, and its two apical stops as voiced and voiceless, respectively; but whereas the aspirated dorsovelar stop is consistently shown as voiceless, its unaspirated partner is shown as voiced in forty-five instances (twelve initial, thirty-three medial), and as voiceless in ten others (six initial, four medial). The new phoneme, hushing affricate /c/ (Ober's *ch*), appears as voiceless in all instances but one, where it was heard as voiced: Ober's *bijúga* = /bicógo/ 'thy head'.

In the modern Central American dialect of Island-Carib, the two series of stops are distinguished by the presence or absence of voicing. But this stage had not yet been reached in 1872, when Henderson wrote initial *k* or *g* with seeming indifference (though only *g* medially), and the *p* sound was said to be "scarcely in use." So, modern CAIC *guríara* 'canoe', *gíbe-* 'much, many', and *gála-* 'having contents', as well as *káta-* 'what; who; thing; (some/no)body', appear in his record with initial *k*; modern *gudá* 'burn' and *gáię* 'egg(s)' as well as *-ciba-* 'wash (clothes)' with initial and medial *g*; while both "kunubu" and "gunubu" are listed for modern CAIC *gunúbu* 'rain' of the men's speech.

The correlation of aspiration was destroyed when what had been spirantized allophones of /ph/ and /kh/ both became generalized, and the correlation of voicing came into being when the remaining bilabial stop, dorsovelar stop, or both were split. The former change apparently took place before, and the latter after, Henderson's time; and there must have been a period of overlapping. Modern /p/ and /k/, though occurring mainly in recent loanwords, are also found, as word-initial only, in some half dozen native morphemes each. And while *páta* 'prickly pear (Opuntia)' is the reflex of Breton's *batta* (with the same meaning), *pátara* 'slap' corresponds to his *páta*, *apátara* and to A *afáthada* 'to slap', in which bilabial /f/ is still sometimes replaced by /pf/, as reflex of former /ph/ (unit phoneme no longer heard as such).[1]

Some of the correspondences tabulated above—such as IC *r* : A *d* and IC *l* : A *h*—may seem surprising. There is no evidence that Island-Carib ever had three apical stops, or that anything but its /r/ ever corresponded to A /d/. But in Taino, initial [d-] and intervocalic [-r-] both correspond to A /d/, as in T *daca* or *dacha* : A *dákia* (> *dái*) 'I; me', and T *yari* : A *-iédi* 'necklace; jewelry', T *guarocoel* : A *oadokónthi* 'our grandfather'. And since there seems to be no sure instance of initial *r-* or of intervocalic *-d-* in the Taino record, these sounds may well have belonged to the same phoneme—as they do today in Warao. So that, if further comparison shows A /d/, /t/, and /th/ to reflect three separate phonemes of the proto-language, Taino of c. A.D. 1500 must have been at a stage in the passage of /d/ to /r/ through which Island-Carib had already passed when it was first recorded.

The second of these correspondences is uncommon, and I can exemplify it by very few instances, even with the help of Guajiro:

CAIC	Arawak	Guajiro	Gloss
búliri	bíhiri	pisíci	bat (zool.)
íli	íhi	-si	tail
alíagua	ihíka	asíkaa	future
agóle	íkihi	aísi	fat; grease
alaakota	ahadakitha	—	ask (interrogate)
íliru	—	asíri	catch (of game; n.)
íleue	—	-síi	flower, blossom
—	áhabo	asápi	back (of man, animal)
—	híkihi	s(i)kí	fire
-íleme	-ihime	—	fire (subordinate form)

This correspondence, if it be one, gains more likelihood when other languages are brought in. So, we find Bare *-hiwi* : Palicur *-riwi* 'blossom, flower' and Baré *-ihibi* : Palicur *-ribu* 'tail'. But the phonology of the Arawakan languages is in want of much more investigation and comparison than it has hitherto received.

---

[1] The replacement of VIC /ci/ by CAIC /gi/ apparently was inhibited by the presence of a dorsovelar stop in the preceding or following syllable: VIC *arici* → CAIC *arigi*, but VIC *nugucili* → CAIC *nuguci;* VIC *anici* → CAIC *anigi*, but VIC *anicigu* → CAIC *anicigu*.

THREE

GRAMMATICAL OUTLINE
OF ISLAND-CARIB

❖

THE MODERN Central American dialect of Island-Carib differs less from that of seventeenth-century Dominica in its grammar than in its phonology and general lexicon. For example, Breton's *aríca nóa tichíbou noúcouchourou* (or *lichíbou noùcouchili*) 'I have seen my mother's face' (or 'my father's face'), *iróponti noùcouchili* 'my father is good', *kanichícotou noùcouchourou* 'my mother is wise', and *cáintium ouacánium* 'our enemies are angry', however different they may appear in modern dress, correspond morpheme by morpheme to their CAIC equivalents (followed here by more literal translations): *aríha na tigíbu núgucu(ru)* 'seen I-have her-face my-mother' (or *ligíbu núguci* 'his-face my-father'), *irúfụti núguci(li)* 'kind-is-he my-father', *ganícigutu núgucu* 'wise-is-she my-mother', and *gáịtiụ uáganiụ* 'angry-are-they our-enemies'. And let me further cite from Breton's *Grammaire* an utterance which he hardly would have composed himself: *Ácai niràheu hàmouca, macótoni lahàmoucae ouáttou*; *àcae maráheu hámouca, cao lahàmoucae nhála* 'if he should be my child, fire would not burn him; if he should not be (my) child, my bench would devour him'. This too can be transposed into the modern CAIC dialect as *áhai niráo hamúga, mágudụ lahamúgai uátu; áhai maráo hamúga, háu lahamúgai nalạ* 'if-he my-child should-be, not-burning it-would-be-him fire; if-he not-(my)-child should-be, eat it-would-him my-bench', although here I cannot vouch for the acceptability of the wording, since *maráo* normally means 'without child, childless' and is not marked for person. In all events, the word order—predicate before subject—is as normal today as it apparently was in Breton's time.

The morphology of the above examples contains some of the most important affixes of the languages; and as most of them have cognates in Arawak and Guajiro, these are also listed in Table 4.

44

TABLE 4. Affixes in Central American Island-Carib, with Arawak and Guajiro Equivalents

	CAIC	Arawak	Guajiro
	Personal affixes		
1st sg.	n-; -na	dA-; -de	tA-
2nd sg.	b-; -bu	b-; -bo	p-
3rd sg. m.	l-; -i	l-; -i	n-
f.	t-; -u ~ -ų	th-; -no, -n, -o	s-, š-
1st pl.	uA-; -ua	oA-; -o	wA-
2nd pl.	h-; -ho	h-; -hɨ	b-
3rd pl.	hA-; -ię, -ią, -ių, -nu	nA-; -ie	hA-
	Attributive and privative prefixes		
Attrib.	gA- ~ hA-	kA-	kA-
Privtv.	mA-	mA-	mA-
	Personal pronouns		
1st sg.	nugúia	dái	tayá
2nd sg.	bugúia	bɨi	piá
3rd sg. m.	ligía	léi	niá
f.	tugúia	théi ~ thɨi	šiá
1st pl.	uagía	oái	wayá
2nd pl.	hugúia	héi ~ hɨi	hiá
3rd pl.	hagía	nái	nayá

In Table 4 the symbol $A = a$ or, more rarely, e or zero. This a or e replaces (or absorbs) a stem-initial vowel other than that of a vowel cluster forming a rising diphthong (for CAIC, those in $-iV$ or $-uV$ where the first element is unstressed and $V =$ any other vowel). For example, $uA-$ + *-úguci* 'father' = *uáguci* 'our father', $hA-$ + *igíbu* 'face(s)' = *hagíbu* 'their faces', $gA-$ + *íleue* 'flower' = *géleue* 'in blossom, having flowers', $mA-$ + *-iurite, iúri* 'tobacco' = *maiúrite* 'without tobacco' (cf. A *-iorithe, ióri, maiórithe* with the same meanings). But with a few stems $A =$ zero, as in $mA-$ (or $gA-$ or $hA-$ or $uA-$) + *-iri* 'name' = *míri* 'nameless'; and with such stems, CAIC second and third plural forms are now homophonous, as in the case of *híri* 'your name(s)' and *híri* 'their name(s)'. And, similarly, in the case of those few stems in CAIC which take the $hA-$ variant of the attributive prefix (normally $gA-$), the product is homophonous with that prefixed by the marker of third person plural, $hA-$, so that either of these two morphemes plus *-ita, hítao* 'blood' gives *háta*, which may represent either possessed 'their blood' or attributive 'having blood, bloody, bleeding' (and contrast A *-ithina, ithihi* 'blood', forming *nathína* 'their blood' and *kathína* 'having blood, bloody').

In Island-Carib, plural number is employed only with reference to animate (or reputedly animate) beings; in Arawak it is usually restricted to humans; but in Guajiro there appears to be no such restriction. In Island-Carib, nouns denoting inanimate objects may call for either masculine or feminine reference; but in Arawak and in Guajiro one gender refers exclusively to males and the other to every one and everything else. Moreover, in Arawak though not in Guajiro, the feminine-neuter gender may be (and usually is) employed in reference to human males who are not Amerindians!

Personal prefixes, which are always word-initial, indicate possessor with nominal stems, subject with verbal stems: CAIC *uágora* : A *oakóra* : G *wa?uulá* 'our hammocks', CAIC *uaríhubaų* : A *oádikhifáno* 'we shall see her/it' (from CAIC *arih-* and A *-dikh-* ~ *-dikh-* 'see'). Attributive and privative prefixes combine with nominal stems (and with those of verbal nouns) to form adjectives which may then be verbalized. Thus, from CAIC *iúri, -iurite,* A *ióri, -iorithe,* and G *yíi, -yiise* 'tobacco' come CAIC *gaiúrite,* A *kaiórithe,* and G *kayíise* 'having tobacco'; and from borrowed CAIC *sabádu, -isábadų,* A *sapáto, -sapáton* 'shoes' come CAIC *masábadų* and A *masapáton* 'shoeless, without shoes'. (Notice the dependent or subordinating suffixes CAIC *-te* and *-Ṿ,* A *-the* and *-n,* G *-se,* whose employment with many, but not all, possessed, attributive, and privative forms will be discussed below, under nouns.)

Attributive and privative prefixes are not always word-initial. This may be the case, for example, in verbal derivatives such as CAIC *agáraniha* 'to deal or to treat with herbal medicines', from *gárani* 'medicinal', from *árani* 'herbal remedy' (perhaps from **ára;* cf. A *áda* 'plant; tree; wood'), or A *-maribend-* 'cleanse', from *maríben* 'clean', from *iríbe* 'dirt' (cf. CAIC *iríbe* 'soot'). In Island-Carib and in Arawak a word may contain both *gA-* and *mA-* (or even two occurrences of either), as in CAIC *magídahadítu* 'it/she is unable (or not disposed) to bear fruit', from *agída(ha)* 'to bear fruit', from *gį* 'having fruit' (cf. CAIC *gítu* and A *kíoitho* 'it has fruit'), from *hį, -į* (A *íoi*) 'fruit', etc.

The personal suffixes of Island-Carib occur in verbs (including auxiliary verbs), verbal nouns, and in two subgroups of a closed word class that I have called locators. Except in one of the latter, they are always word-final. In verbal nouns they always indicate the goal, as in *t-aríhin-i* 'her-seeing-him', but in verbs they may indicate goal (*t-aríhuba-i* 'she-will-see-him') or subject (*t-úmariba-i* 'he will be her husband', *ma-ríhįgíl-i* 'he still does not see; he does not yet see'). Similarly in Arawak, dá-dįkhifá-no 'I-shall-see-her/it', *hadofóthika-dé* 'I sweat' (cf. *da-hadofóthi* 'my sweat'), *th-omárofa-i* 'he-will-be-with-her' or 'he will go to her', *ma-dįkhín dáia-no* 'I haven't seen her/it' (lit., "not-seeing I-have-been-it"), *má-osin bali* 'you must not go', *má-oton balí-no* 'you must not permit her'. Moreover, in Arawak, the personal suffixes and prefixes may both occur with a word class I have called postpositions, as in *damárita boboráno*

'I made it for you' (lit., "I-made you-for-it"), *iaháthe damábo* 'come here with me' (lit., "come-here me-with-you").

VERBS

In Island-Carib, the verb can be defined as a class of primary and secondary words which, apart from whatever personal affixes they may or may not contain terminally, either end in an aspect marker, or begin with a verbalizing prefix (usually *a-*, occasionally *e-* or *i-*) and end in the *a*-form of one of the verbal class-suffixes. Auxiliary verbs are words that consist, apart from personal affixes, of one (or a combination of two) of a small number of aspectual stems and themes. Verbs may be derived from members of any of the other word classes (nouns, particles, locators), from other verbs, or from bound stems. So, from borrowed *gelę́* 'key' (Fr. *clef*), a noun, and *rísi* 'rich' (Fr. *riche*), an adjectival particle, come *egelę́ca* 'to lock', *arísida* 'to get rich' or aspectual *rísitu* 'she is rich', *rísibaᶙ* 'she'll be rich', and *rísiharù* 'she has become rich'; while from the locator *iáhaᶙ* 'hither', itself derived from *iá(ha)* 'here', comes *iáhaᶙbadíbu?* 'wilt thou be (coming) hither?'

The aspect markers are aorist *-ti-* ~ *-t-*, imperfective *-ba*, perfective *-(h)a*, durative ('still, yet') *-gi-*, and progressive *-iᶐ*; and to these correspond the five auxiliary stems *-umút(i)-*, *-uba*, *-a* ~ *-uma*, *-agi-* ~ *-umagi-*, and *-iᶐ*, plus two others, voluntative *-iábu* and conditional *hamúga*. Their use will be explained and illustrated later, for the labels attached to them can serve, at best, only as mnemonic devices.

Productive verb class-suffixes are, in order of their frequency, *-ra*, *-ha*, *-da*, *-ca*, *-a*, forming active verbs, and *-rua*, *-hua*, *-dua*, *-cua*, *-ua*, forming "middle-voice" verbs. Apparently unproductive (since verbs containing them are almost all primary words) are others, such as *-ga*, *-ba*, *-ma*, *-na*, and their middle-voice counterparts, *-gua*, etc. That the productive class-suffixes, at least, may contribute to the meaning of the verbs containing them seems clear from such pairs as *ásora* 'to roast' vs. *ásoha* 'to sting', both derived from the particle *so* 'burning hot; roasting; stinging'; *agᶐiera* 'to gain (earn, win)' vs. *agᶐieha* 'to buy', both containing the borrowed particle *gᶐie* (Fr. *gagner*) 'gain'; *ámuruha* 'to squeeze' vs. *ámuruda* 'to tighten', both containing the particle *murú* 'tight'; *áfaiara* 'to travel (by boat); to float' vs. *áfaiaha* 'to navigate (take an active part in the management of a boat)', both containing the particle *fáia* 'afloat; under way'. Even such primary words as *áfara* 'to beat; to kill', *áfaha* 'to suffer; endure; take pains', and *áfagua* 'to strive; struggle; endeavor'; *arᶖaga* (source of colloquial *erᶗga*) 'to say, tell, speak', *arᶖaha* 'to tell on, report (inform against)', and *arᶖagua* 'to whisper' appear to share a morpheme whose reference is modified by the suffix. Yet such pairs and triads, though not rare, are too sporadic and insufficiently numerous to throw much light on the differential value of these suffixes.

Distinct from the foregoing are the derivative or secondary suffixes—tensive *-ha*, passive *-ua*, stative-reflexive *-gua*, and causative *-goda*—which may be added to the nonaspectual verb either alone or in certain combinations. So, from *á-buna* 'bury; plant' are formed *ábunahà* 'to bury', *ábunagua* 'to plant', *ábunaháua* 'to be buried', *ábunuagua* 'to be planted', *ábunahàgoda* 'to cause to bury', and *ábunaguàgoda* 'to cause to plant'; while from *arámoda* 'to hide' and *arísida* 'to get rich' come *arámodagua* 'to hide oneself' and *arísidagoda* 'to cause to get rich; to enrich'. Tensive *-ha* appears to be incompatible with stative-reflexive *-gua*, and passive *-ua* with causative *-goda*, at least insofar as verbs are concerned; though conversion to a verbal noun makes possible the presence of the last two suffixes, as in *lábunaguágodonúa* 'his being caused to plant'.

The functions of the derivational verbal suffixes here labeled tensive and stative-reflexive vary considerably from one verb to another, as may be seen from the following examples, the last four of which show dissimilatory loss of stem-final consonant:

agába	agábaha	agábagua
hear; understand	*heed; listen*	*be (over) hearing, listening*
-áiba	áibaha	áibagua
go away (injunctive)	*to pursue*	*to run*
áta	átaha	átagua
drink (punctual)	*drink* (iterative)	*be engaged in drinking*
aríha	aríaha	aríagua
see; look at	*peer; peep, stare at*	*to watch, continue looking*
adíga	adíaha	adíagua
to catch (fish)	*to fish*	*to dish up* (food)
ácuga	ácuaha	ácuagua
to chop/fell wood	*to go for wood*	*to chop up* (in lengths)
áluga	áluaha	áluagua
to fetch/seek	*to look for*	*to look out for oneself; to make oneself at home.*

It should be noted that all these verbal suffixes except *-ha* in a secondary word lose their final vowel, *-a*, when followed by passive *-ua*: *aríhua* 'to be seen', *erégua* 'to be said', *áigua* 'to be eaten'. This last verb, from *áiga* 'to eat' + passive *-ua*, should not be confused with homophonous *áigua* 'to fall', which is middle voice and, like most of its kind, a primary word.

INDEFINITE OR NONASPECTUAL VERBS

Only verbs of this subclass have a true infinitive, and only they can underlie a participle or a verbal noun. Such verbs are indefinite in that they rely on context or on total situation to indicate aspect and tense; but they may contain pronominal reference to subject or goal or both, and thus be finite, as in *uarísida* 'we get (got, shall get, are getting) rich', *ká arísidagòdaụ* 'who enriched her?'. They occur in contexts that can leave no doubt about temporal relations: *urínauga baríhana* 'yesterday you saw me', *harúga naríhaụ* 'tomorrow I'll see her', *súạdạ uaríhai* 'we see him often', *higábu baríhana* 'come to see me', *áhana baríha* 'if you see me' (lit., "if-me thou-see"). Total situation may suffice, without contextual aid, in such expressions as *náibuga* 'I'm going', *terę́ga lụ* 'she said to him', *nerę́ga abạ kátai hụ* 'I'll tell you (pl.) something'. In other cases, the syntactic tense-markers—future *me* and past *buga*—may be employed, as in *ída me baríhana?* 'when will you see me?' and *ída buga baríhana?* 'when did you see me?'. And in yet others, one nonaspectual verb may combine with another (*náibuga aríhaụ* 'I'm going to see her'), with an impersonal aspectual verb (*halíaba baríhana?* 'where will you see me?'), or with an auxiliary verb (*aríha numútu* 'I saw her', *aríha náru* 'I've seen her', *aríha nubáụ* 'I'll see her').

ASPECTUAL AND AUXILIARY VERBS

Although these two subclasses constitute a unit, as opposed to the nonaspectual verbs, they are morphologically distinct, aspectual verbs being derived from words of any other class (excepting only the subclass of auxiliaries), while the auxiliary verbs form a closed subclass and usually carry no lexical (as opposed to grammatical) meaning of their own.

The minimal sequence constituting an aspectual verb consists of an underlying form together with an aspect marker, and this may be followed by a personal suffix, with or without the interposition of a relational morpheme. No such "relator" occurs between aorist *-ti-* ~ *-t-* and the personal suffix; and none is employed today before a marker of third person following progressive *-iạ* or imperfective *-ba* when the verb formed by means of the latter either indicates future tense or has what I shall call its relative-subjective function (see below). Nor is one found before the marker of third person plural following perfective *-(h)a* or durative *-gi*. But elsewhere (with one exception which will be discussed below) we find *-di-* ~ *-d-* before the suffixed markers of first and second persons singular and plural, *-l-* before that of third person singular masculine, and *-r-* before that of third person singular feminine.

If we compare two such imperfective verbs as *láfarubàụ* 'he'll beat her', from nonaspectual *áfara* 'to beat; to kill', and *lúmaribaụ* 'she'll be his wife', from nominal *-úmari* 'companion; consort', we are struck by two things: the apparently different functions of the personal suffix -*u̧* in these two verbs (goal in the former, subject in the latter) and the change of stem-final -*a* to -*u* in the first. But *áfaruni*, -*áfaru̧* 'beating', *aríhini*, -*aríhi̧* 'seeing; sight', and *adógoni*, -*adógo̧* 'doing; making' are verbal nouns derived from nonaspectual *áfara*, *aríha*, and *adóga;* and it seems possible that *láfaru-bà-u̧* might, despite the oral character of its first /u/, contain the first of these verbal nouns and so be more closely rendered by 'she'll be his beating'; although the sense is that given above. (Also in Arawak, stem-final -*a* alternates with -*i*, -*o*, or -*i* in many verbs, as in *lofaráno* 'he beat her' vs. *lofarifáno* 'he'll beat her', *dadikháno* 'I've seen her' vs. *dádikhifáno* 'I shall see her', *thobokáno* 'she cooked it' vs. *thobókofano* 'she will cook it'. Here, however, the conditions are more complicated, with many verbs occurring in pairs like *fárin* 'to kill; to beat; to strike', whence *lófarifáno*, and *farán* 'to fight (with)', whence *lofaráfa thóma* 'he-will-fight with-her'. (See Taylor 1970*a*.)

It must not be thought that "imperfective aspect" as employed here is just another name for "future tense." In (*ma sa tugúia*) *láfarubau̧?* '(isn't it she) whom he beat?' and (*ma sa tugúia*) *lúmaribau̧?* '(isn't it she) who is his wife?' we see the imperfective employed in what I have called its relative-subjective function, which is marked only syntactically (by context). So also *ka laríhubau̧?* 'whom (f.) did he see?', *tugúia laríhubau̧* 'it's she whom he saw', *ka taríhubai?* 'whom (m.) did she see?', *ligía taríhubai* 'it's he whom she saw', *ka agágudubáiq̧?* 'who (pl.) awoke?', *hagía agágudubáiq̧* 'it's they who awoke'; but *laríhubau̧ lubára táfaiaru̧* 'he'll see her before she sails' (lit., "before (m.)-it her-sailing"). In such constructions only a suffixed marker of third person can occur, and this refers and attaches the verb to a foregoing antecedent with which it agrees in gender or plural number.

If we now compare with the above such constructions as *ka aríhubarù* (*iráho túra)?* 'who saw her (that girl)?', *ligía aríhubarù* 'it's he who saw her', *ka aríhubali?* 'who saw him?', *tugúia aríhubali* 'it's she who saw him', *larúmugu̧iq̧ buga le taríhubali* 'he was sleeping when she saw him', *ka agágudubáliq̧?* 'who awakened them?', *tugúia agágudubáliq̧* 'it's she who awakened them', *hagía agágudubálina* 'it's they who awakened me', it seems clear that -*r*- (before 3rd sg. f. personal suffix) or -*li* ~ -*l*- (before markers of other persons) relates the following personal suffix to the rest of the verb as its goal.

Comparing now the three functions of the imperfective, we have *badógobau̧ abq̧ bagára nu̧* 'You'll make a shoulder basket for me' (future tense), *ka sa badógobau̧?* 'what is it that you are doing/making?' or 'what do you do/make?' (relative-subjective), and *ida líq̧ badógobarù túra?* 'how is it that you do/make that (f.)' or 'how do you do/make that?' (relative-objective). The last two are clearly indifferent to temporal relations, and it seems plausible to conclude that the factor common to all three is what might be called an *irrealis* mood.

Almost as difficult to evaluate is what I have called the progressive, a label that describes only one of its functions, as in *talúguruiáu* 'she is selling it' or, with postposition of *buga* or *me*, 'she was' or 'she will be selling it'. But added to the tensive verb (containing secondary *-ha*), the same aspect marker indicates the iterative—*talúguraháiau* 'she sells it (habitually)'—while *haliaiàu (búgucu)?* 'where is she (thy mother)?' is functionally distinguished from aorist *halíatu (búbq)?* 'where is it (thy house)?' in that the former, progressive verb refers to transitory whereabouts and the latter, aorist verb to more or less fixed situation. In the main, the progressive is employed in verbs denoting action, process, position, or quantity: *átiriánu tiráhoią?* "how-many-are-they her-children?" = 'how many children has she?'.

The perfective aspect has functions that are not unlike those of our own perfect tense; thus, *coló-ha-di-na, -ha-di-bu, -ha-l-i, -ha-r-u, -ha-d(i)-ua, -ha-d(i)-ho, -ha-ią* 'I have arrived, thou hast arrived, he has arrived, etc.', differing from those of aorist *cólo-t-i* 'he/it arrived', etc., in much the same way as do their English glosses. But perfective *-ha* (which, after stem-final *-a* often loses the aspirate and may be reduced to zero) is frequently employed to form verbs denoting acquisition of a quality, or transition from one state to another, as in *funáaru* 'it has reddened; it is ripe' (contrast aorist *funátu* 'it is red'), from *funá* 'red', and *úali* 'it is finished; there is no more of it' (with which compare *úati* 'there is none of it'), from *úa* 'no; not'.

The durative, *-gi*, may usually be translated by employing 'still' or 'yet' in the gloss: *áfaguagìdina* 'I still strive', *máigigìą buga* 'they had not yet eaten', *bacáruagíli* 'he's still drunk'. But in its commonest occurrences we find as stem a denominal, attributive, or privative particle, as in *gágucigidíbu* 'you still have (a) father', from attributive *gáguci*, from *-úguci* 'father'; and *maráogiru* 'she has not yet had a child', from privative *maráo* 'childless', from *iráho, -iráo* 'child' (cf. nonaspectual *aráoda* 'to beget children').

The aorist verb expresses punctual completion and is therefore usually to be translated by the English past tense in verbs of action—as in *ióbuiti* 'he came', *eréguati* 'it was said'—and by the English present in verbs of state —as in *rísitu* 'she is rich' (cf. perfective *rísiharu* 'she has got rich'), *buíduti* 'he/it is good'. The high frequency of this aspect is due to the fact that adjectival particles are, for the most part, verbalized even where they are employed attributively, so that *uríba* 'bad' becomes an aorist verb in *abą áufuri uríbatu* 'a bad aunt' as well as in *uríbatu abą áufuri* 'an aunt is bad'.

Constructions employing auxiliary verbs offer, in some cases at least, what appear to be synonymous alternatives to aspectual verbs. So compare imperfective *aríha nubádibu* and *naríhubadíbu*, both translatable as 'I'll see you', perfective *aríha bá* and *aríhahadìbu*, both translatable as 'you have seen'. But some informants claimed (and others denied) that the phrasal member of the first (imperfective) pair is concessive (expresses willingness), whereas the aspectual verb expresses intention. And certainly, in perfective, durative, and aorist aspects, only the auxiliary verb can indicate a pronominal goal: *aríha náru* 'I've seen her', *aríha nágiru* 'I still see her', *aríha numútu* 'I saw her'. Note that after a personal prefix of plural number, perfective *-a* is changed to *-umá* and durative *-agi* to *-umági*, as in *aríha humáru* 'you (pl.) have seen her' and *aríha uamágiru* 'we still see her'. (In Arawak, the phrasal construction is usually restricted to the negative: cf. *matórodon thófa* 'she will not lie down' and *mathórodon thófa thokosíoa* 'she will not open her eyes' [note the opposition of *t* ≠ *th* in *torodon* 'lie down' vs. *thórodon* 'open'], but *thotórodofa* 'she will lie down' and *thothórodofa thokosíoa* 'she will open her eyes'.)

The imperfective auxiliary retains the threefold function of its aspectual counterpart: *ligía ibídię tubái nų* 'that's why I don't know her', but more literally "it-is-therefore unknown that-she-be to-me," *ka gía uágu madógǫ bubáli líra?* 'why didn't you do that?', but more literally "what is-it about not-doing that-thou-be-(m.)-it that-(m.)?" In this last example the auxiliary is subordinated by its privative complement, *madógǫ*, for in the positive we have, instead, a nonaspectual verb: *ka gía uágu badógai líra?* 'why did/do you do that?'.

The auxiliary verb stem *-a* ~ *-umá* serves not only the perfective and, with the addition of *-gi*, the durative aspects, but also what we may call the conjunctive mood, which has injunctive and subjunctive functions. When no personal suffix indicating pronominal goal is included, only general situation and tone distinguishes *áfara bá núgucu* 'you've killed my mother' from conjunctive *áfara bá núgucu* 'kill my mother!'. But the conjunctive, unlike the perfective, employs no relator before any personal suffix—*aríha náru* 'I've seen her', but *aríha náų* 'I must see her'; *aríha báru* 'you've seen her', but *aríha báų* 'look at her!', etc.—these forms having the injunctive function except where they occur in a subordinate clause expressing purpose or result, as in (*náibuga túbiaų*) *aríha naų* '(I'm going to her home) so that I may see her', or (*tahámaca nuágu*) *bi tána* '(she pounced upon me) so that (as a result) she cut me'. It should be noted that the prohibitive construction differs from any other negative verb phrase (including the negative subjunctive) in retaining the *a*-form of a nonaspectual verb serving as complement of the auxiliary. So *meręga bái* 'don't tell it!' can only be prohibitive, as compared with subjunctive *lų meręgu bai* '(he thought) that you should not tell it', or aorist *meręgu lumúti* 'he did not tell it', in which *meręgu* is a participle, 'not telling'.

And this same stem, *-a* ~ *-umá*, with the addition of the nominalizing suffix *-ni* ~ *-ne* ~ *-n*, serves to form auxiliary verbal nouns, as in (*luágu*) *aríhi nánu* '(about it) my seeing her', (*subúseti bʉ*) *aríhi nánebu* '(you know) that I saw you' (lit., "[it is known to thee] my seeing thee"), and *aríhi uamánu* 'our seeing her', in which the complement *aríhi* is participial, 'seeing'.

The progressive auxiliary has a variety of functions, largely determined by context. When there is no personal suffix, it usually indicates that the activity or state denoted by the complement is or was contemporary with the present or with the time spoken of; and in this function it is often accompanied by one of the enclitic verbal particles, *ti*, *tia* or *gi*, *gia:* *aríagu nįą* 'I'm just watching', *aríha nįą* 'I've just seen', *fáia tįą* 'she's under way; she's just sailed', *iʉ nią́-ti béiabu* 'I was just sitting by the landing place', *ída bią́-gi?* 'how are you?', *ítara lią́-ti* 'so it is'. But it may also indicate an aptitude, as in *áfara lįą garáuaʉ* 'he beats (knows how to beat) the drum'. With the addition of a personal suffix, the progressive auxiliary takes on an admonitive sense, as in *aríha tią́dibu* 'mind lest she see you', *aríha lią́ru* 'mind lest he see her'.

Also auxiliary *-iábu*, which in Breton's day served to form a sort of proximate future ("appliqué au verbe signifie 'je vais', comme *aíca niábou* 'je vais manger'"), has acquired a special nuance implying that the activity or state is willful: *dína niábu* 'I'm going to embark (whether you like it or not)', *áuca biábu áiga* 'you're going to try to eat' (said to an invalid), and with *lo* 'absent; protracted (time, absence, presence)' (cf. *áloda* 'to linger'), *ló liábu* 'let him stay away (for all I care)'. This auxiliary takes no personal suffix.

There remains the conditional, *hamúga*, which, like the conjunctive, is modal rather than aspectual, but is, unlike the conjunctive, most often employed together with an aspectual verb or with another auxiliary. Moreover, *hamúga* is the only auxiliary that can and often does occur in unprefixed form, although it may take personal prefixes, suffixes, or both. Thus, *áhaị hamúga tia erę́gatibu tʉ* 'if you had told her of it', *buíduti hamúga* 'it would be good', *áburigahádina hamúga bináro áhaị nídi hamúga búma* 'I'd have arrived long ago if I had gone with you', *háu lahamúgai* (Breton's *cao lahàmoucae*) 'he would eat it'. The modal auxiliary *hamúga* enters into composition with the aspectual auxiliary *-a* ~ *-umá* to form a desiderative, thereby losing its first syllable, as in *háu uamámugabu* 'would that we might eat thee'.

Before leaving the subject of the auxiliary verbs, we should mention three cases in which one or another of them may occur without a complement, but with a lexical meaning of its own, and hence is in this case not auxiliary: injunctive (2nd sg.) *bá lʉ!* 'tell him; speak to him!', progressive *má-buga nįą bʉ?* 'didn't I tell thee?', and imperfective ("*kátaių bagóburigubą́ią?*") *lúba búni* '("who are they who are thy parents?") he will say to thee'. Only the first example was heard in colloquial speech, the other two coming from tales that I recorded; and the use of *búni* in place of colloquial *bų* in the last suggests that *lúba* 'he will say', though common in Breton's day (see Breton 1667, pp. 54, 58), may now also be archaic. Except for its meaning, *ką́ią bų?* 'who told thee?' or 'who says so?' might be regarded as an aspectual verb (*ka* 'who, what, which' + the progressive suffix) rather than the verb stem *-ią* 'say' preceded by the interrogative prefix *kA-* 'who?/what?/whose?'; and I think that in *tę́gi nią́-bų* 'thank you' and *mábuiga háią sų mútu bų* 'everybody greets you', *nią* and *haią* must now be regarded as auxiliary (cf. secondary, non-aspectual *etę́gira* 'to thank' and *amábuigara* 'to greet'), despite the possible interpretation as "thanks I-say to-thee" and "greetings they-say every person to-thee."

NOUNS

To the class of nouns may be said to belong any word which, while not a verb as defined above, can take a personal prefix, then indicating possessor. A comparatively small number of words that we should like to call nouns—such as *áudo* 'town', *barána* 'sea', *guríara* 'dugout canoe', and *uátu* 'fire'—which can take no prefix must be defined by their ability to take certain suffixes that occur only with other, prefixable nouns, as in *áudobu* 'at the town', *guríararugu* 'in the dugout canoe'. Moreover, many if not all nouns have suppletive counterparts that occur only in prefixed form: *tíleme* 'her fire', *káleme* 'having a fire'. (Similarly in Arawak, *híkihi* 'fire', *báhi* 'house', *hámaka* 'hammock', and some others can take no prefix, but are replaced by other, suppletive forms which occur only in prefixed form: *daí(h)ime* 'my fire', *oasíkoa* 'our house', *thokóra* 'her hammock'.) Nouns may be (apart from inflection) simple or compound words (*niúmáru* 'my lip(s)', composed of *niúma* 'my mouth' and *áru* 'edge, border'), or they may be derived from verbs (*aríhini* 'my seeing; my sight', from *aríha* 'to see; to look'), from particles (*iuíei* 'dirt', from *uíe* 'dirty'; *irísini* 'riches', from borrowed *rísi* 'rich'), or from other nouns (*líligua* 'his own tail', from *líli* 'his tail').

In Island-Carib and in Arawak many (perhaps most) nouns occur in two shapes, the one possessed or subordinated by a personal, attributive, or privative prefix, or (especially in Arawak) by another noun, and the other absolute or independent. In the case of plant and body parts, kinship terms, etc., the latter is rarely heard, and may not always exist. Sometimes the one and sometimes the other (rarely both) is marked as such by affixation: CAIC *liúrite* and A *liórithe* 'his tobacco', but CAIC *iúri* and A *ióri* 'tobacco'; CAIC *lídiuma* and A *litíima* 'his moustache', but

CAIC *ídiumaha* and A *tíimaha* 'moustache'; CAIC *tóho gáị* "its-extract manioc" = 'starch', but *óhoho* 'extract; concentrate'. The commonest absolutive suffix is *-hV*, in which *V* is identical with stem-final vowel, except that CAIC /ho/ = A /hɨ/ may occur after stem-final /a/: DIC *úihi* 'portion of meat' but *núini* 'my meat', *íthaho* 'blood' but *nítha* 'my blood', *ábuhu* 'bone(s)' but *nábu* 'my bone(s)', and *suliéhe* 'shoe(s)' but *nisuliéni* 'my shoe(s)' (borrowed from Fr. *soulier*). A *íthihi* 'blood' but *lithína* 'his blood', *kathína* 'bloody; bleeding', *mathína* 'bloodless', appear to be somewhat exceptional. And notice the use of the two shapes in *hálikan íthihi?* 'which blood?' vs. *hálikan ithína?* 'whose blood?'.

The same pattern must have been present in the Central American dialect; but today, apart from exceptions like *óhoho* (see above), /h/ has been lost from this suffix or transferred to prefixal position with or without retention of a vocalic suffix: *úii* '(portion of) meat' but *núị* 'my meat', *hítao* 'blood' but *níta* 'my blood', *haráua* 'ax' but *naráuą* 'my ax', *arónao* 'arm; wing' but *naróna* 'my arm', *arónei* 'captain (of a boat)' but *naróne* 'my captain'. After stem-final /e/, the suffix is today *-i* rather than *-e* (a probably unique exception is *ę́u* 'penis' but *lę* 'his penis'); while after stem-final /i/, /o/, or /u/ the suffix (*-i*, *-o*, or *-u*) usually disappears in ordinary colloquial speech, though it can be "reconstituted" on formal or ceremonial occasions. Recent DIC *hálaho* 'bench (seat, chair, stool)', compared with earlier *álaho* (Breton's "álaheu") and CAIC *hálao*, suggests that initial aspiration of such absolute nouns preceded loss of /h/ from the suffix (but cf. Arawak independent *hála* vs. subordinate *lan* with the same meaning).

Besides the dependent suffixes, CAIC *-te* and *-ni* ~ *-ne* ~ *-ę* ~ *V̧* (this last and commonest variant indicating nasalization of stem-final vowel), Island-Carib has a dependent suffix *-ri*, which occurs only in some (but not in all) nominal stems of Karina (Carib) ancestry; thus, *béna*, *-ebénari* 'door', *dóbu*, *-idóburi* 'stone', *dúna*, *-idúnari* 'water; river', *óma*, *-émari* 'path; road'.

With one apparent exception that need not concern us here, dependent or subordinate nominal stems of Island-Carib (forming possessed nouns or attributive and privative particles) containing one of these suffixes have referents that are regarded as alienable, while most of those that are not so marked can be called inalienable. So, compare CAIC *tégite* 'her manioc grater' with *tége* 'her shoulder' (both from *égei* [Breton's "éche"] 'grater; shoulder'), or *tufúlurię* 'her (cultivated and cut) flowers' (from borrowed *fulúri* 'flowers') with *tíleue* 'its (f.) flowers', which can refer only to the plant or tree bearing them. Apparent exceptions such as *lála* 'his bench' (*hálao* 'bench') may be due to errors in recording or to slovenly speech; for the cognate Arawak equivalent, *lilán*, shows nasalization of the stem-final vowel (written as *-Vn*).

If we assume that all nouns having alienable referents take one of the dependent suffixes in their possessed, attributive, and privative forms, but that -V_e, the commonest variant of -ni, may be sometimes almost imperceptible (as may the 're in Eng. we're here), it seems relevant to ask, What determines the choice of one rather than the other? For unlike -ri (or the irregular plurals of English nouns), -te and the variants of -ni cannot be regarded as historical relics, since they are employed not only with inherited forms, but also with loanwords, many of which have been borrowed in fairly recent times.

Informants claim that they do not know; and the shape of the words themselves does not appear to be a determining factor: cf. Breton's echoubára, néchoubàrate (CAIC isúbara, nesúbarate) 'cutlass, my cutlass' (Sp. espada, or perhaps cachiporrea) and acoúcha, noucoúchete (CAIC agúsa, nagúsete) 'needle, my needle' (Sp. aguja) with his bíra, tibírani (CAIC bíra, tibírą) 'sail, its sail' (Sp. vela), pántir, noupántirani (CAIC fanídira, nufánidirą) 'flag, my flag' (Sp. bandera), and carta, nacartani (CAIC gárada, nagáradą) 'paper/letter/book, my paper, etc.' Examination of a considerable number of such words leads me to believe that there is, or was, a semantic distinction between -te and -ni, with forms whose referents the possessor employs for some particular activity or occasion ('harpoon', 'hoe', 'pipe', 'tobacco', 'razor', 'soap', etc.) taking the former suffix, and others whose use does not imply any particular occasion or activity on the possessor's part (such as 'sail', 'finger ring', 'shirt', 'shoes', 'sugar') taking the latter. Admittedly, there are a few counter examples (haráua, naráuą 'ax, my ax', arąsu, narąsute 'orange, my orange'), and in one or two instances either suffix is said to be permissible (áti, nátite, or nátię 'capsicum, my capsicum'; cf. Arawak áthi, dáthia); but by and large this interpretation seems to fit. As cognates of these dependent or subordinating suffixes occur also in Arawak (-the and -n) and in Guajiro (-se and -ni ~ -į), the matter may be of some interest.

The personal and, less frequently, the attributive and privative prefixes also occur with a small group of stems to form words having adverbial and prepositional functions together with some of the morphological characteristics of nouns; thus, tídą 'in it (f.)', tídagię "from within it" = 'out of it', the first showing nominal dependent -V_e and the second the directional suffix -gię (DIC -seę, A -seen, G -hee). These stems are -abu (A ábo, -bo) 'with; by means of; in possession, charge, support of; etc.', -árigi (A adíki, -diki) 'after; footsteps, tracks', -áu (A -áoa) 'over; on; about', -ídą 'in', -íladi 'like', -uágu (A -diáko) 'upon, about', -uária ~ -uái (A oária, -oria ~ -aria) 'from', -ubádu 'opposite', -ubára ~ -ubá (A obóra, -bora) 'for; before (loc. or temp.)', -ugúdu 'for the sake of', -úma (óma, -ma) 'together with', -úni ~ -ų (A omón ~ omin, -mon ~ -min ~ -n) 'for; to (dative); at; etc.', -úrugu (A olóko, -loko ~ -lokho-)

'in; during; in accordance with', -*urúgabu* 'close by', -*urúma* (A *odóma*, -*doma*) 'because, on account, or by reason of'. Most of these combine with one or more of the suffixes—reflexive -*gua*, directional -*gię* 'from', and -uni ~ -*ų* 'to; toward'—to form such derivatives as -*ábugua* 'by ——self', -*unígua* ~ -*ųgua* 'to/for ——self', -*ábugię* 'below', -*áugię* 'above', -*úmagię* 'from (place or person)' (lit., "from with" or "since (time)"), -*úmaų* 'as far as (place); until (time)', -*ídaų* 'into', -*ídagię* 'out of', etc.

In Arawak, such forms are more numerous (I recorded some twenty-seven of them) and freer in their combinations. They may also occur, unlike those of Island Carib, in unprefixed form, and constitute a small class that I have called the postpositions (Taylor 1970*b*).

That such glosses as those given above are quite inadequate to explain the values of the forms will appear from the following phrases, where -*abu* has been placed in attested contexts: (1) *ábą fáluma tábu tí* 'a coconut tree with (bearing) its fruit', (2) *abą ugúnei hábu muládunu* 'a boat with (carrying) mulattoes', (3) *búmari tábu bímenodi* 'thy wife backing up (supporting) thy mother-in-law', (4) *lídi lábu numégegu* 'his going off with (in possession of) my belongings, (5) *náueba lábu* 'I'll die of it (by its agency), (6) *báiba lábu* 'go to the rear of it', (7) *mígira ba lábu* 'don't leave off behind (outdone by) him', (8) *legelęcuni béna lábu iráho lea* 'his locking the door behind (against) the lad', (9) *gųdątina tábu náuori* 'I'm happy with (the possession of) my ax', (10) *goráua tábu tiúrugu* 'tied with (by means of) her pubic hair'. It should be noticed that personal prefixes are present in all these forms in -*abu*, whether their function be adverbial (as in 5, 6, and 7) or prepositional (as in the remainder), although they have been translated in the former case only. In Island-Carib but not in Arawak, this also occurs in regular nominal possession, as in *tebénari lubą uáguci* "its-door his-house our-father" = 'the door of our father's house', with which contrast the Arawak equivalent, *oàthináthi bá(h)isibo* "our-father house-door", a compound of *báhi* 'house' and -*sibo* 'face, front' (the Arawak house being normally open on three sides and having no door).

Insofar as the semantic value of -*abu* is concerned, it may be agreed that most instances of its use contain the notion of underlying position, of support, or of both. And since the bones constitute the underlying support or essential substructure of the body, it seems plausible to suggest that the homophony of -*abu* 'supporting, underlying' and -*abu* 'bones' need not be coincidental (cf. also A *ábo* 'supporting, etc.', *ábon* 'under', and -*abóna* 'bones'). It may also be mentioned that CAIC *uáladi* (from -*íladi*) may sometimes be translated 'our like' and at others 'like us' and that Breton translated his *árici* (CAIC -*árigi*, A *adíki*, G *aciki*) by 'reste, trace' as well as by 'après'.

Island-Carib words formed from these stems by means of the attributive and privative prefixes, CAIC *gA-* and *mA-*, are not plentiful, though *gáma* (from *-úma*) 'being with; having', *máma* 'without', and the aorist verb *máunitu* 'it is useless, without purpose' (from *-uni*) are common enough (cf. A *mamíntho* ~ *máontho*, as in *máontho iónro bósin* 'it's useless for you to go there'). A *abókoton* 'to seize, to lay hold on' is a causative verb derived from the same language's *ábo*; and recent DIC *mábukhu* 'groundless (without valid reason); lacking in resourcefulness' probably contains its *-ábu*.

Some of these stems have reduced forms that must be regarded as suffixal: *-da* as in *ómada* 'in the road', *-rugu* as in *ganálirugu* 'in the canari (earthenware pot)', *-ų* as in *lidáų* 'into it' (cf. *lídagię* 'out of it'). In *turúgabu* (*leskuéla*) 'close by it (the school)' (*túrugu* + *-ábu*), *tégeuagu* 'on her shoulder' (*tége* 'her shoulder' + *uágu*), and *tugúdina* 'her heel' (*tugúdi* 'her foot' + *-íuna* 'stem'; cf. A *dadináina* 'my shoulder', from *dadína* 'my arm'), we may see either derivation or composition, although recent DIC *káirabu* 'leeward side (of an island)' (*akáira* 'island' + *-abu*) and A *-obánabo* 'temporary shelter' (*-bana* 'leaves' + *abo*) are best regarded as compounds. On the other hand, CAIC *árabu* 'woodland' (**ara* 'tree' + *-ábu*) and *áriabu* 'night' (**ari* 'darkness' + *-abu*) reverted to simple forms when their first members became obsolete. It is possible, however, that some native speakers have come to regard these two words, mistakenly, as containing the locative suffix *-bu* 'at; to; in' (of Carib ancestry), by analogy with others like *áudobu* 'at/to town', *béiabu* 'at the landing place', *bórorobu* 'in the courtyard', and *máinabu* 'in the manioc field', which do contain it, since *árabu* and *áriabu*, though unanalyzable at the present time, may also be employed in a locative sense, as 'to the bush' and 'at night'.

A few nouns appear to be anomalous in one way or another; I shall mention only three: *anágani, -anága* 'back (anat.)', *fújieni, -ufújie* 'wrist', and *ilógoni, -ilógo* 'domesticated or semidomesticated animal' (preposed to the name of any animal whose ownership is to be expressed, as in *lilógo áųli* 'his dog' and *tilógo gabáiu* 'her horse'). The suffix *-ni* (or one of its variants) is, as we have seen, common both as a nominalizer (*irísini* 'riches; wealth', from borrowed *rísi* 'rich') and as a marker of dependence in alienable nominal stems (*nubáduni* 'my stick', from borrowed *bádų* [Fr. *bâton*] 'stick'); and it is therefore hard to believe that the same morpheme could also have such a different function as that of marking the absolute noun. Moreover, while it would appear regular for names of body parts and products to require no dependent suffix (as inalienable), Breton's "(n)anágani" and "(n)íliguini" contain *-ni* in both dependent and absolute forms (*fújieni*, containing a loan from Fr. *poignet*, presumably had not yet been borrowed in his time). And this suffix, though now lacking in CAIC *nanága* 'my back', reappears in the compound *nanáganabù* 'my backbone' (with -*ábu* 'bone' or with -*ábu* 'support'?). I suspect that -*ni* is or was nominalizing in all three cases cited; for in one place Breton glosses *anágani* as "le principal, le capital," which suggests that it may be a deadjectival noun meaning 'main', and his "íliguini" is variously glossed as "animal qu'on nourrit; nourrisson; petit fils," which suggests that it contained a verbal stem meaning 'suckle' (Island-Carib and Arawak women often suckle young animals that they wish to raise as pets). As for *fúieni*, the nominalization may well be analogic; for the inherited word that was replaced by the borrowing of Fr. *poignet*, "eleoúchagoni," itself contains -*ni* and is a verbal noun denoting 'that which bends or twists' (cf. now the etymology of Eng. *wrist*).

Some but not all nouns referring to animate beings take a pluralizing suffix which occurs in the same variants as does the personal suffix of third plural: cf. Breton's *cáintium ouacánium* : CAIC *gáįtių uáganių* 'our enemies are angry' (*ágani* 'enemy'). So also, *iráhǫią* 'children', from *iráho* 'child'; *hįár(u)ių* 'women', from *hįáru* 'woman'; *eiérių* 'men', from *eiéri* 'man'; *nidúhęių* 'my kinsmen', from *nidúhe* 'my kinsman/kins-woman'; *nítunu* 'my sisters', from *nítu* 'my sister'; *nibírię* 'my younger brothers', from *níbiri* 'my younger brother'. This last example contrasts with *níbirigu* 'my younger siblings (of either sex)', whose suffix -*gu* may be appended to many nouns with animate or inanimate referents which cannot take the regular pluralizing suffix; so, *numáda(gu)* 'my friend(s)' and *numége(gu)* 'my personal belonging(s)'. But plural pronominal reference is made only to such nouns as denote animate beings: *óroua iráhǫią hára* 'those three children', but *óroua guríara túra* 'those three canoes' (lit., "three canoe that"), *numádagu hára* 'those friends of mine', but *numégegu líra* 'those (lit., "that") belongings of mine'.

On the other hand, a noun's grammatical gender is marked only by third singular pronominal reference to it, as masculine or feminine, in another word; and here there is no distinction between animate and inanimate. So, in *uáiriti tebénari lúbą uáguci* 'the door of our father's house is big', the masculine gender of *béna* 'door' is marked by the -*i* suffix of the aorist verb *uáiriti* 'it is big', the feminine gender of -*úbą* 'house' is marked by the *t*- prefix of *tebénari* 'its door', and the male sex of -*úguci* 'father' by the *l*- prefix of *lúbą* 'his house'. (From a comparison of such pairs as *núguci* 'my father' vs. *núgucu* 'my mother', *náti* 'my brother' vs. *nítu* 'my sister', and *eiéri* 'man' vs. *hįáru* 'woman', it might seem that some nouns contained, etymologically, the mark of their own gender or of the referent's sex; but if so, such vestiges are today non-functional.)

Perhaps the most unusual feature of Island-Carib is the attribution of gender, which in very many cases depends upon the sex of the speaker.

All nouns having abstract referents (such as those meaning 'dance', 'night', 'jealousy', and all verbal nouns) are treated as masculine by the women and as feminine by the men; and this also applies to such impersonal reference as is indicated by the 'it' of Eng. *it is late, it is raining, it is good to see you,* etc. Yet both sexes agree on the gender of nouns having concrete, visible, or tangible referents. And since some nouns, such as *háti* 'moon; month', may have both concrete and abstract referents, such may also have two genders. So, *háti* 'moon' is masculine for both sexes, while *háti* 'month' is feminine for the men, but masculine for the women. (In their concrete senses, *uéiu* 'sun; day' and *háti* 'moon; month' are masculine, it is said, because these heavenly bodies once were men, whereas, since *uarúguma* 'star(s)' is feminine and may have plural pronominal reference, the stars once were women.)

So much for the effects of mythology on grammar. But for the rest, the attribution of grammatical gender seems to follow a logic that one might vainly seek in the most ancient Indo-European languages. Feminine are nouns referring to all kinds of containers: houses and vehicles of all sorts, cloth and clothing, beds, hammocks, boxes, jars, pans, guns, pistols, eggs, etc. Among the articles of clothing, whose names have almost all been borrowed, only *bunídi* 'hat' (Sp. *bonete*) is masculine. Feminine also are the mainly borrowed names of cutting instruments, such as those meaning 'ax', 'hoe', 'knife', 'razor', 'scissors', though the names of piercing instruments, like *agúsa* 'needle' (Sp. *aguja*), *arúfu* 'harpoon' (Sp. *arpón*, Fr. *harpon*), are masculine.

On the other hand, nouns referring to parts and products of the body are for the most part masculine. Out of a list of eighty-seven such items, I find only fifteen that are feminine: these include the words meaning 'belly', 'bladder', 'intestines', 'heart', 'liver', 'lungs', 'nostrils', 'throat', 'tongue', 'vein (or artery)', 'womb'. *Lé* 'his penis' is feminine, while *tógo* 'her vulva' is masculine.

The names of most cultivated plants and their fruits are feminine, notable exceptions being *áti* 'capsicum', *iáiaua* 'pineapple', and borrowed *rį* 'rice', which are masculine. The name of any animal whose sex is known may, in theory, be either masculine or feminine; but usually the words meaning 'bird', 'fish', 'manatee', 'shark', 'snake', and 'turtle' are treated as feminine, irrespective of the animal's sex. Borrowed *aréba* 'cassava bread' (K *are:pa*) and *bínu* 'rum (or other spirituous liquor)' (Sp. *vino*) are masculine, while borrowed *feį* 'bread' (Fr. *pain*) and *diuéį* 'wine' (Fr. *du vin*) are feminine.

Other seemingly arbitrary attributions of gender, while not rare, are comparatively few; and apart from nouns whose referents belong to one of the semantic categories outlined above in which the feminine gender predominates, the great majority of those having sexless concrete referents appear to be masculine at the present time. This is very different from Arawak, in which one of the two genders is restricted (in principle at least) to male human referents who are Amerindians, the other applying to everybody and everything else.

LOCATORS OR DEMONSTRATIVES

Under this label I have grouped together what probably should be regarded as two (or perhaps three) small, closed classes of primary words, each containing a bound stem, which may be simple or complex, and one primary suffix (to which, in some cases, a secondary suffix may be added). All these words contain reference to position (in space or time) or to person; but as most of them refer to both, it is not practicable to separate them on these lines. The stems and suffixes are shown in Table 5. Only those listed for convenience after 4 in the table clearly constitute a set apart. After stem-final /a/, parenthetic (u) = ∅ (zero) and parenthetic (V) = /o/; after stem-final /u/, both (u) and (V) = /u/; and after stem-final /i/, (u) = ∅ and (V) = /i/. Except when followed by secondary -ų, where H = /h/, -Ha loses its aspirate and may undergo crasis with the preceding vowel.

TABLE 5. Locators in Island-Carib

	Primary suffixes						Secondary suffixes		
Stems	-g(u)ia	-Ha	-ra	-g(V)ta	-g(V)ra	-te	-ų	-gię	-i̧
1. ia-	+	+	+	+	+		+	+	
2a. nu-, ua-; bu-, hu-	+								
2b. li-, tu-, ha-	+	+	+	+	+	+			
3. N- + personal suffix		+	+	+	+	+			+
4. hagá-, higá-, áhạ-, káta-				personal suffix					

The first stem, ia- is a "pure" locator, in contradistinction to the others, which are personal or "mixed." So, iágia 'it is here' (emphatic), iáa 'here', iáhaų 'hither', iágię 'hence', iára 'there', iágota 'over there', iagóra 'away yonder', iáraų 'thither', iáragię 'thence', etc.

The second set consists of personal pronominal stems which, unlike the corresponding prefixes, contain stable vowels. Despite the fact that only those of third person take strictly locative suffixes, it is clear that all belong to the same subclass. So, nugúia 'it is I; as for me' and bugúia 'it is thou; as for thee' (instead of which, the men employ, respectively, *áu* and *amóro*) cannot be separated from *ligía* and *tugúia* which, besides 'it is he' and 'it is she', may mean, according to context, 'it is this; it is then; it is therefore' with a following verbal noun. So, *eréga ligía* 'said he' differs only in emphasis from *leréga* 'he said', but *ligía lerégų* 'this is what he said' is, more literally, "it is this (or then or therefore) his saying," and is followed by a quotation. In ordinary colloquial speech *líha* and *túha* 'this' (masculine and feminine, respectively) are reduced to monosyllabic *lea* and *tuo*; *háha* 'these (animate)', to *háa*. These words—like *líra* and *túra* 'that', *lígita* and *túguta* 'that over there', and *ligíra* and *tugúra* 'yon, yonder'—function syntactically either as pronouns or, placed after a noun, as demonstrative adjectives. It should be noted that *ligíra*, *tugúra*, and *líte*, *túte* 'this coming (one)' may refer not only to distance and approach in space, but alternatively to past and future time, this latter sense usually being indicated by the addition of a tense marker: *ligíra buga* 'the other day; some time ago', *líte me* 'soon; shortly; in a few days'. In their impersonal use (to indicate time), these locators take masculine reference in the women's speech, feminine reference in the men's.

Stems of the third set include *anná*, *abú-*, *iní-*, *inú-*, *quá-*, *onó-*, *aniá-*. Clearly they are complex and contain the personal suffixes, but the identity of their first element, which I have called *N*, is obscure. Very possibly it may be the same as obsolete *éni*, which Breton glosses 'voilà', and cognate with Guajiro *ani*, *anu*, or *ania*, which Holmer says is used to express 'here is'. All these locators are, at any rate, predicative, as in *iníte ábą muládu* 'a "Spaniard" (Spanish speaker) is coming', *inúte ábą guríara* 'a canoe is coming', *aniáte óroua iráhǫią* 'three children are coming', *iníha* 'he/it is here; here he/it is', *iníra* 'he/it is there; there he/it is'. The addition of secondary -*į* to third person locators of this subclass makes the resultant form nondemonstrative, *iníhaį* or *iníraį* being employed indifferently for 'there is' or 'there are (some masculine inanimate objects)'. Such a form as *annágora* 'yonder I am' might seem to be a semantic monster, but I found it in a letter, in which a woman, writing to her son, says (my translation): "If you don't help me, you'll soon hear of me that yonder-I-am, come-to-an-end (*luágu annágora lą gumúgua*)"—i.e., 'dead'.

Quite different from the above are the four stems listed after 4 in Table 5, which occur only together with a personal suffix. The first, *hagá-*, is always interrogative and may often replace an aspectual verb derived from *halía* 'where': thus, *hagái?* or *hagái-gi?* 'where is he?', *hagáų?* or *hagáų-gi?* 'where is she?'. These forms are followed by a nominal referent when the situation requires precision: *hagáią barónegu?* 'where are your captains?'. With a second person suffix, the meaning is usually changed, as in *hagábu sa numáda?* 'how goes it, my friend?'

The second of these four stems serves to form words meaning 'come!' (injunctive), as in *higábu iáa, niráo* 'come here, child'. It has an irregular second person plural, *higáugu!* 'come (ye)!' Though rarely employed with a third person referent, I have heard *higái!* 'let him come!' (*higái bába lʉ laríhini nugúdeme!* 'let papa come that he may see my misery').

The third stem may be translated 'if', 'then', or 'when (non-interrogative)', according to context and is peculiar in that its personal suffix may indicate either subject or object of a following verb: *áhana adíga* 'if I catch (fish)', *áhaʉ híla túgucu* '(it was about a week later) when her mother died', but *áhana baríha* "if-me you-see" = 'if you see me' and *áhʉbu naríha* 'if I see you'.

Finally, *káta-* means 'who/what is/are': *kátai gía?* 'what's the matter?', *kátaiʉ bagóburigubáiʉ?* 'who are they who are thy parents?', *narúhudubái kátanaiʉ́dina lʉ́* 'I'll show who it is that I am'. In addition to their interrogative function, *kátai* (m.) and *kátaʉ* (f.) are employed syntactically as nouns meaning 'thing': *kátai líra* 'that thing (m.)', *kátaʉ túra* 'that thing (f.)', *abʉ kátai ítara* '(I never heard of) such a thing'. Though *kata-* is itself bound (but cf. *ní-kata* 'nothing'), it now contains a free form, *ka* 'who; what', nowhere attested in Breton's or in Rat's records of the Dominican dialect.

PARTICLES

Any word which cannot be inflected for person, possession, or number, or marked for position or direction without conversion (by appropriate affixation) into a verb, a noun, or a locator will be called a particle. Like nouns, particles may be simple, complex, or compound words; but unlike some nouns, all complex particles contain an underlying free form (which may, however, be phrasally bound). A particle may underlie a verb (*áhara* 'to consent' contains *áhʉ* 'yes; agreed'), a noun (*iuíei* 'dirt' contains *uie* 'dirty' and *irísini* 'wealth' contains *rísi* 'rich'), or, in one instance, a locator (*kátáʉ?* 'who is she?' contains *ka* 'who, what'); or it may itself have, as an underlying form, a verb (*máiguadi* 'uneatable' contains *áigua* 'to be eaten'), a noun (*máguci* 'fatherless' contains *-úguci* 'father'), or another particle (*buʉ́goda* 'filled' is the causative of *buʉ́* 'full', *máhʉ* 'unwilling' is the privative of *ʉ́hʉ* 'yes; agreed').

Most particles of Island-Carib behave syntactically like adjectives, adverbs, or pronouns, or combine the first with one of the latter functions; but very few can take the place of attribute in a nominal phrase. Those that can do so, including all numerals, precede the noun: *ábʉ (uogóri)* 'a, one, the same (man)', *ábaia (uóri)* 'another (woman)', *sʉ (uéiu)* 'every (day)', *sʉ (lídiburi)* 'all (his hair)', *ka ámu (uogóri)?* 'what other (man)?', *binádo (hábiʉ)*, "former (their home)" = 'their old home', *iséri (urúei)* '(the) new (king)', *káisi* (*hu*) 'like a (hoe)', *ní káta* 'nothing', *ní mútu* 'nobody', *ni halía* 'nowhere', *ni tífe* 'not a scrap of it', *óroua uéiu bía áriabu* 'three days (and) two nights', *ábaia lúmari búguci* 'thy father's other wife'. In an exception, *ítara* 'such; so (thus)' is placed after the noun: *abą kátai ítara* 'such a thing'.

But most adjectival particles are found to occur in verbal phrases together with an auxiliary or other verb, as does *uríba* 'bad' in *áhai uríba lubái bigáburi* 'if thy conduct be bad' and *máma uadímurehạią uríba tuágu hịáru uáladi* 'we are not speaking ill of a woman like ourselves'; and the attributive is, as we have seen (*ábą áufuri uríbatu* 'a bad aunt' vs. *uríbatu abą áufuri* 'an aunt is bad'), usually expressed by an aorist or, more rarely, by a perfective verb placed after the noun.

Very frequent in conversation—though less so in stories, songs and ritual—are what we may call the verbal particles, *tía, ti, gía, gi, sa, ga,* and *rái,* which usually are enclitic to another word, as in *báiba-ti(a)!* 'go away!', *terẹga-ti(a)* 'she said', *saniáti-ti* 'it's impossible', *mútu-ti háa* 'these people', *dísetiuá-ti* 'we're far off', *hanúfudetìna-ti* 'I'm afraid', *hagái-gi?* 'where is he/it?', *kátai gía?* 'what is it'. It would seem that they help to make the meaning more explicit but are not grammatically necessary. And whereas the choice of *ti* or *tía,* like that of *gi* or *gía,* appears to be free or to depend on the fall of stress, one of the first pair cannot be replaced by one of the second without change of meaning.

So, *ída lią-ti?* 'how (like what) is he?' calls for some such answer as 'tall', 'short', 'fat', etc., and contrasts with *ída lịą-gi?* 'how is he?' as an inquiry concerning his health or welfare, and with *ída líą sá?* 'how about him/it?', which calls for an explanation or for news. The difference between the first and second questions is analogous to that between progressive *halíaiàụ* and aorist *halíatu* as described above under aspectual verbs, as is evident when a locator is employed instead of a verb: *hagáụ-ti túbą N?* 'where is N's house?', but *hagáụ-gi túgucu N?* 'where is N's mother?'.

The phrase *ítara lá* 'so be it', employed in some churches instead of *amen,* is said to be ambiguous because it might denote either *ítara lá-tia* 'let it be (remain) as it is' or *ítara lá-gia* 'let it come to be like that'.

Whereas *ti* and *gi* can take no affix, *tia* and *gia* may be verbalized by taking aspectual suffixes, such as the perfective in *terẹga tiaha: "namúlenu, náueba tía"* 'she said, "my juniors, I shall die"' or the aorist in *úati giáti* 'there is nothing (amiss)', which is the conventional reply to the conventional question *ída bią-gi?* 'how are you?'. I believe that both uses of *tia* and that of perfective *-ha* in the former utterance convey a notion of finality, while the two aorist verbs of the latter (which contain the particles *úa* 'no; not' and *gía*) assert the punctually complete fact that there is nothing to report concerning the speaker's phase of being (*gia*).

The particle *sa* is interrogative in most but not all contexts: *gálati ságaụ* 'it contains sand', *gálati sá ságaụ?* 'does it contain sand?'. Elsewhere it may be explanatory or dubitive: *lau sa gudéme lea* 'it's on account of this distress', *áhaị sa naríha, kabá-gi* (or *kabá-sa*) *narẹ́ga lụ?* 'in case I should see him, what shall I tell him?'. And with this last example, compare *áhaị-tia naríha, nerẹ́gubai tia lụ* 'when I see him, I'll tell him of it', and *áhaị-ga naríha, nerẹ́gubai* (*ga*) *lụ* 'if I do see him, I'll (certainly) tell him of it'.

The particle *ga* is emphatic (cf. our auxiliary *do*) and often explanatory at the same time—'why didn't you come earlier?', *náigiạ bugá-ga* 'because I was eating'; 'why don't you do this?', *nadógiaị-ga* 'I am doing it'—but it seems to occur most frequently in restrictive adverbial phrases, as in *siạ́-la sa haríhị mútu magúru-ga?* 'can't people see without touching?', in which the predicate, *siạ́-la sa?* 'can it be impossible?' (dubitive conjunctive), is followed by the subject, *haríhị mútu* 'people's seeing' (lit., "their-seeing people"), and by restrictive *magúru-ga* 'without having to touch'.

Apart from the above (and *rái*, which expresses surprised interrogation, as in *gerẹ́gatti rái lụ garífuna?* 'does he really speak Island-Carib?'), there is another small group of verbal particles that includes negative *ma* and *máma*, quotative *nége*, and the tense markers *buga* (past), *me* (future), and *iébe* (contemporaneous). The first of these, *ma*, occurs most frequently in negative questions to which a positive answer is expected, and may be purely exclamatory: *má-buga niạ́-bụ?* 'didn't I tell you!?', *lubuídụ baránų ma!* 'isn't the sea beautiful!?' The second, *máma*, is usually employed for straightforward negative statements and questions: *máma tia náhurarụiạ búma* 'I'm not playing with you', *máma mútu buídutu* 'she's not a good person', *máma-sa bidúhẹiụ bía eiériụ háa?* 'aren't these two men thy kinsmen?'.

Quotative *nége* is included in any statement for which the speaker cannot personally vouch and may be translatable by 'he said', 'they say', 'it is said', etc., or not at all: *lerẹ́ga nége tụ́ luagu láunaha nége gárada lụ* 'it seems that he told her he would send him a letter'. The tense markers, some of whose uses have already been seen, may combine with aspectual verbs, as in *maríhigidìna buga mútu ítara* 'I had not yet seen such people', *erẹ́ga náụ mé tia lụ* 'I might tell him of it'. Other, less common uses of *me* need not concern us here. The third of these, *iébe*, is employed when the speaker wishes to describe two actions, processes, or states as contemporaneous: *liráo iebe gía Henáru tiráo Bérta?* 'is Berta's child also (at the same time) Henáru's child?', *lubáti larúga bináfi, náibuga iébe D, iụ́ niạ́-ti béiabu,* . . . 'it was before daylight (lit., "its dawn morning"), just as I was going to D, I was sitting by the landing-place, . . .', *tịurahạ́iạ iebe ganáli* 'as she was raising the pitcher', *ábạ iebe caparita agólei* 'even one gill of oil'.

It should be noticed that these tense-marking particles have a use that is not confined to their combination with verbs. Thus, compare *sý dóbu léa-buga niéįbai salígua hárigaų grígia me* 'all these stones (past tense) there changed back into people (future tense)', *iníhaį mè-tia táiginibu íliba* 'there comes a time when a centipede bites you', but lit., 'there-is (future tense) its-biting-thee centipede'. And the future-tense particle may itself be verbalized, as in *nugúia mehá-tia tuo tabúgubaų búgucu*, which means 'she whom your mother drove away (*tuo tabúgubaų búgucu*) has become (*or* was to be) me (*nugúia mehá-tia*)', rather than 'it is I whom your mother drove away'; for the Island-Carib, unlike the latter English sentence, makes it clear that a change in the speaker's condition has taken place.

Particles from which verbs may be derived themselves combine with auxiliary verbs to form verbal phrases, as in *sý-bai* 'finish it!' (cf. *ásura* 'to finish'), *fú-bai!* 'blow it!' (cf. *áfura* 'to blow'), *rú-bai nų!* 'give it to me!' (*ru* 'give, put' underlies aspectual verbs only, such as *rútių* 'they gave'), *uarí-ta!* 'let her come up!' (cf. *auáira* 'to come or go up', with dissimilatory loss of /r/ before *-ra*); but *áfara bái!* 'kill/beat him/it!, *íciga bái nų!* 'give it to me!', *aríha ta!* 'let her see/look!', since *áfara* 'to kill; to beat', *íciga* 'to give; to put', *aríha* 'to see; to look' are primary words.

The function and even the reference of such a particle may change with context (cf., as above, *sų*, which means 'every; all' when followed by a noun, as in *sų uéiu* 'everyday', but 'finish' when followed by an auxiliary verb). So, the particle *darí* has a prepositional function in *darí Alúdu* 'to (as far as) England' and *darí harúga* 'until tomorrow' but combines with a following auxiliary to form such verbal phrases as *darí-baų!* 'meet her, join her, find it!' and *darí náru* 'I've found her/it; I've reached her/it'. And the same particle underlies the nonaspectual verbs *adáira* 'to join, meet, find, come together with' and *adáriha* 'to woo; to try to come together with' (cf. *auáira* 'to mount', *auáriha* 'to creep') and the noun *(n)adári* '(my) sweetheart'. (It should be noted here that while *adáirua* 'to be found' and *adáiragua* 'to find one's self' may be said to belong to the conjugation of *adáira*, *adáriha* is treated as a different verb, in the same way that *agą́iera* 'to gain, earn, win' and *agą́ieha* 'to buy', which have a common borrowed base, are treated as different verbs.)

'When?' and 'how?' are both expressed by means of the particle *ída;* but whereas this is followed by a tense marker (*búga* or *me*) or verbalized as *ídaba*, etc. when it has the former sense, it is instead always followed by an auxiliary verb when it has the latter reference: *ída buga lágorai?* 'when did it bite him?', *ída me badógai?* 'when will you do it?'; but *ída lią sa lágoroni?* 'how did it bite him?' (lit., "how is-it its-biting-him?"), *ída uabá-sa lumą sábų?* 'how shall we be (off) for soap', *ída tią́-gi búgucu?* 'how is your mother?'. And likewise *ítara* in its adverbial function, meaning 'so, thus', is always followed by an auxiliary (*ítara liǫ́-ti* 'so it is; it so happened'), although in its adjectival function, it follows the noun that it determines and means 'such (a)'.

Ka 'what; which; who' also has various functions. It may be adjectival, as in *ka ámu uogóri?* 'what other man?' (cf. *ámu* 'other = different', *ábaia* 'another = additional'); pronominal, as in *ká sa tílabaų?* 'what/who is in it (f.)?' or 'what does it mean?', *ká siuámaį bubáų hádagię?* 'which one (f.) of them (animate) do you like (or prefer)?', (*ibídięti tų*) *ká la tiráobaų* '(she did not know) which one was her child'; or it may be verbalized by an aspect marker, as in *kába láfara?* 'whom will he beat?', *kába áfarana?* 'who will beat me?', *káha átubalì nunię bínu?* 'who has drunk my drink of rum?'. Moreover, *ka* is employed to form phrases meaning 'why?', such as *ká gia uagu?* (lit., "what being about?") and *ká uái-gi?* (lit., "what from?").

A few other, rather heterogeneous particles may be mentioned here: *átiri* 'how much/many' as in *átiri tuágu?* 'how much for it?', or, verbalized, as in *átiriánų tiráhǫią?* 'how many children has she?' (lit., "how-many-are-they her-children?"); *binádo* 'former' has adjectival function, as in *binádo hábię* 'their old home', while *bináro* 'formerly; long ago' is adverbial; *funá* 'can be, maybe, must be' (not to be confused with homophonous *funá* 'red'), as in *ma funá-gia ligía badógobai?* 'isn't that maybe what you do?', may be called dubitive; and *saniá ~ sią* 'impossible, unable', as in *sią lubái gia* 'it will be impossible', inabilitative.

Adverbial *súǫdų* 'often; always' appears to be a compound whose second member is borrowed *dų* 'time' (Fr. *temps*); but the first element is obscure, for *suų-* does not occur as a free form. I can only suggest that it may be a combinative variant of *sų* 'every, all' influenced, possibly, by Fr. *souvent*. Borrowed *le* 'when' (Fr. *l'heure*) and the phrase *dų le* are employed analogously to the French conjunction *lorsque*, as in *darí me dų le hiládina* 'until after I have died', but lit., "until future-tense time when I-have-died." These forms are most often followed by a verbal noun, however, as in *dų nígirų* "time (of) my-leaving" = 'when I leave', *le ladáirų* "when his-finding" = 'when he was found', *dų le tátų árani* "time when her-drinking medicine" = 'when she drinks medicine'. Elsewhere they are followed by an imperfective verb with subordinative function, as in *le láfuacubài iráho* "when that-he-emerge child" = 'when the child emerged'. In this respect, these forms resemble *ábų* 'one; a; same; and', which in its coordinative function is also followed by a verbal noun, as in *abų ladógoni* "and his-doing-it" = 'and he did it'.

Another particle that also appears to be conjunctive is *mámai* 'inasmuch as; ever since'. It is employed as in *sią na adógai mámai sądihadina* 'I have become unable to do it since I have fallen sick', *mámai ámu ubáu lidų uénedo luái dų le básarų* '(but the boy could not go where the old man had shown him) for (*mámai*) the world is different in dreams from the time of your getting up', and *uíetių gię masęsutių sų mútu mámai garúe hą́ią* 'all the people were dirty and penniless ever since they had a king'. To indicate resumption of conversation or narrative, borrowed *uél* (Eng. *well*) or *buénu* (Sp. *bueno*) is employed, and is invariably followed by a slight pause. Exclamations of surprise include *óg!*, *mà-uó!*, *hàu-gą́!*, and *à-ú!* Borrowed *dén* (Eng. *then*) or inherited *gaió!* is employed to reinforce what precedes, as in expostulatory *máma uo áu, gaió!?* 'isn't it I, then!?' or *numáda gaió!* 'my dear friend!'. Postposed *ó* or *uó* is employed as a sort of vocative, especially when calling from a distance, as in *numádagu ó!* 'hey, my friends!', *náibuga aríhaų o* 'I'm going to see her', *ą́hą ó* 'yes indeed'.

One might expect to find *ą́hą* 'yes' and *úa* 'no' listed among the interjections; but these, like the great majority of particles, enter into such morphological constructions as, for example, *máharadítu* 'she is unwilling; she does not consent', an aorist verb derived from the privative particle *máharadi* 'unwilling', itself derived from the indefinite or nonaspectual verb *áhara* 'to consent', which contains underlying (denasalized) *ą́hą* 'yes'. And likewise, aorist *úati* 'there is none', perfective *úali* 'there is no more', durative *úagili* 'there is none yet; there is still none', etc., all contain the particle *úa* 'no', a fact which seems to exclude these particles from the subclass of interjections.

COMPARISONS BETWEEN ISLAND-CARIB AND ARAWAK AND GUAJIRO

To end this chapter as I began it, with a small sample of grammatical comparison, I list in Table 6 two sets of Island-Carib locators together with their Arawak and Guajiro equivalents, the first set (*a*) translatable by our adverbs of place, the second (*b*) by our demonstrative adjectives and pronouns. Words of sets *a* (1–4) may be translated 'here'; 'there'; 'over there' (more distant); and 'yonder', respectively; and to these may be added a secondary suffix denoting direction 'to' (5) or 'from' (6)—as in CAIC *iáhaų*, A *iahámin*, and G *yaámiį* 'hither'; CAIC *iárageę*, A *iarahária*, and G *yaléhee* 'thence'. Stems of sets *b* have third person pronominal reference, distinguish singular and plural number, and in the singular only, have two genders. They combine with the same primary suffixes as do the sets *a* to form words that may be translated (1–4, respectively) 'this', 'that'; 'that over there', 'yon'; 'these', 'those'; and 'those over there', 'yon (plural)'. The secondary suffixes are derived from postpositions: A -*min* from *omín* 'to; for', A -*aria* from *oária* 'from'. Arawak (but not IC or G) has several others, like those seen in *iahámaria* 'on this side' or *iaráamaria* 'on that side (of the border)', and in *iarábo* 'just there'

TABLE 6. Selected Island-Carib Locators, with Arawak and Guajiro Equivalents

Stems		Primary suffixes				Secondary suffixes (examples)	
		I	2	3	4	5	6
		Island-Carib (Central American dialect)					
		-(h)a	-ra	-gVta	-gVra	-u̧	-geę ~ -gię
a.	ia-	iá(h)a	iára	iágota	iagóra	iáhau̧	iárageę
b.	li-	lí(h)a	líra	lígita	ligíra	—	—
	tu-	tú(h)a	túra	túguta	tugúra	—	—
	ha-	há(h)a	hára	hágota	hagóra	—	—
		Arawak (Surinam)					
		-(h)V	-ra(h)a	-kVtha(h)a		-min	-(o)aria
a.	ia-	iá(h)a	iára(h)a	iákitha(h)a	—	iahámin	iarahária
b.	li-	lí(h)i	líra(h)a	líkitha(h)a	—	—	—
	tho-	thó(h)o	thóra(h)a	thókotha(h)a	—	—	—
	na-	ná(h)a	nára(h)a	nákitha(h)a	—	—	—
		Guajiro					
		-V	-l/ra	-sa	-?(y)a	-mii̧	-hee
a.	ya-	yaá	yalá	—	—	yaámii̧	yaléhee
	sa-	—	—	sasá	—	samíi̧	sehée
	ca-	—	—	—	ca?yá	camíi̧	cehée
b.	ci-	cií	cirá	cisá	ci?á	—	—
	ti-	tií	tirá	tisá	ti?á	—	—
	na-	naá	nalá	nasá	na?yá	—	—

NOTE: Phonemes placed in parentheses indicate such as are today actualized only in deliberate or formal speech, or, in the case of Guajiro, in certain dialects.

or *thorábo* 'that other one', which contain the postposition *ábo* 'with'. Thus, not only nouns but also some demonstratives (including interrogatives) can take at least some of the postpositional suffixes; although the possible combinations differ to a small extent from one language to another among the three considered here (suffixes on the words labeled *b* being found only in Arawak). (See Taylor 1970*b*.)

Guajiro, unlike Island-Carib or Arawak, employs its plural number for inanimate objects as well as for animate beings; and unlike Island-Carib but like Arawak, one of its two genders refers exclusively to males. Other abstract differences (such as the single locative stem of Island-Carib and of Arawak, *ia-*, if we exclude IC *halia-* and A *halo-* 'where', vs. the three of Guajiro, *ya-*, *sa-*, and *ca-*) and similarities (such as the analogous expression of four degrees of distance in Island-Carib and Guajiro vs. only three in Arawak) are obvious.

The phonological correspondences among these three languages are complicated and will not concern us here (see Taylor 1969*a*). Suffice it to say that most of the equivalents listed in Table 6 may be recognized as cognate or partially cognate, though regular sound change alone does not explain all the correspondences. Exceptionally, Arawak employs a different suffix under 6, *-(o)aria*, from that employed by the other two languages, IC *-geę* (from DIC *-seę*) and G *-hee*, although A *-seen* occurs elsewhere with a somewhat different meaning, 'around; in the vicinity of'. Also G *-sa* and *-ca* are not represented at all in the other two languages.

It may be worth pointing out that whereas the /g/ of CAIC locators in *-gVra* (4), which have penultimate stress, corresponds to /?/ (glottal catch) in their Guajiro equivalents, the /g/ of CAIC locators in *-gVta* (3), which have antepenultimate stress, corresponds to nothing (zero) in their Guajiro equivalents. As this is only one among many examples indicating consonantal loss brought about, in Guajiro, by immediately preceding stress and/or implosive position, I conclude that stress in Island-Carib words listed under 3 and 4 has remained very much as it was in the parent forms, and that the present ultimate stress in the Guajiro equivalents is an innovation.

Omitted from the lists of locators given in Table 6 are nondemonstrative (anaphoric) CAIC *(n)ieį* and A *ión* 'there' (place already mentioned), which may or may not contain variants of the general locative stem, *ia-* (of both languages).

Prominent among the derivational suffixes of these three languages are those represented in Central American Island-Carib by what I have called iterative or tensive *-ha*, stative-reflexive *-gua*, passive *-ua*, and causative *-gVdV*—as in CAIC *átaha* 'to drink (iterative)', *átagua* 'to be engaged in drinking; to get to drinking', *átua* 'to be drunk (passive; not in the sense of inebriated)', and *átagoda* 'give or cause to drink', from *áta* 'to drink (punctual)'. With this we may compare G *-haa*, *-waa*, *-uwaa* or *-naa*, and *-iraa*—as in "*asáhaa* 'estar bebiendo a sorbos'," "*asáwaa* 'ingerir bebidas alcoholicas; parranda, juerga'," "*asúwaa* or *asínaa* 'ser bebido'," and "*asíraa* 'hacer beber; dar de beber'" (Hildebrandt 1963), from *asáa* 'to drink (punctual)'. The first three of these Guajiro suffixes appear to be cognate with their CAIC counterparts; and as we have seen in the section on verbs in this chapter, there is no exact equivalence in the functions of these suffixes from one verb to another of the same language.

In Arawak many (but not all) "indefinite" verbs occur in sets of two or three, such as punctual *thin* and iterative *than* 'drink'; punctual *bíthin*, iterative *bithán*, and reflexive *bithonoán* 'burn'; punctual *bókon*, iterative *bokán*, and reflexive *bokonoán* 'cook, boil'. Thus *náthifan* 'they will drink it' is punctual, while *natháfa* (or *natháafa*) 'they will drink' is iterative; *thobókofan* 'she will cook it' is punctual and *thoboká(a)fa* 'she will cook' is iterative, while *thobokófa* 'it will boil' is reflexive (in the same way as we have in CAIC punctual *arámoda*, iterative *arámodaha*, and reflexive *arámodagua* 'hide'). The appropriateness of the labels punctual, iterative, and reflexive is not always as clear as in the examples cited here: so, A *dónkon* 'sleep', *donkán* 'sleep out (away from home)', and *donkonoán* 'to be resting; to take a nap'. But while it seems hard to speak here of suffixation, it may be justifiable to say that Arawak verbs in -(*a*)*a* correspond to CAIC verbs in -*ha*, and Arawak verbs in -*oa* to CAIC verbs in -*gua*. For the rest, Arawak has the causative -*kVtV*, which clearly corresponds in form and in function to CAIC causative -*gVdV*, and has nothing corresponding to the CAIC passive -*ua*, although -*kVtVnoa*, a reflexive causative, is occasionally (rarely) employed as a passive: A *amárithin* 'to make', *amárithikítin* 'to have (something) made', *amárithikítonoán* 'to be made'.

These Island-Carib, Guajiro, and Arawak suffixes also occur in certain combinations of two, such as, for CAIC, tensive + passive, passive + reflexive, reflexive + causative, tensive + causative, which for this language gives the order tensive, passive, reflexive, causative. In Guajiro the order is tensive, reflexive, causative, passive, while in Arawak the causative can, apparently (see above), precede the reflexive.

FOUR

THE VOCABULARY
OF ISLAND-CARIB

❁

FROM A LEXICAL standpoint, the most striking changes undergone by Island-Carib over the past three hundred years are a great increase in the number of borrowed forms and a proportionately even greater reduction, through loss or referential differentiation, in the number of men's and women's equivalents.

Whether two words of the same or of different languages are ever absolutely equivalent seems questionable; and it is certainly true that some words of all languages are hard to translate—for example, Du. *lekker*, Eng. *cozy*, Fr. *spirituel* or *effleurer*, Ger. *gemütlich*. Here, I should like to give three examples from Island-Carib.

Breton translates *láona* as "du pain," and *láona hámouca ioúti* as "je voudrais avoir du pain pour manger avec ma pitance," whereas cognate A *aonnaháwa* is glossed in the anonymous *Wörterbuch* as "Essen zum Brod." Yet IC *-áuna*, A *-áona* means neither 'bread' nor 'what is eaten with bread'; and as it is of common occurrence, it merits explanation. Among the Black Carib, the Arawak, and in many rural districts of the Lesser Antilles, a meal is regarded as a combination of two components: (1) CAIC *áigini* '(starchy) food'—such as cassava, yams, plantains, sweet potatoes, tannias—and (2) *úii* 'portion(s) of fish or flesh together with a sauce' (Breton's "pitance"). Either one of these components may be regarded as the *-áuna* of the other; so that *láuna náigi̜* 'its-accompaniment my-food' = *úii* 'portion of prepared meat', and *láuna núi̜* 'its-accompaniment my-meat' = *áigini* '(starchy) food'. In place of *núi̜*, one may still hear the men's term, *iúdi* (Breton's *ioúti*) 'my portion of meat'.

Under *gâter*, Breton enters: "*Le requin gâte ma pêche*, kabíchati nàtikini." But the Island-Carib phrase contains no word for 'requin (shark)'; and although the last word is correctly translated "ma pêche," the first (CAIC *gabísati*) is an attributive aorist verb whose literal meaning

72

is 'it has predators'. Modern CAIC *hibísao, -ibísa* 'animal (or human being) that preys upon or plunders another' is very frequently employed today both as a noun and as the base of adjectival and verbal derivatives. So, the chicken hawk's commonest name is *habísa gáiu* "their-predator fowl" = 'the fowl's predator' (CAIC *gáiu*, DIC *káiu*, an old loan from Sp. *gallo*), and the attributive *gabísa* 'having predators' is usually verbalized, as in *gabísati nadígi* (the modern form of Breton's entry), which might be freely rendered 'my catch is often plundered'.

Somewhat similarly, verbs expressing love or hate, like or dislike, are based on a noun, Breton's *icheem* or *íchiem* "ce que j'aime," modern *-isie*, perhaps better if badly translated 'likableness'. So, Breton's *minchínti tóne* (CAIC *mísieti tu*) "he-is-without-likableness for-her" = 'she dislikes him/it'; and his *kinchíntou lóne* (CAIC *hísietu lu*) "she-has-likableness for-him" = 'he loves/likes her/it'. These forms contain, respectively, the privative and attributive particles *mísie* 'without likableness' and *hísie* 'having likableness'; while the possessed noun *tísie* 'her likableness' is contained in *ligía tísiebai lu* "it-is-this that-is-her-likableness for-him" = 'that is what he likes about her'.

BORROWING

Probably all speech communities have borrowed linguistic forms, although some—like Island-Carib and English—have been more hospitable in this respect than others, like Hopi and German. But it is one thing to adopt an exotic term for an exotic referent (e.g., CAIC *arásu*, Eng. and Fr. *orange*, Ital. *arancia*, Ptg. *laranja*, and Sp. *naranja*, from Persian via Arabic *nārandj*), and quite another to replace the inherited word for something familiar by a foreign lexeme, as CAIC *uéiu* 'sun', borrowed from Karina, has replaced inherited *kási* (still current in Breton's day), and as Eng. *take*, borrowed from a Scandinavian dialect, has replaced inherited *nim*. "Intimate borrowing," as that of the latter type is called, usually indicates that at one time there were widespread and prolonged intimate relations between members of different speech communities; and it probably matters little, under these conditions, whether the languages thus in contact are or are not related. Why Island-Carib should have come to prefer the borrowed word for 'sun' and the inherited word for 'moon' may probably be explained as follows:

In Carib (Karina), the sounds [u] and [o] are distinctive, and have been so for as far back as our records go. Thus, for example, in modern K /nu:no/ 'moon' but /no:no/ 'earth', Pelleprat's (1655a) *noúno* and *nóno*. But in Island-Carib of all dialects and times (men's and women's speech alike), both sounds were heard as allophones of a single back rounded vowel phoneme as is evident from the shapes of many items in Breton's

Island-Carib dictionary (1665 and 1666), and especially from that of his "*nónum* la lune; la terre," in which the two words had become homonyms.

It is therefore not surprising that this word of the men's speech was gradually superseded, first by *múa* 'earth', and then by *káthi* 'moon' of women's and general speech. On the other hand, inherited *kási* 'sun' went out of use in favor of the men's *uéiu* (K *we: yu*) with the same meaning —probably because /kási/ ['kaši] and /káthi/ ['kači] (CAIC '/háti/ ['hati]) were felt to be insufficiently distinguished.

Inherited CAIC -*íleue* 'blossom, flower(s)' and -*į* 'offspring; fruit; egg(s)' can be grammatically possessed only by their bearers, as in *tíleue* (*uéue*) 'its blossom (of the tree)', *tį* (*uéue*) 'the fruit (of the tree)', *tį bágai* 'the fruit of thy womb'—much in the same way as, in English, *her hair* normally refers to that which grows on her head, or *her child* to that which she has borne. But the introduction of cut and cultivated varieties of fruit and flowers brought with it a need to express de facto ownership by nonbearers; and this has been met by borrowing: *nufúlurię* 'my flower(s)', from *fulúri* (from Sp. *flor*) 'flower(s)'; *nufúrudą* 'my fruit', from *furúda* (from Sp. *fruta*) 'fruit'.

Similarly, the Island-Carib referred to eggs as the 'fruit' or 'the little one' of the mother bird. Thus, in Dominica, hens' eggs were called indifferently *thį káiu* 'her-fruit fowl' or *thiráho káiu* 'her-child fowl'. But in St. Vincent, probably owing to an increased consumption of this commodity, a new compound was formed; and this was passed on to the Vincentians' Central American offshoot: *gáię* 'hen's egg(s)', from borrowed *gáiu* 'fowl' plus inherited *hį*, -*į* (with dissimilation of /į/ to /ę/ after /i/).

It may seem surprising that the introduction of milk (chiefly canned) as a commercial food considered fit for adult human consumption should have led to the borrowing of *míligi* 'milk' during the present century. But whereas the inherited compound, *húrirao*, -*úrira*, from -*úri* 'breast' plus -*íra* 'juice', sufficed in reference to the product of natural lactation, it was felt that such a commodity as Pet Milk demanded a shorter appellation than *túrira bágasu Pet* 'her-breast-juice cow Pet' (CAIC *bágasu*, DIC *bákasu*, 'cow', an old loan from Sp. *vacazo* or *vacacho*).

The concept of marriage was expressed in Breton's time by derivatives of the terms for 'wife' (-*iáni*) and 'husband' (-*iráithi*, itself analyzable as a compound meaning 'child's father'): *karáithithu* 'she has a husband' = 'she is married', *kaiánię* "(he) takes wife" = 'gets married'—with which compare Ital. *ammogliarsi* 'get married (of a man)'. But the Christian wedding, with which the Island-Carib only later became familiar, was new and different enough to warrant the borrowing of Fr. *marier* as DIC *amaríeta*, CAIC *amárieda* 'to get married (in church)'. The old terms for 'husband' and 'wife' continued to be employed regularly in all three communities (Dominica, St. Vincent, and Central America) until the beginning of the present century, when both were replaced in Central America (though not in the islands) by *-úmari* 'companion' (cf. Breton's "*nómari* mon compagnon"), as in *túmari* 'her husband' and *lúmari* 'his wife'. Today, CAIC *-iráiti* (DIC *-iráithi*) is unknown, while *-iáni* is archaic and seems to have acquired a humorous connotation. Although I cannot account for the decay of these older terms, the prevalence of "companionate marriage" may well have determined the choice of the new one.

Kinship terms occupy a very special place in the vocabulary of a language, reflecting as they do both conservatism and change in the structure of the society that employs them; it is therefore not surprising to find that Karina influence in this domain has been greater than in most others of a more general nature; see Table 7.

Borrowing from European languages had begun before Breton's time and was then mainly from Spanish; but it had not yet affected

TABLE 7. Kinship Terms of Central American Island-Carib

1. náruguti	FF, FFB, MF, MFB	21. nirá(h)ihaię	step-K
2. nagíti	FM, FFM, MM, MMZ	22. isáni	K + KK (collective)
		23. nirániu	mBW, wZH
3. núguci, baba	F, FB	24. uaránigu*	WZ, HB
4. núguciháię	step-F, FB	25. naníre	WZ, HB, mBW, wZH
5. núgucu, dada	M, MZ		
6. núgucu dúnaru	step-M	26. nídiu	m/wSW, wDH
7. iáu, niáurite	MB, MMB	27. nágiri	HM, wSW
8. náufuri	FZ, FFZ	28. nígatu	HZ, wBW, wMBD, wFZD
9. níbugaię	mEB, wEZ, mFBS, wMZS	29. nígeru	K$F/M
10. írui*	mEB	30. nilígi(ni)*	wKK
11. (n)íbiri	mYB, mFBS	31. (n)íme-dámuru	WF, HF
12. namúleę	wYB, wMZS	32. (n)iménidi	WM, HM
13. namulélua	wYZ, wMZD	33. (n)ibári	m/wKK
14. nítu	mZ, mMZD, mFBD	34. (n)ibárimu	mDH
		35. (n)ibámu	WB, mZH
15. náti	wB, wFBS, wMZS	36. (n)ibáse	mZD, wBD, HZD, mWBD
16. niráiti*	H	37. (n)ibádumu*	wBS, HZS
17. níani*	W	38. (n)ígiriri*	wMBS
18. númari	$ (H/W)	39. (n)iuíriri*	mFZD
19. nubuíamį	co-$	40. (n)inądáganį*	mZs
20. nirá(h)į	m/wK (S/D)	41. niníbu*	mZS

KEY: F = father, M = mother, E = elder, Y = younger, B = brother, Z = sister, S = Son, D = daughter, K = child (S/D), H = husband, W = wife, $ = spouse (H/W), m = man's, w = woman's.

NOTE: Most kinship terms are basically possessed by a personal prefix; that of first person singular, *n-* 'my', has been so employed here. Terms numbered 7, 8, 10, 11, 31–40 are (and 41 may well be) derived from Karina; the remainder are inherited Arawakan.

* Terms no longer in common use and considered as archaic by my informants. (No. 30, though obsolete as a kinship term, retains in current usage its reference to 'domesticated or pet animal'.)

the basic vocabulary, which already contained a considerable proportion of Karina (Carib) items, some in general use, others employed only in the "men's speech" and paralleled by inherited Arawakan equivalents. Today, the number of these men's and women's synonyms in Island-Carib has been drastically reduced, and the proportion of Arawakan terms greatly increased. Table 8 shows the numbers of words of Arawakan, of

TABLE 8. Distribution of Inherited Arawakan and Borrowed Karina Loanwords in Basic Central American Island-Carib Vocabulary

Word categories	Arawak only		Arawak and Karina		Karina only		Total number of items
	1650	1950	1650	1950	1650	1950	
Flora and fauna	2	2	4	2	2	3	8
Nature	1	6	8	1	6	8	15
Adjectival bases	6	15	10	0	3	4	19
Verb bases	6	17	13	1	0	1	19
Grammatical	4	6	4	2	0	0	8
Body and plant parts	14	31	17	0	0	0	31
All categories	33	77	56	6	11	16	100

both Arawakan and Karina, and of Karina ancestry in Swadesh's 100-item diagnostic test list filled in for the year 1650 (Breton's time) and again for 1950 (the time of my own field work), and divided into six "domains": flora and fauna ('woman', 'man', 'person', 'fish', 'bird', 'dog', 'louse', 'tree'), nature ('sun', 'moon', 'star', 'water', 'rain', 'stone', 'sand', 'earth', 'cloud', 'smoke', 'fire', 'ash', 'path', 'mountain', 'night'), adjectives ('all', 'many', 'one', 'two', 'big', 'long', 'small', 'red', 'green', 'yellow', 'white', 'black', 'hot', 'cold', 'full', 'new', 'good', 'round', 'dry'), verbs ('drink', 'eat', 'bite', 'see', 'hear', 'know', 'sleep', 'die', 'kill', 'swim', 'fly', 'walk', 'come', 'lie', 'sit', 'stand', 'give', 'say', 'burn'), grammatical ('I', 'thou', 'we', 'this', 'that', 'who', 'what', 'not'), and body and plant parts and products (the remaining thirty-one items). To this list must be added the modern Central American word for 'person' (omitted from the table), *mútu*, apparently a loan from some Bantu language. The comparatively heavy borrowing from Carib in the first three categories and its absence or scarcity in the last three seems to be worth notice, although I can offer no plausible explanation for this difference.

The cultural or general vocabulary of the modern Island-Carib dialects contains a large number of French, Spanish, and, more particularly in British Honduras, English loanwords. In my own field notes on the language of the Black Carib of British Honduras (1947–48), I find 377 integrated and apparently stabilized European loans, 41 of which (plus 35 others now lost or replaced) are listed in Breton's seventeenth-century dictionary of the Dominican dialect. The distribution of their apparent models is as follows: 209 French, 119 Spanish, 49 English, besides a few others of doubtful ancestry. From this it appears (if my lists are representative) that the heaviest European borrowing was from French and occurred between 1653 (the date of Breton's return to France) and 1797 (the date of the deportation from St. Vincent); for whereas Spanish and English models were adopted both before and after these dates, French models were not available to the deportees and their descendants in Central America.

Whatever the status of their models, borrowed lexemes belong to the class of particles (for example, *rísi* 'rich' and *maríe* 'married', which, in conjunction with auxiliary verbs, function as predicate adjectives) or to that of nouns (for example, CAIC *gelé* 'key', from Fr. *clef*, and *fáifa*, DIC *páipa*, 'pipe', from English). Or they may be bound (for example, DIC *suliéhe* 'shoes' and *nisuliéni* 'my shoes', based on Fr. *soulier(s)*, both contain inherited affixes). In CAIC *gágugilí tia, maiúsugìli-ga spéko* 'he still has eyes (= sees well enough), since he doesn't yet use spec(tacle)s', one English loan (*spéko*) is free, while another (*-ius-* 'use') was never heard otherwise than bound. But whether elsewhere bound or free, borrowed lexemes can underlie verbs only in conjunction with inherited derivational affixes, as in the case of *risi* 'rich', from which are derived the verbs *arísida* 'to get rich', *arísigoda* 'to be made rich (causative)', etc., and the noun *irísini* 'wealth, riches'. Similarly, from the borrowed noun *gurásu* (from Fr. *courage*) 'patience' are formed the attributive and privative particles *gagúrasụ* 'patient' and *magúrasụ* 'impatient', while the latter may be reconverted into a noun as *umágurasúni* 'impatience'. Of course, some borrowed and likewise some inherited lexemes yield no derivatives (for example, *murúsu* 'a bit, a little', from Fr. *morceau*), but it is clear that the number of "dictionary words" containing borrowed bases is several times as great as that of borrowed lexemes; and I am sure that well over a thousand can be constructed from the 377 borrowed bases which I noted.

Some further examples of nonaspectual verbs with borrowed bases are the following: CAIC *abúlieda* 'to forget' (Fr. *oublier*), *asúsereda* 'to happen' (Sp. *suceder*), *ebégira* 'to beg (pardon)' (Eng. *beg*), *abúsẹra* 'to want' (Fr. *besoin*), *afaịra* 'to provide with' (Eng. *find*), *afálara* 'to follow' (Eng. *follow*), *agáiera* 'to win; to earn' and *agáieha* 'to buy' (Fr. *gagner*), *agúdara* 'to make happy' (Fr. *content*), *aháiara* 'to hire (labor)' (Eng. *hire*), *arásera* 'to repair' and *aráseha* 'to get ready; to arrange' (Fr. *arranger*), *asádira* 'to be or to become sick' (Fr. *sentir*), *aságara* 'to withdraw (money)' (Sp. *sacar*), *asígenera* 'to doubt' and *asígeneha* 'to argue' (Fr. *chicaner*), *adúeha* 'to owe (money)' (Fr. *devoir*), *afurédeha* 'to borrow' (Fr. *prêter*), *alámiduha* 'to starch (clothes)' (Fr. *l'amidon*), *eleskuéleha* 'to school' (Sp. *la escuela*), *amúliha* 'to grind' (Sp. *moler*), *apuríciha* 'to preach' (Eng. *preach*), *arúeha* 'to reign' (cf. *urúe* 'king', from Fr. *roi*), *egeléca* 'to lock' (cf. *gelé* 'key', from Fr. *clef*).

Understandably, the earliest loans from European languages consisted for the most part of names for newly introduced animals, implements, and weapons, and contained few verbal derivatives. Of those found in Breton's dictionary (some seventy-five in all) the following have survived:

Modern CAIC	17th-c. DIC	Gloss	Presumed model
badía	batía	watermelon	Sp. badea
badíse, a-báste-ra	batísse, a-batissé-ra	(get) baptized	Fr. baptisé
bágasu	bácachou, bácacho	cow, ox	Sp. vacazo
bínu	bínê	wine, rum	Sp. vino
bíra (nibírą)	bíra (nibírani)	sail	Sp. vela
buíruhu	bouírocou	pig	Sp. puerco
bunídi (nubúnidj)	bonéttê (nibonétini)	hat	Sp. bonete
burígo	boúrriquê	donkey	Sp. borrica
búroburo	boúrbrê	gunpowder	Sp. pólvora
fádiri	pátri	priest	Sp. padre
fáluma	pálma	coconut	Sp. palma
fanídira (nufánidirą)	pántir (noupántirani)	flag	Sp. bandera
a-furíe-da	a-pouriérou-ta	to pray	Fr. prière
mégeru	méguerou	Negro	? (cf. Sp. negro)
mésu	méchou	cat	Sp. micho
múdų	mouton	sheep	Fr. mouton
sabádu (nisábadų)	sabátto (nichabáttoni)	shoe	Sp. zapato
sálu	sálou, chálou	salt	Sp. sal
siára (nisíarą)	sciérra	saw	Sp. sierra
isíbuse, isúbuse	(i)chiboúchi	mirror	Sp. espejo
simúni (nisómunj)	chimononi (nichimónoni)	rudder, helm	Sp. timón
sírasi (nisíreste)	chírachi	scissors	Sp. tixeras
isúbara (nesúbarate)	echoubára (néchoubàrate)	cutlass	Sp. espada
súgaro	choúcrê (nachoúcaronê)	sugar	Sp. azucar
arágabusu	racaboúchou	gun	Sp. aracabuz
arírą	allíran	cock or hen	Sp. gallina
gabáiu	cabáyo	horse	Sp. caballo
gábara	cábrara	goat	Sp. cabra
gaburána	caboúranê	billhook	? (cf. Sp. caparona)
gáiu	cáyou	cock or hen	Sp. gallo
gamísa	camícha	cloth	Sp. camisa
gániesi	caníchê	sugarcane	Sp. cañas
gárada (nigáradą)	cárta (nacártani)	book, paper, letter	Sp. carta
a-gáradaháti	a-gardácati	guard	? (cf. Fr. garde-côte)
garádų	carattóni	rat	Sp. ratón (?)
gasúru	cachoúrou	rassade (beads)	Ptg. casulo

Modern CAIC	17th-c. DIC	Gloss	Presumed model
aŭgléisi	Anglichê	Englishman	(Fr. or Sp.)
grábu (nogórabų)	crábou	nails, iron	Sp. clavo
áŭguru	ancoúroute	anchor	(Fr. or Sp.)
agúsa (nágusete)	acoúcha (noucoúchete)	needle	Sp. aguja
gusįiu (nugúsįiu)	couchígno, couchígnê	knife	Sp. cuchillo
ligílisi	eglisê	church	Fr. l'église

Hyphens separate borrowed bases from verbalizing or other inherited affixes. Forms in parentheses are possessed nouns prefixed by inherited *n-* 'my'. The shape of the verb *abástera* (whose base is the particle *badíse* 'baptized') is probably due to dislocation of stress from penult (Breton's *abatiséra*) to the word's second syllable, with syncope of the /i/ and metathesis of the sibilant and the apical stop. Since CAIC voiceless /t/ normally reflects DIC aspirated /th/, and CAIC voiced /d/ corresponds to DIC unaspirated /t/, while /s/ of both dialects is normally though nondistinctively voiceless, we might have expected this change to produce **abásdera*, with or without nondistinctive voicing of the /s/, rather than attested *abástera*.

In the meager record of the recent Dominican dialect, I find (excluding numerals) eighteen European loans unknown to Breton, of which thirteen reappear in my own record of the Central American dialect:

Recent DIC	Modern CAIC	Gloss	Presumed model
páipa (nupáipathe)	fáifa (nufáifate)	pipe	Eng. pipe
pulátu	—	dish	Sp. plato
pútu	fúdu	mug, jug	? (cf. Sp. pote, Eng. pot)
a-maríe-ta	a-márie-da	to get married	Fr. marier
mulátu	muládu	half-breed	Sp. mulato
múthu	mútu	person	? (cf. Bantu múntu)
tábula	dábula	table	Fr. table
thásu	tásu	cup	Fr. tasse
e-théki-ra	e-tégi-ra	to thank	Eng. thank 'ee
sápu	—	hat	Fr. chapeau
sáuteru	sáudieru	cauldron	Fr. chaudière
siménu	—	week	Fr. semaine
simísi	simísi (nisímisį)	shirt	Fr. chemise
suliéhe (nisuliéni)	—	shoes	Fr. soulier(s)
rúbu	—	woman's dress	Fr. robe
kabána	gabána	bed	Fr. (Creole cabane)
kúieru	gulíeru	spoon	Fr. cullier > cuiller
uéru	uéru	drinking glass	Fr. verre

Early borrowing in other Amerindian languages of the area was often from the same European models as in Island-Carib (except that loanwords from Karina [Carib] are much more rare). So, with the above lists compare the following Arawak and/or Guajiro words:

Arawak	Guajiro	Karina	Gloss	Presumed model
báka	paá?a	pa:ka	cow	Sp. vaca
oéla	—	pi:ra	sail	Sp. vela
póroko	—	piiru:ku	pig	Ptg. porco, Sp. puerco
—	pilíiku	—	donkey	Sp. borrico
—	piĺtpila	—	gunpowder	Sp. pólvora
—	pántteera, wántteera	pandi:ra	flag	Sp. bandera
arakabúsa	—	ara:kapu:su	gun	Sp. arcabuz
karíina	kalíina	—	domestic fowl	Sp. gallina
kaoáio	—	kawa:ri	horse	Sp. caballo
—	kaá?ula	kabiri:to	goat	Sp. cabra
kimisa (-kimisan)	kamíisa	kami:sa	cloth	Sp. camisa
karta (-kartan)	karálautta	kare:ta	book; letter; paper	Sp. carta (+ G -utta 'skin'?)
akósa (-akosáthe)	—	aku:sa	needle	Sp. aguja
aránso (-aransóthe)	—	—	orange	Fr. orange (?)
páipa (-páipan)	—	—	pipe	Eng. pipe or Du. pijp
sapáto	sapáata	sapa:to	shoes	Sp. zapato

However, the same model was not always chosen to express the same concept; thus A *kasipara* 'machete, cutlass' is a loan from Sp. *cachiporra*, whereas IC *isubara* and K *su(m)ba:ra*, which have the same meaning, appear to come from Sp. *espada*. Dominican Island-Carib, from Breton's day until it became extinct at the beginning of the present century, employed a stem borrowed from Sp. *querer* to express the concept 'wish or want'—*kréethi* 'he wants/wishes'—but the only equivalent known to speakers of the Central American dialect—CAIC *busẹti* 'he wants/wishes'—has a stem borrowed from Fr. *besoin*. IC *mésu* 'cat' comes from Sp. *micho;* but its Guajiro equivalent, G *muúsa* or *muúsu*, comes (like Hopi *mó:sa* 'cat') from Sp. *mozo, -a* 'youth, waiter; girl, waitress', which acquired the extended meaning of 'cat' in eighteenth-century Spanish (see Bright 1960, pp. 167–68). On the other hand, the reference of a traditional word may be changed to fit a new or borrowed concept, as was pointed out by Nils Holmer (1949, p. 54) in the case of G *amá, -?amáị* 'horse', which is almost certainly cognate with A *kama* 'tapir' and its equivalent in other Arawakan languages.

LOSS, REFERENTIAL DIFFERENTIATION, AND CHANGE

We have seen how, since Breton's time, the number of apparently synonymous pairs of noncultural words used, respectively, in the men's speech and in that of the women has shrunk from fifty-six to six, while the number of Arawakan words in general use has increased from thirty-three to seventy-seven, and one African and sixteen Carib words are now found in general use by both sexes. Some doubt may subsist with regard to suppletive *uátu, -íleme* 'fire'—counted as Carib although the dependent form, *-íleme*, is Arawakan—and the quasi-synonymous *acólora* 'arrive, come' (Arawak), *nióbui-* 'come' (Carib), which are counted as a pair by both Breton and me.

The Arawakan affiliation of even the men's speech of Breton's time is evidenced mainly by its grammar, grammatical morphemes of Arawakan ancestry being used—and some of Cariban ancestry being misused—with Cariban lexemes. Moreover, generally employed Arawakan words without Cariban equivalents in the men's speech then included not only grammatical (or functional) words like those meaning 'that', 'this', 'they', 'he', 'she', 'we', 'you (pl.)', but also the names of such body parts as denoted 'claw', 'ear', 'feather', 'hand', 'liver', 'nose', 'tail', and 'tongue'.

In a few cases, words "lost" before Breton's time are recoverable. Thus, his *bánna* (*-oúbana*) 'feather; liver; leaf; house', which is Arawakan, enters into composition with borrowed Cariban words for 'bird' and 'tree' to give his *toúnoulou bánna* ('bird-*banna*') 'feather' and *huéhue oúbana* ('tree-*oúbana*') 'leaf'—besides syntactic *toúbana huéhue* 'feuille d'arbre'. But glossed identically with the latter, he elsewhere lists another word written *árou-bánna*—a faulty division, as may be seen from the cognate Arawak equivalent, *adobána*, containing A *áda* 'tree' + *obána* 'leaf; liver'. And another word which almost certainly contains older Island-Carib (or should we then say Eyéri?) **ára* 'tree; wood' is Breton's *arábou* ("*íkira bélouha arábou* 'il est entré dans le bois"), CAIC *árabu*, and T *arcabuco*, all meaning 'woodland, forest, bush' and having as second member of the compound *-(kh)ábu* 'comprising, taking in, underlying; with' (possibly identical with the root of the word meaning 'hand'). And similarly, G (*w*)*uná?api* 'woodland, forest, bush' appears to be a compound of its (*w*)*unú?u* 'tree; wood' with its *api* (as in G *huyápi* 'rainy season', containing G *huyá* 'rain') 'that which supports or sustains or holds'.

The old word for 'water' is probably contained in the Guadeloupe river name *Coyoúini* /kuiúini/, perhaps meaning 'spirit water' (cf. A *kóioha* 'spirit' and *óni* or *óini* 'rain; water'), whose utterance while upon its waters was said to bring on abundant rain, according to Breton. And the old word for 'stone' (cf. A *síba* (*-isiban*) 'stone') may well be seen in Breton's *ichíbani*, which he gives as the name of the Island-Caribs' 'anchor', and describes as a large rock secured in a sort of cage made of sticks.

Similarly, Cariban forms for 'leaf', 'root', and 'ear', though not listed by Breton as such, are recognizable in compounds like his *monochíali* 'twin leaf' (the name of several species of *Carludovica* which have swallow-tailed leaves), with which compare Akawaio *yale* and Wayana *ali*, both 'leaf'. And K *sa?rombo* 'leaves' appears to be contained in Breton's DIC *massalómboe* 'half-rotten leaves massed and deposited by the river'. K *mi:ti* 'root' is seen in Breton's *mábi-míti* 'sweet potato roots', and its *pa:na* 'ear' in his DIC *nibánali*, 'my hearing', *tibánali* 'her hearing', etc., whose personal prefixes are Arawakan! None of these forms has survived.

On the other hand, the inherited Island-Carib cognate (if such existed) of A *híkihi* (Robert Dudley's *hicket*), G *s(i)kí*, Palicur *tiketi*, etc., all meaning 'fire', has left no trace, although IC *íleme* and A *íhime*, which are the suppletive subordinate forms of the same meaning, appear to be cognate. But independent IC *uáthu*, borrowed from K *waxto* 'fire', can hardly be called equivalent to its dependent *íleme* since the one may enter into construction with the other, as in CAIC *líleme uátu* 'the fire's blazing'.

Neither of the words that Breton gives for 'person' has survived with this reference. But if his *ilácou* of the women's speech (cf. its Arawak equivalent, *lóko*) contains his *íla* 'contents', and his *itánoucou* of the men's speech contains his *-itan-* 'in; inside', the former subsists as CAIC *ilágu* 'collective contents; load', while the stem *-ídą* and the suffix *-da* (K *ta*) still mean 'in; inside'. Modern CAIC *mútu* (recent DIC *múthu*) 'person; people; human being(s)' is certainly a loanword (cf. common Antillean French Creole *mun*, whose reference is identical), and may well have a Bantu ancestry.

The explanation for this rather surprising change is to be found, I think, in modern Surinam Arawak, which has no word equivalent to our 'person', and in which one must choose between *kákitho* 'living creature' and *lóko* (pl. *lokóno*) 'member(s) of the tribe' (a Negro or a white man is not a *lóko*, understandable when one learns that *lóko* also means 'in; inside'). I conclude that the change in Island-Carib was brought about by the adoption of a more liberal attitude toward the rest of humanity, and that the concept 'person' = 'individual human being' is not as basic as some might suppose.

Breton's *oulíbignum* 'bird' of the women's speech (now replaced by Cariban *dunúru* for both sexes), which appears to be cognate with its Arawak equivalent *kódibio*, may well subsist in the name of a species of bird, CAIC *guríbiua*, otherwise known in British Honduras as 'pork-and-dough boy'. And as was mentioned at the end of Chapter I, Breton's *iouánni* 'heart; soul; life; courage' of the men's speech subsists as common CAIC -(*i*)*uáni* 'vitality, courage' or 'soul (in particular, that one of several souls which is situated in the heart)'; while his *aníchi* 'heart; soul; will; desire' of the women's speech retains, as CAIC *anígi*, the referents 'heart (as an organ); mind; inclination' of the general vocabulary.

Given the last example and that of the pairs glossed 'bite' and 'hot', there is some suspicion that some of these men's and women's "equivalents" were not regularly interchangeable. Yet, a few that, short of quibbling, are interchangeable still subsist; and such pairs evidently were much more numerous in Breton's time. The cases of Breton's *cáo* (or *cáho*) 'eat; bite' and *cheu* 'hot'—besides his *áica* 'eat', *ácrêcoua* 'bite', and *bacha-* or *ara-* 'hot'—are somewhat different. The first, CAIC *háu*, is not a verb but a particle which takes the place of *áiga* 'eat' in some aspectual verbs (such as perfective *háuhadina* 'I've eaten') and verbal phrases (such as injunctive *háu-bai!* 'eat it!'). And similarly *gurá* 'drink' takes the place of regular *áta* 'drink' in these same forms. This is because, though *áiga* and *áta* are in no way defective, certain of their moods and aspects have acquired undesirable connotations, namely, 'eat/drink to excess' or 'take food/drink on the sly'. (Cf. English, in which *he's already drunk* is, to say the least, ambiguous, though *he's already eaten* is not.) As for CAIC *so*, the reflex of Breton's *cheu*, this particle means 'burning; roasting; stinging' rather than 'hot' and underlies the verbs *ásora* 'to roast' and *ásoha* 'to sting' (Taylor 1961c, pp. 30–34). So also, denominal attributive *gagóle* (Breton's *kakêlle*), which is inherited, and borrowed Cariban *dibúnaį* (Breton's *tiboúnaim*) are usually both translatable by 'fat'; but the former now refers to 'fat (greasy)' and the latter to 'fat (obese)'.

Ninety-three of the modern CAIC terms in the 100-item list on which Table 8 is based are reflexes of those given by Breton as part of the women's speech or as then common to both sexes. Three more (those glossed 'bird', 'swim', and 'sun') correspond to the equivalents Breton listed for the men's speech; and a fourth, *subúdi-* 'know' (Breton's "*chouboútoui* connaître"), has changed its meaning from 'know (be acquainted with)' to 'know (facts)'. (CAIC *subúse-* now has the former reference; while its *agába* 'hear; understand' formerly covered the latter.)

For 'good'—apart from inherited *seméę* 'good (pleasant to the senses of taste, smell or touch)'—both Breton's and the modern dialects have only Cariban words, which still subsist. But Breton's *íropon* 'good (in general)' has become modern CAIC *irúfų* 'good (kind)', and his *bouítou* 'good-looking' (which is also Cariban though he attributes it to the women's speech) has become modern CAIC *buídu* 'good (in general)'.

The word given me for 'yellow', *dumári*, is Breton's *tomáli*, the name of a yellow sauce made from manioc juice, which reference the word in its modern shape has retained, while also supplanting Breton's *houhereti* 'yellow'. The only CAIC form on the list not found in Breton's work is *mútu* 'person' (for which, see above).

Extension, narrowing, or change of reference seems to have taken place in at least 4 percent of the lexemes recorded. Many of those that were borrowed from European languages had a much wider reference than that of their models until the adoption of further loanwords brought about a narrowing—which was not always in the direction of the model's reference. Thus, Sp. *vino* 'wine' gave Breton's DIC *bínê* 'wine or brandy', which then became modern DIC and CAIC *bínu* 'rum (or other strong distilled liquor such as whiskey, brandy, gin)', *diuéi̧*, from Fr. *du vin*, having replaced it in reference to 'wine'. And Sp. *camisa* 'shirt', which gave Breton's DIC *camícha* 'cloth or clothing of any description', was subsequently narrowed in its reference to become CAIC *gamísa* 'cloth (woven stuff)' by the borrowing of such words as *simísi* (Fr. *chemise*) 'shirt', *gúdu* (Fr. *cotte*) 'skirt', *galásu̧* (Fr. *caleçon*) 'trousers', etc.

On the other hand, accommodation to acculturational change has more usually brought about extension or change of reference in older, inherited lexemes. So, *-iáua* 'shadow; reflection' has been extended to include 'picture; photograph', *uádigidígi* 'firefly' to include 'electric torch'. The reduplicated particle *balábala* 'rolling over and over' may be employed as a noun meaning 'wheel', and the aorist verb *bacáti* 'it is warm' also functions as a noun meaning either 'tea (any infusion taken as a beverage or as a medicine)' or 'breakfast', the meal at which such infusions are usually drunk. Breton's *mámba* 'honey' has become CAIC *mába* 'bee(s)', his term for 'bee(s)' having been *mámba-étegnon* 'honey begetter', and the modern word for 'honey' being *hára mába* 'their-juice bees'. The change seen in Breton's "*alloúcoura* donner" to CAIC *alúgura* 'sell' should be familiar from the history of our own word *sell*, which is the same; and the creation of a tensive (or iterative) verb *abúgaha* 'to drive (a vehicle)' from inherited *abúga* 'to drive/chase off/out/away' at least is logical.

Deterioration, already evident in Breton's DIC *caouánam* 'gold or brass' (cf. T *caona* 'gold'), has gone still further in CAIC *gáuana* 'penny, cent, copper' (perhaps owing to a sort of Gresham's law); and the change in reference from Breton's DIC *chébi* '(coral) reef' to CAIC *sébi* 'white lime' will perhaps require explanation for most readers. In the Lesser Antilles, white lime for mortar (unknown there in pre-Columbian times) was and often still is made by burning coral prized from the reef; and therefore both 'coral' and 'white lime' are known in the local creoles by the French term for the latter, *la chaux*.

More obscure are the reasons for some other changes of reference. So, Breton's DIC *áouere* 'well; happy; satisfied' now has a pejorative sense as CAIC *áuere* 'served right'; and his *ébechoua* 'to become; to take shape' has become CAIC *ébecua* 'to speak ill of; to slander'. The former word's change probably began as an extended meaning, in the same way as Fr. *bien* 'well' has an extended meaning in *c'est bien fait pour toi* 'it serves you right'. But Breton's DIC "*mébechouatítiũ tébou ouekêliem* les hommes ne deviennent pas pierres" and cognate CAIC *mébecuadítių dóbu uogórię* 'men do not slander stones' seem to have no connection. It may be that the semantic thread took the course 'take or change shape' → 'transform' → 'misrepresent' → 'slander or speak ill of'; but the shape of this now active verb indicates that it was once reflexive or passive.

Still more perplexing is the change in reference of a kinship term which Breton lists as follows: "*Nígatou*, c'est ainsi que les cousines appellent leurs cousins maternels lors que leurs soeurs ne se marient pas avec eux: & les cousins en tel cas les appellent *niouelle átonum*." And since he also makes it perfectly clear that the preferred type of marriage was that of a man with his father's sister's daughter (real or classificatory), it follows that Breton's *nígatou* was the name by which a girl called her (real or classificatory) mother's brother's son when intermarriage between the two nuclear families was not contemplated. But today, CAIC *nígatu* refers to 'my (woman speaking) brother's wife or husband's sister', thus showing change in the sex of the referent though not in that of the "propositus." Thus one may speak of *tígatu* 'her brother's wife', but not of **lígatu*, since the relationship is and always has been that of someone to a female. I shall not attempt a solution to this problem here except to suggest a possible relationship with the Arawak kinship term *daiokatho* 'my (man speaking) mother's brother's wife', which clearly contains the same language's *dáio* 'my mother'; so that *-katho* seems to refer to a woman's brother's wife, as does also modern CAIC *-(í)gatu*.

COMPOUNDS AND
COMPARISON

It often happens that an old lexeme whose earlier shape and meaning have been quite forgotten is preserved in "petrified" state as part of synchronically simple words that once were compound or complex. So, for example, though OEng, *niman* 'to take' and *stígan* 'to climb' have no reflex in the English of today, their stems, *nim-* and *sti(g)-*, may still be recognized in modern words such as *nimble*, *stile* (OEng. *stigel*), and *stirrup* (OEng. *stírap*). This fact may be of small interest to the Germanicist, who has at his disposal a vast amount of historically attested data; but the search for cognates among related "exotic" languages like those of the Arawakan family or stock is not so fruitful that petrified forms may be ignored. In what follows, a few instances of lexemes that are still alive in at least one language but petrified in others will be cited; more may be found in two articles having the same title as has this section (Taylor 1958*a* and 1960*a*) and in a third called "Teknonymy in Arawakan" (Taylor 1961*b*); many certainly remain to be discovered.

IC -*iúma*, A -*réroko*, and G *aániki*, which are those languages' current forms for 'mouth (external orifice in the head)', appear to be unrelated; whereas their forms meaning 'moustache'—CAIC -*ídiuma*, A -*itíima*, and G -*líima*—show regular correspondences and are almost certainly cognate (cf. CAIC -*ugúdi* : A -*koti* : G -*?úlii* 'foot'). But the Island-Carib form for 'moustache' is a compound of *ídi*- 'hair' with -*iúma* 'mouth'; and we may presume that its Arawak and Guajiro equivalents, which today are probably unanalyzable to native speakers, once contained cognates of both these lexemes. (For Arawak, only -*iima* 'mouth of a river', and for Guajiro, only -*líi* 'fur; body hair', are attested.) Moreover, while CAIC -*iumáru*, from -*iúma* 'mouth' and -*áru* 'edge; border', and A -*rérokoda*, from -*réroko* 'mouth' and -*da* 'skin', are both compounds meaning 'lip' but sharing no cognate members, G -*íimata* 'lip' cannot be seen as a compound containing attested G -*tá* 'skin' (cognate with the second member of the Arawak compound) unless it is recognized that unattested G *-*iima* is or was another lexeme cognate with CAIC -*iúma* 'mouth'. And similarly, DIC *áriuma* 'anus', composed of *ári*- 'after' and -*iúma* 'mouth'—analogous but unrelated to its Arawak equivalent, *énakoréroko*, containing *enako* 'behind'—is most probably cognate with its Taino equivalent, written both as *marima* and as *tarima*, in which the initial letters probably represent prefixes.

Attested eighteenth-century A (*d*)*ádithi* '(my) son', from *adi*- 'after; beyond' + -*thi* 'father', has now been reduced to (*d*)*áithi*, and so presumably lost its motivation; but A *iréno* 'children' (-*no* is a nominal pluralizer, but there is no attested singular of this word) and *dáthi* 'my father' should suffice to make the composition of *deréthi* 'my husband (my child's father)' clear to the native speaker. Yet DIC *iráithi* 'husband' could hardly have been felt to contain the stem of its *iráho* 'child' by the native speaker of Island-Carib, whose only term for 'father' was and is DIC -*úkusili*, CAIC -*úguci*.

A -*thi* 'father' and -*io* 'mother' (*dáio* 'my mother') appear to be contained in that language's -*tithi* or -*tethi* 'daughter's husband' and -*tio* 'son's wife', with which we may compare Breton's DIC -*ítiti* (probably /-ítithi/) 'daughter's husband' and -*ítignon* or -*éteignon* (probably /-ítịiụ/ ~ /-étẹiụ/) 'progenitor; husband; husband's father; husband's mother; daughter's husband' (alternatively with the foregoing), and *keteignókêta* 'engenderer' —literally, 'cause to have progenitor'. If these terms are compounds, the first member of the Arawak and the second member of the Island-Carib seem to have been obscure at the time of recording. But DIC -*éte* means 'stock; base; bottom'; and it is at least plausible to assume that a son-in-law might have been designated as a father or begetter of stock and a daughter-in-law as a mother, parent, or breeder of stock; though if DIC *-iŭ* or *-niŭ* is cognate with A *-io*, it is evident that the former lexeme specified neither the sex nor the generation of its referent. So, DIC *nirániŭ* 'my (female speaking) sister's husband' or 'my (male speaking) brother's wife' apparently contains, together with *-niŭ* as second member, the stem of *iráho* 'child'; and we know that among the Island-Carib, father's brothers were classed as fathers, mother's sisters as mothers, and their children as brothers and sisters. It therefore follows that *lirániŭ* 'his child's parent' refers to 'his brother's wife', and *thirániŭ* 'her child's parent' to 'her sister's husband', these terms being taken in their classificatory sense. And even in Arawak, whose *-io* refers primarily to females, we find plural *daionóthi* 'my parents', *óioho* 'multiplicity', *ióhon* 'many', *híme oio* 'a great fish', *mába óio* 'bee(s)' (with *mába* 'honey'; cf. DIC *mába étĕiŭ* 'bee/bees', with *mába* 'honey').

A *isí(h)i* (*-si*, *-sin*) 'head; tip; seed' occurs as the second member of a compound in A *-kósi* 'eye(s)', whose first member—also seen in A *-kóke* 'eyelid(s)' (containing *éke*, *-ke* 'covering; container')—evidently is cognate with DIC *áku* and G *a?ú* 'eye(s)', though unattested as a simple form in Arawak. And DIC *-íuna* 'stem' occurs as the second member of a compound in DIC *-isíuna* 'neck', whose first member, though unattested in simple form, is evidently cognate with *isìi*, the Arawak for 'head'. Also DIC *-óko* (CAIC *-ógo*, G *á?i*) 'kernel; nucleus' occurs as the second member of a compound in DIC *-isík ~ isóko* (CAIC *icígo*) 'head', whose first member is the same as that of DIC *-isíuna* 'neck'.

On the other hand, Piapoco *íwita* 'head' seems to be cognate with A *íoida* or *ìida* 'calabash' (a compound of A *íoi* 'fruit and *-da* 'skin') and partly cognate with G *ekíwi* (*-ikíi*), Ipurina *ikiwi*, S *-kewiri*, etc., all meaning 'head' and all of whose first members may well be cognate with IC *-óko* (for which see above). Whether Piapoco *íwita* 'head' and *íwina* 'blossom, flower' are or are not analyzable in that language I do not know; but in any case they probably share a lexeme that is cognate with A *íoi* 'fruit', as in *íoida* 'calabash' and *íoisi* (*-si* 'seed') 'testicle(s)', and with the last part of Adzaneni *eliwi* and IC *íleue*, both meaning 'blossom, flower' (the Island-Carib form is unanalyzable, though it might be thought to contain *ila-* 'contents').

Finally, G *epíamiį* 'co-wife; husband's brother's wife; wife's sister's husband' appears to be cognate with Breton's DIC *-oubouyámoni* and CAIC *-ubúiamŭ* 'co-mate; sexual co-rival (relationship between two men or two women who have had intercourse with the same partner)', which I have hitherto been unable to analyze. Hildebrandt (1963) says that the Guajiro term comes from G *epía* 'vivienda; casa'; and G *amiį* (*-miį*) 'para (for); a (to)' presumably constitutes the rest of this word. This fits well with Breton's DIC *-óbogne* 'habitation' and CAIC *-úbię* 'home' (*lúbię* 'his home' . . *-ų* 'to' = *lúbiaų* 'to his home'), and with Breton's *loubouyáoni* 'his secondary wife'. But are Breton's *-moni* and *-oni*, CAIC *-mų* and *-ų*, to be regarded as the same or as different morphemes? If they are the same, as appears to be the case when we compare them with the apparently cognate Arawak equivalents—A *omón* ~ *omín*, *-mon* ~ *-min* ~ *-(o)n* 'for; to (dative); at, etc.', which are variants of one and the same postposition—then we are again indebted to one language for explaining another; for in Island-Carib *-moni* and *-mų* occur nowhere else with this function, whereas *-oni* and *-ų* are productive.

The above may suffice to illustrate the interest for the study of these languages in matching "live" lexemes of the one with "petrified" members of erstwhile compounds in another or others.

FIVE

FORM AND FUNCTION
OF KARINA LOANWORDS
IN ISLAND-CARIB

❀

THERE PROBABLY ARE few Amerindian languages that have borrowed lexemes from another Amerindian language so extensively as has the Arawakan idiom misleadingly known as Island-Carib from Karina, the type language of the Cariban family. This borrowing must have taken place in pre-Columbian times from the speech of Karina invaders of the Lesser Antilles, who did not, however, succeed in bringing about a shift of language among their native wives and descendants, any more than did the Normans in England.

These Karina loanwords, acquired under socially deplorable but linguistically favorable circumstances, should show as close a resemblance to their models as the phonetic and phonemic systems of the two languages in contact allowed. But since these models may well have differed in some respects from their modern Karina counterparts, we are lucky to have, beside Hoff's phonemic transcription for the latter (Hoff 1968) and my transcription of the modern Central American dialect of Island-Carib (Taylor 1955, 1956a and b, and 1958b), two seventeenth-century sketches of Karina (Pelleprat 1655a and Biet 1664) and a dictionary and grammar of the Dominican dialect of Island-Carib (Breton 1665, 1666, and 1667). All three seventeenth-century authors were French missionary priests, whose spelling conventions were based on the French orthography of their time. But Pelleprat and Breton both did their best to explain such difficulties and differences as they observed; and their comments cannot be ignored in any attempt to reconstruct either of these languages.

It would have been desirable to compare Breton's record with that of the recent Dominican dialect; but the latter became extinct about 1920, and even records made in the fifty years before that date are scanty and not always reliable. I have therefore preferred to employ the Central American dialect of Island-Carib, a living language and an offshoot of

89

the dialect of St. Vincent, whose mainly phonetic differences from that of Dominica were allophonic, not phonemic. In the following list of sixty-four loanwords I have given the recent Dominican form (DIC) in just six cases, either because the Central American counterpart could not be found and may not exist (14, 30, 31, 50, 51), or because of some considerable difference in shape (52; for recent Dominican *ima* 'path', *uikíri* 'man; male' and many other recorded words make it clear that this recent dialect did not lack the high back unrounded vowel /i/).[1]

Karina		Island-Carib		Apparent
Hoff	*Pelleprat*	*Breton*	*Taylor*	correspondences
1968	*1655*	*1665/67*	*1955*	
I	II	III	IV	
1. ma:po	mapo	mábou	mábu	a : a : a : a
2. ta:ta	—	—	dáda	Ibid.
3. pa:pa	bába	bába	bába	Ibid.
4. sa:kau	sácau	chácao	ságau̜	Ibid.
5. pa:u	oubáou	oubáo	ubáhu	Ibid.
6. waxto	oáto	ouáttou	uátu	Ibid.
7. ya?wan	yáoua-	ianhouanni	iá̜ua̜-	Ibid.
8. ka?ma	cáman	cáïman	kaimą	Ibid.
9. axka:ri	—	acáli	áhari	Ibid.
10. pena:ro	bináro; penaré	binále	binári	Ibid.
11. koiya:ro	coignáro; coiaré	cognále	gu̜iári	Ibid.
12. maina	maina; maigna	máina	máina	ai : ai : ai : ai
13. au	aoù	áo	au	au : au : ao : au
14. e:ne	ené	énni	éni (DIC)	e : e : e : e[2]
15. we:yu	huéiou	huéyou	uéiu	Ibid.
16. we:we	huéue	huéhue	uéue	Ibid.
17. we:rino	eróno	huéronum	—	Ibid.
18. eme:ri	emére	emére	emére	Ibid.
19. ore:ku	erécou(rou)	erécou(lou)	—	Ibid.
20. me:nu	moínou	moinou(lou)	—	Ibid.
21. pepeito	pepéito	bebéite	bebéidi	ei : ei : ei : ei
22. iseiri	—	ichéri	iséri	ei : — : é : e
23. pi:pi	bíbi	bíbi	—	i : i : i : i
24. pi:ri	bíou	íbiri	íbiri	Ibid.

[1] The nondistinctive character, in Island-Carib and in Arawak, of the difference between the sounds [o] and [u] has allowed us to represent both by the same phoneme, written IC /u/ and A /o/. In order to facilitate printing, the high back unrounded vowel of Central American Island-Carib has hitherto been represented by (CA)IC /o/. But this practice is clearly impossible when comparing any dialect of Island-Carib with Karina, in which the difference between [o] and [u] is distinctive and therefore represented by different phonemes, K /o/ and K /u/. In this chapter, therefore, the high back unrounded vowels of both Karina and the Island-Carib dialects will be represented alike in phonematic transcriptions by K /i/ and IC /i/.

[2] Alternatively, Hoff's demonstrative *e:ni* 'this (inanimate)' could be the reflex of the other forms listed in item 14.

Karina		Island-Carib		Apparent correspondences
Hoff 1968	Pelleprat 1655	Breton 1665/67	Taylor 1955	
I	II	III	IV	
25. siri:ko	sirícco	chíric	sirígi	Ibid.
26. pu:tu	boútou	boútou	búdu	u : u : u : u
27. tipu:na	—	tiboúnaim	-dibúnai̯	Ibid.
28. iruxpa (E)	iroúpa	irópon-	irúfu̯-	u : u : o : u
29. tu:na	toúna	tóna, tónê	dúna	Ibid.
30. nu:no	noúno	nónum	núni̯, núnu̯ (DIC)	Ibid.
31. no:no	nóno	nónum	núni̯, núnu̯ (DIC)	o : o : o : u
32. wo:to	ouótto; óto	óto, aóto	údu	Ibid.
33. yo:rokaŋ	yólocan	iouloúca	hiúruha	o : o : u : u
34. ito:to	eitóto	etoútou	idúdu	Ibid.
35. tono:ro	tonólo	tonnoúlou	dunúru	Ibid.
36. poito	bouíto	bouítou	buídu	oi : ui : ui : ui
37. koine (E); koiye	— cóié	cógne	gu̯ie	oi : oi : oi : ui
38. o:roi	—	oúloui	úrui	o : — : u : u
39. to:pu	tóbou	tébou	díbu	o : o : e : i̯
40. wo:ku	ouócou; ouácou	ouécou	ui̯gu	Ibid.
41. o:ma	óma	éma	íma	Ibid.
42. o:ruwa	óroa	él(e)oua	ír(i)ua	Ibid.
43. ko:wei	cóué	kéoue	gi̯ui	Ibid.
44. wo:rii	ouóri; ouáli	ouélle	ui̯ri	Ibid.
45. poro:ro	—	bouelléle	biríri	Ibid.
46. oxkatombo	acápo	acámbouée	áhambue	o : a : a : a
47. oxko	occóné; acné	ákeu; hac; háakê	áhi̯	o : a : a : a
48. oxtoro	óttoro	átili	átiri	o : o : a : a
49. mo:pii	móboui	mábouica	mábii̯ga	Ibid.
50. o:ro	—	ála, álê	ála, ali̯ (DIC)	Ibid.
51. (a)no:ki	(a)nóke nec	anáki	anáki (DIC)	Ibid.
52. amo:ro	amólo; amoré	amánle; amoúle; ámourou	amúle (DIC); amíri	o : o : a/u : u/i̯
53. i:ri	—	eúllê	—	i : i : i : i
54. wi:wi, wi:ri	ouíoui	houéhoue	-uíri	i : i : e : i
55. wi:pi	ouíboui	ouébo	ui̯bu	Ibid.
56. woki:ri	oukéli	ouekélli	ui̯gíri	i : e : e : i
57. piri:wa	bléoua	bouléoua	—	Ibid.
58. wixsa	oússa	huíchan	uísa(ha)	i : u : i : i
59. tixse	tíche tissé	tíche	díse	i : i : i : i
60. tixka	—	-tícali	-díhari	Ibid.
61. ixpe	—	hípe, -ipe	-ífe	Ibid.
62. i:rui	—	íloi	írui	Ibid.
63. i:ʔme	—	im, íme-	hi̯, íme	Ibid.
64. a:mu, am	ámu, am	ámou, ámien	ámu, ámie̯	a : a : a : a

Glosses

(Where glosses differ considerably from one to another of the four records, this is shown by use of the Roman numerals I, II, III, and IV.) 1. ashore (I), way or path by land (II and III), way or journey (IV). 2. mother. 3. father. 4. sand. 5. island. 6. fire. 7. bad. 8. let's go. 9. shadow (I), soul or form (III), the spirit of one who died recently (IV). 10. long ago, formerly. 11. yesterday. 12. garden (provision ground). 13. I, me. 14. to see (I), here is . . . , voilà . . . (II–IV). 15. sun; day. 16. wood; tree. 17. ashes. 18. custom. 19. war. 20. blood. 21. wind. 22. new. 23. grandmother (I), mother (II–III). 24. younger brother. 25. year (I), the Pleiades (II–IV). 26. wooden club. 27. fat (obese). 28. good (I), handsome, good (II), good, kind, wise, handsome (III), kind (IV). 29. water. 30. moon. 31. earth. 32. fish. 33. evil spirit (I–II), God (III), elemental (good) spirit (IV). 34. upland Indians (I), enemy (II–III), Miskito Indian (IV). 35. bird. 36. young, handsome, nice (I, II, III), good (IV). 37. evening. 38. cashew. 39. stone, rock. 40. cassava beer. 41. path, road. 42. three. 43. fishhook. 44. woman, female. 45. yard (space before house). 46. spirit of the dead. 47. come! (imper.) 48. how much/many? 49. have you come? (usual greeting to new arrival) (I–II), a meaningless greeting only (III–IV). 50. would that . . . (expressing wish). 51. who is it? (I), who/what is it? (II–IV). 52. thou. 53. to give. 54. ax. 55. hill or mountain. 56. man or male. 57. type of arrow. 58. I'm going (as farewell of departing guest) (I–II), as greeting only (III–IV). 59. far. 60. be afraid. 61. (type of) arrow. 62. elder brother. 63. child, son. 64. some, somebody, something (I), other, different (II–IV).

Forms under column I of the preceding list are from the western Surinam dialect of Karina except for those followed by *E*, which are from the eastern dialect. Where two forms are given under column II, the second is that given by Biet (see 10, 11, 12, 32, 37, 40, 44, 47, 51, 52, 59). Not all the Karina loanwords in Island-Carib have (or had) the same currency, indigenous synonyms being known and employed for about a third of them—in theory only by women and children, but in practice also by most men. Thus homonymous 30 and 31 are no longer even known to speakers of the Central American dialect of Island-Carib.

This wordlist is by no means exhaustive. It attempts to show, in the first place, Island-Carib correspondences to the long vowels (*a: e: i: u: o: i̴:*) and diphthongs (*ai, au, ei, ui, oi, ii*) of modern Karina. The first three present no difficulty for the borrowing language, which has the stressed vowel phonemes *á, é, í, ú, i̴;* diphthongs *ai, au, ei, ui, ii;* and their nasalized counterparts (*V̨*). Nor do about half (26–38) the correspondences to K *u:* and *o:, ui* and *oi*, which are in both cases IC *ú, ui*—with [u] and [o] as apparently free allophones, according to Breton (column III).

But we also find in seeming correspondence to K *o:* IC *é* and/or *í* (39–45) and *á* (46–52); while in seeming correspondence to Karina *i:* we find (columns III/IV): *í/i* (53), *é/í* (54–57), and *í/i* (58–63). I do not believe that such a muddle can represent true correspondences and shall try to show that Breton's "é" in these words represents—as do his "eu" and "ê" in 53 and elsewhere—the "high nonfront unrounded" vowel *i*. I shall also try to show that IC *i*, *á*, and *í* here correspond to *i:*, *a:*, and *i:* of the dialectal Karina model from which they were borrowed, and not to *o:* and *i:*.

Both Pelleprat (for Karina) and Breton (for Island-Carib) describe "three kinds of E," which they call masculine, feminine, and neuter. The first, Breton says is long when marked with the acute accent and otherwise like the *e* of Latin. The second is like "the feminine *e* in French, because it is only half pronounced"; and the third "has some resemblance to our dipthong *eu* and to the vowel in French *de, ne, me, te, se.*" Breton says that he wrote the second and the third both as circumflexed ê or, when long, as *eu*. Actually, he wrote both *arênna* and *areúnna* 'arm or wing', though only the latter spelling allowed him to mark stress, a double diacritic being precluded in the former. Pelleprat exemplifies the three *e*'s by K *ené* 'voilà', *noke* 'who', and *ipótele* 'the muzzle of an animal' (/e:ne, no:ki, ipo:tiri/ in phonemic transcription of the present-day forms).

Such evidence of dialectal difference within Karina itself as I dispose of is meager; but á in place of Hoff's *o:* is attested in Biet's *ouácou* (40), *ouáli* (44), and *acné* (47, which like Pelleprat's *occóné* contains an emphasizing enclitic, *ne*), as well as in Pelleprat's *acápo* (46); while *í* for Hoff's *i:* is seen in *ouíoui* (54) of both Biet and Pelleprat, in the latter's *ouíboui* (55), the former's *tissé*, and Pelleprat's *tíche* (59)—as against the latter author's *é* for Hoff's *i:* in 56 and 57. But Pelleprat, as he tells us himself, does not distinguish his feminine and neuter *e*'s (which I take to represent the phoneme /i/, as in his examples *anóke* 'who, what', *ipótele* 'muzzle', *enétale* 'nose') from his masculine *e* (= [e], as in *ené* 'voilà'). And although the vowel of Biet's *nec* (51), and the final vowel of his *penaré* (10), *coiaré* (11), *amoré* (52), together with that of their Island-Carib counterparts under III, may represent either /e/ or more probably /i/, it cannot at the same time correspond to the final *o* of Pelleprat's *bináro, cognáro, amólo* (same numbers)—nor to that of Hoff's phonemicized equivalents.

And equal if not more convincing evidence that we are dealing with dialectically different models is the imperative suffix, which Hoff gives as /-ko ~ -go/ and Pelleprat writes as *-co* or *-go* (*occo-!* 'come!'), contrasting with Biet's *-que* or *-gue* (*am eneque!* 'bring it!') and Breton's *-keu* or *-kê* (*icákeu!* 'make it!'). Unfortunately, Biet gives only the contracted form of /axki/ 'come!' as *ac-* (47), where Breton gives *hac!, ákeu!, haakê!,* and (in addressing more than one person) *haakêtêkê!* 'come!', thus showing in one word what appear to be correspondences of both *á* and *i* to Hoff's *o*, but must in fact go back to a Karina model with *axki* instead of *oxko*. As it is, I can find only one other imperative form common to all three records: *itángo!* (Pelleprat), *itangue!* and *itanque!* (Biet), and *itánkê!* (Breton), 'go (away)!'.

Turning now to the consonants, Pelleprat tells us that in Karina, *l* and *r*, *b* and *p*, were interchangeable; and as examples he cites (inter alia) *amólo* and *amóro* 'thou', *aboitópo* and *aboitóbo* 'handle'. He could have added *d* and *t*, *g* and *c* (= *k*), to this list; for their lack of differentiation seems to be attested by such examples as Biet's *itangue!* as well as *itanque!* 'go!', his *acado* and Pelleprat's *acáto* 'hammock', his *segaliti* and Pelleprat's *secáliti* 'I have told'. And Breton, writing of the same sounds in Island-Carib, says: "Where the mainland Caribs say *p* and *r*, those of the Islands often them change them for *b* and *l*." This is only partially borne out by our wordlist, in which half of the twelve occurrences of *r* under column II become *l* in column III, but *b* is far more frequent than *p* in both (thirteen *b*'s for six *p*'s in II, sixteen *b*'s for one *p* in III).

Breton goes on to say: "In pronouncing the *l* they bend the tongue back against the palate, then let it go, which makes it seem as though they pronounced two, particularly when they say *amánle* 'thou'." This is interesting because *l*-like and *r*-like sounds are allophones of one phoneme in Karina but are distinctive in Island-Carib, as in *mála* 'without contents, empty', but *mára* 'without skin'. And in a recent study of Karina phonology (Peasgood 1972), the *r* and *l* allophones are explained as follows: "*r* is an alveolar tap following *e* or preceded by and followed by *i*: . . . *r* after *u*, *o*, *i* and *a* is a reverse flap [ř] varying freely with a flap having slight lateral opening [l]. . . . *ara:bó* [ara:bó˘ ~ ala:bó˘] 'eel-like fish'." On applying these criteria to the items on our wordlist, I was surprised to find that whereas only eight out of seventeen instances in column II (Karina) conform to them, eighteen out of twenty-three in column III (Island-Carib) do so. Yet all those items that survive in the modern Central American dialect now have phonetic and phonemic *r*, although *l* is still a phoneme of the language. Since this can hardly be a coincidence, I can only conclude that the [l] of the Karina loanwords in Breton's record always differed sufficiently from the /l/ of inherited forms never to be confused with it by native speakers of Island-Carib.

At the time of Breton's and Pelleprat's writing, both Dominican Island-Carib and Karina had unaspirated labial, apical, and dorsal occlusives with voiced and voiceless allophones [b ~ p, d ~ t, g ~ k]. Except for [b], which was clearly more frequent than [p] in all positions, the voiced allophones seem to have been comparatively rare (especially *d*) and confined to intervocalic position and to that following a nasal, *m* or *n*.

But Island-Carib (though not Karina) also had, unrecognized by

Breton, three aspirated occlusives (also labial, apical, and dorsal) which, though unit phonemes, I write *ph*, *th*, and *kh*. And Karina had, unrecognized by Pelleprat, a velar or glottal fricative *x*, occurring only before *s* or a voiceless occlusive. And apart from other evidence, the former must have corresponded to the latter in order to account for the different development of, for example, the apical stop in *waxto*, which has become *uátu* 'fire' (6) and (*w*)*o:to*, which has become *údu* 'fish' (32). In the Central American dialect of Island-Carib, *ph* has become *f*, *th* has become *t*, *kh* has fallen together with preexisting *h*, and the voiced variants of the unaspirated stops have been phonemicized as /b d g/ (see 6, 9, 28, 46, 47, 48, 60, and 61).

One of the most striking features of modern Karina phonology, the allophonic palatalization of consonantal phonemes when they are preceded by *i* or by a diphthong ending in *i*, is all but absent from the loanwords and from seventeenth-century Karina, where it seems to have occurred only (but not always) in the cases of [s ∼ š] (spelled *ch*) and [n ∼ ñ] (spelled *gn*). The palatal nasal is reduced to vowel nasalization— sometimes in Breton's record and always in the modern dialect of Island-Carib. In some Karina dialects it is omitted or replaced by *i* or *y*, a development that seems to result from overpalatalization. Also, since it was first recorded, Arawak (but not Island-Carib) has developed palatalization of the apical consonants *s*, *th*, *t*, *d*, and *n* when these are followed (rather than preceded as in Karina) by *i*. So A *káikusi* ['kajkuši] 'cayman', but K *kaiku:si* [kajču:si] 'jaguar'.

It seems probable that the semivowels *w* and *y* were phonemes of Karina in the seventeenth century, as they are today. But, as I have tried to show elsewhere, they were not and are not distinctive in Island-Carib (or in Arawak); the occurrence or nonoccurrence of these sounds cannot affect the meaning, although displacement of stress can do just that: *úii* ['u(w)i:] 'meat' and *íuu* ['i(y)u:] 'body hair', but *uátu* 'fire' and *úatu* 'there is none'.

But the consonants do not present any serious difficulty once we have understood the rather drastic changes that some of them have undergone. And in the foregoing I have tried to show that if IC *á* < K *a:* (as in 1–13 of the wordlist), IC *é* < K *e:* (as in 14–22, or in *iégi* < *ye:ki* 'my pet animal'), IC *í* < K *i:* (as in 23–25), IC *ú* < K *u:* or K *o:* (as in 26–38), and IC *i* < K *i:* (as in 53–57), then IC *á* cannot, in the same or very similar environment, come from K *o:*, and IC *í* cannot come from K *i:*, nor IC *i* (and Breton's *é*) come from K *o:*, as might be suggested by numbers 46–52, 58–63, and 39–45. These numbers therefore show false and not irregular correspondences, or, rather, correspondences that are probably regular in comparison with their models, which must have belonged to a dialect of Karina other than that recorded by Hoff.

If such a dialect could be located, this might be some indication of that part of the mainland from which the Carib invaders set out to conquer the Antilles. And in the meantime it may be of interest to note that in closely related though now extinct Yao, both *e* and *a* seem to have corresponded to *o:* of modern Karina: Yao *-ewyn* : K *o:wiŋ* 'one', Yao *-age* : K *o:ko* 'two', Yao *-errewaw* : K *o:ruwa* 'three', Yao *-pata* : K *po:ta* 'mouth', Yao *tapou* : K *to:pu* 'stone', and Yao *kenape* : K *kono:po* 'rain'. Like the Karina, the Yao at the time of first contact had already settled in the Antilles, though only in southwestern Trinidad; but unlike the former, they are said to have been friendly with the Arawak and to have followed the latter's migration to the mainland.

Breton's avowed aim was to describe the so-called men's speech (he wrote rather slightingly of "the children's jargon and the women's dialects"), but he never considered that he was dealing with two languages, one of which was very imperfectly known to even his oldest native informants. So, while his dictionaries list considerably more lexemes of Karina ancestry than are current today, his *Grammaire* has no section devoted to the men's speech; and the use of such grammatical and functional morphemes of Karina ancestry as are—almost casually—mentioned is nowhere explained.

As personal prefixes employed with nouns of the men's speech, Breton gives *i-* 'first singular', *a-* ~ *e-* 'second singular,' and *k-* 'first plural' (but in fact a dual, first and second); says that the prefixes of third singular masculine (*l-* 'his'), third singular feminine (*th-* 'her'), second plural (*h-* 'your'), and third plural (*nh-* 'their') were "common to men and women alike"; and then, on the next page, gives the paradigm of *uhémbou* (K *uwémbo*) 'belly' with all seven personal prefixes of the women's speech: *nuhémbou, buhémbou*, etc.! The borrowed prefixes are now obsolete, as are likewise the postpositions (Breton's) *-bónam* (K *po:na*) 'to', *-ouíne* (K *wiino*) 'from', and *-ouála* (K *wa:ra*) 'like' to which they might be prefixed; the negative suffix *-pa* and, except in petrified form, demonstrative *anáki* 'who' (51) and *ié* 'here'; and the imperative suffix (DIC *-khi*, CAIC *-hi*), as in *áhi ié, hị!*, the men's equivalent of *higábu iáa, nirái!* 'come here, my child!'.

On the other hand, the men's demonstrative *au* 'I, me' (13) and *amíri* 'you (sg.)' (52) are still very much alive (as are their nouns *uíri* 'woman' and *uigíri* 'man'); and the Karina nominal pluralizer *-kon* has been adopted by both sexes as a collectivizer, *-gu*, to supplement inherited pluralizers, which are irregular in shape and restricted in use to some but not all animate beings. Functional morphemes of Karina provenance that subsist are suffixal *-bu* (K *po*) 'at' (as in *béiabu* 'at the landing place' and in only a few other nouns), *-da* (K *ta*) 'in' (either suffixed to one of a few nouns, or as a postposition with personal prefix: *múnada* 'in the house', or *tidạ múna* [DIC *muína*] with the same meaning), *-rána* (K *ra?na*) 'in the middle of' (*haránaguatu* "she-in-between-them"), -*uábu* (K *uwa:po*) 'in front of' (DIC *ála kuábuthu* "may it be set before us" = 'let's have a drink'). To these may probably be added DIC *ákha-* and CAIC *áha-* 'if; when; then; as', which must bear a personal suffix (as in *áhana baríha* "if-me thou-seest" = 'if you see me' and *áhabu naríha* 'if I see you') and whose meaning but not shape is the same as that of K *axta*, and IC *me* 'to-be (future); will, may or might', which has the same shape but not meaning as K *me* 'as; when; in order to be or become'.[3]

But ignorance or confusion of Karina grammatical morphemes is most evident in the verbs, where, by Breton's time, personal and temporal-modal relations usually had to be made explicit by grammatical morphemes belonging to the so-called women's speech. Only in one place (1667, p. 132; 1877, p. 71) does Breton attempt to explain an apparently verbal prefix of Karina provenance by citing three utterances all meaning 'you have made me drunk' (I have put forms of presumed Karina ancestry in SMALL CAPITALS): NITÍMAIN ÁO *boróman* (*boróman* 'because of you'), NITÍMAIN*kêta boátina* (-*kêta* 'causative', *boátina* 'you have . . . me'), and CHITÍMAIN *biátina* (*biatina* 'you did . . . me'). Breton concluded that the men's prefix *ch-* was equivalent to the women's causative suffix -*kêta*, but did not mention the men's prefix *n-;* and modern Karina does not help. His interpretation of *ch-* is certainly supported by such a pair as *chitícae liátina* and *niticae áo loróman*, both 'he frightened me' (cf. 60, and CAIC *madíhari bá* 'don't be afraid'). But what of such a form as Breton's *chenebouíkêta* (*tiem taónicoua*) '(she) show(s herself)', which appears to contain, besides both *ch-* and -*kêta*, a Karina verb *ene:po* 'cause to see; show' based on *e:ne* 'to see'? Both *keúleukê* and *cheúlê bana* 'lead/take/ accompany me' are given as men's equivalents of women's *íchiga bana* or (*caïman*) *bíchigana;* but *b-* 'second person singular', -*a-* 'imperative', and -*na* 'first person singular' are inherited Arawakan, not Karina. Moreover, it is not clear what part a causative could have in this context. Both *icákeu* and *chicáboui báe* are said to mean 'make it!', *achicabouero-yéntina* to mean 'he made/begat me'; yet both the latter appear to contain a loan from Karina *sika:pii* (Pelleprat's *sicáboui*) 'I have made it', together with inherited *b-á-e* 'thou-do-it' and -*royentina* 'did/does . . . me'.

Breton's *mábouica* (49) and *huíchan* (58) are classified as adverbs meaning only "bonjour; salut" and "bonsoir; adieu," respectively; whereas synonymous *chileátibou?* and *náyoubouca* (CAIC *cilíhadibu?* and *náibuga*) of the common tongue—which were and are also employed as greetings—are correctly analyzed and translated 'You have come?' and

---

[3] I have here assumed a Karina provenance for both CAIC -*gu* and CAIC *áha-*. Yet either or both could be Arawakan, by irregular correspondence with A -*kho*, a nominal pluralizer, and *kha*, a functional word with much the same meanings as those listed for CAIC *áha-*.

'I'm going'. Had forms similar to K *wo:pii* 'I have come' (as well as *mo:pii* 'you have come') and *mixsa* 'you are going' (as well as *wixsa* 'I'm going') then been current in the men's speech, Breton would not have mistaken finite verbs for adverbs, and there would have been no room for hybrid monsters such as his *namábouicaroyéntibou* 'I greet you' and *nahuíchanroyéntibou* 'I take leave of you', which are still current and whose inherited affixes have nullified those once present in the borrowed verbs. Finally, I should like to cite a four-word CAIC utterance in which a lexeme and a functional of Karina provenance combine with inherited grammatical morphemes: *ka siuámaį bubáų hádageę?* 'which one of them do you like?'. The interrogative *ka* 'who, what, which' is inherited, the lexeme *siuámaį* 'like' borrowed, the auxiliary verb *bubáų* "you do her" inherited, and the functional *ha-da-geę* "them-among-from" has a Karina base (*-da*, K *ta* 'in') with inherited affixes. But the lexeme; though treated as a particle in Island-Carib, is itself an inflected verb form in Karina, *si-wama-e* 'I please him/her/it'.[4]

I conclude that by Breton's time not two languages but a kind of diglossia was employed by the men. This had probably arisen out of necessity, been maintained through interest so long as dealings with the mainland Karina were kept up, and finally nurtured through a sort of *machismo* as the language of a more prestigious nation. This attitude may perhaps be illustrated in an utterance recorded and translated by Breton (1665, p. 24) as "ala ioueletétín lam, ibouikênoumapa oua aó-lam ichanummun-lam michígatou catou niránnium aléiba nóne. *J'ai envie de me marier, on n'a point soin de moi, parce que je n'ai plus de mère, ma belle-soeur ne me présente pas seulement de la Cassave.*" Beginning in what is clearly men's speech (note the triple *lam* = K *ra*, an interjection only used by men), the speaker lapses with *michígatu* and the remainder into the common, everyday speech: "she-does-not-give affirmative my-sister-

---

[4] The type of language mixture current in the men's speech of Breton's time may be further exemplified by the following ten utterances taken from his dictionary, in which most of the grammatical morphemes (here italicized) are Arawakan, and most of the lexemes Cariban. The early Dominican forms are given in Breton's spelling; the English translation is mine, including the parenthetic morpheme-by-morpheme translation of the Arawakan forms.

1. chichanoumain *nienli.*
I love/like/want him. (*I-do-him.*)

2. anichanoumapa *loměti.*
He does not love/like/want him. (He-does-him.)

3. chitímain *báe!*
Make him drunk! (*Do-you-him!*)

4. nitímain*hátina.*
I am drunk. (*I-am.*)

5. caïman cheneboui *bánum* imáboulou ibónam!
Come and show me my way! (*Do-you-it!*)

6. chiouamain *boměti.*
You like him. (*You-do-him.*)

7. chiouamain *ba!*
Accept!/agree!/approve! (*Do-you!*)

8. *náyouboucoúba* acan chiouamai*na.*
I shall go when it pleases *me.* (*Me.*)

9. tiouama*ti itarati nóne.*
It is pleasing to me (nóne) *thus* (ítara).

10. iouámêpati *nóne.*
It is not pleasing *to me* (nóne).

in-law cassava-bread to-me." And the same thing happens in Dominica today when a native speaker of the local French Creole embarks upon an utterance in English, but reverts to Creole when he gets stranded.

But not all words of Karina ancestry were or are regarded as belonging to the men's speech, a case in point being *aréba* 'cassava bread' (see above), the inherited name for which has been restricted to a particular variety. Borrowed *uéiu* (15) has ousted inherited *kási* 'sun', most probably because palatalization of the consonant preceding /i/ threatened a homonymic clash with *káthi* 'moon'. And in the same way the borrowed Karina words for 'moon' (30) and 'earth' (31), which became homonyms in Island-Carib, failed to subsist in Central American Island-Carib, where first one, then the other were abandoned. Only twenty-five out of the sixty-four items of Karina provenance in our list are or may still be regarded as men's words, since inherited synonyms are also in use. In some other cases the inherited equivalent has been lost since Breton's time and is therefore known only through his record, as are the inherited words for 'sun' and 'bird' ((k)oulíbignum; cf. 35). But in yet others—such as the words for 'fire' (6), 'wood' (16), and 'water' (29)—the loss was prehistoric, and the only possibility of recovering the displaced words is by the study of compounds and toponyms: thus, IC *arábu* 'bush, forest' probably contained **ára* 'tree, wood', and the Guadeloupe river name *Coyoúini* probably contained **uini* 'water, river'.

On the other hand, gains have almost certainly outnumbered losses, for synonyms are rarely absolute and tend with time to lose such synonymity as they once had. So, in Central American Island-Carib, the reference of *máina* (12) has been restricted to 'manioc field', inherited *icári* having been retained for 'gardens' with more general cultivation (and cf. the semantic evolution of *fowl* and *bird, hound* and *dog* in English). Number 64, said to have been borrowed (as also 5) by Karina from Tupí, occurs in two forms in each of the three languages—Tupí *amu, mu,* K *a:mu, am,* and IC *ámu, ámię*—both having or having had such meanings, attested by both Pelleprat and Breton, as 'other; different' (lost in modern Karina?) and 'one; some, somebody or something' (lost in modern Island-Carib?). Number 23, which according to Biet, Pelleprat, and Breton meant 'mother' (particularly in address), now means 'grandmother', while its former place has been taken by modern K *ta:ta* and CAIC *dáda* 'mother', not attested elsewhere. (But cf. *dada* of several West Indian creoles with meanings such as 'elder sister; aunt; mother or grandmother', varying with family and local usage, perhaps ultimately from Ewe *dàdá* 'elder sister'.) In these and in numerous other cases the language has been enriched and/or made more precise—not by the men's speech, but by all the Karina lexemes that have been adopted and adapted by both sexes of Island-Carib speakers.

SIX

AMERINDIAN TEXTS
AND WORDLISTS

❧

TEXTS

Arawak. Story told by Michel Sabajo, Sawariweg, Bernharddorp
0. tho diáhi daakásiafa iáha Harioánli-khonán hálika lán-koba ósin anoána óio síkoa-banáro. 1. abahán tha lii Harioánli lomároadoákole tha karáobandi, lothikákoba aba boádotho hisíro khotaha óma. 2. táaoei ki théi lidikhín thora hamátali, likánaba tha aoákothan tho kákithobe. 3. lii iakhatoá tha táaoesabo diáro ki éredan thádano hamáa thaníha. 4. lidikhá tha tho anoánabe thókodon, thidináoa sakhan thátha ribothín, sikínno aba mária, kákithobébia thebésoa—hiároberon. 5. thokonáka tho hiárobe ósin tho hísitho bithíro, thínata thokon tho hisíro.
6. thíboa thokonária, iaráka lii Harioánli, dikhákoana hamáa thaníbo. 7. abá tha tho híaro lidikhisiásia thokobóroko, kia tha sasábotho híaro thokobóroko, harán thómakoa ádin. 8. thoráa tha lidikhín lii Harioánli, mi lá thakho liloábo ansin thorá híaro. 9. laithá thakho hálika láma dián thora híaro óma. 10. kiádoma ki théi, abahánda loaiábo kenda, lebesóhada aba hísitho koiárabia. 11. kia kída abáhan kída, lánika lísidikitoá thoborán.
12. lisidonoánbena kí, káboin kásakabo diáro, ki thibíithilokon thidíidin oéi thandá tha abáro anoána lámin. 13. thitiná tha lámin, thithókoda tha hororónro. 14. akonán lokosádi, thidikhá thái: 15. "sá thakho hisinkoándai," kia tha diáhi. 16. thósa kíka tho abáiriki anoánabe bithiróda: "sákhokoáin!".
17. maothéboan diáro kída, thánda oáboka dikhin oábondai hísitho kakosíro. 18. haráda tho anoánabe ándin tho hisíro ámin. 19. harátho anoána thokodónthe libithíro. 20. thoráa ki abáro híaro lidikhisiásia kobáa, kia ki théida kakoiáthima ándin lámin. 21. oádiasábo diáro ki théida, thandá tha lámin. 22. lidikháno. 23. thothokodá libithíro, thidináoa thiribothá, aba mária thisikáno. 24. díkhakoá láno halón

thisikin thidináoa. 25. thandáthe lokosán. 26. thidínamadáboka thoráa tho abáiriki anoánabe, thotokáthika tha baríndai. 27. rokosáberon látha thomín. 28. "aka!" thátha tho abáirikibe anoána; 29. "hálikathi thákan tho hísitho thoráa diathidínda?" thátha tho abáirikibe anoána thónoa. 30. "aóseróntho thora! oáriboráron thora!" moro thátha tho abáirikibe anoána, (a)ónaban kidabáno. 31. thorá thakho khonan thidikhá, thorá tha tho híaro lansínsiasia kobá, thokonánloko ki théida. 32. lidiidinbia thidína bithíro, liniká, lobokotáno thidína thória. 33. thorá ki thidikhín, tho abáiriki anoána thomorodá harán thora abáro anoánaória.

34. thoráa íbara iáraha, thobokoáiaa. 35. thiiá tha lii Harioánlimin: 36. "dakhóiabiiadabo, bii oadíli, bísikan kho tho dadínáoa dan, damorodónbia kídaba dásikoa-banáro?" 37. "dáiama kho sikin(ba) tho bidínáoa biminda," látha lii Harioánli tho anoána híaro omín. 38. likiádoa tha sikín thidináoa thomín. 39. kiádoma ki théi, losá-tha lisikoánro thabo.

40. lándin ki théi ión lísikoan, lóio ámin thabo, lidiáka tha lóiomin: "dandá aba híaro abo, dáio," látha lóiomin. 41. "kénkhan; hálika móthokhan tho híaro abo bandá dadiakónda, Harioánli?" thátha lóio lomín. 42. "daothikísia thoraa karáobana, tho híaro," látha lóiomin. 43. ken tha lokhóiaba tha loióoa máadakoton thánbia tháda thoráa liréitho hálika mothón kirikiiádano. 44. oáadiasabo diáro ki théida, tháadako-tamádano hálika móthon kirikiiádano. 45. kídin ki théida tho loióda máadakotónka tho anoána híaro hálika mothon kirikiiádano. 46. kabénasabon béna ki théidano, aba maothiáda kasakónroda, thoráha Harioánli oióda aadákotonbia thoraa híaro hálika mothón kirikiiádano. 47. "hamáa mothóiakho kírikiiá baríndade, téete?" thátha thomín. "anoána kirikiiá déi," thátha thikíribiamón. 48. "sáre tháse!" thátha Harioánli óio aónabándano.

49. ioári ki théi, háliman nanbena nabokoáoa kákin, bádakhabo oíoa diáro ki théida. 50. aba maothiáda thánbia tha lii Harioánlimin: 51. "bódekha, Harioánli; tanó(h)o keiá kho bóma hibíndade. 52. kiádoma ki dakhóiabádabo bosínbia dabo daiomáro," thátha lii Harioánlimin. 53. "kiakho kaimároadanon," látha leréithomin; "oaósali." 54. "hálikha?" thátha lomón. 55. "maothéboan oaósali," látha leréithomin.

56. lidián-lokhodí ki théida, nái sádoa maothéboan, kia máothia kida lísika tho liréithoamin thidináoa. 57. lii Harioánli kho kadína, kiadoma ki théida abáda lebethérathi, tho báriri koikóio maro dián, thidína litinabá. 58. máothi máothia diáro ki théida namórodaha haiomónro anoána óio síkoa banáro. 59. liréitho tha ósa libóra, Harioánli thiinabóka. 60. hádia lána thakho díisian, morodónbia thiinabo kíadóma ki théida basadáka lósin thínabo.

61. táaoei ki théida, ánakibo nandínbo, tho abáiriki anoánabe kaia-dáthe nakhonán. 62. "kakithinonthe," thátha, "korarínonthe!" 63.

nomontoásabon ki théi, tho anoána óio dikhá théidaie, thisáoa théida ándinbothé thibithíro. 64. nandá tha ión thoráa haiomon sikoábana diáko. 65. nándinmakí, abáren thá tho kákithobe dikhíndaie Harioánli, dikhin hálika mothin kakithobe ion andínbo thisikoábana diáko. 66. "dandáda, dáio," thátha tho Harioánli réitho thóiomin. 67. "bandíroakhanáda," thátha onabándano. 68. "hálika móthi oadíli berethída líra?" thátha áadakotón thothóoa; "hái líra iaráabo?" 69. "sáre láse," thátha thónoa. 70. kiadóma ki théi ki nanda, tho anoána óio siká aba báhi nabóra ión thomádaie.

71. ión tha lándin, lii Harioánli, tho lireithóda lokhonán saboka kho hadiaken, thoiomáriaro thátha lória. 72. iónka thádaie háliman! 73. abáiriki tha anoánabe tha dikháthedai, diádiadoánthe lóma, hálika mothon iaraa tho sikoa, hálika nan ión kakín.

74. ioári ki théi abahánda, aba maothiáda, liréitho andáthe lámin, áakanthe tha lomín: 75. "téetekhan tha khóiabikitáthebo maósin banbiá tha bodedánrokhan thomín; mi thátha kho funásian," mótho tha diáhi lomín. 76. "kiákho kaimároadano, deréitho," látha Harioánli onabándano; "daósali." 77. kiadóma ki théida ki thándoma lomín, lisádononbia tha, liniká libodéoa, losáda, losáda ónikhan síirokonro bodedábia.

78. ión lándin libodedáka, libodesiáka tháda hímesabe. 79. thoráa hímesabe ki théida, linikádan dikhithíndano. 80. thoráabo ki théida lokóioa bahínro. 81. lándin ki théi, lisimaká tha liréithooa: 82. "dandada; háitho bóio iabodiniáoa," látha, sikin thoraha díkhithahí thomínda. 83. thosínbia tha thóio bithíro. 84. "háitho tho bóiabidiniáoa, téete," thátha thóiomin. 85. thorá tha díkhithehé thidikhin tho anoána óio, mi tháthakho ímatonoán: 86. "khíi!" thánbia tha; "tho diáron thokho dáma mánama, lii koratáribekhan!" 87. kiadóma tha thibiréda thora díkhithahá bodáli abónroda thíbithonoánbia. 88. thoráa tho díkhithahá itéme rikánbia, thoraa lidíkhithehé Harioánlida, thithikidáka, ken tha thoraa koratári sabékhan sakhan la besókotonno fírotho hímebiáda. 89. kiadóma ki théi thoraa anoána óio dikhínda, thobokoáia: 90. "khíi!" thánbia tha, "thoráa diakénthioáli, lii sáthi. 91. daitháia kho thoráa diakénthindaí," thátha thónoa.

92. thisímaka thothóoa thobokánbia tha thomín. 93. thobokáka thoióomin. 94. sátho khoton, horosíkanon, hamaasábo khoro. 95. thoraa thóda abáro kisidáa thisikísia lii Harioánlimin. 96. kiadóma ki théida thoraa abáro kisidáa, lobálika lóroa. 97. thibiánthedinoán kisidáa óthikiháli lii Harioánli kídaba.

98. abá máothia ki, thanda kíkathe leréitho libithíro. 99. "Harioánli," thátha lomín; "abá hamátali kíba téete áadakotaiáthebo maní bámano thomínno." 100. "hamákhana thóra?" látha leréithoamin. 101. "bikísakhaniáma tha siókothokhan oniábo téeteminda," thátha lomín. 102. "dakisáiama thomíndano. daósali kisánro tho oniábo thomín." 103.

kiadóma ki théida losínbia onirebónro. 104. ken thora hamátali likisíisiá-haloko thisiká lomín kéeke. 105. thoraa kéeke liniká, losá thabo. 106. thoraa onirébon landin, baríka likisáthin. 107. fatábo lá kisídinoan kisábia barínno, maoadílika kho thobokotón oniábo, balíro tha lória. 108. kiadóma ki théida kobórokoatoá tha thisiká lii Harioánlimin hálika lánfa kisin tho(raa) oniábo kéeke abo.

109. kobórokoatoá lan kha ki théida, lidikhínbiathe tho moníri óio balíthobo ládi. 110. thidikhíndoma tha lii Harioánli, thidiáka lomin: 111. "Harioánli, hamá aníthibo iaháda bii?" thátha tho moníro óio lomín. 112. "hamákhoro, moníri óio," látha thomín. 113. "oniáboron kisáthibo dei barín dei. 114. hamáken kho oadílika dákisin tho oniábo." 115. "kenkhan hamábo kisíthibóda bii?" thátha lomín. 116. "kéeke abo dakisábo tho oniábo." 117. "báiama kho oádilin kisin thorá oniábo," thátha tho moníri óio aónabandái. 118. "daboroátalíbo tho hamátali lokoária." 119. kia thadóma thiniká tho kéeke lória, thoaiá tha thikisá thoráa oniábo tho kéeke abo. 120. thoráa thikisinmakithe tho oniábo, abáren thobokotá tho oniábo tháboa. 121. "háitho tho oniáboda, Harioánli; daboroáta hibín dabo," thátha limín. 122. kiadóma ki théida, mi lá thakho hálekheben lii Harioánli. 123. "oáan!" látha thomín. 124. lisifudáka, lósa bahínro kídaba, landá tho oniábo abo, lisimaká tho leréithooa. 125. "háitho tho oniábo abo dandínda; dandá thabo hibín." 126. thiniká tho oniábo lória, thosáda thoiomáro thabo. 127. thoráa thidikhín tho anoána óio, thimitadáka tha thónoa. 128. "sáre báa bii, oadíli," thátha thonoa. 129. thoraa thóda thibiánthedonoán kisidáa lii Harioánli bálika lóroa.

130. thikabóintheha kídaba. 131. aba máothia kídaba thánda kíkathe leréitho libithiróda. 132. "Harioánli," thátha lomín; "téete tha khóia-bikitáthebo abá tha hála bomáritínbia thomín. 133. thoraa hála, Harioánli, dáio sí diáretali tha," thátha lomín. 134. limitadánbia tha lii Harioánli: "damáritali thomínno," látha, leréitho aónaban. 135. khakoánrikinei kia kásakabo lósa lii Harioánli konokonro, losá ribotánro thoraa áda. 136. landá thabo bahínro, lokobórokoatoáha hálika lánha maritinha tho hála. 137. laithá-kho hálika móthon síi-thora anoána óio. 138. kiadóma ki théida limikodá thoráha hadírikiri háio tho anoána óio bithíro. 139. limikodádano, thandá tho hadírikiri thomín, kodoábon thithíboko kobórokhodi barin. 140. barin hálika than tho hadírikiri arídin thokhonán barin, rokosákotoro tháno tho hadírikirinon. 141. hamáa ken thakho oadílikoma thiribotin tho thadóoa thisídiakoaria. 142. nasífodáka naa hadírikirinon kídaba. 143. "hamáa kenkhanbo danikomá díkhin thisída?" látha lii Harioánli lónoa.

144. kiadóma ki théida, thibiánthedonoán háio limikodá kika thibithi-róda kia kitha thoda háorere náromin. 145. rokosákotoron thátha tho háorere anoána óio. 146. nái kíba sifodá kíkaba.

147. thikabónthedonoán ki théida, lánika míkodon tho háio oaromóri náromin, thei kia ki théida andá thokhonán. 148. kia ki théida abárema simakákoton tho anoána óio: 149. "ákasée!" thátha simakán; "hoboroátathéde! hamátali ándabothé dakhonán; háikhaha báa thora," thátha simakán tho anoána óio. 150. boroatá thánsika. 151. kiadóma ki théi thoráa oaromóri orodon thithíboko lokhodi, iakoáboka thobokóro lokhodi. 152. kia ki maoadílisaboka thobokotón thiridan tho háio thokhonán. 153. ioári ki théida thiribotínbia thisí adóoa, fádokodón thoroádano. 154. kaboníbon ki théi thifádokodon thoroádano, Harioánli dikhádano tho anoána síida. 155. abáren tho tha hólolon síida thora. 156. kabáratho thakho sí(i)-thora. 157. "thoráa diantho oáa-thora," látha loloálokoa. 158. limitadáka tha lii Harioánli. 159. "sádano!" látha lónoa.

160. liniká thora adáda, lebesókotabódano, thifíro lomaritá tho hála thisíbia ki, lomáritinháda. 161. thandá tho leréitho lámin kídaba. 162. thoráa thidikhínbo tho halasíi maritonoánbo, thimitadáka tha thónoa. 163. "sáre báa bii, kakithí," thátha thónoa. 164. maothéboan diáro ki théida, líbida oáboka tho hála. 165. lisímaka tho leréithooa thinikínbiathe tho hála, hibinádano. 166. lisiká tho hála thomín; 167. thosáda thóio bithíro (th)abo.

168. thisiká tho hála thoiomín; thóio niká tho hála. 169. sá tha tho haláda thisídin. 170. kiadóma, tháda, thátha tho anoána óio thónoa: 171. "hálika doákhan (= dafákhan) lidiánthi kákithi farínda?" thátha thónoa. 172. "haráia tho amátali dakisidísia hibíndai, laníno." 173. kiadóma ki théida thokobórokoatoáka thónoa. 174. "abákoan iaráka," thátha thónoa; "oabókotohái!" 175. aba máothia ki thisímaka hará tho anoánabe hamáa thaníhali lii Harioánli óma. 176. "sanoái!" thátha. 177. kia tha tho Harioánli reithóda kanabá hamáa than tho thóio diántho abáirikibé anoánamin.

178. ioári ki théida, aba bákhilamáda, thandáthe lii Harioánli bithíro leréitho. 179. "Harioánli, bobálata dámin; dáakaha aba amátali bon." 180. thobálatikitái lii Harioánli, thiniká thibáridaniáoa, sá tha thobaribaridínbodai. 181. thibaridinbo ki théida, thibaridin lokhodi ki théidai, tháakaha thádai: 182. "Harioánli, báitha hamáa danha bomín? 183. máothi maothéboan diáro ki, nafáraiahádabo (= nafárifabo)." 184. "kia thokhonán baakabódade?" látha leréithooamín. 185. "kiakho kaimároadano," látha thomín. 186. "kiáron khonán daakabóthebo," thátha theréthimin. 187. kiadóma ki théida, thidián lokhodí, ki théida thobokotáthedai.

188. maothéboan diáro ki bákhilamáron thobokotádai, lii Harioánli. 189. thisikádai iáraloko. 190. laadákota liréithooa liiánkaboárin; thisiká tho liiánkaboárin lomín. 191. iónka thádai tho iáraloko. 192. liiẹiendoákita tho liiánkaboária abo. 193. "aoséronthi héi anoána; 'datokohai'

haakhobata dámin." 194. "atídithiha dai máothi maothiáron déi," látha lónoa. 195. kasakóda nakán diáro ki théida, liéntoa kíkadaba thoraa lientoan-oáriki.

196. "anoána ilio,
anoána ilio;
dabókotará,
hisísiro senee."

197. líboa ientoán. 198. thoraa anoánabe kánabon kha tho nóma leiéiendoanda. 199. "óseronthibo líra kákithi dibádibadoánbo," thátha kánabon leiéntoan liiánkaboária abo.
200. líkisi andásibo, kiadóma tháda tho iánkaboarída lokórotá tho iára ári lokhodi, táamaria bálikitín. 201. ioária ki théida maoárakathibía lebesoá taamária tha lofóthikidá. 202 liniká tha lidináoa, abáren ki líra morodáthe tha ioária onabónrobia. 203. háliman lá ósin lomorodá. 204. landásinbo ki hororónda, libiráka tho liiánkaboariniáoa kídaba.

205. "anoána ilió,
anoána ilió;
dabókotarán,
dabókotará,
oria liba dadikin,
tha senee!"

látha. 206. thoraa ki théi thikánabon tho liiánkaboáriniáoa tho anoánabe. 207. "hálika lákhan mafathiáken bíranli lii Harioánli tho liánkaboária?" thátha thonabe. 208. thosínbia tha dikháhinro, thoraa thósin tháda thidikhá tha lii Harioánli kaoán. 209. thoraa thídikhin tháda, abáren tha tháda bokonoanbeia. 210. abáren tha thisadáka hamáron thidináoa, thínikabé harán tho anoánabe ósin tha lii Harioánli ínabo.
211. halimán tha osín thosá tha línabo ao thikábia barín' 212. *ma* lii Harioánli tha ándá thobóra hibín, hororón. 213. hadia lánma ki théi ándin hóroron, litínikitín láboa, tho anoánabe ánda kíka línaboda, áda sakáro dínabo diáko. 214. "oakibodá bii, Harioánli," thátha lomín. 215. limithákanon, lii Harioánli. 216. "háiama kho thokóndade, héi anoánanon," látha lii Harioánli tho anoánabemín.
217. thoraa diakéntho ki tho diáhi Harioánli khonán. 218. hálika lánkoba anoána óio síkoa-banáro ósin. 219. íboa thátha tho adiáhida.

Translation
0. This story tells how Hariwanli went to the country of the Vulture Mother.
   1. Once while Hariwanli was bird shooting in the savanna, he came across a rotten, stinking carrion. 2. He saw this thing from afar and heard

the cries of living creatures. 3. He hid somewhat farther off in order to watch what they would do. 4. He saw the vultures descend, take off their wings, put them on one side, and turn into human beings—only women. 5. These women walked up to the stinkard and began to peck at it.

6. When they had finished their pecking, Hariwanli was still there watching what they were doing. 7. There was among them especially one woman whom he saw, the most beautiful of all among them. 8. That woman Hariwanli loved with all his heart. 9. He didn't know how he could talk with that woman. 10. And so once he himself will take the form of a deer's carrion. 11. And once he did so, turning into carrion in front of her.

12. After his turning into carrion, about three days passed, and when the fourth day broke, a vulture came to him. 13. It alighted by him; it came down on earth. 14. Walking beside him, it looked at him: 15. "He still doesn't stink enough," it said. 16. It went back to the other vultures: "He's not good yet!"

17. About the next day but one, they came together to inspect the deer's carrion. 18. All these vultures came to the carrion. 19. All the vultures alighted by him. 20. That woman whom he had singled out came shyly towards him. 21. She came towards him more slowly. 22. He looked at her. 23. She landed by him, took off her wings, (and) put them on one side. 24. He watched where she put her wings. 25. She came beside him. 26. Those other vultures were walking about; they wanted to peck at him. 27. He just shook himself at them. 28. "Och!" said the other vultures; 29. "how can this carrion be like that?" said the other vultures to themselves. 30. "How foolish! That's for our beaks only!" the other vultures added again. 31. She, the woman whom he loved, was walking unconcernedly about. 32. So he jumped at her wings, took them, and held onto them. 33. Seeing which, the other vultures all flew off and away from that one vulture.

34. Left behind there, she was startled. 35. She wept, and said to Hariwanli: 36. "You man, I implore you. Won't you give me my wings so that I may fly back to my country again?" 37. "I won't give you your wings back," said Hariwanli to the vulture woman. 38. He refused to give her her wings. 39. And so it was that he took her home with him.

40. When he arrived home and brought her to his mother, he said to his mother: "I've brought a woman with me, Mother," he said to his mother. 41. "Well then, what sort of a woman have you brought me, Hariwanli?" said his mother to him. 42. "I found this woman in the savanna," he told his mother. 43. Then he begged his mother not to ask his wife to what clan she belonged. 44. Later on she might ask her which was her clan. 45. And so it was that his mother did not ask the vulture woman the name of her clan. 46. And it was long afterwards, one morning before dawn, that Hariwanli's mother asked this woman to what sort of

clan she belonged. 47. "What matter which is my clan, Mamma?" she said to her; "I'm of the vulture clan" she said to her mother-in-law. 48. "That's fine!" said Hariwanli's mother in reply.

49. From then on, they lived together a long time, something like five years. 50. One morning she said to Hariwanli: 51. "Look, Hariwanli, it's not just since yesterday that I've been with you. 52. So I beg you to take me to my mother," she said to Hariwanli. 53. "That's nothing to worry about," he said to his wife; "we must go." 54. "When?" she said to him. 55. "The day after tomorrow we'll go," he told his wife.

56. According to his word, they got ready the next day but one; and in the morning he gave his wife her wings. 57. Hariwanli did not have wings, so he borrowed the wings of one of his friends, the sparrow hawk of *koikoyo*-like[1] speech. 58. Next morning they flew up to the country of the Vulture Mother. 59. His wife went in front, Hariwanli behind her. 60. Not being very accustomed to flying, he therefore went behind and followed her slowly.

61. The other vultures perceived them from afar whilst they were in the midst of their flight. 62. "Human beings are coming," they said; "strangers!" 63. When they got nearer, the Mother Vulture saw them— saw her own child coming towards her. 64. They arrived there, high up in the sky country. 65. As soon as they arrived, Hariwanli saw those creatures, saw what kind of creatures came to their country.

66. "I've come, Mother," said Hariwanli's wife to her mother. 67. "You've come at last," she said in reply. 68. "What sort of man is that husband of yours?" she asked her daughter; "he there?" 69. "He's all right," she said to herself. 70. And so it was that they came; and the Vulture Mother gave them a house for them to stay there.

71. After Hariwanli arrived there, his wife did not occupy herself much with him any more, but turned from him to her mother. 72. They stayed there a long time. 73. Some of the vultures came to see him, chat with him about his home and how they lived there.

74. Some time after that, one morning, his wife came to him and said: 75. "Mamma wants me to ask whether you wouldn't go and fish for her a little; she's very hungry." That is what she said to him. 76. "That's no trouble, wife," said Hariwanli in answer, "I must go." 77. Therefore because of what she had said to him, he got ready, took his fishing tackle, and went to fish at the head of the creek.

78. When he got there, he fished; and little fish were what he caught. 79. He took these small fish and wrapped them up. 80. With them he returned home. 81. When he arrived he called his wife: 82. "I've come. Here's something for your mother to roast," he said, giving her the parcel. 83. She went to her mother. 84. "Here's something for you to

[1] Onomatopoeic of the whistle made by the sparrow hawk.

roast, Mamma," she said to her mother. 85. When the Vulture Mother saw that parcel, she was very angry: 86. "Pshaw!" she said; "this sort of thing is not enough for me. The little sprats!" 87. So she threw that parcel under the griddle to let it burn. 88. The string broke, and the parcel that Hariwanli had wrapped burst open, and all those little sprats turned into big fish. 89. So when she saw this, the Vulture Mother was startled. 90. "Good gracious!" she said, "So the dear fellow is like that. 91. I didn't know he was that sort," she said to herself.

92. She called her daughter to cook for her. 93. She cooked for her mother. 94. The food was good, she was satisfied, and wanted no more. 95. That was the first test that she set Hariwanli. 96. And so Hariwanli passed that first test successfully. 97. He will also meet a second test.

98. One morning his wife came to him again. 99. "Hariwanli," she said to him; "Mamma is asking whether you would not do something else for her." 100. "And what is that?" he said to his wife. 101. "Draw a little water for Mamma," she told him. 102. "I could draw it for her. Let me go and draw that water for her." 103. And so he went to the waterside. 104. And as to the thing into which he was to draw it, she gave him a carrying-basket. 105. He took the basket and went with it. 106. When he arrived at the waterside, he tried to draw water. 107. Time and again he tried to draw it, but the water would not hold: it ran out. 108. So that made Hariwanli ponder as to how he would draw water with a carrying-basket.

109. While he was thinking about it, he saw the Muniri[2] Mother passing by. 110. As she saw Hariwanli, she said to him: 111. "Hariwanli, what are you doing here?" said the Muniri Mother to him. 112. "Nothing Muniri Mother," he told her. 113. "In fact, it's only water that I'm trying to draw. 114. However, I'm unable to draw the water any way." 115. "And with what are you drawing it?" she said to him. 116. "I'm drawing water with a carrying-basket." 117. "You won't be able to draw the water," answered the Muniri Mother; 118. "I must help you out of this." 119. And so she took the carrying-basket from him and herself drew the water with it. 120. The water held by itself as soon as she drew it. 121. "Here's the water, Hariwanli; I've already helped you," she said to him. 122. So Hariwanli was very happy. 123. "Thank you!" he told her. 124. He turned around, went back home, arrived with the water, and called his wife. 125. "Here's the water I brought; I've brought it already." 126. She took the water from him, and went with it to her mother. 127. When she saw it, the Vulture Mother smiled to herself. 128. "You must be good, you man," she said to herself. 129. That was the second test that Hariwanli overcame.

130. There's to be yet a third. 131. One morning his wife came to him

[2] The name of a large species of ant, *Ponera clavata.*

again. 132. "Hariwanli," she said to him, "Mamma sends to ask you to make a bench for her. 133. This bench, Hariwanli, must resemble my mother's head," she said to him. 134. Hariwanli laughed: "I'll make it for her," he said in answer to his wife. 135. The very same day and time Hariwanli went to the forest to collect the wood. 136. He came home with it, and pondered how he would make this bench. 137. He didn't know what shape the Vulture Mother's head had. 138. So he sent the hadárakara ants to the Vulture Mother. 139. He sent them; they came to her and penetrated her clothing. 140. But however much they bit her, yet she only shook the ants off. 141. It was in no way possible to make her take the kerchief off her head. 142. The hadárakara ants turned around and came back. 143. "Whatever could I do in order to see her head?" said Hariwanli to himself.

144. And so he sent a second sort of ants to her again, those that they call háorere. 145. The Vulture Mother only shook them off. 146. They too turned back.

147. The third time he sent the ants that they call warumúri, and they went at her. 148. The Vulture Mother immediately called out: 149. "Ouch!" she shrieked; "help! Something is walking on me; it may be dangerous," shouted the Vulture Mother. 150. She wants help. 151. So the warumúri ants crowd into her headcover and penetrate her clothing. 152. She was no longer able to bear the biting of the ants. 153. Then she took off her headkerchief and shook it away from her. 154. The third time she shook it away from her, Hariwanli saw the vulture's head. 155. The head was bald. 156. The head did not have hair. 157. "So that's the way it is," he said in his own heart. 158. Hariwanli laughed. 159. "That's good," he said to himself.

160. He took the wood, shaping it, and making this bench into the semblance of her head; he will do it. 161. His wife came to him again. 162. Seeing the head-bench being made, she laughed to herself. 163. "You're pretty good, human being," she said to herself. 164. About the next day but one, he completely finished the bench. 165. He called his wife for her to come and take the bench, which was ready. 166. He gave the bench to her; 167. she went with it to her mother.

168. She gave the bench to her mother; her mother took the bench. 169. The bench was truly like her head. 170. And so it is that the Vulture Mother said to herself: 171. "Whatever shall I do to kill a human being like him?" she said to herself. 172. "Everything I have already set him as a test, he has done." 173. So she pondered. 174. "There's still one way," she said to herself; "we'll catch him!" 175. And one morning she called the vultures together to say what they must do with Hariwanli. 176. "Fine!" they said. 177. But Hariwanli's wife had heard what it was that her mother had said to the other vultures.

178. Later, one afternoon, Hariwanli's wife came to him. 179. "Hariwanli, sit down by me; I've something to tell you." 180. She made Hariwanli sit down; she took her own comb and began to comb him gently. 181. While still combing him, she tells him: 182. "Hariwanli, do you know what I'm going to tell you? 183. About tomorrow or the next day, they will kill you." 184. "Is that what you're telling me about?" he said to his wife. 185. "That's nothing to worry about," he told her. 186. "It's only about that that I've come to tell you," she said to her husband. 187. And so it was, according to her word, that they came and seized him.

188. It was in the afternoon of the next day but one that they caught Hariwanli. 189. They put him in a cage. 190. He asked his wife for his flute; she gave him his flute. 191. There he was in the cage. 192. He sang and played on his flute. 193. "You vultures are powerless; 'I'll peck him' you imagine concerning me." 194. "Early tomorrow morning I'll escape," he said to himself. 195. When it was about the middle of the night, he sang again.

196. "Vulture tribe,
Vulture tribe;
What I catch/caught,
Stinking ————[3]."

197. He stopped singing. 198. Every time he sang, those vultures heard. 199. "That human being is powerless; it's just a lot of nonsense," they said, listening to his singing and his flute.

200. His time was approaching, so he passed the flute between the bars of the cage, through to the far side. 201. Then he turned into a mudfly, and came out on the far side. 202. He took his wings and straight away flew off and down. 203. He flew as hard as he could. 204. When he was about to reach the earth, he played his flute again.

205. "Vulture tribe,
Vulture tribe;
What I catch/caught [?],
I caught,
Went from me, behind me,
———— ————,"

he said. 206. And so it was that the vultures heard his flute. 207. "How is it that Hariwanli plays his flute so faintly?" they said to themselves. 208. They went to see, and when they went, they saw that Hariwanli was not there. 209. When they saw this, they were startled. 210. At once they all got their wings ready, and all the vultures took off after Hariwanli.

211. As hard as they could they went after him so as to try to catch him.

[3] The raconteur himself was unable to give the meaning of these snatches of song.

212. But Hariwanli reached the ground, still ahead of them. 213. He had no sooner reached the ground, alighting by himself, than the vultures came after him again, onto the branch of a dry tree. 214. "We missed you, Hariwanli," they said to him. 215. Hariwanli laughed at them. 216. "You vultures are unable to peck me," said Hariwanli to the vultures. 217. And so goes the story about Hariwanli, 218. and how he went to the country of the Vulture Mother. 219. The tale is ended.

Commentary

Hariwanli is the name of an Arawak culture hero about whom many stories are (or were) told. Since he is (or was) an Arawak, he is always referred to by the markers of male-Indian gender, *l*- and *-i;* and when the reference is to him together with his wife, the human plural number is employed (*nA*-, *-ie*, and nominal *-no*). On the other hand, the vultures are nearly always referred to by singular female-neuter gender, *th*-, *-o*, although nominal plurality may be indicated by the suffix *-be*. So *hiárono* 'women', but *hiárobe* 'females'; *kákithinon* 'human beings; people', but *kákithobe* 'living creatures'. Exceptionally, the ants helping Hariwanli are referred to by human-plural *nA*- in 142 and 144, though they were treated as singular in 138–39 and again become so (*tho háio*) in 151–52. Exceptional also is the form *anoánanon* in 216 ("*héi anoánanon* 'you vultures'"), where Hariwanli addresses the vultures, thus, apparently, necessitating the use of the human plural nominal suffix *-no* ∼ *-non*, although in the same paragraph we find *tho anoánabe* 'the vultures', and in the same sentence *tho anoánabemín* 'to the vultures'; while *thátha lomín* in 214 must be translated 'they said to him'.

Many words take or omit with seeming indifference a suffix *-da* which may displace the stress but adds nothing to the meaning: *óio* ∼ *oióda* 'mother', *máothia* ∼ *maothiáda* 'morning', *lánda* ∼ *landáda*, *lósa* ∼ *losáda*, *hará* ∼ *haráda* 'all' (without change of stress). According to my informants, "it sometimes sounds nicer"; and I therefore take it to be purely stylistic.

Arawak. Besoána Kírikiiá. Story told by Ferdie Sabajo

1. lihída aba lokokhánda mánsikhináthi kobá, tháda, baríron látha oáadin libianthéoakhan. 2. hamáron kenkho kidin lóthika. 3. abanbóda losá-tha loaiákoan, tháda, sikoatoánda lepéeron tha omáda. 4. aba balíthiakhanín tho tha lepéeron lonaká lomaoáda. 5. kidin ki théi loaiákoa látha ionin, losá-tha konokónro. 6. lósa konokón, ken tha landínthe kída, lóthika béletho kháli loboránoa.

7. "hamáronkhan sikáthe khálikhan dánda?" látha. 8. "dáiorodátho ki sikáthe khali dáni," latháda. 9. lekéno tho khálioanádan; léke thadano.

10. ken tha lepéeronkhan tha, éme oábo lándin kónokoariáda, hálekhebetoáka laoáda, didábon lokhóndi. 11. léke tho kháli, ken tho ioári ki lósa kíkaba konokónro. 12. bé(l)-thirikhan tha loborán kinbiáda. 13. kia tha lithá kíkaba, ken tha ioári ki kia balinbéna ki lósa kíka konokónro kíba. 14. kasíri tha aba ko(r)iáraoei lothikínbia. 15. "hamáronkhan kasiridá-kika daboránda ba? 16. dáiorodáthokhan báto maritá kasiriné," látha. 17. *ma dan* (= kénda) péeroron tha diki lidikha báikokhodi. 18. kídin ki théi losáda loiorodáthokhan bithíro: 19. "bíi tho maritá kasíri dánda, béebe?" látha thon. 20. "máosin dáia bibithíro; déiakhoro dáno," thátha lomínda. 21. "kasíri damoniáda; oáthi báthekhanádano," lánbia tha thomínda. 22. kia lokóioa. 23. naosínbia tha athín tho kasirída, nathádano. 24. kia íboa, ioária máothi diáro ki tha, lósa konokonróda. 25. "hamáronkhan tho diamáda dikhin iáa dakhonáda, baría dáiorodáthooa daadákotoni?" lánbia tháda. 26. kiadóma tha lósa tháda. 27. ken tha tho lósin, tháda, lepéeron hálekhebetoáka. 28. "iáakoan béi (= báli)!" látha thon. 29. dikhákoa thánbia tha linabóda, iónro tho losínda. 30. tho péero balákoan, dikhákoan línabo. 31. ken tháda ki thána lokóionoánbia tha. 32. "dádikho(h)á (= dádikhofá) tho tánoho (h)amá thodin," lanbia tha. 33. lepeerónda besonoán-tha abáren tha, kéeke thinikáda, ósin tha konokónro/kaboiánro. 34. "émesée! depeeronoa bátho tho diamáne," lánbia tha. 35. lisíbon ki théi thandáthe ion líakhatoa. 36. oáa thakho thósin tho péero kaboiánro. 37. lisíbon ki théi thansáka, iorodán, korán tho béletho, íbakin tho khalídaba. 38. ken landínbia thíbidonoánbena. 39. mondákoa thátha tho lepéeron bálisikolokoákoan tha lándin ki théi. 40. thósa libithíro, didábon lokhóndi, hálekhebetoán. 41. leké tho kháli, dikhin lána thádan. 42. lokobórokoa-toáthi látha thámin. 43. ken ioári ki tha lósa kíkaba, máotheboan diáro ki théi. 44. "dádikhoa (= dádikhofa) kíbabo," látha; "thóiorohánkhan iarahána."

45. abáren tha thósa ikihínro kídaba. 46. leredá kikathé. 47. thosána ikihínro, andínthe íkikhodobo, thóbodaléoa (= thobodáliaoa) tha thokhotónbia tha, koránfa. 48. kídin ki théi thekéoa thofulidínbia thiiáboano, 49. doradoábon thanbia tha koránbo. 50. "tanoho dabókoto-fádabo!" lánbia tha, dáridin thidiákon tho tha thída *fosída* (= (th)abánia). 51. lóbokotá, birédin thádan íkikolokón thobodále (= thobodália) abónroda. 52. thiiínbia tháda: "bisiá (= busiká) tho déke dani! 53. thoáriakho tho dásabohádabo," thátha lon. 54. "bidikháthiakhan dakhonánda; bidikhakhán thodin dakhonánda. 55. kamonéikathiakhanádade," lánbia tha thomínda.

56. thebesonoánbia kobá tha lokóbia oamádin. 57. kídin ki théi thebésonoan lónda, bálisikolokónro thaibeka, harán máothiabeka likídakídaiafádan. 58. hímilibéka, lominbéka hímili. 59. bálisikolokónro tháibe kia lon. 60. ki diánthi kobá thanáda, ná(h)a Besoananonkhan otoróda, náa Besoananonbia oakharohoda oakharohoda naióotoada.

daiboroáda.

Translation. *The Besoana Clan*

1. He was, they say, an unloved little fellow who sought in vain for a mate. 2. But none such did he find. 3. So he went off somewhere by himself apart, they say, and made a home together with his dog. 4. Rather a nasty looking dog it was that he brought with him. 5. And so it was that, still living all alone there, he went to the forest. 6. He went to the forest; and when he came back again, he found soft cassava bread awaiting him. 7. "Whoever can have given me cassava?" he said. 8. "It's my sister who has given me cassava," he said. 9. It certainly was cassava; and he ate it. 10. And his little dog, whenever he came from the forest, made much of him and jumped about him joyfully.

11. He ate the cassava, and afterwards went back again to the forest. 12. Then it was *beltiri* [a kind of drink] that awaited him. 13. This he drank; then after some time had passed, he went back to the forest again. 14. This time it was a boatful of cashiri that he found.

15. "Whoever can have made this cashiri for me? 16. It must be my sister who made cashiri," he said. 17. But then, he saw only the dog's tracks in the house. 18. So he went to see his sister:

19. "Did you make cashiri for me, Sister?" he said.

20. "I haven't been to your house; it's not I who did it," she said to him.

21. "I have cashiri, so come and let's drink it," he said to her. 22. Then he went home.

23. They went to drink the cashiri; they drank it. 24. That done, about the following day, he went to the forest. 25. "Although I've already asked my own sister, who else is there here would look after me like that?" he said. 26. And so he went.

27. And as he went, they say, his dog rejoiced. 28. "Stay here!" he told it. 29. It remained looking after him in the direction he took. 30. The dog was still sitting, still looking after him. 31. And then it was that he turned back. 32. "Today I shall see how it is," he said.

33. His dog changed form right away, took the carrying-basket and went to the provision ground. 34. "Good gracious! It must be my own dog that is like that," he said. 35. She came right in front of him there where he was hiding. 36. Without delay the dog went to the field. 37. Then right in front of him she grated, pressed, and baked soft cassava bread, and left the batch.

38. When she had finished, he came in. 39. His dog was still lying quietly in the ashes when he came. 40. It went up to him, jumped about him, and rejoiced. 41. He ate the cassava he had seen her make. 42. He thought it over. 43. And then, about the next day but one after that, he went away again. 44. "I'll watch you again," he said; "her pressed manioc is there (still)."

45. Right away she returned for more firewood. 46. He spied on her again. 47. She went for firewood, came back with it, and made up the fire under the griddle in order to bake. 48. And so she took her covering from off her back, 49. and stooped down to bake. 50. "This time I'll catch you!" he said, running up to her, and first to her skin. 51. He seized and threw it into the fire below the griddle. 52. She wept: "Give me my covering! 53. From now on I'll not do this to you any more," she said to him.

54. "You want to look after me; then look after me like that. 55. I'm wont to be a little poor", he said to her.

56. She was changed into an Indian/person like us. 57. And so it was, when she took another form for his sake and often crept into the ashes, every morning he bathed her. 58. It was cold; on his account she felt cold. 59. On his account she often crept into the ashes. 60. And so in this way originated the Besoana clan; and up to the present time they have continued to increase.

I've finished.

Commentary

I was told different version of this tale in creole in Dominica's Carib Reserve, and an English translation, under the title "The Carib and His Dog," appears in Taylor 1952, p. 277. Roth (1915, sects. 64B and 362) gives two somewhat similar stories, one of which is adapted from Brett.

The Arawak version given here purports to explain the origin of Besoana clan and of its name, the verb *besonoán* meaning 'to turn or change (into)', *thebésoa* 'it changes shape, becomes, etc.'

Borrowed from Sranan Creole are *ma dan* 'but then' (17) and *fosída* 'first' (50) (SN *fósi* 'first', to which has been added an Arawak expletive suffix). In both these cases, Arawak "equivalents" are given in parentheses. Parenthetic forms given under 32, 44, 47, and 52 indicate careful pronunciation of contracted forms that I had failed to understand. Future tense *-fa* (formerly *-pha*) often becomes *-(h)a*, with or without the aspirate. In 33, the raconteur at first used *konokónro* 'to the forest', then changed it to *kaboiánro* 'to the garden (= provision ground)'. In 56, I hesitate between 'Indian' and 'person' in the translation of *lokóbia* 'to become X', since in Arawak, Negroes and white people are not *lokóno* (pl. of *lóko*).

Arawak. Orisábe Oionátho. Story told by Ferdie Sabajo

1. tho abá bíkidoliátho thíkithíma tho áni. 2. thíkithi óma thokán, kathoáthikan k(ien) aba thilikinthokan thá. 3. aíboa thadikoáoa, kia hámaka nathobodáka thobóra. 4. kídin ki théida iónda ónabose orída kása kobá thomónda. 5. kien tha máithin nádano kadibéiokathe nándan. 6. "khíi! hamáron kasásia omin bíi, dalikíntho?" thatha tho hébethokhan thomónda. 7. kidin kída, thidéinthikhan, abálikhan thidéinthida: 8. "khíi, dáio! hamáronkan kasásia tho daoínthomónda?" látha. 9. "harán kásakabo tháda thósa kaboiánro. 10. hamárikin thábo thandáthe: ada íoi, kokoríthi, bóroe íoi." 11. kia tha domáda, abáhan ki théida, losínbia tha thidéinthi thinabóda, éredan thádano kia tha domáda kiáda bíkidoliathóda dikháboka aiomónda thoáadada bóroe kioítho bithiróda dikhábonda.

12. thidikhá tha bóroe kíoithóda. 13. kien tha líra thidéinthi dikhákoamabódano. 14. kien tháda, thodorádonoanbiáda tho bóroe otórokhonánda, lidikhínbia tha thidéinthída óri thitélokoária fóthikidin, ósin modínda tho bóroesínro. 15. ken tha ión thándin tho óri tho bóroe thísin, thebesoáda aba ilónthibiáda, 16. aoiínthe tha bóroe íoi onabónro thádi loiomínda. 17. thibotháda thioída. *so!*

18. "mebénko tha bekéekere, dáio?" látha thátha.

19. "ehée! hebéiadano, sádano. bothókodathé!" thánbia tha lomón. 20. thokodónbiathe tha kien—tha líida thidéinthida dikhákoamabódano. 21. thosénbiathe thá tho orída thokodónthe tho bóroe idaiakhóndida. 22. ión ki théi thandásinbo, lósa thidéinthi thibithíro likásiparánbo, 23. losokónbia tha khólebethábono tho óri.

24. límatonoán; kídin ki théi kia thidikhin doma tho lioíntho thidaridínbia tha. 25. dinamákoan than kha loborán, kia oábo ki tho lofaráman barínda. 26. thiiákhatoá tha lória.

27. límatonoándoma thidéinthikhan, kídin ki théi losokáka tho órikhona. 28. libádano, lósa lokóioa. 29. ken tha tahárioei diáro leredákathe kíkathebáno. 30. kia lokhólebethísia óri thiboténbia tháda anida kónokobóroko ibíndano. 31. thórodokotá thádano, kídin kída hárithibána abo thobókoro tha thidiakóda. 32. kía lidikhin thiíboa thiiákhatan kiáda kasároda. 33. kianáda ki thána thidéinthikhan akóioa. *tééé* . . .

34. báthian (= abáthiman) kásakabo díkhidi, tháda, lósifa díkhin. "dádikhabáli hamáa balín," lánbia tha. 35. kien tha mabóri firobéro thára: "daririn!"; 36. mánbia tha thidiakoária aósin kálemebéro. 37. lothorodónbia tha thaoáda. 38. lidikhínbia tha hibírokho iséhi, biámbe tháda, kakhónemedákoantho, isehída. 39. kídin ki théida lokóioada kíkada, litaká thisíbo kíba. 40. kien tháda maothéboan diáro ki théi, lósa kikádaba (= kíka thádaba). 41. lidikhínbia tha tho ibírobe, abáro oadíli, abáro híaro, mótho bálabálabán loborán. 42. thórodoró látha

tháoa, libínbia tháda. 43. dikhákoa thátha libithíro. 44. losá-tha thória.
45. kien tho lósen ki théi, kia lioíntho ándiha lidíkilokon.
46. thidian tho thóma: "ehée," thánbia tha thisábeminda, "hidikhába
héi líi hidéinthináthi monáikatánhi, sókan hokhóna. 47. háliman han
kákin, 'dadéinthi' man háli lóni (= lomín). 48. kídin kída, hírikisáboha
kho namádoo. 49. hisikoátali iahádaoo. 50. déi háboha, hóionathok-
hánda," thánbia tha thisábemin, biáninomin káiorodáthida.
51. a! abáren, tháda, nasíkoatoakitáda hárithibána abóda. 52. síkoato-
noánda ioníbia kobádaie. 53. kídin kída oái lokonónda, líi thidéinthikilída
isábe. 54. ió(h)otonon kobá; nabákhokoasiáka oéida akharóbiada basári
óma.

Translation. The Snake Children's Mother

1. It's about an adolescent girl and her grandmother. 2. She was living
with her grandmother, who had but one daughter and one granddaughter.
3. She reached puberty, so they slung up a hammock for her. 4. And
there it was that a boa snake got her with child. 5. And they didn't know
what it was that had made her pregnant for them.

6. "Well! Whatever has got you with child, granddaughter?" the old
woman said to her. 7. And so said her mother's brother, her only maternal
uncle:

8. "Well, mother! Whoever got my niece with child?" he said. 9.
"Every day she goes to the garden, it seems. 10. She comes back with
all kinds of things: fruit, maripa nuts, balata fruit." 11. And so one day
her uncle went after her and watched to see why the girl looked upwards,
seeking fruit-bearing balata trees. 12. She saw a tree with fruit. 13. And
that uncle of hers was still watching her. 14. Then her uncle saw her
crouch at the foot of the balata tree and a snake emerge from her entrails
and climb up to the top of the tree. 15. Then the snake, having reached the
top of the balata tree, turned into a little boy, 16. plucked the fruit, and
cast it down over his mother. 17. She gathered up her fruit. So!

18. "Isn't your basket full, mother?" he—it said to her.

19. "Yes; it's full; it's enough. Come on down!" she said to him. 20.
It was just coming down—and he, her uncle, was still watching her. 21.
The snake was just coming down the trunk of the balata tree. 22. As it
was about to arrive, her uncle went up to it with his cutlass, 23. and
chopped the snake to pieces.

24. He was angry, so that his niece, seeing this, ran away. 25. Had she
still been standing there, he really would have killed her. 26. She hid from
him.

27. It's because he was angry that her little uncle chopped at the snake.
28. He left it and went away. 29. Then, from some distance off, he watched
her again. 30. She gathered up the pieces of the snake left thus in the forest.

31. She placed them in a heap and covered them over with leaves of wild plantain (Heliconia spp.). 32. He saw the pregnant one finish hiding them. 33. Then her little uncle went away. Téee . . .

34. Six days later, it seems, he will return: "I must see what happens," he said. 35. There were big flies—"darering!"—36. off from it came shining flies. 37. He opened it up. 38. He saw big worms, two of them lying side by side, worms! 39. Then he went back and covered them up again. 40. Then, about next day but one, he went back again. 41. He saw the little ones, a male and a female, just sitting there in front of him. 42. He just opened it up, then left it. 43. They were looking in his direction. 44. He went away from them. 45. And as he goes, his niece will come in his footsteps.

46. She spoke to them: "Yes," she said to her children; "you have seen your uncle who humiliated you by chopping at you. 47. As long as you live you must not call him 'uncle.' 48. So we shall no longer be together with them. 49. You must make a home for us here. 50. I, your little mother, shall care for you," she said to her two children, brother and sister.

51. Ah! At once they made a house of wild plantain leaves. 52. They made their home there where they were. 53. And so it is we Arawaks who are her uncle's children. 54. They multiplied; and up to the present time we and the Caribs cannot get along together.

Commentary

The story whose text and translation are given here is one of two Arawak versions that I recorded in Surinam in 1968. Like very similar Warao and Carib tales recorded by Walter E. Roth (1915), nos. 55 and 56), it purports to explain the origin of the Caribs and of the enmity between them and the Arawaks; and has in common with an Island-Carib story recorded by me in Dominica (Taylor 1952) and another Warao story recorded by Wilbert (1965) the motif of a girl pregnant by a snake, whose offspring leaves and reenters her body and climbs a balata tree in order to gather the fruit for its mother.

The story emphasizes the matrilineal character of Arawak society: the grandmother has only one daughter and one granddaughter, whose duty it was to ensure the continuity of the family and clan. But the offspring of a snake were not acceptable; and when the girl went off with her children, it was her mother's brother who, contrary to all the rules, undertook to prolong the line of descent, while the snake's children became Caribs.

Under 3, *aiboa thadikoáoa* 'she attained puberty' means, more literally, 'her transitory state ended'. When an Arawak girl first menstruates she undergoes a period of segregation, during which her hammock is slung high up under the roof and certain restrictions imposed upon her activities and diet as a protection against, inter alia, the attentions of the *ório* 'water spirits' (cf. *óri* 'snake' + -*io* 'parent; mother'), to which she is particularly exposed at this time. Here, the girl's impregnation is regarded as an affront (notice the ethical dative *nándan* 'to/for them', that is, to members of the matrilocal household) whose burden falls mainly on her maternal grandmother and on her mother's brother. Her father is not even mentioned.

A not uncommon attempt to conciliate grammatical and sex gender is seen in 18, where *látha* 'he (male Indian) said' is followed by *thátha* 'she/it/he (non-Indian) said'. As a boy and son of an Arawak mother, pronominal reference to the child should be *l-;* as a snake or only half-human creature it should be *th-*. And in 41, the noun *oadíli* 'man; male' is preceded by the feminine-neuter form of the determinant, *abáro* 'one/a', instead of the male-Indian form, *abáli*.

I cannot explain why the future tense (or mood?) is employed in 34 and 45, and so have carried it into the translation unchanged. Perhaps it is a kind of narrative future, analogous to the narrative present of French.

The word *káiorodáthi* 'brother and sister' (the final -*da* of *káiorodáthida* in 50 is expletive) contains the same stem as the kinship term for 'a (man's) sister', *óiorodátho*, in construction with the attributive prefix *kA-* and the male-human nominal suffix -*thi*.

Loans from Sranan (Surinam coastal creole) are seen in the exclamations *so!* (17) and *téee* . . . (33) (lit., "until," but employed also, as in the creole, to indicate passage of time), the latter most probably itself borrowed from Ptg. *até* 'until'. In 22 the Spanish loanword *kasipára* 'cutlass' (Sp. *cachiporra*) combines with inherited possessive *li-* . . . -*n* and postpositional -(*a*)*bo* to form *likásiparánbo* 'with his cutlass'.

Several rather typical contractions occur in this text: *nándan* (5) < *namíndano* 'to/for them', *báthian* (34) < *abáthiman* 'six', but literally, 'one across' (i.e., on the other hand), *kikádaba* (40) < *kíka thádaba* 'back again'.

Whence comes the word *basári* 'Carib(s)' (in 54) I cannot say. It is now the usual Arawak term for members of that nation, although *kalipína* (cf. IC *karifuna*) is also known. If *basári* should have been a nickname, any other meaning has now been lost.

Arawak. Hábori. Story told by Mrs. Williams

1. bíamano tha hiárono kásathie tháda. 2. nakonáka kónokothé, aba hébetho amin nánda. 3. kien tháda: "dasanóthi, dáminthe héi!" thátha náonda. 4. ken tha iarahádaie naosaósada kaboiánro kenkhebón. 5. thiniká nása, abáli oadíli nasa tháda, thiniká. 6. "hiba dáoni, mani!" 7. ken tháda nándin kaboiária, mekheboária, thóiothi náothikifa. 8. hálika lán abáten líi nása! (9. nána tho thóiothi damónda, dakánabon

dái. 10. maithínkano sánbo diáro dadián.) 11. aioáda, laitháfa tha loionóthi áoa, *taki:* "daionóthi tha héi!"
12. lisináka loiokhákole, lisináka. 13. kodibío lofára, hamáiron lofára.
14. ken tháda, íbirokhán lisiká namón tha líi Hábori nasiamónda, líi thóiothi oadíli. 15. ibírokhan lisiká loionóthimon.
16. abá kásakabo lisináfa thérebon ándin. 17. likiáfa, tháda, sákoantho módekeléloko. 18. ken tha hasírobe tha módekelé thora, lidáinothi. 19. "táha máosin balí; bidáinothi sakadáfa bóma," thátha tho hébetho lonída. 20. *ma,* lisináka tha móroni, likiáfa onirébo. 21. limóda tha aiomónro aiákhatonoánbia. 22. likánabofáthe koriára kíri-kiri dakoánthe, koriára tháda. 23. ken tha limodá áiomon. 24. thandá tho hasírobe, abá koriáraren kákithobe thandáthe. 25. ken tha ítika nadimísifa—hm! hamairon! 26. "maithánkoro tháoa híme, Hábori!" nátha náa lidáinothida. 27. "bothókodathé, biidiáro! máithanthi báoa, bíi Hábori, bobrédathe bitikáoa!" náa tháda. 28. lothokodá, lobirédiha, laakáka: "émehée!" 29. 'kídiabana báika amonáikatarón boionóthioa," nátha lomón. 30. "thonbenáda, aibóra balída! 31. bóio tho thoráabo. 32. thokíthokoro ki tho bóio oábo, thitiláthokoro tho boiaboátho," thátha tho hasírobe lomónda. 33. ken tha lokóionoan lóiokhan.

34. lóthikifa kódibio diántho. 35. hamáron lóiokhofá kia lana. 36. ken tha thora lándin, íbiro thisikáthika tho hébetho namínthe. 37. "tha khoro, hébe, tánoho kásakabo. 38. ifírobe thó bisíkifa mámakho omín; daionóthibekáiaie," látha. 39. "emée! 'táha máosin balí', dáiada bóni," thátha tho hébetho lonída. 40. "bidáinothi óma diáro bisákadaia," thatháda. 41. ken tháda loionóthimin, káoa than kha tho hébetho, laádakotáfa: "kidianthi kho déi?" látha. 42. "hehéi! dáokitho ki tho boióda, dái tho biaboátho," thátha lon. 43. "sanoáironi! oaósali thória tho hébetho," látha náonda. 44. "hikhaletoáli; oaósali thória." 45. nakhaletoáka—hm, hamáiron. 46. "hikhaletoábo," thátha tho hébetho.

47. *téee* áioa, tánoho kásakobo lobotontoáka tha líi bikidoliáthi. 48. lokoriáran atinoákoro tha fímthika ábo lomarita. 49. hamáa khoro! máothi maothia thomasoá tho koriára. 50. lomárita kíka aba kíba kia tháda iorádifa lónda. 51. sanoáironi! 52. "hikháletoa baa híbidinoáron!" látha loionóthimin. 53. "ken tha tánoho oaósifa kaboiánro, ken tha holokhótali tho koriára. 54. dandínrikini oaósifa thória tho hébetho," látha loionóthimin. 55. *ma,* lósa, hádali thére. 56. "dakóioábo, mamá," látha thon tho hébethomin. 57. ken tha: "hehéi! sáre bali ósin! kasíri thora iarahána, bitháli!" thátha lon. 58. lándinrikíni tháda: "oabirédathe tha, oasikáa!" 59. ken tha náika bótoloko, aosínbo.

60. ken tha: "hamáa baa asímakaka 'nàosabóo!'?" thátha tho hebethóda thónoa. 61. thidaridá tha thikasarónan abo tho hébetho, abokotáthin lobóton khonan. 62. thobádoa thikasarónan thória. 63. ken tha thérebo khóna konáloko: "dasá-dasa, Hábori," thátha aián. 64. hm!

thin! thiborédin thisiriráoa, kia tha tho sibábiaka. 65. háliman thokonáka thérebo khónathe, kídia koan: "dasá-dasa, Hábori," dakoán. 66. ken tháda Káota-Wáota ámin thándifa. 67. 'táo táo dakoánthobo, mába aoákidithóbo. 68. "halónro ósathobo bíi, mamá?" thátha thomín. 69. "hm! hm! dása Hábori osáa dáoria," thátha aiián tho hébetho. 70. "maián ba, mamá! dái iahá-iaháthebo; aba mába botháthe," thátha thon. 71. atórodokotón áda kálokotho óloko, kia tháda ión tháda thitáka thisíbo, ebesókoton sibérobiáda.

dáiboa.

Translation. *Haburi*

1. There were two women who had a child. 2. Walking in the forest, they came upon an old woman. 3. Then: "My children, come stay with me," she said to them. 4. So there they remained and took to going to the garden to work. 5. She took their child, a boy child it was. 6. "Leave him to me!" she said. 7. Then when they come back from the garden, from work, they find a grown man. 8. How their child has altered! (9. So the old people told and I heard. 10. I don't know whether I tell it right.) 11. Later he will know about his mothers; say: "You are my mothers."

12. He got lost while hunting; he strayed. 13. He killed birds; he killed everything. 14. Then he whom they call Haburi, he the grown man, gave them the small ones. 15. He gave the small birds to his mothers.

16. One day he strays and comes to the waterside. 17. He shits, they say, on a nice landing place. 18. And it is the landing place of his uncles the water dogs. 19. "You must not go far or your uncles will meet with you," the old woman had told him. 20. He strays nevertheless and shits at the river bank. 21. He climbs up in order to hide. 22. He hears the noise of an approaching canoe: kre-kre, it is a canoe. 23. Then he climbed up. 24. The water dogs came, a boatload of creatures came. 25. Then they smell the shit—hm! everything. 26. "It's on account of that ignorant fish Haburi," said his uncles. 27. "Come on down, you ignoramus, you Haburi, and throw away your own dirt!" they said. 28. He came down, went to throw it away, and said: "O dear!" 29. "So it's like that you only make your own mothers suffer," they said to him afterwards. 30. "From now on, finish with that! 31. That one is your mother. 32. It is her younger sister who is your real mother; the older sister is your aunt," said the water dogs to him. 33. Then he returned to his hunting.

34. He finds so many birds. 35. He shoots everything. 36. Then when he arrives, the old woman wants to give them the little ones. 37. "Not so today, old woman. 38. You'll give the big ones to my mammas; for they are my mothers," he said. 39. "O dear! I told you you must not go far," the old woman said to him. 40. "It seems that you met with your uncles,"

she said. 41. Then, in the absence of the old woman, he asks his mothers: "What sort of a man am I?" he said. 42. "Aye, this younger sister of mine is your mother, and I am your aunt," she said to him. 43. "Very well, then we must go away from this old woman," he told them. 44. "You must bake cassava; we must leave her." 45. They baked cassava; did everything. 46. "Hm! So you are baking," said the old woman.

47. And later on, the same day, the young man made a canoe. 48. The first one he made of wax. 49. No good! The next morning it sank. 50. He again made another which floated for him. 51. Fine! 52. "Finish your baking!" he said to his mothers. 53. "Then today we'll go to the garden; then the boat must be loaded. 54. As soon as I arrive, we'll go away from the old woman," he said to his mothers. 55. Well, he went; the sun was hot. 56. "I'm going back home, Mamma," he told the old woman. 57. "All right; walk well! There's that cachiri there; drink it!" she said to him. 58. As soon as he arrived, he said: "Let's go; let's clear out!" 59. Then they embark and are on their way.

60. "Whatever can be shouting 'They are going!'?" said the old woman to herself. 61. The old woman ran with her hoe, wanting to hold the boat with it. 62. Her hoe fell into the water. 63. Then walking along the bank weeping, she said: "My child, my child Haburi!" 64. Atchum! She blew out her snot, which turned into stone. 65. For how long she walked along the bank lamenting: "My child, my child Haburi." 66. Then she comes upon Kauta-Wauta. 67. 'Tau-tau' it is sounding [as when] breaking up honey. 68. "Where are you going, Mamma?" he said to her. 69. "Hm! hm! My child Haburi has left me," the old woman said weeping. 70. "Don't cry, Mamma; I'm here with you; come and drink honey!" he said to her. 71. Lying down in a hole in the tree, it was there that she covered her face, turning into a toad.

I've finished.

Commentary

A longer version of this story is given in English translation by Roth (1915), who got it from the Warao. The name, Haburi, however, is an Arawakan word (/hábori/ [haburi]) meaning 'shame'.

The raconteuse, Mrs. Williams, was born and brought up in Oreala, British Guiana, but has lived in Fosi Bergi, Surinam, for the past sixty years or more. Nevertheless, her Arawak differs in several respects from that of my Bernharddorp informants (e.g., *hamáiron* instead of *hamáron* 'everything; anything whatever'). The sprinkling of loanwords from Sranan Creole (*taki* 'saying; that', *ma* 'but', *té(ee)* 'until') is usual, as is the frequent use of future tense where English requires past or narrative present. Note also borrowed *-boto-* 'boat' in 47.

Haburi and his mothers (*loiaboátho* 'his mother's sister' being treated as another mother) are taken to be Indians (reference to him is by male-Indian *l-* and to them by plural human *nA-*), while reference to the water dogs is in the singular (in 24, *thandá tho hasirobe* 'the water dogs came', with sg. fem.-neuter *th-*). The status of the old woman (spirit or human) and the sex of Káota-Wáota (male or female) are not made explicit; but I was given to understand that both were spirits of the woods, the latter being male. In other versions of this tale, the old woman is identified with the toad (into which she turns at the end of the story given here) and is named Wáota, while the one who consoles her by the offer of honey is her son-in-law.

Central American Island-Carib. *Úraga tuága abǫ áufuri uríbatu*

1. luágu abǫ dǫ, inúhaị iráho, híla túgucu; ítara líǫ tagánaụ túma táufuri. 2. luágu-ti abǫ uéiu, táunaharu tiráo túma-ti iráho tùo adábura dúna. 3. tíciga-ti ábǫ búgidu tụ tiráo, abǫ ganáli tụ iráho tùo. 4. hacólorǫ-ti láru dúna, ítara líǫ tadáburuni iráho tùo tidúnari, tịurahǫ́iǫ iebe ganáli, ligía tálagacagụ, láiguada ganáli tuái, báugua gubái. 5. ítara líǫ tagúmeserụ aiáhua. 6. téherahà-ti tiráo áufuri táu. 7. hacólorǫ iaráfa tụ múna, taríhinu táufuri úali là ganáli túma, ligía terégụ tụ: "mebélubadíbu núbiaụ madáiri-ga bái nigánali nụ; báiba gia iágię!" 8. abǫ tídi iráho tùo aiáhuahàina.

9. óroua uéiu bía áriabu táu luágu mábu, ligía tadú́ragụ túma Uanúi. 10. teréga Uanúi tụ: "gadí-biǫ?" 11. teréga tụ: "báugua rogá-liǫ tigánali náufuri nuái. 12. le nídi adábura dúna, nálagacagúa, ligía láiguadụ. 13. táunahaiǫdina-ti ibíha lamíǫgua." 14. teréga Uanúi tụ: "madíhari bá! bibíhuba lamíǫgua. 15. baró-bai óma lèa, badú́ragua lúma ugúdi abínaha; méheraha bà! 16. badú́ragua lúma úhabu lúma icógo abínaha; méheraha bà! 17. basógoruni báibugu dímisǫ bǫ́du luáiburi kátai lèa, baríhuba abǫ múna. 18. bacólorǫ niéị, babúsuragua lụ uáiriai mútu lèa baríhubai niéị. 19. uíeti; maháhone bà lụ! 20. barúmadahà me láu. 21. adóga bai me lèa lubáliti bụ. 22. bibíhuba kátai buíd(u)ti búgua."

23. ligía tadógobai. 24. tacólorǫ lúb(u)ię uáiriai mútu ligía, leréga tụ: "báiga núma!"; abǫ táigị lúma tídagię tágai fáluma. 25. lau gúiedu-ti leréga-tụ: "baró-baụ báulu tùo! 26. ladǫorǫ sísi harúga bináfi, beréga-me kà la babúsęrubài, bacóraụ-me lubáraụ uéiu." 27. ligía tadógubai. 28. tadáiragua túgua tídǫ abǫ tagóto múna hau boróbu saráuạdu lúma hísigalę.

29. luágu-ti abǫ uéiu lídagię sụ uéiu, ligía tiábi tùo-buga tiráo táufuri alúguraha féị. 30. teréga-ti saráuạdu tụ: "nuhá-ba iráho alúguraha féị iáa." 31. teréga tụ: "uarí-ta iáhaụ!" 32. tacólorǫ ịu, teréga tụ: "subúse bumútina? 33. nugúia mehá-tia tùo tabúgubaụ búgucu." 34. uágati alúgurahàtu féị. 35. ába-ti tagǫ́iehanu sụ féị, ába-ti terégu tụ: "baró-bai lèa tụ búgucu!" 36. tíciga darǫ́di murúsu síliba tụ. 37. táibagua águiu,

teréga tų túgucu: "rísiharú-tia iráho tùo-meha babúgubaų iágię." 38. teréga tų: "báiba aríha ída líą lá tibíhini." 39. ábaia tídi iráho tùo álagodaų tùo rísibaų ída líą lá tibíhini. 40. abą teréguni. 41. abą tagíribudų erégai tų túgucu. 42. teréga túgucu tų: "áhąbu nabúga, bídiba?" 43. teréga iráho tùo tų: "ąhą!"; abą tabúgunu. 44. tídi óroua uéiu táu, bía áriabu. 45. lamáru-ti lau umágurasùni. 46. tadúragua túma Uanúi; teréga tų: "halíabadíbu?" 47. teréga tų Uanúi: "málagodagùa bána; lamádina." 48. abą tásogǫ. 49. tadúragua lúma úhabu, ugúdi, icógo, abą téheraha tau. 50. tacólora tídaų múna. 51. uíaugati! 52. taríhai uáiriai mútu ligía nieį, abą terégu lų: "ká badógobai lidą liuíauga lèa?" 53. leréga tų: "báiga gia núma!" 54. teréga lų: "uíaugati iáa nų. 55. marúmugubádina gię tídą tiuíe gabána." 56. leréga uáiriai lèa tų: "baró-baų báulu tùo! 57. báguraų me lubáraų uéiu ladǫorǫ sísi, bibíhubai lèa babúserubài." 58. abą tagíribudų. 59. tacólorǫ hábię, teréga tų túgucu: "uarísida!" 60. marúmugutíų áugurabai ladǫorǫ sísi. 61. ladǫorǫ sísi abą tacóronu báulu tùo lubáraų uéiu. 62. hadáiragua háųgua lamídą barána hau boróbu uáibaiaua háma údu, abą háiginių.

63. nieį lagúmuca úraga hauágu uríbatių. 64. lų-iebe hagúmucagua uríbatių luái ubáu.

Translation. Story about a Bad Aunt

1. Once upon a time there was a girl whose mother had died; and so it was that she lived with her aunt. 2. One day she sent her daughter together with this girl to draw water. 3. She gave a bucket to her daughter, a pitcher to this girl. 4. When they reached the bank of the river, and this girl went to draw her water, it so happened that as she was lifting the pitcher she slipped, the pitcher fell and was completely smashed. 5. And so she began to cry. 6. Her aunt's daughter laughed at her. 7. When they arrived near the house and her aunt saw that she no longer had the pitcher, she said to her: "You'll not come into my house unless you find my pitcher for me; so go away from here!" 8. And the child went away weeping.

9. She was three days and two nights on the way, and then she met Wanuhi. 10. Wanuhi said to her: "What's the matter with you?" 11. She told her: "It's only because I let my aunt's pitcher get broken. 12. When I went to draw water I slipped and it fell. 13. She's sending me to get another to replace it." 14. Wanuhi said to her: "Don't be afraid! You'll manage to replace it. 15. Take this path; you'll meet feet dancing: don't laugh! 16. You'll meet hands and heads dancing: don't laugh! 17. When you've passed some fifty yards beyond these things, you'll see a house. 18. When you reach it, greet the old man whom you'll see there. 19. He's dirty: don't spurn him! 20. Clean him, and 21. do whatever he tells you! 22. You'll get something good for yourself."

23. And that is what she did. 24. When she reached this old man's house, he said to her: "Eat with me!"; and she ate with him out of a coconut shell. 25. In the evening, he told her: "Take this ball! 26. On the stroke of six tomorrow morning you'll say what it is that you want, and throw it toward the sun." 27. That is what she did. 28. She found herself in a huge house with lots of servants and treasure.

29. One day of all days, she who had been her aunt's daughter came selling bread. 30. The servant told her: "A girl has come here to sell bread." 31. She said: "Let her come up here!" 32. When she arrived upstairs, she said to her: "Do you know me? 33. I am she whom your mother drove away." 34. The bread-seller was speechless. 35. And she bought all her bread, and said to her: "Take this to your mother!" 36. She gave her thirty pieces of silver. 37. She ran back home and said to her mother: "The girl whom you drove away from here has become rich." 38. She told her: "Go and see how it is that she got it!" 39. And the girl went again to the one who was rich and asked her how it was that she had got it. 40. And she told her. 41. And she returned to tell it to her mother. 42. Her mother said to her: "If I drive you away will you go?" 43. The girl told her: "Yes!"; and she was chased away.

44. She went on for three days and two nights. 45. She was hungry and full of impatience. 46. She met with Wanuhi, who said to her: "Where are you going?" 47. She told Wanuhi: "Don't question me! I'm hungry." 48. And she passed on. 49. She met with the hands, feet, heads, and she laughed at them. 50. She came to the house. 51. How dirty! 52. She saw the old man there and said to him: "What are you doing in this filth?" 53. He said to her: "Eat with me!" 54. She told him: "It's (too) dirty for me here. 55. And I won't sleep in a dirty bed either." 56. The old man said to her: "Take this ball! 57. You'll cast it toward the sun at the stroke of six, and you'll get what you want." 58. And she returned home. 59. When she reached their home, she said to her mother: "We're going to get rich." 60. They didn't sleep waiting for the stroke of six. 61. On the stroke of six she threw the ball toward the (rising) sun. 62. They found themselves in the middle of the sea with lots of sharks and great fish; and these ate them up.

63. There ends the story of the wicked ones. 64. And just so, bad people disappear from the world.

Commentary

This, like almost all the stories I recorded among the Black Carib of Central America, is obviously a tale of Old World provenance, in which it is not hard to recognize a version of Grimm's *Frau Hölle*, otherwise known as *The Good Child and the Bad*. It differs notably from the German tale, however, in extolling discretion and forbearance instead of beauty and diligence; and in this it resembles a Dahomean version of the story recorded by Herskovits (1958, no. 69). It is much shorter than most of the tales told by the Black Carib today; and its moralizing trend suggests that it is a version composed for telling to small children. But the hardships endured by the underdog, who triumphs in the end over those who are more privileged, is a theme that is common to all of them.

This short text (some 500 words) contains no fewer than thirty-nine borrowed forms (not counting repetitions), some of which are free (loanwords), while others occur in construction with Arawakan affixes. The following apparently had Carib (Karina) models: *áufuri* 'father's sister', *bináfi* 'morning', *boróbu* 'lots of', -*dihari* 'fear', *dúna* 'water; river', *gu̧ie-* 'evening', *múna* 'house', *óma* 'path; road', *óroua* 'three', *subuse-* 'know', *ubáu* 'world' (cf. *ubáuhu* 'island'), *údu* 'big fish' (the diminutive, *údurao*, is employed for fish of ordinary size), *uéiu* 'sun; day', *uríba-* 'bad, wicked', -*ida-* 'in'. The verb *am(u)íagua* 'to exchange' contains *ámu*, *am-* 'other (different)' (cf. *ábaia* 'another [additional]'), which is found with the same form and meaning in Tupí, and with the same form in Carib, where the meaning is, however, 'somebody; something'.

From French or from a French creole come -*busę-* 'want' (*besoin*), -*busu-* 'greet' (*bon jour*), *da̧* 'time' (*temps*), *darádi* 'thirty' (*trente*), *dimisa̧* 'fifty' (*demi cent*), *féi̧* 'bread' (*pain*), *gabána* 'bed' (*cabane* in dial. Fr. or creole?), -*gái̧e-* 'buy' (or, with different affixation, 'win; earn') (*gagner*), -*gumese-* 'begin' (*commencer*), -*gurásu-* 'patient' (*courage*), *hísigalę* 'treasure, money, wealth' (*escalin*, the name of old coin and/or money of count), *le* 'when' (probably creole, which has *lè* with the same meaning; cf. Fr. *lors* and *l'heure*), -*midą* 'in the middle' (*mitan*), *murúsu* 'piece(s); bit(s); a little' (*morceau*), *risi-* 'rich' (*riche*), *saráuqdu* 'servant(s)' (*servante*), *sísi* 'six' (*six*).

Probably from English models come *báulu* 'ball', *bu̧gidu* 'bucket', and *síliba* 'silver'; from Spanish, *bádu* 'yard(s)' (cf. Sp. *vara*) and *fáluma* 'coconut' (Sp. *palma*). CAIC *mútu* 'person; people' probably comes, as I have suggested elsewhere, from some Bantu language.

Except for its paucity in Spanish loans this text appears to me to be representative of the distribution of borrowed and inherited forms in Island-Carib as spoken in its Central American (and especially its British Honduran) dialect at the present time.

Central American Island-Carib. *Úraga hauágu sísi tiráhq̧ia̧ abą uóri: lèa amuléię Bagámu, Ebédimu haránaguati, íbugaiá̧ Sirígo, líbugaia̧ Sirígo Uráu, hámati bíama ibidiḛ́ti híriu̧*

1. *onúhai̧ abą hi̧áru hísięti Ebédimu tu̧*. 2. *luágu-ti abą uéiu táibuga alúguraha badía lidą faníe turúgabu leskuéla*. 3. *lídą aura ligía háhurarú̧ia̧*

iráhǫią turúgabu leskuéla. 4. óuara luma haríhinų, habúdaha idóburi hacóragua tuágu. 5. liábui Bagámu lacóroni lidóburi, ábą tígiragodóni faníe tabadía—báuguagubái! 6. teréga lų: "lų basáfarų nuái, maríegubai la Ebédimu numa." 7. ábą lídi Bagámu erégai lų; ábągubái lamáredų Ebédimu túma. 8. lárigię maríehaią lą́, lanógai áucahani (/adíahani) lifísiute me. 9. le lídi áucaha, úati údurao uái(h)ali ladigį lų dáiarubái lą; hanią́buri tia dáiarubái. 10. luágu-ti ábą uéiu ladų́ragua túma Uanúi. 11. teréga lų: "masą́ditibu sa abą kátai núma? 12. mámatių gorígia búmari tábu bímenodi." 13. leréga tų: "ka gia uágu?" 14. teréga lų: "dą le bídi áucaha, dáiarutíų údurao uáinamuhą́ią badígį?" 15. leréga tų: "úa." 16. teréga lų: "bagą́ieha lámbara; bágora me bubúre lau." 17. leréga tų: "tę́ki nią bų!" ábą lídi águiu. 18. lacíloro ábą laguméseru ágorahái lubúre. 19. teréga lúmari lų́: "ída-ti gię lai mágorahaiahádibu bubúre lau lámbara?" 20. leréga tų: "ígira bána! basubúserubái ka la uágu nágorai nubúre lau lámbara."

21. larúgati ábą lídi áucaha. 22. íderagua tumúti límenodi anógaų liámadi lau. 23. eréga tugúia lų lau tiáb(u)iba lą lubáraų. 24. lacóloroti ganálirugu, furúmie údorao ladígį tamídą. 25. tibíama, áhaų derégoda lifítaru dą le ladíginų, abą tagóto uáibaiaua. 26. ábą libíhunų murúsu murúsu, ábą lacágarunų baránahaų. 27. sų́ buga murúsu lèa líbugubái salígua lų uáibaiaua mé. 28. calati tau lugúne. 29. hanúfude(h)agua, bírogo láli láųgurute, ábą lafágaiuha múarugu.

30. lacólorǫ, ligía terę́gų lúmari lų: "áfara bá núgucu!" 31. leréga tų: "ma funá gia. tugúia anagubali buga numégegu nau; an tiáb(u)iba negeia buga nubáraų." 32. ábą terę́gų lų: "áfara bá núgucu!" 33. ligía tasáliragų uáibaiaua mé, táibagua lárigi, máragodǫ tumúti, tidi agáradaha lubá lamúlę turúgabu leskuéla. 34. óuara lúma tadíleru leskuéla taríhini Bagámu abą táibagų lárigi. 35. máufųti. 36. táragodóni ábą tíbuguni (/tibiaguni) ábą liáda. 37. iurúguaru; ábą tadáburų baránahaų. 38. lagámbubali iebe Sirígo, málali; ábą lagą́iodų lų Ebédimu. 39. ligía hadíseguabái dą le háfuacų siélurugu (/ubéurugu). 40. le lagámbubalí gię Uráu lídą dísi háti, málali. 41. ligía kési habái uáibaiaua lídą háti líra.

Translation. Tale of a Woman's Six Children: Bakamu the youngest, Ebetimu the middle one, his elder Siríko, Siríko's elder Urao, together with Two Others Whose Names I Have Forgotten

1. There was a woman who loved Ebetimu. 2. One day she went in front of the school with a basket of melons to sell. 3. At that time the children were playing in front of the school. 4. As soon as they saw her, they gathered stones and threw them at her. 5. When Bakamu came to fling his stone, she let go of the basket of melons, which were completely smashed. 6. She said to him: "For you to escape from me, Ebetimu

must marry me at once." 7. And Bakamu went and told him of it, and Ebetimu married her right away.

8. After they were married, he took to fishing as his occupation. 9. When he went out to fish, none of the big fish he caught was whole, but the little ones were whole. 10. One day he met with Wanuhi. 11. She said to him: "Don't you feel the same thing as I do? 12. Your wife and your mother-in-law are not human." 13. He said to her: "For what reason?" 14. She said to him: "When you go fishing, are the big fish you catch whole?" 15. He told her: "No." 16. She told him: "Buy some wire, and tie your hooks with it." 17. He told her "Thank you!" and went home. 18. When he arrived he began to bind his hooks. 19. His wife said to him: "And how is it that you never before bound your hooks?" 20. He told her: "Let me be! You'll find out for what reason I bind my hooks with wire."

21. On the following day he went fishing. 22. His mother-in-law helped him to carry down his basket. 23. She told him that she would come to meet him. 24. When he reached the deep water, the first fish he caught was (cut) in half. 25. The second, which stretched his line tight as he was pulling it in, was a huge shark. 26. Then he cut it into little bits, and scattered them over the sea. 27. All those pieces he had cut turned back into sharks. 28. His canoe was being swamped. 29. He grew afraid, cut the anchor, and paddled for shore.

30. When he arrived, his wife said to him: "You've killed my mother!" 31. He told her: "That cannot be. It was she who carried my tackle for me; and she said that she would come to meet me." 32. And she told him: "You've killed my mother." 33. Then she turned into a shark, ran after him, did not catch him, and went to lay in wait for his young brother by the school. 34. As soon as the school let out, she saw Bakamu and ran after him. 35. He did not hurry. 36. She caught him and severed one of his legs. 37. She was satisfied and plunged into the sea. 38. When Siriko heard of it, it was of no avail; and he quarreled with Ebetimu. 39. That is why they are far apart when they emerge into the sky. 40 When Urao too heard of it in the tenth month, it was of no avail. 41. And that is why sharks are scarce in that month.

Commentary

Clearly, this is but a fragment of a much longer story having to do with a number (varying from eight to twelve, according to informant) of brothers, identified with different Carib constellations thought to control different seasons or "months" of the year. In other versions of this tale, Ebetimu is the youngest; and it is certainly he who had his leg severed, as the name itself indicates: *ipe:tima* 'without a thigh', from *pe:ti* 'thigh'. (See Taylor 1952, pp. 270–73, and Taylor 1951, pp. 153–57.)

Borrowed items are perhaps unusually common in this short piece. I find eleven different loans from Carib (Karina): *uóri* 'woman', *uéiu* 'sun; day', *úa* 'no', *-ímenodi* 'mother-in-law', *-dise-* 'far', *idóburi* 'stone', etc. There are six from Spanish (including *batía* 'badea', *leskuéla* 'escuela', *áura* 'hora', *-físiu-* 'oficio', and *lámbara* 'alambre'); fourteen from French (including *-marie-* 'marier', *fanie* 'panier', *dą* 'dans', *le* 'lors' or 'l'heure' [probably from a French creole], *-gáie-* 'gagner', *-gumése-* 'commencer', *-ide-* 'aider', *-mídą* 'mitan', *murúsu* 'morceau'); and three from English (*tęki* 'thank 'ee', *an* 'and' [an undigested loan], and *kési* 'scarce').

Alternative forms are given in parentheses, preceded by a slash.

Wanuhí, the old soothsayer of Dominican Carib stories, changes sex to become Uanúi of the Central American Island-Carib. Bakamu is met with again in a Lesser Antillean creole story of that name (given in Chapter 12, below).

Karina. *Paki:ru:mi*

a:mú / mirexkoko / kini:sáɲ / wota:ró / ko:koro // mo:r(o) o:má ta kini:sáɲ // irombo kinixsaɲ teee / a:mú tono:mi / epo:yáɲ // moxko tono:mi / e:marí / (ix)koto:yáɲ / kino:saɲ ma:n(oɲ) ipo:ko // irombo / ipo:ká se maɲ moxko tono:mi kínixsaɲ // kinixsaɲ teee / irombo kini:kó:maiya(ɲ) // irombo kine:páxka:no / mo:ró emandó:kon da:ka // kine:pó:yaɲ / o?wí tampo:ko / naŋga moxko ipi:tí // emiirí // iyo:ruwá:norikoɲ // irombo / "yu:pa ro:ripo maɲ he tamu:sí" kiŋga:no // "a:a se pa:ri / yu:pa su ro:ripo // amo:ro ra:pa" / "ha yu?pa weitáɲ se tamu:si" // "o:ya ko mi:saɲ" // "a yu:ta:pii se tamu:sí" "irombo e:ro pó o?ní:ko" // "ha:há" // irombo tomiirí kó:ma:no // "ye:miirí / mo:r(o) apa:tí aro:kó / mo:n(i) ita:ribin da:ka // irombo kinixsáɲ moxko / emiirí tipa:t(i) aiye / (t)uwo:wá:to kinixsaɲ // irombo moxko / akaxtopó ma:ro ase:na o?ní:toko // kiŋga:no iyu:mi // "a:ha pa:pa" // kiŋga:no moxk(o) emiirí // i:ro wa:ra ro mandóɲ / nexkiríndoma:toɲ tuwe:sa:pimarik(oɲ) a?moyá:ton // . . . .

English translation. *Peccary Girl*

In the morning a young man went hunting. On the path he went. Then he went on and on; he found a game animal. The animal crossed his path; obliquely (leaving the path) he came after it. Then he wanted to shoot it, the animal went away. It went on and on until it became dark, it became dark. Then he came out (from the bush) into their dwelling place. He found one old man, with his wife. His daughter was the third of them. Then "Are you fairly well, grandfather," he said. "Yes, my grandchild, fairly well indeed. And you?" "I may be doing well, Grandfather." "Where are you going?" "I, eh, have lost my way, grandfather." "In that case sleep here." "Yes, please." Then he called his daughter. "My daughter, take your hammock into yonder empty house." Then his daughter went

to take her her hammock, she went to tie it. Then "You and your uncle must sleep side by side," her father said. "Yes, father," said his daughter. And so they did; they lay down and began their play. . . .
Text and translation from Hoff 1968, p. 306.

Arawak Translation. Abíia híaro
abá tha maóthia losá iokhánro abá bíkidoliáthi. losá líbonáa lokhodí, ken tha losáosadáka. ken tha abá khotáama lothikáka. ken tho khotaha thimáka lobóra. losá thínabo. ken tha loiokháthikan, ken tha thosa lória. thosáosadáka bákhilamaderen, téee . . . landá tha aba síkoa-banán. lóthika aba hébethi leréithoma. nátho nakabóntheka. "hálika diáko bá, dókothi?" látha lomín. "hehéi, sákoa dá, dalikínthi. ken bíi?" "sakoa dáida, dókothi." "halonro bósabo?" "dasinaka (dabonáalokoária), dókothi." "kiadóma bodónka iáa." "hehéi." ken lisimáka lothóoa: "dátho, bónika tho bokoráoa thókothaa malokhódokoro báhi." ken tha thosá tha lótho nikánro thokoráoa, thosá thibodánro. ken tha: "bodónkali bidainthima kadokákoan," látha thithí thomín. "hehéi, dáthi," thátha lon. ken ki náa. nátorodá, ken náinata birán. . . .

Apology and commentary
Under the title "Peccary Girl" (K *paki:ru:mi*), I have given here just the beginning (text and English translation) of the tale, so-called, in Dr. Berend Hoff's excellent work, *The Carib Language* (1968, pp. 306–13). When I received a copy of this book, I was in Surinam, studying Arawak, and found this story so delightful that I induced my informants to work on an Arawak version. They seemed to be pleased with the result; and I, at least, found the exercise very helpful. But to repeat the whole story here in three languages would serve no useful purpose; and the short extract that I have given will suffice to show the difference between the Karina and the Arawakan contributions to Central American or other dialects of Island-Carib.

To the Karina layer belong (ll. 1, 2) K *a:mu* 'some' and earlier 'other', CAIC *ámu* 'other'; (ll. 1, 2) K *o:ma* and *e:mari*, CAIC *íma* and *-émari*, all 'path'; (l. 1) K *ta* and CAIC *-da* 'in'; (l. 6) K *-o:ruwa-* and CAIC *íriua* 'three'; (l. 6) K *yu:pa* and its fuller form *iru:pa* 'good', CAIC *irúfy* 'kind'; (l. 7) K *pa:ri* and CAIC *-ibári* 'grandchild'; (l. 7) K *amo:ro* and CAIC *amíri* 'you (sg.)'. Finally, K *mi:san* (l. 8) 'you (sg.) are going' has the same stem as CAIC *uísą* 'goodbye', derived from K *wi:sa* 'I'm going'; and K *wa:ra* (l. 13) 'so; likewise' provided the stem of CAIC *íuara* (K *o:wa:ra*) 'at the same time', though the last two Island-Carib examples have long been monomorphemic.

Turning now to Arawak, which, like Island-Carib but unlike Karina, distinguishes sex-gender in its personal prefixes of third person singular, we see that those of the two related languages (A *l-* and *th-*, CAIC *l-* and *t-*) are cognate, whether the verbal, nominal, and postpositional stems to which they may be attached are so or not. Examples from the Arawak version of the Karina extract are (l. 3) *thosa lória* "it-went-away from-him," (l. 6) *látha lomín* "he-said to-him," (l. 10) *látha thithí thomín* "he-said her-father to-her," and *thátha lon* "she-said to-him" (A *lon* and *thon* are commonly employed reduced forms of *lomín* and *thomín*); and their Island-Carib equivalents, CAIC *táibuga luária, leréga lụ, leréga túguci tụ, teréga lụ*.

All the personal prefixes of Arawak (*dA-, b-, l-* and *th-, oA-, h-,* and *nA-*) except that of first person singular are cognate with their Island-Carib equivalents (*n-, b-, l-* and *t-, uA-, h-,* and DIC *nhA-* → CAIC *hA-*) and combine with stems of the same classes, as in A *bodonka* : CAIC *barumuga* 'you sleep', A *bonika* : CAIC *baniga* 'you take', A *bokora* : CAIC *bígira* 'your hammock', A *natho* 'their daughter' : CAIC *hatu* 'their sister', A *loária* : CAIC *luária* or *luái* 'from him'. In lines 5, 7, and 10 we see suffixal forms of A *oma* : CAIC *-úma* 'with' and A *odoma* : CAIC *-uruma* 'because; on account of', and in line 5 a free postposition, A *diako* (earlier *adioáko*) : CAIC *uágu* '(up)on'. The privative prefix A *mA-* : CAIC *mA-* occurs in A *malokhodo(koro)* '(which is) without contents'—i.e., 'empty' (l. 9)—and its Island-Carib equivalent, *mála*. A *aba* : CAIC *abạ* 'a; one', A *dokothi* : CAIC *aruguti* 'grandfather', A *híaro* : CAIC *hịáru* 'woman, girl, female', A *iáa* : CAIC *iá(h)a* 'here', and A *thókothaa* : CAIC *túguta* 'yon(der)' require no explanation; but this is not true of A *dalikínthi* 'my grandson' compared to CAIC *nilígín(i)* 'my pet animal'.

Earlier A *dalikin(i)* and IC *nilikin(i)* seem to have both referred indifferently to 'my pet animal (animal que je nourris)' or to 'my grandchild'. With the former meaning, the Arawak form has remained unchanged; but with the latter meaning, /i̵/ has replaced /i/ of the stem, and a suffix indicating human male (*-thi*) or female (*-tho*) has been added, thus giving *dalikínthi* 'my grandson'. In Island-Carib this stem has retained only the former meaning; but the vowels of the stem have been replaced similarly by /i̵/, so that now we have CAIC (*i*)*lígini* 'pet or domestic animal', *níligị̵ (áụli)* 'my pet (dog)'.

WORDLISTS

The following lists, and those in Chapter 12 of this volume, are based on Morris Swadesh's diagnostic lists (Swadesh 1966).

Arawak (*list A*): Sawariweg, Bernarddorp, Surinam, 1968

1. I   dái ~ déi
2. thou   bíi ~ bíi
3. we   oái ~ oéi

4.	this	thó(h)o; lí(h)i
5.	that	thóra(h)a; líra(h)a
6.	who?	hálika(n)
7.	what?	hámaha
8.	not	kho(ro); mA-
9.	all	hára(-)
10.	many	ió(h)o (cf. 135)
11.	one	abá(-)
12.	two	bíama ~ bían
13.	big	(i)firo-; (i)fili-
14.	long	oadi-
15.	small	ibi-; sióko-
16.	woman	híaro
17.	man	oadíli
18.	person	lóko (but see p. 82 above)
19.	fish	híme
20.	bird	kodibío
21.	dog	péero (< Sp.)
22.	louse	iéhi, -ie
23.	tree	áda
24.	seed	isíi, -si
25.	leaf	adobóna, -bana
26.	root	iíkirahi, -íkira
27.	bark	ádada, -da
28.	skin	ída, -da
29.	flesh	sírokoho, -síroko
30.	blood	íthihi, -thína
31.	bone	abónaha, -bona
32.	fat	iki(h)i
33.	egg	kodibíosa, -sa
34.	horn	-(o)koa
35.	tail	i(h)ítoko; -í(h)i
36.	feather	(o)bára, -bára
37.	hair	(o)bára, -bára
38.	head	isíi, -si/sin
39.	ear	-dike; -kóioko
40.	eye	-kosi
41.	nose	sírihi, -siri
42.	mouth	-réroko
43.	tooth	aríi, -ári
44.	tongue	-iée
45.	claw	-báda
46.	foot	-kóti
47.	knee	-kóro
48.	hand	-khábo
49.	belly	-dibéio; ité ('gut')
50.	neck	-nóro
51.	breast	-dio
52.	heart	-oásina; óloa; kákin
53.	liver	-bána
54.	drink	(a)thin (v.t.); (a)than (v.i.)
55.	eat	(e)kin (v.t.); khoton (v.i.)

56. bite	rídin
57. see	díkhin
58. hear	kánabon
59. know	áithin
60. sleep	dónkon
61. die	(h)ódon
62. kill	fárin
63. swim	thímin
64. fly	mórodon
65. walk	kónan
66. come	ándin
67. lie	tórodon; iákadan (in hammock)
68. sit	bálatin
69. stand	dínamin
70. give	síkin
71. say	aakan; dián; man
72. sun	hádali
73. moon	káthi
74. star	oíoa
75. water	oniábo, -niá
76. rain	óni
77. stone	síba, -síban
78. sand	móthoko, -móthokon
79. earth	hóroro, -órora
80. cloud	oráro
81. smoke	koréeli
82. fire	híki(h)i, -ihime
83. ash(es)	bálisi
84. burn	bíthin, bithán, bithonoán
85. path	oabóroko; abónaha
86. mountain	hororo sin (= 79 + 38)
87. red	koré(e)-
88. green	(ímoro-)
89. yellow	(héhe-)
90. white	haríra-
91. black	khareme-
92. night	oríka; kásakodá
93. hot	thére-; oerébe- ('warm')
94. cold	mímili-
95. full	(h)ébe-
96. new	(h)emeléa-
97. good	sa-
98. round	balala-
99. dry	oaa-; sare-
100. name	-íri

Arawak (list B): Sawariweg, Bernharddorp, Surinam, 1968

101. ye	híi ~ héi
102. he	léi ~ líi
103. they	nái ~ néi
104. how?	hálika-, hálidi
105. when?	hálikha

106.	where?	hálon, hálo-
107.	here	iáha
108.	there	iáraha
109.	other	abán(o), abáro
110.	three	kábiin
111.	four	bíithi, biábithe
112.	five	(a)ba-dakhabo
113.	sky	kasáko
114.	day	kásakabó(h)o
115.	wind	àoadóli
116.	flow	maladin
117.	river	óni(khan)
118.	wet	ióio-
119.	wash	sokóson, sokosán
120.	snake	óri
121.	worm	iséhi
122.	back	aháboroko
123.	arm	adína
124.	wing	= 123
125.	navel	ókoio
126.	guts	itéhi, -te
127.	saliva	orároni
128.	fruit	-íoi
129.	flower	otókoro
130.	grass	kárao
131.	with	óma; ábo
132.	in	lóko
133.	at	-min ~ -n
134.	if	farókha
135.	mother	óio, -ió
136.	father	íthi, -thi
137.	husband	iréithi, -rethi
138.	salt	pamo
139.	children	iréno (no sg.)
	child	ísa
140.	dark	oríroko
141.	cut	ríkin, rikán, bíkin
142.	narrow	míbiloko
143.	far	oáikili
144.	near	iá(h)adi; iaháboron
145.	thick	hánahana
146.	thin	oakara-
147.	short	moadi-
148.	heavy	khidi-
149.	sharp	kamana-
150.	dirty	iribe-
151.	bad	oakaia-
152.	rotten	toro-
153.	smooth	folifoli-
154.	straight	misi-
155.	correct	= 97
156.	old	hebe-; oa(h)adi-

157. rub	lítin
158. throw	borédin; borédan
159. hit	bórikin; also as 62.
160. split	oalasan
161. stab/pierce	thíadin; aiákonoan
162. dig	thíkin, thíkan
163. tie	kírin
164. sew	kisán
165. fall	thíkidin; khin (of rain)
166. swell	aákonon
167. think	kobórokoatonoán; ikisikin
168. sing	ientonoán
169. smell	dímisin
170. puke	oédin
171. suck	sóroton
172. blow	fódin, fódan
173. fear	hamáron
174. squeeze	samórodin
175. hold	bókoton
176. down	abomin
177. up	aiomin
178. ripe	hebe- (= 95 = 156)
179. year	= 74

Segmental unit phonemes are *th kh; p t k; b d; f s h; m n; l r; i e, a o i;*
VV, V́. Nasalized vowels are also distinctive, but in the vast majority of
cases occur only in preconsonantal and word-final positions, where they
can be shown, as above, by -*Vn*. Stylistically or otherwise, nasalized
vowels may always be replaced by a nasal consonant flanked by oral
vowels (*VNV*). Arawak /i/ is mid to high back *un*rounded, Arawak /o/
mid to high back rounded.

Guajiro (*list A*): Guajiro peninsula, Venezuela

1. I	tayá
2. thou	piá
3. we	wayá
4. this	tií; cií
5. that	ti(r)á; ci(r)á
6. who?	harái
7. what?	haman; kasa-
8. not	noho
9. all	apišua?a
10. many	maima/waima
11. one	wanée
12. two	piama
13. big	milia?u
14. long	ka?ápu
15. small	mottso; cinkini
16. woman	hiéri
17. man	toólo; hašici

18. person	wayúu
19. fish	himé
20. bird	(w)ucíi
21. dog	(y)érí
22. louse	e ʔe; mapíi
23. tree	(w)unú ʔu
24. seed	á ʔɨ
25. leaf	(a)pána
26. root	aúrala
27. bark	sta unú ʔu (28 + 23)
28. skin	atá ~ -ta
29. flesh	eiruku
30. blood	ašáa ~ -ša
31. bone	hímpu/hiípu
32. fat	aísɨ
33. egg	-šuku
34. horn	o ʔuwá
35. tail	así ~ -si
36. feather	olíi
37. hair	waláši ~ -walá
38. head	ekíwi ~ -ikíi
39. ear	acé ʔe
40. eye	o ʔú
41. nose	e(ʔ)icí
42. mouth	aánikɨ
43. tooth	a(l)íi
44. tongue	iyée
45. claw	-patta ʔu
46. foot	- ʔulíi
47. knee	asápain
48. hand	ahápɨ
49. belly	alé ʔe
50. neck	anúlu
51. breast	acíra
52. heart	á ʔin
53. liver	= 25
54. drink	asáa
55. eat	ekáa
56. bite	ekáhaa; ohóttaa
57. see	eráa
58. hear	aápaa
59. know	atíhaa
60. sleep	atunkaa
61. die	áukktaa
62. kill	aukktáa á ʔin
63. swim	katínaa
64. fly	awátaa
65. walk	a(ʔ)unáa
66. come	ánttaa
67. lie	ahúleraa
68. sit	áikkalaa; ikátaa
69. stand	atámat-; šawatáa

70.	give	asílahaa
71.	say	máa
72.	sun	ka ʔí
73.	moon	kaší
74.	star	herótsi; šilíwala
75.	water	wíin
76.	rain	huyá
77.	stone	(h)ipá
78.	sand	muáku
79.	earth	umá ~ -ma
80.	cloud	sirúma; misái
81.	smoke	misái
82.	fire	s(i)kí
83.	ashes	palí ʔi
84.	burn	epéhaa; a ʔaháa; hotá a
85.	path	wopú; apínaa
86.	mountain	uúci; urápa
87.	red	išá, išó (cf. 30)
88.	green	wíittaa
89.	yellow	maláukataa
90.	white	kasu-
91.	black	mittsiia-
92.	night	á(l)i
93.	hot	ha ʔisi
94.	cold	hemíaa; saámataa
95.	full	wotaa (solids); pirátaa (liquids)
96.	new	hekéci
97.	good	anáa-
98.	round	palápalaa-
99.	dry	huláa- (veg.), hosóo-(other)
100.	name	anília

Guajiro (list B): Guajira peninsula, Venezuela

101.	ye	hiá
102.	he/she	niá/šiá
103.	they	nayá
104.	how?	?
105.	when?	haúha
106.	where?	halá, halayaá
107.	here	yaá
108.	there	yalá
109.	other	wané ʔeya
110.	three	apiniin
111.	four	pienci
112.	five	ha ʔrái
113.	sky	sirúma (cf. 80)
114.	day	= 72
115.	wind	houkktai
116.	flow	palátaa
117.	river	scí
118.	wet	ci ʔláa

119.	wash	ašíhawaa; olohóo, o?óhaa
120.	snake	wíi
121.	worm	hokoma
122.	back (n.)	asapi
123.	arm	atina
124.	wing	= 123
125.	navel	omoco
126.	guts	ayilain
127.	saliva	aliha
128.	fruit	-cón
129.	flower	-asíi
130.	grass	alama; hi?ici
131.	with	amáa
132.	in	alu?u
133.	at	amiin
134.	if	miikka
135.	mother	eíi, eyí
136.	father	ašíi
137.	husband	eécili; eérili *wife*
138.	salt	icíi
139.	child	= 128; tepici; hiínttii (m.), himó?olu (f.)
140.	dark	piuuši; hu?iši
141.	cut	oyotoo; oyotowaa; alatáa
142.	narrow	moúšin (adj.); moulee (vb.)
143.	far	wátta
144.	near	pehé
145.	thick	kohóo
146.	thin	arílaa
147.	short	?
148.	heavy	hawátaa
149.	sharp	kasáa
150.	dirty	eríttaa, -iin (niá)
151.	bad	muhusu
152.	rotten	?
153.	smooth	sirátaa
154.	straight	lotóo
155.	correct	?
156.	old	alaílaa, alaklaa
157.	rub	oló?otaa
158.	throw	aleéhaa
159.	hit	ahátaa; ašé?etaa
160.	split	opóttaa
161.	stab/pierce	oótohoo
162.	dig	opótoo
163.	tie	ahittawaa
164.	sew	?
165.	fall	éittaa; ahúttaa
166.	swell	štáa
167.	think	soótoo a?in
168.	sing	éirahaa
169.	smell	eénhulaa
170.	puke	eétaa

171. suck   acúlaa
172. blow   ahú?laa
173. fear   éema (n.); momóloo (vb.)
174. squeeze   ?
175. hold   a?ápawaa
176. down   unápɨ(miin); óupɨnaa
177. up   iípɨnaa
178. ripe   hakɨtaa; ocoótuuši
179. year   = 76

Segmental unit phonemes are *p t c k ?* (glottal catch); *s š h; l r; m n;
w y; i e a o u ɨ; CC, VV, V́* (cf. 61 and 62), and nasalized vowels (unmarked
as such here). As in Arawak, these latter apparently occur only or almost
only in preconsonantal and word-final positions, and are here indicated
by *Vn* or *Vm* (oral vowel plus nasal consonant). /c/ is a palatal affricate,
/š/ a hushing sibilant, /ɨ/ a mid to high back unrounded vowel.

Central American Island-Carib (list A): British Honduras

1. I   nugúia
   (M.S.)   áu (K)
2. thou   bugúia
   (M.S.)   amóro (K)
3. we   uagía
4. this   tùa; lèa
5. that   túra; líra
6. who?   ka ~ káta-
7. what?   = 6
8. not   mA-; úa (K)
9. all   sų́(gubai)
10. many   gíbe
11. one   ábana ~ ábą
12. two   bíama ~ bía
13. big   uáiri-
14. long   migífe- (K)
15. small   niórao-
16. woman   hį́áru
    (M.S.)   uóri (K)
17. man   eiéri
    (M.S.)   uogóri (K)
18. person   mútu (Afr.)
19. fish   údu(rao) (K)
20. bird   dunúru (K); sóso
21. dog   áųli
22. louse   įe
23. tree   uéue (K)
24. seed   t-íla; t-íį
25. leaf   -bána
26. root   -ílagolá
27. bark   -úra
28. skin   = 27
29. flesh   -ógorogo

30. blood	hítao ~ -íta
31. bone	-ábu
32. fat	-agóle
33. egg	t-íį (cf. 24)
34. horn	arígai
35. tail	-íli
36. feather	= 25
37. hair	-ídiburi
body hair	-íu
38. head	icógo/icígo
39. ear	= 34
40. eye	-águ
41. nose	ígiri
42. mouth	-iúma
43. tooth	-ári
44. tongue	-iéie
45. claw	-(ú)bara
46. foot	-(u)gúdi
47. knee	-gácorogo
48. hand	-(ú)habu
49. belly	-(u)rágai
50. neck	-igíina
51. breast	-úri
52. heart	anígi
53. liver	= 25
54. drink	áta ~ gura-
55. eat	aiga ~ háu-
56. bite	ágoragua
57. see	aríha
58. hear	agába
59. know	subúdi- (K); subúse- (K)
60. sleep	arúmuga
61. die	áue ~ hilá
62. kill	áfara
63. swim	áfuliha (K base)
64. fly	ahámara
65. walk	áibuga
66. come	acólora; nióbui (K)
67. lie	ráų-
68. sit	niuru- ~ (n)ių
69. stand	rárama-
70. give	íciga; ru-
71. say	eréga ~ aríaga
72. sun	uéiu (K)
73. moon	háti
74. star	uarúguma
75. water	dúna (K)
76. rain	húia
(M.S.)	gunúbu (K)
77. stone	dóbu (K)
78. sand	ságaų (K)
79. earth	múa

80. cloud	huárių; ubé(h)u
81. smoke	gumúlali
82. fire	uátu (K) ~ -(í)leme
83. ashes	balígi
84. burn	águda ~ gudá
85. path	óma (K) ~ -émari (K)
86. mountain	uóbu (K)
87. red	funá-
88. green	urígi- (= 91 + -gi 'still')
89. yellow	dumári
90. white	harú-
91. black	urí-
92. night	áriabu
93. hot	hára-; bacá-; so
94. cold	dili-
95. full	buį
96. new	iséri (K)
97. good	buídu (K)
98. round	giríri-
99. dry	mábai-
100. name	-íri

Central American Island-Carib (list B): British Honduras

101. ye	hugúia
102. he	ligía; tugúia (f.)
103. they	hagía
104. how?	ída líą
105. when?	ídaba, ída buga
106. where?	halía
107. here	iá(h)a
108. there	iára
109. other	ámu; ábaia
110. three	óroua (K)
111. four	gádoro; biáburi (arch.)
112. five	ségo
113. sky	siélu (Sp.); ubéhu
114. day	= 72
115. wind	garábali
116. flow	auíara
117. river	= 75
118. wet	dódo-
119. wash	acíba(gua)
120. snake	(h)éue
121. worm	ígei
122. back	anágani
123. arm	-aróna
124. wing	= 123
125. navel	-ári, -áribiri
126. guts	-isása
127. saliva	-aróre
128. fruit	= 24

129.	flower	íleue
130.	grass	sagádi
131.	with	-(ú)ma; -ábu
132.	in	-(í)dą (K); -rugu
133.	at	-rugu
134.	if	áha-
135.	mother	-(ú)gucu
136.	father	-(ú)guci
137.	husband	-(ú)mari
138.	salt	sálu
139.	child	iráho ~ -(i)ráo
140.	dark	búre-
141.	cut	íbuga, ibíagua
142.	narrow	borórao-
143.	far	díse- (K)
144.	near	iaráfa-
145.	thick	durú-
146.	thin	ibíbię-
147.	short	láugua-
148.	heavy	hóro-
149.	sharp	gamána-
150.	dirty	uíe-
151.	bad	uríba-; ią́uą- (K)
152.	rotten	nią́la-
153.	smooth	gurána-
154.	straight	surú-
155.	correct	ríca-
156.	old	uáiha- (cf. 13)
157.	rub	arágaca; acógora-
158.	throw	acóra
159.	hit	= 62
160.	split	abáuca-; agúca-
161.	pierce; stab	áfuduna; ímiraha
162.	dig	acíga
163.	tie	agóra(gua)
164.	sew	áhoca(gua)
165.	fall	áigua(da)
	fall (rain)	áhuia
166.	swell	áluda
167.	think	arítagua
168.	sing	erémuha (K)
169.	smell	irímica
170.	puke	euéreha
171.	suck	acúra
172.	blow	áfura
173.	fear	anúfudei
174.	squeeze	ámuruha
175.	hold	ágoda, áragoda
176.	down	ónabu
177.	up	íu
178.	ripe	funáli/-ru (cf. 87)
179.	year	irúmu (K)

Segmental unit phonemes are: *p t c k; b d g; f s h; m n; l r; i e a u o V̥ V́.* Note that CAIC /o/ is mid to high back unrounded; CAIC /u/, mid to high back rounded except before /i/ or /e/, where it is high front rounded. CAIC /c/ varies from the palatal affricate of English *church* (when it precedes a stressed vowel) to the hushing sibilant of French *cherche* (when it follows a stressed vowel). When they do not bear stress, CAIC /i/ and /u/ followed by another vowel are nonsyllabic ([y] and [w] respectively).

M.S. indicates words employed in the men's speech only; *K* indicates words of recognizable Karina ancestry.

CAIC *-ári* 'tooth' (43) and *-ári* 'navel' (125), though homophonous, are not cognate; the former corresponds to A *-ári* 'tooth', and the latter to A *-ádi(-)* 'upon; after'.

Karina, or True Carib (list A): Surinam

1.	I	au
2.	thou	amo:ro
3.	we	a?na
4.	this	e:ro
5.	that	mo:ro
6.	who?	no:kɨ
7.	what?	oxtoro, o:tɨ
8.	not	adj. + wa:tɨ
		n. + ka:pɨ
9.	all	paxporo
10.	many	apiime
11.	one	o:wiñ
12.	two	o:ko
13.	big	po:to
14.	long	mosi:pe
	length	mo:siñ
15.	small	imimbi
16.	woman	wo:rɨi
17.	man	wokɨ:rɨ
18.	person	kari?na
19.	fish	wo:to
20.	bird	tono:ro; wañsi:ri
21.	dog	pe:ru
22.	louse	o:mɨ
23.	tree	we:we
24.	seed	epixpo
25.	leaf	sa?rombo
26.	root	mi:tɨ
27.	bark	pi:po
28.	skin	= 27
29.	flesh	pu:nu
30.	blood	me:nu
31.	bone	ye:po
32.	fat	ka:tɨ

33. egg	i?mo
34. horn	reme:ti
35. tail	andi:ki-
36. feather	uxse:ti (head)
	i:poti (body)
37. hair	= 36 (head)
	= 36 (body)
38. head	upu:po
39. ear	pa:na
40. eye	o:nu
41. nose	onaxta
42. mouth	inda; po:ta
43. tooth	ye-
44. tongue	nu-
45. claw	amo:seiki
46. foot	pu:pu-
47. knee	oku:na
48. hand	aina (E), aiya (W)
49. belly	uwembo
50. neck	pi:mi
51. breast	mana:ti
52. heart	turu:po
53. liver	o:re
54. drink	eni:ri
55. eat	o:no (of flesh/fish)
	ena:pi (otherwise)
56. bite	e:ka
57. see	e:ne
58. hear	e:ta
59. know	uku:ti
60. sleep	oni:ki
61. die	rombi
62. kill	wo; po:ka)
63. swim	epo:numi
64. fly	ari:rumi
65. walk	ixta:mi; wi:to
66. come	wo:pi
67. lie down	exkirindo
68. sit down	otandi?mo
69. stand up	awo:mi
70. give	i:ri
71. say	i:ka
72. sun	we:yu
73. moon	nu:no
74. star	siri:ko
75. water	tu:na
76. rain	kono:po
77. stone	to:pu
78. sand	sa:kau
79. earth	no:no
80. cloud	enu:puru
81. smoke	ekiini

82. fire   waxto
83. ashes   we:ri
84. burning koro:ti
85. path   o:ma ~ e:mari
86. mountain wi:pi
87. red   tapi:re (adj.); a:pi (n. ['redness'])
88. green   take:neire (adj.); ake:nei (n.)
89. yellow   tixki:re (adj.); i:ki (n.)
90. white   tamu:ne (adj.); a:mu (n.)
91. black   tixkaraire (adj.); ka:rai (n.)
92. night   ko:ko
93. hot   a:siñpe
    heat   a:siñ
94. cold   i:sano (n.); tixsanore (adj.)
95. full   ta?no:se
    be full a?no:pi
96. new   iseiri
97. good   yu:pa/iru:pa
98. round   tamo:merexke
99. dry   taru:re
    dryness a:ru
100. name   e:ti

Karina (list B): Surinam

101. ye   amiiyaro
102. he   moxko
103. they   moxka:ro
104. how   iine⎱wa:ra
           oine⎰
105. when   o:ti ya:ko (cf. 7)
106. where o:we
107. here   e:ro po (= 4 + 133)
108. there   mo:ro po (5 + 133)
109. other   a:mu ro:teŋ
110. three   o:ruwa
111. four   o:kopaime
112. five   aiyato:ne
113. sky   ka:pu
114. day   kuri:ta
115. wind   pepeito
116. flow   apei-na (vb.)
           apeini (n.)
117. river   = 75
118. wet   tike:pure (ke:pu = n.)
119. wash   ku:mi (face)
           a:ti (things)
           sa:wo (cloth)
120. snake   oko:yu
121. worm   oru:ko
122. back   inga:na
123. arm   apo:-ri
124. wing   apo:ri-ri

125. navel	ipo:weti
126. guts	uwembo yo:poto:ri (49 + 13)
127. saliva	eta:kuru
128. fruit	epe:ri
129. flower	epi:ri
130. grass	itu:pu
131. with	ma:ro; ke; po:ko
132. in	ta
133. at	po
134. if	a:ta ~ axta
135. mother	sa:no, ta:ta
136. father	yu:mi, pa:pa
137. husband	iiyo
138. salt	waiyo
139. child	i?me
children	pita:ni (-koŋ)
140. dark	towa:rume
	(ewa:rumi = n.)
141. cut	ixko:to
142. narrow	sira:pime
143. far	tixse
144. near	senge
145. thick	tipiime
146. thin	ipi:piye
147. short	sani:me (sa:niŋ = n.)
148. heavy	awo:simbe (awo:siŋ = n.)
149. sharp	tiye:ke (cf. ye:ri 'tooth')
150. dirty	tixko:ne (ixko:ne = n.)
151. bad	ya?wa:me (ya?waŋ = n.)
152. rotten	tiko:re (ko:ri = n.)
153. smooth	tonamiiye
154. straight	sa:pato:ro
155. correct	ita?ro, ipo:ro
156. old	pena:to; tati:se (person)
157. rub	kiri:rima, merema
158. throw	e:ma
159. hit	= 62
160. split	ra:ka
161. pierce	pu:ka
162. dig	ato:ka ('make a hole')
163. tie	mi
164. sew	eta:mi ('lace with liana')
165. fall	wo:ma (cf. 158)
166. swell	pu:na ('get flesh'); cf. 29
167. think	enu:meŋga
168. sing	wa:reta, (wa:re = n.)
169. smell	ponu:ku ('perceive smell')
170. vomit	uwe:nata, (uwe:na = n.)
171. suck	= 54; nu (cf. 44)
172. blow	u:ro
173. fear	ena:riri ('nervousness')
	wetixka ('to be afraid')

174. squeeze   aki:ka
175. hold   apo:i ('hold; get hold')
176. down   poxpona:ka (poxpo = adj.)
177. up   ka:wona:ka (ka:wo = adj.)
178. ripe   = 87
179. year   = 74

Segmental unit phonemes of Karina are *p t k; b d g; m n ñ ŋ; r; s; x, ?* (glottal catch); *h; w y; i(:), e(:), a(:), o(:), u(:), i(:); au, ai, ei, oi, ui, ii.* See Hoff 1968. I should like to thank Dr. Berend Hoff for supplying me with the Carib (Karina) data in these lists.

Warao: Orinoco Delta, Venezuela

1. I   iné
2. thou   ihi, ihé
3. we   oko
4. this   tamaha
5. that   tai; amaha
6. who?   sina; kasika
7. what?   bitu; ka(tukane)
8. not   -na(ka); -yana
9. all   kokotuka
10. many   -sebe; era
11. one   hisaka
12. two   manamo
13. big   (er)ida; uri-
14. long   (w)ari; kawa-
15. small   sanuka
16. woman   tida
17. man   -nipora/-nebora
18. person   -rao
19. fish   homakapa
20. bird   domu/romu
21. dog   behoro/beroro
22. louse   ami
23. tree   -rau/-dau
24. seed   -mo; namuna
25. leaf   -roko
26. root   -hokonamu
27. bark   dau ahoro
28. skin   -horo
29. flesh   -toma/tuma
30. blood   hoto/hotu
31. bone   -muhu (müehüe)
32. fat   -toi
33. egg   -hi
34. horn   hĭōhi
35. tail   -hu; ahu
36. feather   huhi
37. hair   -hio, -hi
38. head   -kʷa

39. ear	-kohoko
40. eye	-mu
41. nose	-kari
42. mouth	-roko
43. tooth	-i
44. tongue	-hono
45. claw	muhusi (müehüsi)
46. foot	-omo/-omu
47. knee	-muku
48. hand	-mõhõ
49. belly	-ubono
50. neck	?
51. breast	kameho
52. heart	kobe
53. liver	?
54. drink	hobí-; kora
55. eat	nahoro-
56. bite	abu-n-
57. see	mi-
58. hear	noko-
59. know	namina-
60. sleep	upa-
61. die	wapa-
62. kill	na-; kuba-
63. swim	nako-
64. fly	?
65. walk	koho-; yã-
66. come	nabaka-; naru-; yaro; oa-
67. lie	tona-; yahi-
68. sit	duhu-n-
69. stand	karamu-
70. give	mõãũ; mo(a)-
71. say	dibu-n-
72. sun	hokohi; ya
73. moon	waniku
74. star	-kura
75. water	-ho
76. rain	naha
77. stone	hoyo
78. sand	waha
79. earth	hobahi; hota
80. cloud	kohe
81. smoke	hehuku
82. fire	hekunu
83. ashes	huhu-hoko
84. burn	hota-; doku
85. path	sisi; omonoko
86. mountain	hota(-kʷaira)
87. red	simo
88. green	?
89. yellow	hehehe
90. white	hoko

91.	black	ana
92.	night	-ima
93.	hot	ihi(da)
94.	cold	daida/raira
95.	full	?
96.	new	ahidama
97.	good	yakera
98.	round	kopo-
99.	dry	= 78
100.	name	-wai

According to both Henry A. Osborn and Johannes Wilbert (see my review of the latter's *Warao Oral Literature* in *IJAL* 31:104-6), Warao, spoken in several mutually intelligible dialects, has the following segmental unit phonemes: /i e a o u/ together with their rare though distinctively nasalized counterparts, /ĩ ẽ ã õ ũ/, and /p t k kʷ m n s h r w y/. /p/ = [p] or [b], /r/ = [d], [r], or [ľ] ([d] being more common initially, and [r] being more common in intervocalic position). The above list has, however, been compiled from several sources, which I have thought best to follow, writing both *b* and *p*, *d* and *r*.

Warao is not known to be related to any other language, though affiliation with Chibchan has been suggested. Items that seem to be shared with neighboring languages therefore probably show borrowing. Such include W(arao) *ipihi*, A *íbihi*, K *e:piti*, and IC *ibíę*, all meaning 'remedy; medicine'; W -*roko* and A -*reroko* 'mouth'; W *wari* and A *oádi*- 'long'; W *hehehe* and A *hehe*- 'yellow'; W *barabara*- and IC *balá-bala*- 'roll(ing)' (cf. A *balala*- 'round'); W -*koina* and A -*koana*, both instrumental suffixes; W (*hekunu*) *eku* and A (*hikihi*) *ako*, both meaning 'in/on (the fire)'; W *hio* and IC *híu* 'body hair; thorn'; W *matáro* and Breton's IC *matállou* 'calabash'; W *waha* and A *oaa*- 'dry'; W *duhu-n*- 'sit', which may well be related to T *duhu* and G *tulú*, both meaning 'bench'; W -*rapo* and -*rapo* of several Cariban and Arawakan languages, all meaning 'knife'; and W *mo(a)*- 'give', which may be compared to G *maa*-, with the same meaning; W *hahe* and T *nahe*, both 'paddle (n.)'.

II
CREOLE LANGUAGES
❈

SEVEN

THE CARIBBEAN
CREOLES

❖

ALTHOUGH THE FIRST Negroes to reach the New World were *ladinos*—that is to say, such as had spent at least a couple of years in Spain or in Portugal—the vast majority of slaves subsequently brought to the Americas came straight from Africa; and it is usually assumed that almost none of these knew anything of a European language on arrival. This assumption may be correct; but it is well to remember that the Afro-Portuguese pidgin which arose about the middle of the fifteenth century prospered and spread till it came to be used, some two centuries later, by Dutch, English, and French as well as Portuguese traders on the West Coast of Africa and in the Congo. Jean Barbot (1732), who was himself engaged in the slave trade, lists this pidgin under the name of *lingua franca* as one of the languages that would-be travelers to those parts of Africa or to the West Indies would do well to learn before setting out.[1] It is therefore not unlikely that it should have served, in parts of the New World other than Brazil, not only as a means of communication between African-born slaves of different mother tongues, but also as a sort of framework or model upon which later pidgins and creoles came to be built.

By *pidgin* is usually meant an auxiliary language empirically evolved and adopted by two or more speech communities in their dealings with one another, but native to none; by *creole*, a former pidgin that has become the native language of a group. But the latter definition is admittedly unsatisfactory, depending as it does on historical knowledge that may well be lacking (very few such languages are attested in both their pidgin and their creole stages). And if there should be any likelihood

---

[1] It is interesting to note that while Dutch, English, French, and Portuguese are also mentioned, Spanish is not. For a sample of what may have been one kind of French pidgin, see Taylor 1961*a*.

that one pidgin (or creole) arose under conditions of changed contacts by means of massive replacement within the framework of another, it is clear that neither definition would hold good. The testing of this hypothesis will be one of the objects of our inquiry.

In the meantime, the principal Caribbean creoles may be listed and grouped according to what seems to be the predominant source of their basic vocabularies, as follows:

Dutch	*English*
Negro Dutch (ND)	Jamaican and others (JC)
Berbice Dutch* (BD)	Sranan (SN)
Essequibo Dutch* (ED)	Saramaccan and Matuari (SM)
	Djuka and Aluka (DA)
French	*Iberian*
Louisiana Creole (LC)	Papiamentu (PP)
Haitian Creole (HC)	Palenquero (PQ)
Lesser Antillean (LA)	
Cayenne Creole (CC)	

Negro Dutch, formerly spoken in the Virgin Islands (principally in St. Thomas and St. John), is nearing extinction, but has lingered on to the present (Hesseling 1905; Josselin de Jong 1924 and 1926; and most recently Sprauve 1976). It appears to have evolved between the times of first and last recording, but there is no indication in the data of local or other contemporaneous varieties. Data on the two Guyanese Dutch creoles, first reported in August 1976, are not yet sufficient for description.*

The English creoles are somewhat heterogeneous; and at least one of them—Saramaccan—has such a large proportion of Portuguese elements in its lexicon that one may well hesitate to place it in this group (Donicie and Voorhoeve 1963; Voorhoeve 1959, 1961b, and 1973).

On the other hand, the creoles of Jamaica, British Honduras, and Antigua seem to be in the process of disintegration and replacement by normal English; for while they have a number of lexical and structural features that are shared by the Surinamean creoles, they differ from all others discussed here in shading off without any cleavage into the country's noncreole language, as the creoles of Haiti, Guadeloupe, Martinique,

---

* This book was already in press when I received "A Preliminary Wordlist of Berbice Dutch," compiled by Ian Robertson of the University of Guyana. The list contains 423 items in the Dutch Creole of Berbice, and 124 equivalents in that of Essequibo. "The speakers of these varieties claim that they are not mutually intelligible"; indeed, while the provenance of most words is clearly Dutch, that of some very common items is obscure (such as the Berbice negative suffix *-ka* 'not' and the words for 'eat', which are *jefi* in Berbice and *skaf* in Essequibo).

Cayenne, and Palenque do not (Bailey 1962, 1966, 1971; Bickerton and Escalante 1970; Cassidy 1961, 1971; Cassidy and Le Page 1967; De Camp 1968, 1971; Le Page 1957/58; Le Page and DeCamp 1960; Reisman 1968).

Sranan (also called Nengre, Negerengels, or Taki-Taki) consists of several mutually intelligible dialects spoken by various local, racial, and social groups inhabiting Surinam's coastal region. Some 30 percent of the country's total population have it as their first language, and more than 86 percent of the remainder employ it as a lingua franca (Eersel 1971; Voorhoeve 1957, 1959, 1961a, 1961b, 1962, 1973).

The other Surinamean creoles apparently constitute only two languages, spoken—with local differences—by four distinct groups of Bush Negroes: the Djuka (Ndjuka or Auka, a large group settled on the Tapanahoni River) and the Aluku[2] (or Boni, a small group settled on the Lawa River) on the one hand, the Saramacca and the Matuari on the other (the former's settlements extending for a considerable distance along the Surinam River, the latter and smaller group established on the upper reaches of the Saramacca River). Very little has so far been published on Djuka, Aluku, or Matuari (see, however, Hurault 1965; Huttar 1972 and MS).

The four French creoles, though lexically very similar, show enough diversity in phonology and grammar to make it unlikely, in my opinion, that mutual intelligibility between native—especially unilingual—speakers of any two of them could be any greater than that which obtains between the standard languages of Czechoslovakia and Poland, or Germany and the Netherlands. (*Pace* David DeCamp 1971, who writes: "The French creoles of the Caribbean and of the Indian Ocean are all mutually intelligible. Within each community the French creole is also quite uniform.") Lesser Antillean may be subdivided into Guadeloupean, Dominican, Martinican, St. Lucian, Grenadan, and Trinidadian, which are to a large extent—though not altogether—mutually intelligible; while in each island or territory one may distinguish an indeterminate number of varieties peculiar to a particular locality, age group, or social milieu. Varieties of Lesser Antillean are also spoken in French Guiana, a large proportion of whose inhabitants are Antilleans by birth or descent; and these should not be confused with Cayenne Creole. (See Ducoeur-Joly 1802; Goodman 1958, 1964; Hall 1953; Horth 1949; Jourdain 1956; Lane 1935; Marbot 1931; Morgan 1959; Saint Quentin 1872; Sylvain 1936; Taylor 1947, 1951b, 1956d, 1958c, 1961a, 1962b, 1963; J. J. Thomas 1869, reprinted ed. 1969.)

Varieties of Papiamentu—spoken in Aruba, Bonaire, and Curaçao— seem to differ chiefly by their employment of a greater or lesser number

[2] *Alukuyana* is the name given by the coastal Arawak to the Wayana Indians.

of Dutch loanwords. The vocabulary of this language, like that of Saramaccan, contains a considerable proportion of Portuguese-derived words; and while Spanish sources appear to predominate, almost half the lexicon might, with equal probability, be attributed to either ancestry (Goilo 1953). Palenquero—spoken only (so far as is known) in the village of Palenque de San Basilio, near Cartagena, Columbia—has not yet been adequately studied. It appears to be Spanish-based and to contain African but no Portuguese elements (Bickerton and Escalante 1970).

The first question that arises is, What is the relationship of one English (or French) creole to another, and to English (or French) itself? And secondly, What, if anything, do the creoles have in common that distinguishes them from other languages? Only by comparing the lexicons, phonologies, and grammars of the languages concerned can we hope to give answers to these questions; and according to Karl V. Teeter (in *Language* 39:648), "lexical similarities are the only place to start." And since Saramaccan, because of its vocabulary's very mixed ancestry, invites a wider range of comparison than do any other of the creoles listed above, we shall begin by discussing lexical and phonological similarities and differences between it and some other creoles.

EIGHT

SARAMACCAN
AND SOME OTHER
CREOLES

❧

SARAMACCAN AND
SRANAN

Saramaccan and Sranan are said to be clearly and closely related, but to have evolved in different directions with comparatively little opportunity for mutual influence; so that, on account of phonological and lexical divergence, they are not mutually intelligible at the present time (Donicie and Voorhoeve 1963, p. 1). Saramaccan, unlike Sranan, has two relevant tonal heights, four degrees of vocalic aperture, prenasalized as well as plain voiced stops, implosive as well as explosive bilabial stops. Swadesh's 100-item test list, when filled in for these two creoles, points to a common model for sixty-three of their equivalents (see figures given under list A in Table 9), but when this list is expanded, there is a considerable increase in the proportion of Portuguese-derived words in Saramaccan and of Dutch-derived words in Sranan, with a corresponding decrease in the proportion of apparent cognates (see figures under list B in the table, which refer to seventy-nine equivalents belonging to Swadesh's supplementary list). I have distinguished Dutch from English sources insofar as seemed possible; but since the ancestry of many forms is clearly Portuguese, whereas that of none is clearly Spanish, these two possible sources are grouped together. Some forms appear opposite more than one item of the list; in these cases the number of *different* forms attributed to a particular ancestry is shown by figures in parentheses. Readers who wish to make their own estimates will find the actual lists and forms in Chapter 12 of this volume.

Saramaccan and (as we shall see) Papiamentu are exceptional among the West Indian creoles in showing a considerable Portuguese element in their basic vocabularies—a phenomenon that is usually attributed to the presence of Sephardim among the early settlers of Surinam and Curaçao.

TABLE 9.   Derivation of 179 Saramaccan and Sranan Words (Based on Swadesh's Test Lists)

Presumed source	Saramaccan (SM)			Sranan (SN)			SM/SN words with common model		
	List A	List B	A + B (%)	List A	List B	A + B (%)	List A	List B	A + B (%)
English	36	24 (23)	33.5%	63	46 (44)	61%	35	21 (20)	31%
Eng./Du.	11	2	7	11	4 (3)	8	10	2	7
Dutch	5	4	5	9	13 (12)	12	3	3	3
Ptg./Sp.	31 (30)	40 (37)	39.5	4	5 (4)	5	4	4	4
Other languages	6 (5)	4	6	2	3	3	2	2	2
Dubious	11 (9)	5	9	11 (8)	8	10	9 (6)	3	7
	100	79	100%	100	79	100%	63	35	54%

NOTE: Figures in parentheses indicate number of *distinct* forms attributed to a particular ancestry, excluding repeated forms.

But this explanation ignores the fact that the same people's presence in Jamaica has left no such mark on the local creole, and it accounts for the Saramacca-Sranan divergence by what seems to be no more than a myth: that it was the slaves of these Jews who suffered the greatest ill-treatment and therefore they who constituted the bulk of the fugitives.

A more plausible hypothesis, and one that would also account for the greater proportion of African words in Saramaccan than in Sranan, is that proposed by Melville J. Herskovits in 1931, and by others since then, which seeks to explain this divergence as due to a preponderance among those who fled to the bush of African-born slaves. Their long detention in West Coast factories and passage to America had familiarized them with the Afro-Portuguese pidgin, henceforth the readiest means of communication between those whose native African languages were not mutually intelligible. Understandably, this pidgin would have come under heavy pressure from the speech of masters and missionaries, to whom it was quite incomprehensible, and would have been best preserved by the descendants of those who won their freedom a hundred and fifty years or more before the abolition of slavery.

In Curaçao there was no such opportunity for escape as existed in Surinam; but here, owing to the exertions of missionaries from the adjacent mainland, the principal external influence came to be that of Spanish—a language so closely related to Portuguese that its native speakers could have found little difficulty in learning to understand the pidgin and in contributing to the reshaping of many of its words. This circumstance could explain why Papiamentu still contains a greater proportion of clearly Portuguese elements than does Sranan, though fewer than does Saramaccan.

A thorough comparison of these and other West Indian creoles with those now spoken in Africa and the adjacent islands might settle the question as to just what in the former originated in Africa and what was acquired in America. Unfortunately, comparatively little has so far been published on the African creoles; and I dispose only of brief sketches of Portuguese Guinea Creole (Wilson 1962), here abbreviated as PGC, and of Sãotomense (Valkhoff 1966), here abbreviated as ST, both Portuguese-based, the latter spoken on the island of São Tomé in the Gulf of Guinea. To this may be added some as yet unpublished material on Krio, an English-based creole spoken in Sierra Leone (here abbreviated as KR). Something, however, may be gleaned from a comparison of the data contained in this material with those available for Saramaccan.

SARAMACCAN AND PORTUGUESE GUINEA CREOLE

Portuguese Guinea Creole has the same number of segmental vowel phonemes with the same allophones as has Saramaccan: *i, e* ([ɪ], [e]), *è* ([ɛ]), *a, ò* ([ɔ]), *o* ([o]), and *u* ([ʊ]). Vocalic length, distinctive in both these creoles, is shown by sequences of identical vowels (PGC *túudu* : SM *túu* 'all'). The acute accent (replaced by the circumflex over lower-mid *è* and *ò*) marks free stress in Portuguese Guinea Creole (as in Sranan), high tone in Saramaccan. Portuguese Guinea Creole has the following consonantal unit phonemes: *p t tj k; b d dj g; m n nj ng; f s; r l; w j*. This differs from Saramaccan in having an *r/l* opposition (modern Saramaccan has *l* but not *r*), and in lacking, like Sranan, the implosive stops *kp* and *gb*, the aspirate *h*, the oppositions of *f/v*, of *s/z*, and of prenasalized vs. simple voided stops (*mb/b, nd/d, ndj/dj,* and *ng/g*). The presence or absence of these latter oppositions may be a question of analysis, however; for Portuguese Guinea Creole has at least the phonetic counterpart of prenasalized voiced stops (i.e., as consonant clusters instead of unit phonemes), as in *mbõ!* 'good!', *nturúdja* 'deceive', *ndjêènja* 'try', *nggáaba* 'praise' (/ng/ of this language being a simple velar nasal occurring, for example, in *ngônki* 'be crooked').[1]

Under "Phonetic irregularities in derivation from Portuguese", Wilson lists "infixed -*n*- following unstressed initial *mV*- or *nV*-," as in *minjôòr* (Ptg. *melhor*) 'better', *mantjáadu* (Ptg. *machado*) 'ax'. Similarly in

---

[1] In order to facilitate comparison with Saramaccan I have made certain substitutions for the symbols employed by Wilson: *è* for his *ɛ*, *ò* for his *ɔ*, *tj* for his *c* [č], *dj* for his *j* [ǧ], *nj* for his *ny*, *ng* for his *ŋ*, and *j* for his *y*. For the same reason I have made similar changes in the spelling of other Portuguese and English creoles cited here insofar as this was found to be possible without invalidating whatever phonematic bases such orthographies may have. But *ɛ* and *ɔ* had to be retained for Papiamentu, in which the circumflex accent is employed to indicate a distinctively falling tone, as in *bêbe* 'drink' and *kôme* 'eat', and stressed half open vowels are shown as in *pêntji* 'claw' and *kóra* 'red'. The spelling of all French creoles cited here has been adapted to that which I employ for Dominican Creole. Each of the basic wordlists given in Chapter 12 is followed by a phoneme inventory insofar as this is known.

Saramaccan we find such forms as *mandú* (Ptg. *maduro*) 'ripe', *miindjá* (Ptg. *mijar*) 'piss', *munjá* (Ptg. *molhar*) 'to wet, moisten'. And also in other positions, an intrusive nasal element occurs in some words of both these creoles, as in PGC *ánsa* : SM *hánza* (Ptg. *asa*) 'wing', where it is unlikely, despite Lat. *ansa*, to be etymological (cf. also SM *súndju* 'dirty' with Ptg. *sujo*) and although -*nC*- of Saramaccan, which has no consonant clusters, here indicates only nasalization of the preceding vowel. This feature is found in yet other creole languages; thus, SN *míndri* < Eng. *middle*, *njun* < Eng. *new;* ST *munjá* < Ptg. *molhar*, *nãsé* < Ptg. *nascer;* PP *nanísji* < Ptg. *nariz*, *nẽnga* < Ptg. *negar*, *frumínga* < Ptg. *formiga;* JC *sampat* < Ptg. *sapato;* HC and LA *nẽ* < Fr. *nez;* LA *pẽthwi* < Fr. *pétrir*, *sẽcèy* < Fr. *cercueil*, etc.

Another "irregularity," Wilson's "*y-* [here written *j-*] added to verbs with initial 'e' or 'a' in Portuguese," is likewise common to Portuguese Guinea Creole and Saramaccan: PGC *jáasa* : SM *jasá* (Ptg. *assar*) 'roast', SM *jabí* (Ptg. *abrir*) 'open'. (Papiamentu often has *h-* in the same position, as in its *hása* 'wing', *hábri* 'open'.) And analogously, some words otherwise beginning in *ó-* have, in both these creoles, variants in *wó-:* PGC (*w*)*ójtu* (Ptg. *oito*) 'eight', SM (*w*)*óbo* (Ptg. *ovo*) 'egg', (*w*)*ógi* (Eng. *ugly*) 'bad', (*w*)*ójo* (Ptg. *olho*) 'eye', (*w*)*ómi* (Ptg. *homem*) 'man', *w*)*ósu* (Eng. *house*) 'house'. Both these features are also found in other creole languages, although the *j-* or the *w-* often cannot be dropped: PP *jíu* (cf. Sp. *hijo*, Ptg. *filho*) 'son, daughter' and *wówo* (Ptg. *olho*) 'eye'; CC *yeg* (Fr. *aigre*) 'sour' and *wõm* (Fr. *homme*) 'man', *wot* (Fr. *autre*) 'other', *wey* (Fr. *oeil*) 'eye' (but cf. ST *we* with the same meaning; so that both CC and ST forms may possibly stem from some such model as Provencal *uelh* 'eye'); LA *ywit* (Fr. *huit*) 'eight', (*y*)*isj* (cf. Sp. *hijo*) 'son or daughter', and *wõz* (Fr. *onze*) 'eleven', (*w*)*ẽde* (Fr. *aider*) 'help'. I have found prosthetic *j-* (but not *w-*) in four other creoles: SN *jápi* (Du. *aap*) 'monkey', *jépi* (Eng. *help*) 'help', *júru* (Du. *uur*) 'time; hour'; JC and KR *jaj* (Eng. *eye*) 'eye'; and ND *jet* or *jit* (Du. or Eng.) 'eat'.

Corresponding to the hushing sibilants of modern Portuguese (orthographic *ch* and *j* or *g*, formerly affricates), Portuguese Guinea Creole and Saramaccan usually have their affricates *tj* and *dj*, as in PGC *katjúur* (Ptg. *cachorro*) 'dog' and *òrlôòdju* (Ptg. *horlógio*) 'clock or watch', SM *tjúba* (Ptg. *chuva*) 'rain' and *djulá* (Ptg. *jurar*) 'swear'. But in some words we find instead *s* in both these creoles, as in PGC *fúusi* : SM *fusí* (Ptg. *fugir*) 'flee'. And like those Portuguese creoles which have (as PGC has not) an *s/z* opposition, Saramaccan occasionally has its *z* showing this correspondence, as in *zúntu* (Ptg. *junto*) 'together, near' and *zuntá* (Ptg. *juntar*) 'join, bring together', with which compare ST *zúta* (Ptg. *junta*) 'joint; knee'. The reverse process, seen in SM *síndja* (Ptg. *cinza*, ST *šíža*) 'ashes', may well result from dissimilation, which, together with assimilation and metathesis, has produced such Lesser Antillean forms as *sãsiv* (Fr. *gencive*) 'gum', *zizye* (Fr. *gésier*) 'gizzard', *zes* (Fr. *geste*) 'gesture', *siče* (Fr. *chiquer;* the affricate, like that of SM *tjumá* < *tjimá* < Ptg. *queimar* 'burn', resulting from palatalization) 'chew (tobacco)', *sjasfãm* (Fr. *sage-femme*) 'midwife', *sjes* (Fr. *sèche*) 'dry'—although in the case of *zibye* (Fr. *gibier*) 'bird hunted for food or sport' no such factor can be proposed.

Turning from phonetic to semantic similarities, PGC *fála* and SM *fan* 'say' (cf. Ptg. *falar* 'speak, talk') have replaced Ptg. *dizer* 'say'; Portuguese Guinea Creole and Papiamentu alike have *papia* 'speak, talk' (cf. Ptg. *papear* 'chatter'). PGC *matêèrja*, ST *matéja*, SN *mantéri*, and LA *matyê* all mean only 'pus', while SM *mateéa* refers only to 'slime (as left by a snail)', contrasting with Ptg. *matéria* and Fr. *matière*, which refer primarily to 'matter, material, substance'. PGC *pádi*, SM *pa(l)í*, and ND *parí* alike mean not only 'give birth to', as does Ptg. *parir*, but also 'be born' (Ptg. *nascer*) and 'beget' (Ptg. *gerar*): SM *dí óto ómi paí wán wómimíii* 'the other man got a son'. PGC *pilông*, LA and Mauritian Creole (MC) *pilõ* (cf. Ptg. *pilão* and Fr. *pilon* 'pestle') both mean 'mortar' (Ptg. *almofariz*, Fr. *mortier*), 'pestle' being expressed as PGC *pòò de pilông* 'mortar-stick', LA and MC *mãsj pilõ* 'mortar-handle'; and Wilson says that the same thing is true in the creoles of the Cape Verde Islands. PGC *seréenu* and LA *sehwẽ* (cf. Ptg. *sereno* and Fr. *serein* 'evening mist') both mean 'dew' (Ptg. *orvalho*, Fr. *rosée*).

Among words of apparently non-Portuguese ancestry found in this sketch of Portuguese Guinea Creole, the following also occur in other creoles: PGC *búnda* : HC *bũda*, LA *bõda*, all meaning 'backside, buttocks' (cf. Mandinka *buu-daa* 'anus'); PGC *fandáng* : ST *fènené* : SM *fáán* : SN *fan* 'dazzling (white)' (intensifiers employed together with these creoles' words for 'white'); PGC *pupúu* : SN *pupú* : HC and LA *pupu* 'excreta'; PGC *tjóki* 'tap (palm-tree for wine)' (Ptg. *furar*), which seems to be paralleled by SM *tjòkô* : SN *djukú* : LA *coke*, all meaning 'stab, pierce, prod, poke, stick into' (as well as PGC *fúra* : SM *fulá* with much the same meaning).[2] PGC *ka* and BD *-ka* both mean 'not'.

Finally, a few grammatical similarities and differences seem worth mentioning here. PGC *i ta kúuri* and SM *a tá kulé* may both mean 'he runs (repeatedly)', with *ta* of either language then indicating the iterative function. But here the similarity ends, for the *ta*-aspect of Portuguese Guinea Creole also includes the future ('he will run'), and the *ta*-aspect of Saramaccan also includes the progressive ('he is running'), the former function being marked in Saramaccan by *sa* or *ó*, the latter in Portuguese

---

[2] Under "Words of non-Portuguese origin," Wilson cites "*bulbuli* 'flutter about, wave, shake' (equivalent to Ptg. *agitar*)." But this word might well come from a reduplication of Ptg. *bulir* 'stir; move': cf. SM *bulí* 'move; stir', whence SM *bulí-bulí baafu* (lit., "agitated broth"), a name given to the spider!

Guinea Creole by *na*. And here I should like to introduce for purposes of comparison Igbo, a West African language, as well as Sãotomense, Papiamentu, and Krio, which have already been mentioned. So, compare:

For 'he is running':	For 'he is in the house':
Igbo *ɔ na agba*	Igbo *ɔ nɔ na ulo*
PGC *i na kúuri*	PGC *i sta na káasa*
SM *a tá kulé*	SM *a dê na wósu*
PP *e ta kôre*	PP *e ta na kas*
ST *e ska kulé*	ST *e sa na kê*
KR *i de rɔn*	KR *i de na os*

The Igbo, Papiamentu, and (as we have seen) Saramaccan forms for 'he is running' are also employed for the iterative function 'he runs', whereas the others are only progressive. The Sãotomense progressive in *ska* appears to include the iterative *ka* (*e ka kulé* 'he runs'), contracted with the "substantive verb" *sa* (seen in the second column above).

All six of these languages (not to mention a number of other creoles; see the last section of this chapter) have locative *na*, variously translatable, according to context, by 'at, by, from, in, off, on, to' (cf. meaning 'he came from the house': Igbo *o sitɛrɛ na ulo*, PGC *i saj na káasa*, SM *a kumútu na wósu*, etc.). But only Igbo, Portuguese Guinea Creole, and Saramaccan have a special form for 'be (in a place)'—Igbo *nɔ*, PGC *sta*, and SM *dê* (ST *sa* is the same as the copula, for which Saramaccan has *da*, earlier *na*, as in *mi da nêngè* 'I am a Negro')—and only Igbo and Portuguese Guinea Creole agree in employing *na* as an aspect marker. Yet Saramaccan has a compound, *nán-gó*, that is completely concordant with its phrase *tá gó* (the verb meaning 'go' preceded by the aspect marker *tá*); and Voorhoeve (1961*b*, p. 153) has stated as his opinion that this compound is a survival pointing to an earlier, more general use of *nán* as an aspect marker.

It seems clear that PGC *sta* 'be (in a place)' and the PGC aspect marker *ta* are different forms today, whatever their ancestry (cf. not only Ptg. *estar*, *está*, but also Guang *ta* 'stay, be in a place', used to form the iterative, as in *n ta tsa* 'I dance', and Swahili *-ta-*, which forms the future as in *ni-ta-soma* 'I shall read'); while SM *tán* 'stay' and the aspect marker *tá* may well have had a common origin, for both were recorded in 1778 as *tann*. Whether locative *na* and aspectual *na* of Portuguese Guinea Creole and/or of Igbo should be considered as the same or as different morphemes must be left for the Africanist to decide.

The above necessarily sketchy comparison of elements belonging to an Afro-Portuguese creole with others belonging to a West Indian "English" creole reveals several similarities of both form and function (or meaning) that are not attributable to the presumptive model, and therefore tend to support the hypothesis of common origin. Other similarities, of function alone, are usually held to be evidence only for membership in a common convergence area; but this area must then include the West Indies, the Guianas, and much of West Africa.

SARAMACCAN AND SRANAN AGAIN

What seems to be a close relationship between Saramaccan and Sranan shows up not only in the similarity of their grammars and the large proportion of their lexical equivalents which appear to have the same ancestry but also in certain of the latter's "irregularities" or shared deviations from the model. Thus, two such features that we have seen to be common to Portuguese Guinea Creole and Saramaccan—the addition of a palatal semivowel to some words whose models began in a- or e-, and an intrusive nasal element in others (whether by addition or by substitutuion)—occur likewise in Sranan: cf. SM *jéi* : SN *jére* : JC and KR *jèri* 'hear', SM *jési* : SN *jési* 'ear(s)' (and cf. KR *jerín* 'earring'), SM *míndi* : SN *míndri* 'middle', SM *nêngè* : SN *néngre* 'Negro' (Du. *neger*, Eng. *nigger*), SM *kpínji* : SN *kwínsi* 'squeeze', SM *mángu* : SN *mángri* 'thin' (although this last pair may derive from two different models, Ptg. *magro* and Du. *mager*). And similarly, in the case of such semantic deviation as is seen in SM (w)*ógi* : SN *ógri* 'bad', whose presumptive model was Eng. *ugly*. Yet unless these two creoles had separate origins, one or both of them must have undergone "relexification" to an extent that has hitherto been considered impossible in so short a time as has elapsed since the first African slaves were brought to Surinam, in 1651; and it is hard to believe that the less affected by this process should be Sranan, which has long been exposed to much greater external influence than has Saramaccan.

Moreover, the view that many Portuguese-derived words preceded their equivalents of English ancestry in Saramaccan is supported by records showing the gradual disuse of forms like *baíka* (earlier *baríka*; cf. ST *bêga*, Ptg. *barriga*) 'belly', *kòmê* (ST *kumê*, Ptg. *comer*) 'eat', and their replacement by what appear to be loans from Sranan, SM *bêè* and *nján* (SN *bére* and *njan*). SM *bebé* (Ptg. *beber*) and *diíngi* 'drink', though said to be synonymous today, were distinguished by Schumann, who recorded both in 1778, attributing the same general sense to the former as it still has, but restricting the latter, English-derived word to "alles starke Getränke". SM *djái* : SN *djári* 'garden; yard' and SM *djaaí* 'small enclosure in which the women bathe' both go back to Schumann's "*djaralí* 'Garten; alles Umzäumte; Hof am Hause; der Zaun selbst'."

Accentuation of the final vowel of SM *djaaí* < *djaralí* and the initial affricate of both Saramaccan and Sranan forms (contrast SM *jái* : SN *jári* 'yard [measure of length]'), make it clear that the model was Ptg. *jardim* and not Eng. *garden* or *yard*; and it may be doubted whether the creole words' wide reference, though etymologically justified, could have been learned from Sephardim as late as (or later than) the 1660s.

Saramaccan shows evidence not only of lexical replacement but also of what might be called lexical remodeling, by which words of apparently Portuguese ancestry become more like their Sranan equivalents of apparently English ancestry. So, compare Schumann's SM *sindá* (Ptg. *sentar*) > modern SM *sindó* with SN *sidón* (Eng. *sit down*), both meaning 'sit'; SM *tán-a-pê* (Ptg. *estar em pé*) ~ *taámpu* with SN *tanápu* (Eng. *stand up*), both meaning 'stand'; SM *póndri* (Ptg. *podre*) > *póndi* with SN *póri* (Eng. *spoil*), both meaning 'rotten; to rot; spoil(ed), decay(ed)'. The English ancestry of this last Sranan form is far from certain, however, as becomes evident when we compare it with SN *spéri* 'spell', *spíti* 'spit; spittle', *spun* 'spoon'.

Partial adaptation (semantic and/or accentual) of Saramaccan forms in the direction of Sranan and English is seen in SM *nínga* (cf. PP *nênga;* Ptg. *negar*) 'deny; refuse; renounce' (according to Schumann), which has now acquired the same meaning as SM *tínga* 'think; mean'; SM *píndja* (cf. Ptg. *pinchar* 'heave up; leap') 'pinch; nudge' (by confusion with SN *píndji* 'pinch'?); and SM *pusá* (cf. Ptg. *puxar* 'pull, draw') 'shove;-move up' (confusion with SN *púsu* 'push'?). SM *tampá* (cf. Ptg. *tampa*) and SN *tapún*, both 'lid', apparently have been equated, while SM *tapá* (Ptg. *tapar*) and SN *tápu* (Eng. *stop*) have both come to mean 'close, closed; stop'. SM *tjalí* (cf. Fr. et al. *chagrin*) and SN *sári* (cf. Eng. *sorry*), both 'grief', might well end—or have begun—as the "same" word; and in SM *giin* ~ *guún* 'green' we observe a word of apparently English ancestry in process of becoming, by way of free variation and probably influenced by its Sranan equivalent, *grun*, a word of apparently Dutch ancestry! Could it not be that Sranan had led the way in both types of lexical change—replacement and remodeling?[3]

---

[3] In Dominica, LA *espehwe* 'wait; wait for; expect; hope' (cf. Fr. *espérer*) is losing the last of these senses to borrowed *howp*, and is beginning to be replaced by borrowed *espek* in the sense of 'expect'. Moreover, various adaptations of Eng. *because, behave, drop, enjoy, feed, gamble, guess, pants, pliers, print, razor, right, wrong, use* (vb.), and *use* (n.) are gradually ousting their older, French-derived equivalents: *pis* 'puisque' or *pas* 'parce que', *kõpôte kô* 'se comporter', *kite tõbe* 'quitter (laisser) tomber', *apwesye* 'apprécier' or *mize kô* 's'amuser' or *jwi* 'jouir', *nuhwi* 'nourrir', *jwe pu lajã* 'jouer pour de l'argent', *divinē* 'deviner', *cilot* 'culotte', *letenay* 'les tenailles', *ẽpwime* 'imprimer', *hwazwê* 'rasoir' (retained in the restricted sense of 'barber's razor', an instrument widely used for castrating pigs!), *ni hwezõ* 'avoir raison', *ã tô* '(être) en tort', *sêvi* 'servir', and *sêvis* 'service'. And there are many others.

SARAMACCAN AND
PAPIAMENTU

Papiamentu, like Sranan, has long been subject to strong external influence, but in its case the main pressure has been that of a language so closely related to Portuguese that the reshaping of words belonging to an underlying Portuguese pidgin would have been at once easier and less necessary than in the case of Sranan. Today, at any rate, and insofar as the words contained in Swadesh's 100-item list are concerned, one might assign the ancestry of forty-nine to either Spanish or Portuguese (e.g., *grándi* 'big'), that of thirty to Spanish (e.g., *tjikítu* 'small'), thirteen to Portuguese (e.g., *nóbo* 'new'), four to Dutch (e.g., *hópi* 'many'), and regard the remaining four (e.g., *dûna* 'give') as of dubious etymology. But evidence of remodeling is even clearer in Papiamentu than in Saramaccan: PP *harínja* (Ptg. *farinha*, Sp. *harina*) 'flour, meal', *héru* (Ptg. *ferro*, Sp. *hierro*) 'iron', *manjáng* (Ptg. *amanhã*, Sp. *mañana*) 'tomorrow', *palomba* (Ptg. *pomba*, Sp. *paloma*) 'dove, pigeon'. And in some cases it is Dutch rather than Spanish which is ousting the older form: PP *blátji* (Du. *blaadje*) or *fója* (Ptg. *folha*) 'leaf', the former having been first recorded in the sense of 'leaf (of a book)'.

As do Portuguese Guinea Creole and Sranan, so also Papiamentu shares with Saramaccan certain phonological and other deviations from the presumptive model. So, it will be noticed that whereas the final vowels of SM *sándu* 'sand' and *sónu* 'sun' (cf. Eng. *sand, sun;* Du. *zand, zon*) are regular, since all syllables of this language now end in an oral or in a nasal vowel (the latter here transcribed as *-Vn* or *-Vm*), those of PP *sántu* 'sand' and *sólo* 'sun' (cf. Ptg./Sp. *sol*) are anomalous because Papiamentu does have closed syllables, as in *laat* 'late', *ferf* 'paint', *dos* 'two', *tur* 'all', *hel* 'yellow', and *bong* 'good'. Cases like PP *sántu* and *sólo* are therefore best explained as coming from an older stage of the language when its phonology was more like that now found in Saramaccan. And if Papiamentu has four relevant degrees of aperture, as seems to be the case (cf. *kɔrá* 'red' vs. *korasóng* 'heart' and *péntji* 'claw' vs. *djénte* 'tooth' or *hénde* 'person'), it resembles in this respect both Saramaccan and Portuguese as against both Sranan and Spanish.

The /w/ of PP *wébu* 'egg' may be clearly attributable to that of Sp. *huevo;* but not so either /w/ of PP *wówo* 'eye' (Ptg. *olho*, Sp. *ojo*). These are at least plausibly explained as resulting from assimilation following the generalization of a "movable" *w-*, as in SM *(w)ójo* 'eye' (but cf. CC *wey* and ST *wé*, both 'eye').

We have already seen that Papiamentu shares with other creoles the intrusive nasal element (cf. PP *lamáng* 'sea' from Sp./Ptg. *mar*) and the prosthetic palatal semivowel (e.g., PP *jíu* 'son or daughter', with which cf. Ptg. *filho* and Sp. *hijo* 'son'); and if PP *rondó*, SM and SN *lóntu*, both meaning 'round', should derive from Ptg./Sp. *redondo*— as the earlier recorded Saramaccan form *lolóntu* (cf. ST *lõnlõndɔ*) seems to indicate—the similarity of its evolution in these three creoles is remarkable.

SM *túu* and PP *tur* 'all' clearly come from Ptg. *tudo* (/'tudu/) rather than from Sp. *todo* (/'todo/); and likewise, SM *duumí* (earlier *drumí*) and PP *drûmi* 'sleep' (cf., with the same meaning, PGC *dúrmi* and ST *dumíni*) appear to have had Ptg. /dur'mir/ rather than Sp. /dor'mir/ as their model. It therefore seems at least possible that earlier HC *drumi* ("droumi") and *dromi* (> modern *dômi*), earlier Mauritian Creole *durmi* ("dourmi") but modern *dômi*, CC *drõmi*, and LA *dômi* all go back to a Portuguese-derived model. Deviations from the Spanish or Portuguese model common to Papiamentu and Sãotomense are seen in PP *lânda* : ST *lãda* (Sp./Ptg. *nadar*) 'swim', and in the occurrence of hushing sibilants in such forms as PP *sjinísji* (Sp. *ceniza*) : ST *sjĩzja* (Ptg. *cinza*) 'ash' (cf. SM *síndja*), PP *nanísji* (Sp./Ptg. *nariz*) : ST *lisji* 'nose'.

Spanish influence on Saramaccan as well as on Papiamentu is suggested by equivalents such as SM *teéa* (earlier *teréja*) and PP *strea* 'star' (cf. Sp. *estrella*, Ptg. *estrela*), SM *puúma* and PP *plúma* 'feather' (cf. Sp. *pluma*, Ptg. *pena; pluma*), SM *líba* and PP *ríba* 'on top, up, above' (cf. Sp. *arriba*, Ptg. *acima, em cima, arriba, em riba*); but at least one of these forms is echoed in PGC *ríiba* 'on top, up, above' (cf. PGC *ríba* 'to return' and Sp./Ptg. *arribar* 'to put into port; to arrive'), just as Spanish-looking PP *nótji* 'night' (Sp. *noche*, Ptg. *noite*) is echoed in its Sãotomense equivalent, *nótji*.

The choice of Sp./Ptg. *garganta* 'throat' for reference to the 'neck' is shared by Saramaccan (*gangáa*), Papiamentu (*gargánta*), Sãotomense (*glagãtji*), and (with alternatives) Haitian Creole (*gagãn*); while rejection of the usual words for 'tree' (Ptg. *árvore*, Sp. *árbol*, Fr. *arbre*) in favor of those for 'stick' (Ptg. *pau*, Sp. *palo*) or 'stalk' (Fr. *pied*) is all but general in those creoles which have a Romance word for this concept—SM *páu*, PP *pálu*, PGC *pòò*, ST *po*, HC, LA, and CC *pye* (*bwa*), MC *pye* (*dibwa*)— although Mauritian Creole also has *zâb* 'tree', Louisiana Creole has *nab* 'tree', and Lesser Antillean has *zâm* in the restricted sense of 'cultivated fruit tree'. Do PP *adéŋ* : LA and HC *adã* 'inside' have a common source in Ptg./Sp. *adentro*, or was the latter derived directly from Fr. *dedans*?

To make further individual lexical and phonological comparisons of Saramaccan with this or that Dutch-, English-, or French-based creole would serve no useful purpose because these have, in the main, rather homogeneous basic lexicons, whose apparent provenance has been our only criterion for so grouping them. But before passing on to a comparison of some grammatical words and patterns, it may be well to take a more general view of lexical similarities.

SOME COMMON ITEMS IN CREOLE VOCABULARIES

SM *mángu*, SN *mángri*, PP *márga*, JC *máaga*, and ND *mága*, all meaning 'thin (lean)'—wherever each or all may come from—probably owe their wide extension in some degree to the occurrence of similar equivalents in a number of European languages: Du., Ger., and Scand. *mager;* Ital., Ptg., and Sp. *magro, -ra*. And surely there is more than one reason for the persistence and spread of locative *na* and disjunctive *ma* 'but'. Both occur in Saramaccan, Sranan, Papiamentu, Negro Dutch, and Portuguese Guinea Creole; the former also occurs in Lesser Antillean (attested only for St. Lucia), Krio, the three Philippine creoles, and Sãotomense (where it is *na* ~ *ni*). This is in addition to HC *nã* ~ *lã* and CC *la*, which have the same functions, and general LA *ã*, which, though homophonous with Fr. *en*, is functionally identical with *na*, etc., of the other creoles. These reasons seem to be (1) the presence of both *na* and *ma* with the same functions in some West African languages (e.g., Igbo), and (2) these words' formal and functional similarity not only to Ptg. *na* 'in the' (< *em* 'in' .. *a* 'the', feminine form of the definite article) and *mas* 'but'. but also, in some contact situations, to Du. *naar* 'to' and *maar* 'but'. And is it a mere coincidence that ND *lo* 'go' (cf. Y *lò* 'go' and Du. *lopen* 'walk') was employed to form the future in the same way as is PP *lo* (cf. Ptg. *logo* 'then; soon')?

That there should have been some linguistic borrowing among Dutch, English, French, and Spanish creoles spoken in the West Indies is not surprising: cf. LA or HC *kabãn* and ND *kabán* 'bed'; LA or HC *kuhwi* and ND *kurí* 'run'; PP *mâta* and ND *máta* 'kill'; HC, LA, and ND *tete* 'breast; to suckle'; SM, SN, and ND *tutú* 'horn'. But if a Portuguese pidgin or creole was never known and employed there, it is remarkable to find that West Indian Spanish (*not* Spanish Creole) "*pae, pai* 'padre', *mae, mai* 'madre', *compae, compai* 'compadre', *comae, comai* 'comadre', extendidas hoy día en el habla popular de Puerto Rico y de Santo Domingo (sobre todo en las zonas rurales), y también, respecto de *compae, comae*, en el español que aún sobrevive en Trinidad" (Alvarez 1961, p. 184). Ptg. *pai, mãe*, and *compai* are represented also in the West Indian creoles: SM *pái* is the term of reference for DaHu, WiFa, and HuEBr; SM *mái* is the term of reference for WiMo, HuMo, as well as for a man's SoWi and BrDa. SN *paj* is glossed 'old man'. PP *kompáj* as well as LA *pai*, *mãi, kõpai* are employed as affectionate terms of address to adults or children of the appropriate sex, though without any implication of actual alliance (for the co-sponsor and parent-sponsor relationships LA *kõpê* and *makumê* are employed).

Like SM *kambósa* and SN *kabósa* 'co-wife', LA *kõbôs*—employed as a term of reference (rarely of address!) for the relationship between two men who have had intercourse with the same woman, or between two women who have had intercourse with the same man—clearly comes from Ptg. *comboça, comborça* 'concubine of married man; sexual rival'. (The term's semantic evolution in Lesser Antillean, however, may have been influenced by the occurrence of an Island Carib equivalent, *-(u)búiamu*.) SM *kambó*, employed reciprocally for the relationship between an older and a younger woman in general, and more particularly for that between HuMo and SoWi, looks like an abbreviation of *kambósa;* but as this extension of reference may seem unlikely, the term *kambó* may possibly be of African ancestry (or perhaps a derivative of Ptg. *cambóu* 'transferred', which is 3rd sg. past indic, of the obsolete verb *cambar*).

Apparently isolated forms like HC *sãmaye* 'resemble' (Ptg. *semelhar*), LA *sjapote* 'splash (water)' (Sp. *chapotear*), CC *briga* 'fight; quarrel' (Ptg. *brigar*), as well as agreements limited to the Guianas—such as CC, SN, and SM *fiká* 'stay, remain; be' (Ptg. *ficar*)—may be ignored; but among those that are more widespread, the following deserve mention:

HC, CC, PP, SN, and SM *kabá* 'finish'. Cf. Sp./Ptg. *acabar.*
Anobom *káži*, HC and LA *kay*, ST *kè(è)*, all 'house'. Cf. Ptg. *casinha* and Fr. *case*. But word-final /y/ from Fr. /z/ is unusual in HC and LA, though /y/ from Fr. /ž/ is common in this position, as in HC and LA *bagay*, from Fr. *bagage*, and HC and LA *sjay*, from Fr. *charge*. And in ST, /ɛ/ from Ptg. /a(za)/ is unusual, though /ɛ/ from Ptg. /ay/ is common, as in ST *pè*, from Ptg. *pai*, and ST *bè*, from Ptg. *vai* (contrast ST *be* from Ptg. *ver*). I conclude that ST *kè(è)* comes from an earlier ST **kay* (homophonous with the HC and LA equivalents), and that this in turn resulted from a contraction of still earlier **káži* (homophonous with the attested Anobom (AB) form, [káži]), itself a shortening of Ptg. *casinha.* Cf. also ST *sè* : AB *say* 'this', Ptg. *essaqui.*
LC *kẽñ* and northern HC *kin* 'share, portion', corresponding to *pa* (Fr. *part*) in the rest of Haiti. Cf. Ptg. *quinhão* 'share, portion'.
HC *koko* 'female genitalia', LA *koko* '(male or female) genitalia', SM *kôkò* 'scrotum', SN *kóko* 'scrotum; lump (swelling); kernel', Y *kókó* 'lump'. Cf. Ptg. *coco*, to which a number of apparently disparate references have been attached; and contrast LA *kuku* 'small, cup-shaped container'.
HC, LA, and CC *makak* and SM *makáku*, the generic name for 'monkey' —as is Ptg. *macaco*, but not Fr. *macaque.*
LA and CC *mi* 'maize'. Cf. Ptg. *milho* rather than Fr. *maïs.*

HC *sjinta, sinta, sjita,* or *sita* (the forms with /n/—or /ĩ/?—apparently being older), PP *sînta,* SM *sindá* (> *sindó*), LC *asit,* and LA *asid,* all meaning 'sit'. The hushing sibilant in two of the Haitian forms has given rise to a belief that Sp. *sienta* 'sit!' (imperatv.) or 'sits' (3rd sg. pres. indic.) was the model; but it might reflect nothing more than an apical *ś* in Ptg./Sp. *sentar.* HC *sita* might well have come from dialectal, west-of-France *sita* 'assis' (past part.). And similarly, LA *asid* (varying locally with *asiz*), though less likely LC *asit,* could have come from a dialectal French *assid* '(s')asseoir' (infinitv.), or from the remodeling of an Ibero-Romance form. HC *kãpe* 'stand' may originate in a reinterpretation of Fr. *se camper* 'se tenir dans une attitude fière, provocante'; but it seems just as likely to have resulted from the remodeling of an earlier HC **tãpe,* itself derived (like SM *tánapê* 'stand') from Ptg. *estar em pé.* Other examples of remodeling are SN *doro* 'door' from English and SN *doro* 'to arrive' from Twi *dru* 'to arrive'; SN *tapu* 'to close, shut' from English and SN *tapu* 'to cover' from Ptg. *tapar* 'to cover'.

SM *mòfína,* SN *mofína,* and MC *mofin,* all meaning 'unfortunate, unhappy'. Cf. Ptg. *mofino, -a* 'wretched'.

SM *zugúu* (earlier "sukro"), PP *skur,* CC *suku,* PK *skúru* and MC *sikur,* all meaning 'dark'. Cf. Ptg. *escuro;* and compare SM *sikáda* 'stair, ladder', from Ptg. *escada.*

SM *djêndè* (earlier "gendri") and KR *djêntri,* both meaning 'rich'. This word, which appears to come from Eng. *gentry,* has not been found in any other creoles.

CC *wey* and ST *we* 'eye(s)'. I am willing to believe that the former comes from Fr. *oeil* (though if CC *ye* 'they' comes from Fr. *eux,* one might have expected *oeil* to yield **yey*), but not that the latter comes from Ptg. *olho.* And if ST *we* should come from some form of the old Lingua Franca similar to Provençal *uelh* or Mozarabic *welyo,* both 'eye', there seems to be no reason why CC *wey* should not have the same etymology.

PP and CC *so,* PGC *sò,* meaning 'only', appear to derive from Ptg. *só* 'alone; single; only'. But Wilson remarks that PGC *sò,* like KR *djès* (Eng. *just*), "has acquired meanings found in local vernaculars" such as 'only just' and 'nothing but'. Whether this also applies to PP and CC *so* I do not know; but JC and SN *sóso* mean 'nothing but, no one but; for nothing'. And with these forms compare ND *súsu* 'for nothing', LA *soso* 'only; bare(ly); poor(ly)' (contrast AB *sosó* 'alone; only'), SM *sôsò* 'poor(ly); empty'—meanings which do not attach to their presumed models, Eng. *so so* and Du. *zo zo* (cf. LA *mwẽ soso ti-bwẽ mal mêsi* 'I'm only a little bit ill, thank you'). One would like to know more about Y *šošo* 'only', which may or may not include other meanings.

Finally, some words that appear to come from non-Indo-European models, and which occur in two or more creoles belonging to different groups, may be listed here:

SM *akala* : JC *akra* : LA *akhwa* '(kind of) pancake or fritter'. Cf. Y *ðkàrà* with the same meaning.

SM *ambolo* : LA *abôlô* '(sp. of) lizard'.

PGC *bunda* : LA *bõda* 'buttocks' : HC *bũda* (cf. Mandinka *buó-daa* 'anus').

SN *dáda* 'aunt', MC *dada* 'elder brother', and LA *dada* or *da*, term of address to a female member of the family who looks or looked after the speaker as a child (usually an elder sister, but sometimes grandmother, mother, or aunt), appear to reflect Ewe *dàdá* or *dàá* 'elder sister (term of address)'.

JC *djondjo* and HC *djõdjõ* 'mushroom or other fungus or mold', SM *djòdjò* 'old rag or disused object', SN *djódjo* 'ghost, spook', LA *djõdjõ*. This last, Lesser Antillean form refers to an intrinsically worthless object which incites unreasoning fear or attachment in another person (often a child), but it may also refer to a mushroom or fungus or mold (including a kind of skin disease).

SM *dokúnu* 'lump, ball, plug (of anything)', SN *dokún* 'bundle (as of wet clothes); peanut butter; (kind of) sweetmeat', LA *dukun* (and borrowed by the Black Carib of Central America as *dukúnu*) '(kind of locally made) sweetmeat'.

SM, SN, JC, and KR *dóti* 'earth'. Cf. Twi *dòté*, Y *dòtí* 'earth'; but now influenced in the last three creoles by Eng. *dirty*.

SM, SN, and CC *gogó* 'backside, buttocks'. Cf. Fõn *gogo* 'anus'; MC *gogòt* 'penis'.

SM *leletí* and LA (*batõ*) *lele* 'swizzle stick'.

SM *sómbi* and LA *súmbe* 'Calandra palmarum' (a fat, white, edible grub found in fallen or felled palm trees).

SM *tjaká* (and earlier *saká-saka*), SN *saká*, and LA *sjak-sjak*, all 'maraca (rattle)'.

SM *tjakaa* 'dry; unhappy, upset, disturbed', JC *tjakra* 'untidy', and KR *tjakrá* 'troublesome'.

SM *tjòkŏ* : SN *djúku* : LA *čoke*, 'stab; poke'. Cf. PGC *tjòkki* 'tap palm wine'. SM *djòkòtŏ*, SN *djokotó*, CC *djokoti*, all 'to squat'. Cf. Y *djókŏ* 'to sit'.

SM *fónfón*, SN *fonfon*, LA *fõfõ* 'a flogging'. Cf. Y *fɔnfɔn* 'soundly'.

SM *tjólóló*, LA *čôlôlô*, and CC *čaloló* 'watery, thin (said of weak coffee or of liquid food)'.

SM, SN, and JC *únu* 'you, your (pl.)'. Cf. Igbo *unu* 'you, your (pl.)'. With the same meaning (and probably from the same source) as the foregoing are HC *nu* 'you, your (pl.)' (in contradistinction to HC *nu* 'we, us, our', from Fr. *nous*), KR *úna*, and Wes-Kos *wuna*. SM *vunvu* and LA *fufu* 'humming-bird'.

LA *vôkô* 'sp. of black worm' appears to be related to Sango *vɔkɔ* 'black'; but I have not found it in another creole.

Other forms—such as LA and CC *beke* 'white person' (cf. Igbo *bɛkɛ*, which has the same reference); SM *pòtò-pòtò*, SN and JC *poto-póto* 'mud', said to come from Twi—may be confined to only one group of West Indian creoles, but some of the forms cited above probably have a wider distribution than I have been able to ascertain. For example, whatever its ancestry, the last item may be compared with Warao *potopoto* 'soft', *poótsji* 'mud', and AB (*móle*) *potópoto* 'extremely (soft)'.

The facts cited above and the accompanying discussion admittedly prove nothing; but they may perhaps make it seem rather more likely that a considerable number of slaves brought to the New World before the middle of the eighteenth century had, besides their native languages, some other and common means of communication, however rudimentary. In theory, this could have been an African, Portuguese, Spanish, Dutch, English, or French pidgin, or one composed of elements from various African and all five European languages. But apart from obviously recent loanwords, the only lexical items that have a wide distribution among West Indian (and other) creoles of supposedly different origin are those which appear to have an African or a Portuguese ancestry; and we know that the Dutch—and, to a lesser extent, the English and French—slave traders generally employed an Afro-Portuguese pidgin as their "business language." To "panyar," from Ptg. *apanhar* 'to catch', became for a time almost an English verb.

NINE

A GENERAL
GRAMMATICAL SURVEY
OF THE CARIBBEAN
CREOLES

❀

INTERROGATIVE WORDS
AND EXPRESSIONS

Papiamentu and the creoles of Louisiana, Haiti, the Lesser Antilles, and Cayenne all have an interrogative determinant (or adjective) *ki . . .?* 'which . . .?' that cannot clearly be derived either from Ptg./Sp. *que* or from Fr. *quel*. It is employed extensively, as in PP *ki-ko?*, HC and LA *ki sa?* 'what?' (cf. PP *kos* 'thing', HC and LA *sa* 'that; the one'); PP *k'énde?*, HC and LA *ki mun?* 'who?' (cf. PP *hénde*, HC and LA *mun*, both 'person'); PP *ki témpu?* or *ki óra?*, LA *ki tã?* or *ki lê?*, all 'when?' (cf. PP *témpu* and LA *tã* 'time; weather' or relative 'when'; PP *óra* and LA *lê* 'time of day' or relative 'when'). For interrogative 'where?', Papiamentu has *únda?* (cf. ST *ãdji;* both from Ptg. *onde*), as against HC and LA *ki kote?* (*kote* 'place; side') or *o-la?* (*la* 'there') and AB *ke kamá?* (*kamá* 'place'); but in its noninterrogative functions, PP *únda* is commonly replaced by PP *kamína* 'place; where; road', while 'nowhere' is expressed always and only by PP *ninggúng kamína*. Since PP *kamína*, SM *kamía*, and ST *kamjá* (cf. PP *galínja*, SM *ganía*, ST *ganjá*, all 'fowl, hen') all show the same formal and referential differences (i.e., word-final /a/ and the meanings 'place; where') from Sp. *camino* and Ptg. *caminho* 'way, path, road' of the standard languages, it seems plausible to assume that the creole forms derive from the same model—perhaps the verb Ptg. *caminhar*.

Analogous constructions are found in the Portuguese creoles spoken in the Gulf of Guinea on Principe, São Tomé, and Anobom, and in the English creole, Krio, spoken in Sierra Leone. Thus, in Sãotomense, we have *ke kwa?* "what thing?" = 'what?', and *ke nge?* "which person?" = 'who?'. And the semantic pattern of the interrogatives in the Surinam creoles is very similar to that described above for Papiamentu, Haitian, and Lesser Antillean, and to that of such a West African language as Igbo. Compare SM *andí?* and SN *san?* 'what?' (SM *sondí* and SN *sani* 'thing'), SM *ámbè?* and SN *súma* or *o-súma?* 'who?' (SM *sèmbè* or *sòmbè* and SN *súma* 'person'), SM *ún-júu* or *ún-té(n)?* and SN *o-júru* or *o-tén?* 'when?' (SM *júu* and SN *júru* 'time of day' or relative 'when', SM *té(n)* and SN *ten* 'time' or relative 'when'), SM *ún-sê* or *ún-kamía?* and SN *o-pé?* 'where?' (SM *sê* 'side, direction' and *kamía* 'place', SN *prési* 'place' and *pe* 'where'). And likewise in Igbo, interrogative *olεε* is preposed to substantives in order to form the same questions as are listed above: *olεε nkε?* 'what?' (*nkε* 'the one'), *olεε onyε?* 'who(m)?' (*onyε* 'person'), *olεε mgbε?* 'when?' (*mgbε* 'time; when'), *olεε εbε?* 'where?' (*εbε* 'place; where').

TABLE 10. Analogous Interrogative Constructions in Various Creoles

Gloss	LA	PP	ST	SM	SN	KR	Igbo
what?	ki sa?	ki-ko?	ke kwa?	andí?	san?	wé-tin?	olεε nkε?
who?	ki mun?	k'énde?	ke nge?	ambê?	o-súma?	údat?	olεε onyε?
when?	ki lê?	ki óra?	ke ôla?	ún-júu?	o-júru?	us-tèm?	olεε mgbε?
	ki tã?	ki témpu?	ke témpu?	ún-tén?	o-tén?		
where?	ki kote?	(únda?)	(ãdji?)	ún-sê?	o-pé?	us-saj?	olεε εbε?
				ún-kamía			

These creoles are less uniform in their expression of 'why?' and 'how?'. PP *pa ki-ko?* "for what?" = 'why?' may be paralleled by LA *pu ki sa?* with the same meaning, but in the latter creole 'why?' may also be expressed by *puki?* or *puci?* (which recalls Ptg. *porquê* rather than Fr. *pourquoi*), by reinforced *pâs pucí koz?* ('because for which cause?'), or by *sa ki fê . . . ?* 'what makes . . . ?'—this last analogous to JC *wa mek . . . ?*, KR *wé-tin du . . . ?*, and Igbo *gene mεrε?* On the other hand, SM *fu ándí édi?* and SN *fu san éde?* (commonly reduced to *sayde?*) "for what head" = 'why' are analogous to Twi and Ewe equivalents. 'How?' is expressed by PP *kɔng* (cf. Sp./Ptg. *como*), PGC and ST *kumá* (cf. OPtg. and Provençal *coma*), HC and LA *kumã* (cf. Fr. *comment*); but SM *ún-fa?* and SN *o-fási?* "which fashion/manner?" = 'how?' appear to be loan translations from an African model.

PERSONAL PRONOUNS

The personal pronoun pattern of Papiamentu is similar to those found in the Afro-Portuguese creoles like Sãotomense and Portuguese Guinea Creole, though much simpler than the latter. The personal pronouns of these three languages are shown in Table 11, along with those of Palenquero (PQ), an apparently Spanish-based creole spoken in the village of El Palenque de San Basilio in Colombia (see Bickerton and Escalante 1970), and of Anobom Creole (indicated by AB).

TABLE 11. Creole Personal Pronouns: I

		1st sg.	2nd sg.	3rd sg.	1st pl.	2nd pl.	3rd pl.
PP:	sbj.	mi	bo	e	nos	bóso	nang
	obj.			-(l)e			
	gen.			su			
	emp.	ami	abo				
PQ:	sbj.	i	bo	ele	suto	utere	ané
	obj.	mi		e			
	gen.		si	ele			
ST:	sbj.	m ~ n ~ ng	bo	e	nŏ	năse	nĕ
	obj.	mũ, -m		-le ~ -y			
	emp.	ami		ele		inăse	
AB:	sbj.	m-	bo, ati	el	no	namesédi, bútulu	(i)neng
	obj.	mi		li, -l			
	gen.	(di) mu		d'el			
	emp.	amí		el			
PGC	sbj.	ng	bu	i	nò	bòs	è
	obj.	-ng	-u ~ -w	-l	nòs		êlis
	gen.	nja	bò	si	nò	bò, bòs	sè
	emp.	amí, mi	abò, bò	èl	anôs, nòs	abôs, bòs	êlis

NOTE: In the absence of any indication to the contrary, forms employed in objective (obj.), possessive or genitive (gen.), and emphatic (emp.) functions are the same as those given for the subjective (sbj.). PGC *mi, bò, nòs,* and *bòs,* though listed here as emphatic, are the forms employed after a preposition.

Most of these forms may be explained as having arisen from an Ibero-Romance model (*amí* from Sp./Ptg. *a mi; nja* from Ptg. *minha;* etc.); but they are also reminiscent of some African equivalents such as Efik *ámí, mî* and Gã *mi* for first singular; Efik *afo, fò* and Gã *bo* for second singular; Mende *nyá* 'my'; while PP *nang,* PQ *ané,* ST *nĕ,* and AB *(i)neng* for third plural appear to derive from Bantu.

The personal pronouns of the four West Indian French creoles may, for the most part, be assigned to French models; those of Saramaccan, Sranan, and Afro-English Krio, to English models (see Table 12). But

TABLE 12. Creole Personal Pronouns: II

		1st sg.	2nd sg.	3rd sg.	1st pl.	2nd pl.	3rd pl.
LC:	sbj.	mo ~ m	to ~ t	li	nu ~ no ~ n	vu ~ vo	yè
	obj.	mwẽ	twa				
	gen.			so			
HC:		mwẽ ~ m	u ~ w	li ~ l	nu ~ n	nu ~ n	yo ~ -y
LA:	sbj.	mwẽ	u ~ w	i ~ y	nu	zot	yo
	obj.			-li ~ -ni ~ -y			
CC:	sbj.	mo ~ m	to; u	li ~ l	nu ~ n	zot	ye
	gen.			so			
SM:	sbj.	mi	ju ~ i	a	u	únu ~ un	de
	obj.			hên			
SN:	sbj.	mi ~ m	ju ~ i	a	únu ~ un ~ u	únu ~ un ~ u	den
	obj.			en			
ND:	sbj./						
	obj.	mi	ju	am	õs	—(?)	sel
	gen.			sji			
KR:	sbj.	a	ju	i	wi	úna	dèm
	obj.	mi		am			
	emp.			im			

for the second person plural, Haitian, Saramaccan, Sranan, and Krio have forms that appear to be related to Igbo *unu* 'you, your (pl.)'; while those for the first person singular in the same languages could as well be African as European (cf. Igbo *m* and Gã *mi* 'I, me, my').

The similarity in the forms used in Louisiana and in Cayenne, at the extremities of the French-Creole-speaking area, is worth noting—particularly when viewed in conjunction with grammatical similarities which differentiate these two from the intervening creoles: LC and CC *mo tas* 'my cup', *so tas* 'his or her cup', vs. HC and LA *tas mwẽ*, *tas-li* with the same reference.

Such similarities and differences are not confined to the French creoles. So, compare PP *bo rumáng* and PGC *bò irmông* with their Sãotomense equivalent *lumṍ bo* 'thy brother' or 'thy sister' (Ptg. *irmão* 'brother', *irmã* 'sister'). And Palenquero—like Haitian, Lesser Antillean, and the Gulf of Guinea creoles, but unlike Papiamentu, Louisiana, Cayenne, and Portuguese Guinea creoles—postposes the pronominal determinant, as in *mailo mi* 'my husband', *moná si* 'thy child (son or daughter)'. The Lesser Antillean third singular objective forms are employed as follows: -*y* after a vowel (*i fê-y* 'he did it', *pye-y* 'his feet'), -*li* after a consonant or semi-vowel (*yo bat-li* 'they beat him', *tet-li* 'his head', *kay-li* 'her house'), while after /n/ (though not /m/) -*ni* usually replaces -*li* (*u tãn-ni* 'you heard it', *sãn-ni* 'its ashes'). There is no possessive form, and postposition alone distinguishes *determinans* from *determinatum*, so that an expression such as *funet kay papa mwẽ* 'the window(s) of my father's house' is equivalent to "(the) window(s) (of the) house(s) (of the) father (of) me."

SOME PRONOMINAL AND NOMINAL EXPRESSIONS

Table 13, which follows, shows the various forms of the demonstrative and definite determinants in construction with a noun for three dialects of Lesser Antillean and for six other creoles. As in Yoruba and in most of these creoles (to which I might add Louisiana Creole, Palenquero, Sãotomense, and Papia Kristang), the demonstrative is postposed to its referent.

The noun is invariable in all these creoles, singular or plural number being indicated only by context or situation. Thus SM (*w*)*ómi*, HC and LA *nõm*, CC *wõm*, JC and SR *man* may refer to either 'man' or 'men'. But forms meaning 'those men', 'these men', 'the men (in question)' may be distinguished from others meaning 'that man', 'this man', 'the man (in question)' by means which differ considerably from one creole to another (see Table 13). It should be noted that the creole definite articles (LA -*la* ~ -*na* ~ -*a*, varying as do the objective personal pronouns

TABLE 13. Demonstrative and Definite Determinants in Construction with the Noun

Gloss	LA-G*	LA-D*	LA-M*
this man	nõm sila	nõm sa-a, nõm sala, nõm-la sa	nõm ta-a, nõm tala
that man	nõm-la sa	(id.)	(id.)
these men	se nõm sila	se nõm sa-a, etc.	se nõm ta-a, etc.
those men	se nõm-la sa	(id.)	(id.)
the man	nõm-la	nõm-la	nõm-la
the men	se nõm-la	se nõm-la	se nõm-la

Gloss	HC	CC	PP
this man	nõm sa-a	sa wõm-la/a	e hómbər akí
that man	nõm sila-a	(id.)	e hóbər ej/ajá
these men	nõm sa yo	sa wõm ya (< ye + a)	e hómbər nang akí
those men	nõm sila yo	(id.)	e hómbór nang ej/ajá
the man	nõm la	wõm-la/a	e hómbər
the men	nõm(-la) yo	wõm y'a	e hómbər nang

Gloss	JC	SN	SM
this man	dis man(-ya)	a man dísi	dí ómi akí
that man	dat man(-de/yánda)	a man dáti	dí ómi alá
these men	dem man-ya	den man dísi	déé ómi akí
those men	dem man-de/yánda	den man dáti	déé ómi alá
the man	di man	a man	dí ómi
the men	di man dem	den man	déé ómi

* LA-G, LA-D, and LA-M refer to the Guadeloupean, Dominican, and Martinican dialects of Lesser Antillean, respectively.

-li ~ -ni ~ -y described above, HC and CC -la ~ -a, etc.) are employed only to particularize the noun or pronoun that they determine, so that they would not be employed in the creole equivalents of such expressions as Eng. *the sun* and Fr. *de la viande* 'meat' (LA *soley* and *vyãn*).

Here, apart from lexicon, concordance among the French or among the English creoles seems to be no greater than that between them. In all except the three Lesser Antillean dialects listed in Table 13 (which employ a special pluralizer *se;* cf. Fr. *ces*), plurality is indicated by forms having in other contexts the function of third plural personal pronoun (see above, p. 172), although SM *déé* may be regarded as a partial exception since it differs in tone and vocalic length from the personal pronoun of third plural, *de*. Expression of relative proximity ranges from one degree in Dominican (*sa*), Martinican (*ta*), and Cayenne (*sa*) to three degrees in Papiamentu (*akí, ej,* and *ajá*) and possibly in Saramaccan (*akí, dê, alá*). And whereas both Papiamentu and Saramaccan (and also, in part, Jamaican) employ in this function words elsewhere meaning 'here' and 'there' (JC *ya, de, yanda*), the other creoles shown in the table have distinct forms for 'this' and 'that', placed before the substantive in

Cayenne and Jamaican creoles, but after it in Sranan, Haitian, and the Lesser Antillean creoles. (And note that whereas HC *sila* means 'that', LA-G *sila* means 'this'.)

None of these West Indian creoles has simple words equivalent to our possessive pronouns in predicative or elliptical use, such as Eng. *mine*, *thine*, *hers*, Fr. *mien*, *tien*, *sien*, etc. The phrases by which this function is fulfilled differ from one dialect to another, only Guadeloupean and Martinican, among the French creoles, showing complete agreement in this respect, while northern Haiti (HC-N) employs forms different from those current in the rest of the country (see Table 14). So, 'These books are his. Where are mine?' is expressed by LA-D *se liv-la se sa-y. o-la sa mwẽ ye?* and by PP *e búki nang akí ta di dje. únda di mi nang ta?* And likewise, 'that book is mine' is expressed by SN *a búku dáti (n)a fu mi*, JC *dat buk a fi mi*, and KR *da buk na mi yown*, in which *de* 'there' might well be inserted after the word for 'book' in Jamaican Creole and in Krio, though not in Sranan. (Notice that the demonstrative is placed after the substantive it determines in Sranan as in Haitian Creole and Lesser Antillean, but before it in Jamaican Creole, Krio, and Cayenne Creole.)

TABLE 14.   The (Pronominal) Possessive Absolute

	1st sg.	2nd sg.	3rd sg.	1st pl.	2nd pl.	3rd pl.
LC	mo kẽñ	to kẽñ	so kẽñ	no kẽñ	vo kẽñ	yè kẽñ
HC-N	kin-a-m	kin-a-w	kin-a-l	kin-a-n	kin-a-n	kin-a-yo
HC	pa-m	pa-w	pa-l	pa-n	pa-n	pa yo
LA-G/M	ta mwẽ	ta-w	ta-y	ta nu	ta zot	ta yo
LA-D	sa mwẽ	sa-w	sa-y	sa nu	sa zot	sa yo
CC	mo pa	to pa	so pa	nu pa	zot pa	ye pa
PP	di mi	di bo	di dje	di nos	di bóso	di nang
ST	di mũ	di bo	dj'e	di nõ	di nãse	di nẽ
SM	fu mi	fu jú	fu hên	fu u	fu únu	fu de
SN	fu mi	fu ju	fu en	fu únu	fu únu	fu den
JC	fi mi	fi ju	fi im	fi wi	fi únu	fi dèm
KR	mi yown	ju yown	im yown	wi yown	úna yown	dèm yown

Jamaican seems to be exceptional in employing the forms listed above, for greater emphasis, also before a noun, as in *dat a fi-mi buk* (as well as *dat a mi buk*) 'that is *my* book'.

CREOLE AND THE ROMANCE VERBS

To distinguish a class of creole verbs from other predicative words and expressions would be difficult and, I think, artificial. This will appear more clearly in the following sections of this chapter; and here it will suffice to compare, for example, LA *i sav sa* 'he knows that' or *i ĕmme mwĕ* 'he likes me' (cf. the French verbs *savoir* and *aimer*) with LA *i pê mwĕ* 'he's afraid of me' or *i swef dlo* 'he's thirsty' (cf. Fr. *peur* and *soif*, which are nouns), *i las mwĕ* 'he's tired of me' (cf. Fr. *las*, an adjective) *i la* 'he's there' (cf. Fr. *là*, an adverb), and *i ã jâdĕ* 'he's in the garden' (cf. Fr. *en*, a preposition, and *jardin*, a noun). Now while the adverbial expression *ã jâdĕ* is clearly predicative in this context, neither of its components (*ã*, *jâdĕ*), taken separately, ever is—a fact that makes it impossible for us to find any "verb" in this construction. And if the expression *ã jâdĕ* cannot be called a verb, why should *la* '(be) there', which may likewise have a purely adverbial function (*mwĕ jwĕn-li la* 'I met him there', *mwĕ jwĕn-li ã jâdĕ* 'I met him in the garden)? Nor can predicative constructions in *la* be formerly distinguished from those in *las, swef, pê*, or the latter from those in *ĕmme* or in *sav*, etc. Nevertheless, a great many (probably most) creole "predicatives" derive from verbal models; and it may be of interest to inquire what parts of the Romance verb contributed to this end.

Apparently, it was the infinitive of the Romance verb that served most commonly as model for the creoles: SM *buá*, PP *bûla*, LA *vole* (Ptg. *voar*, Sp. *volar*, Fr. *voler*) 'fly'; SM *bebé*, PP *bêbe*, LA *bwê* (Ptg./Sp. *beber*, Fr. *boire*) 'drink'; SM *duumí* (< *drumí*), PP *drúmi*, LA *dômi* (Ptg./Sp./Fr. *dormir*) 'sleep'; LA *kõpwãn* (Fr. *comprendre*) 'understand'; LA *(v)wê* (Fr. *voir*) 'see' (and cf. LA *hwisivwê* 'receive' and *avwê* 'obtain; possessions', from Fr. *recevoir* and *avoir*). But in some cases it was the third singular present indicative that served as model: SM *sábi* and PP *sábi* 'know', from Ptg./Sp. *sabe* 'knows' (cf. PP *fálta* 'lack' vs. *fâlta* 'fail', the circumflex in Papiamentu denoting a complex falling tone present in most dissyllabic predicatives); PP *baj* and PGC *baj* (ST *bè*) 'go', from Ptg. *vai* 'goes'; PP *ting* and PGC *tèng* 'have', from Ptg. *tem* 'has' (whence come PP *téne* and PGC *tènè*, which also mean 'have', is not clear); LA *bay* 'give', *dwe* 'owe', *pwã* 'take', *sãm* 'seem', etc., from Fr. *baille* 'gives', *doit* 'owes', *prend* 'takes', *semble* 'seems', etc. And some French creole predicatives derive from the French past participle: LA *cwit* 'to cook', *mô* 'to die' (as well as 'dead'), *sufê* 'to suffer', *uvê* 'to open' or 'to be open', *pwi* 'to light or kindle' (contrast *mwĕ pwi lãp-la* 'I lit the lamp', but *mwĕ pwã lãp-la* 'I took the lamp'), from Fr. *cuit* '(have/be) cooked', *mort* '(have) died; (b) dead', *souffert* '(have) suffered', *ouvert* '(have) opened; (be) open', *pris* '(have) taken'.

Exceptionally, a few creole predicatives that appear to derive from French verbs seem to conform to none of these patterns: CC *save* and LA *sav* 'know', CC and HC *tãde* 'hear' (LA *tãn* 'hear' is derived regularly from the infinitive, Fr. *entendre*), HC and LA *mete* 'put' (contrast *met-ba* 'give birth' and *pwomet* 'promise' of the same creoles), HC and LA *môde* 'bite' (but *môd* 'take the bait', derived regularly from the French infinitive *mordre*). There are three possible explanations for these apparent exceptions: anomalous derivation from another person or number of the French present indicative (*savez, savent,* etc.), analogical leveling of the French infinitive (cf., in French itself, *puir* > *puer* 'stink' and *tistre* > *tisser* 'weave'), or derivation either from the infinitive or from the third singular present indicative of an Ibero-Romance verb: *saber* or—more probably in view of LA *sav—sabe,* Ptg. *entende(r)* (cf. AB *tendé,* ST *tĕde,* and PP *tênde,* all 'hear'), *mete(r), morde(r).* We have already seen that remodeling may affect form or meaning or both (cf. LA *mate* 'upset, overturn, turn over', which probably goes back to Ptg./Sp. *matar* 'kill; quench'; and Ptg./Sp. *entender,* which now means 'understand; know; perceive', once meant 'hear').[1]

SM *sá,* PP *sa,* and LA *sa* 'can, be able to, may' are usually taken to be allomorphs (variants) of the same creoles' *sábi, sábi,* and *sav* 'know'. But whatever their origin, the two forms must be considered as different morphemes today, since either may occur in all three creoles with different reference in the same context: LA *mwĕ pa sa* (*pwi lãp-la*) 'I can't (light this lamp)', but *mwĕ pa sav* (*pwi lãp-la*) 'I don't know (the price of this lamp)', with the first *pwi* 'kindle' derived from the French past participle *pris,* and the second *pwi* derived from the French noun *prix* 'price'. And in Haitian Creole, in which 'know' is always *kõnĕ* and *save* means 'wise', *sa* is employed for 'can, be able to, may'. It therefore seems possible that

---

[1] Penultimate stress in Portuguese Guinea Creole verbs might suggest that here the third singular of the Portuguese present indicative had provided the usual model. Wilson believes this feature to be an innovation, however, because "when an object pronoun is suffixed this stress is shifted to the last syllable, with lengthening of the final vowel": so, PGC *i kúnsi kil ôòmi* (Ptg. *conhéce aquele homem*) 'he knows that man', but *i kunsíi-l* (Ptg. *conhéce-o*) 'he knows him'. Cf. also Cape Verde and São Tomé creoles, in which the unstressed vowel of the model is often lost, as in CV and ST *fla* vs. PGC *fála ~ faláa-* 'say', from Ptg. *falar* 'speak, talk'.

Problems are raised by a few other Lesser Antillean verbs; e.g., *ni* or *tini* 'have'. (LA *avwê* 'avoir' occurs in very few contexts: in *fê avwê,* lit., "make have" = 'procure, get', and as a noun meaning 'wealth; possessions'.) The shorter form, which is employed from Trinidad to Dominica, recalls Y *ni* 'have'; but Guadeloupe has *tini,* which may formerly have been current elsewhere, and points to a Romance model. Perhaps the most likely is Fr. *tenir,* except that it does not mean 'have'! Neither *avwê* nor (*ti*)*ni* can be employed as an auxiliary verb. One would also like to know whence came PP *téne* and PGC *tênè,* employed as free variants of PP *ting* and PGC *tèng,* which they regularly replace before pronouns. LC and LA *cĕn* 'hold', LA *cêbe* together with LC and MC *côbo* 'take hold; seize; capture', are also puzzling, because the palatal affricate of Louisianan and of Lesser Antillean creoles usually results from /k/ (but not /t/) plus front vowel of the model—[lačɛt] < Fr. *la quête,* but [tɛt] < Fr. *tête* and [tjɛd] < Fr. *tiède*—although there are a very few counter examples like [kite] < Fr. *quitter* and [čчe] < Fr. *tuer.* So that *cĕn* 'hold' suggests some such model as **kendre,* or perhaps **tiendre,* the former to be sought possibly under Lat. *cingere.*

sa of these creoles should derive from a model other than that or those which gave *sábi, sav*, etc. 'know'. But if they should have arisen from the splitting of one morpheme, then it is legitimate to regard this as a shared innovation and as another argument in favor of common origin.[2]

THE PREDICATIVE SYSTEMS

The most striking characteristic of those creole languages with which I have any acquaintance, either at first hand or from published descriptions, is the lack of congruity between basic lexicon and basic grammar: the former clearly derives, in most cases, from this or that European language; the latter shows a remarkable analogy to what we find in such West African languages as Twi, Ewe, Igbo, Yoruba, and Efik, but little resemblance to the presumed "parent." And this divorce is further accentuated by the fact that whereas the basic lexicons of, say, two French creoles may be almost identical, their basic grammars may differ from one another more than does either from that of some English creole.

Thus, in their predicative systems, Lesser Antillean and Haitian creoles with French-derived lexicons, and Sranan and Jamaican creoles with English-derived lexicons, all show a fundamental dichotomy between two grammatical aspects, the one marked by preposed or prefixed LA *ka*, HC *ap-*, SN *e-*, JC *a-* or *de-*, or by allomorphs of these forms, the other negatively indicated by the absence of these markers. But the values of the two aspects differ—not, as might be expected, between the French and the English creoles, but between Lesser Antillean and Sranan on the one hand and Haitian Creole and Jamaican Creole on the other.

In Lesser Antillean and Sranan alike, the presence of the aspect marker indicates incompletion of the event or state predicated, which is regarded

---

[2] Both Saramaccan and Sranan have a modal marker *sa-*, most often indicating future tense. In the former creole, this is distinguished from *sá* 'can, be able to, may' by its low tone and by the fact that it cannot occur after a negation, as *sá* may. But Sranan shows no such distinction: cf. *m sa-tak nang a bákra* 'I shall talk with the white man' vs. *mi tak nang a bákra* 'I talked with the white man', and *i sa go taig a man dáti!?* 'you could go tell the man that!?' (expressing incredulity and/or indignation) vs. *i go taig a man dáti?* 'did you go tell the man that?' (as a simple request for information). Or again, *lúku na mófo na óro, éfu ju no sa-sí Konkóni* 'look in the mouth of the hole whether you can't see Konkoni'. Here, despite differences in translation, we can hardly speak of homonymy (rather than identity) unless and until a context can be found in which *sa* with the sense of 'can, be able to, may' is clearly *not* the modal prefix. But comparison with the other creoles mentioned in the text makes it likely that Sranan once had (and possibly still has) a form *sa* indicating potentiality, identifiable neither with its modal prefix *sa-* nor with its *sábi* 'know'.

either as recurrent (iterative) or as in process of achievement (progressive) according to context or situation:

LA	SN	Gloss
i ka fê-y	a e-du en	he does it; he is doing it
i ka sav	a e-sábi	he knows (recurrently); he gets/is getting to know
i ka las	a e-wéri	he gets tired; he is getting tired

Without it, these utterances would indicate completion of the event or state predicated: LA *i fê-y* and SN *a du en* 'he has done it' or 'he did it', LA *i sav* and SN *a sábi* 'he knows (now)' or 'he has known (it for ages)' (but *not* 'he knew', which is past completive LA *i te sav* and SN *a ben-sábi*), LA *i las* and SN *a wéri* 'he is tired'.

But in Haitian Creole and Jamaican Creole alike, the presence of the aspect marker indicates only that the event or state predicated has yet to be achieved:

HC	JC	Gloss
l'ap-fê-l	im a-du i	he's doing it; he's about to do it; he'll do it
l'ap-kõnẽ	—	he's getting/going to know; he'll know
l'ap-buke	—	he's getting/going to be tired; he'll be tired

(Jamaican Creole forms corresponding to the last two examples are not attested in the data available to me, and perhaps do not occur.) Without the aspect marker, these utterances indicate either recurrent or completed achievement of the event or state predicated: HC *li fé-l* and JC *in du i* 'he does it (recurrently)' or 'he has done it' or 'he did it', HC *li kõnẽ* 'he knows (now or recurrently)', *li buke* 'he is tired' or 'he gets tired'.

It is important to notice that the difference between the values of these two categories, in Lesser Antillean and Sranan as in Haitian Creole and Jamaican Creole, is one of aspect, not tense. Thus, the unmarked aspect of one of these creoles may correspond either to a past or to a present tense of French and English, or to both: LA *mwẽ mãje* 'j'ai mangé', but *mwẽ sav* 'je sais', and JC *mi njam kisáada* 'I eat cassava (recurrently)' or 'I ate/have eaten cassava'. On the other hand, French and English alike must depend on context or resort to paraphrase in order to express some concepts that are contained in the marked aspects of these creoles: cf., above, LA *i ka sav*, SN *a e-sábi*, HC *l'ap-kõnẽ*. One of the greatest difficulties encountered by the native creole speaker in learning a Western European language is caused by the incompatibility of the creole aspects with the tenses of English, French, etc. For he finds it hard to attach the same importance to the temporal difference between, let us say, Eng. *I know* and *I've eaten* as to the aspectual difference between "completive" *I know (now)* and "incompletive" *I know (sometimes)*—the former expressed by LA *mwẽ sav* and SN *mi sábi*, the latter by LA *mwẽ ka sav* and SN *mi e-sábi*—or, in the case of the other two creoles under consideration, to that between "achieved" *je le fais* (*de temps en temps*) and "unachieved" *je le fais (en ce moment)*—the former expressed by HC *mwẽ fê-l* and JC *mi du i*, the latter by HC *m'ap-fê-l* and JC *mi a-du i*.

The marked aspects of these creoles always have the same values, irrespective of context: incompletion in Lesser Antillean and Sranan, nonachievement in the Haitian and Jamaican creoles. So, in subordinate clauses, LA *gade se mun ki ka fê-y* 'look at those people who are doing it' or *mwẽ tãn i ka fê-y* 'I've heard that he does it' (contrast LA *mwẽ tãn-ni ka fê-y* 'I heard him doing it'), and HC *u kwê l'ape-muri?* 'you think that he's dying?' or *di-m lô l'ap-vini* 'tell me when he is to come'. But their unmarked aspects do not necessarily indicate completion or achievement when they occur in other than independent or principal clauses: LA *mwẽ le u fê-y* and HC *m'vle u fê-l* 'I want you to do it', LA *si u fê-y, . . .* and HC *si u fê-l, . . .* 'if you do it, . . .', LA *mwẽ pa te la lê u fê-y* 'I wasn't there when you did it' and *mwẽ pa ke la lê u fê-y* 'I shan't be there when you do it', HC *lô l'sjita m'wê yo* 'when he sat down, I saw them' and *lô l'sjita m'a-wê yo* 'when he sits down, I'll see them'. And the same is true in the cases of Sranan (which agrees with Lesser Antillean) and Jamaican Creole (which agrees with Haitian Creole).

It therefore seems more logical that the marked aspects should have positive labels, their unmarked counterparts negative labels; and I propose to employ the terms *continuative* and *noncontinuative* (instead of *incompletive* and *completive*) in the case of Lesser Antillean and Sranan, *pursuant* and *nonpursuant* (instead of *unachieved* and *achieved*) in that of Haitian Creole and Jamaican Creole. Most if not all the other West Indian creoles appear to have grammatical aspects that conform rather closely to one or the other of these patterns: Cayenne Creole, Saramaccan, and Papiamentu (aspect markers *ka*, *tá*, and *ta*) to the former; Louisiana Creole (aspect-marker *ape*) to the latter (although here complications arise from the fact that many predicative words occur in two forms).

Predicates in either aspect may be put in the past tense by the addition, before the aspect marker where this is present, of LA *te;* HC *te* or *t';* SN *ben, be,* or *b';* JC *ben*. Thus LA *i te ka fê-y* and SN *a b'e du en* 'he did it (recurrently)', 'he used to do it', or 'he was doing it'; LA *i te fê-y* and SN *a ben du en* 'he had done it'; LA *i te ka sav* and SN *a b'e sábi* 'he knew (recurrently)' or 'he was getting to know'; LA *i te sav* and SN *a ben sábi* 'he knew (then)' or 'he had known'; LA *i te ka las* and SN *a ben-e-wéri* 'he got tired (recurrently)' or 'he was getting tired'; LA *i te las* and SN *a ben-wéri* 'he was tired'; HC *li t'ap-fê-l* and JC *im ben-a-du i* 'he was doing it' or 'he was about to do it'; HC *li te-fê-l* and JC *im ben-du i* 'he did it (recurrently)' or 'he had done it'; HC *li t'ap-kõnẽ* 'he was getting to know' or 'he was going to know'; HC *li te kõnẽ* 'he knew (then or recurrently)'; HC *li t'ap-buke* 'he was getting tired' or 'he was going to be tired'; HC *li te buke* 'he was tired' or 'he got tired (recurrently)'.

In Lesser Antillean, Sranan, and Haitian Creole, predicates in either aspect and in either tense may be put in what I shall call the *prospective* mood by preposing, after the tense marker and before the aspect marker when either is present, LA *ke-*, SN *sa-*, HC *ava-* ~ *av-* ~ *va-* ~ *a-*. Past tense forms so obtained usually have the value of a conditional or an optative, non-past tense forms, that of a future tense. Jamaican *wi-*, which does not combine with *ben-*, may be regarded as a marker of future tense. So, with LA and HC *mãje*, SN and JC *njam*, both meaning 'eat', we have:

	LA	HC	SN	JC
1.	mwẽ mãje	m'mãje	mi njam	mi njam
2.	mwẽ te mãje	m'te mãje	mi ben-njam	mi ben-njam
3.	mwẽ ka mãje	m'ap-mãje	mi e-njam	mi a-njam
4.	mwẽ te ka mãje	m't'ap-mãje	mi ben-e-njam	mi ben-a-njam
5.	mwẽ ke mãje	m'a-mãje	mi sa-njam	mi wi-njam
6.	mwẽ te ke mãje	m't'a-mãje	mi ben-sa-njam	(mi wuda njam)
7.	mwẽ ke ka mãje	m'av-ap-mãje	mi sa-e-njam	mi wi-a-njam
8.	mwẽ te ke ka mãje	m't'av-ap-mãje	mi ben-sa-e-njam	mi wud ben a njam

In the above list of creole forms, Haitian has been placed next to Lesser Antillean, and Jamaican next to Sranan, the better to show similarities of shape; but functionally, Lesser Antillean belongs with Sranan, and Haitian Creole with Jamaican Creole. Thus, if the creole forms as numbered above from 1 to 8 are matched with the lettered English translations given below, we find the following agreements and differences:

	1	*2*	*3*	*4*	*5*	*6*	*7*	*8*
All four languages	b, c	d	h	i	e	f, g	j	k
LA and SN			aa	bb			ee	ff
HC and JC	aa	bb			ee	ff		

The English (or other) translation of these forms, of course, depends to some extent on context but may usually be given by one of the following: (*aa*) 'I eat (twice a day)', (*b*) 'I ate (an apple yesterday)', (*bb*) 'I ate (whenever I was hungry)', (*c*) 'I've eaten (it already)', (*d*) 'I had eaten (before he came)', (*e*) 'I shall/will eat (there tomorrow)', (*ee*) 'I shall/will eat (there throughout the holidays)', (*f*) 'I should eat (it if I were hungry)', or 'I would (like to) eat', (*ff*) 'I should eat (it all the time if I could get it)', (*g*) 'I should have eaten (had I been well)', (*h*) 'I am eating', (*i*) 'I was eating', (*j*) 'I shall be eating', (*k*) 'I should be eating'.

Forms and translations expressing a concept by lexical paraphrase rather than by a particular grammatical category have been avoided insofar as possible. So, 'I shall have eaten' may be expressed by LA *mwẽ ke ja fini mãje* (more lit., "I shall be already finished eat"), but 'I shall have known him ten years' only by LA *sa ke fê dizã depi mwẽ kõnet-li* (more lit., "that will make ten years since I know him"). And similarly, the translation given above under *bb* might be paraphrased as

'I used to eat'; though LA *hwamã i te ka mãti* 'he rarely lied', which is in the same category, could hardly be rendered by the habitual 'he rarely used to lie'!

When we compare the translations of LA *mwẽ sav* or SN *mi sábi* 'I know', LA *mwẽ mãje* or SN *mi njam* 'I ate; I have eaten', and LA *mwẽ te sav* or SN *mi ben-sábi* 'I knew', LA *mwẽ te mãje* or SN *mi ben-njam* 'I had eaten', we are apt to accuse these creoles of ignoring or confusing temporal relationships. But a native speaker of either might with as much justification accuse English and French of ignoring or confusing aspectual relationships. For whereas the present no less than the past indicative of English verbs like *believe, have, know, love*, etc., may be completive or incompletive in an independent or predicative syntagm, the present indicative of others like *come, eat, give, tell*, etc., is now always incompletive (and therefore rendered by the continuative aspect of these creoles). So, in LA *i kwê tut sa yo di-y* 'he believes everything they told him' and *i mãje tut sa yo ba-y* 'he ate/has eaten everything they gave him', 'he believes' is no less completive (or noncontinuative) than 'he ate' or 'he has eaten'; but in LA *i ka kwê tut sa yo ka di-y* 'he believes everything they tell him' and *i ka mãje tut sa yo ka ba-y* 'he eats everything they give him', 'he believes' is incompletive (or continuative), just as 'he eats' always is in modern English.

A further example may not be superfluous: A person asked to do something might, if momentarily occupied, respond by LA *mwẽ pa ni tã*, SN *mi no ábi ten* 'I haven't time'; since the lack of time is then regarded as of the moment (noncontinuative). But the same person, if asked such a question as "Why don't you come to see us more often?", could give the same excuse only in its continuative form, LA *mwẽ pa ka ni tã*, SN *mi nee* (< *no + e-*) *ábi ten*, since the lack of time is then regarded as extending over a period that includes at least some past and some future—though not necessarily the present occasion.

But English grammar ignores this aspectual distinction, as the grammars of these creoles ignore the temporal distinction between reference to present state and past activity or process when both are seen as noncontinuative, LA *i kwê* and *i mãje* both being treated as present—or better, as nonpast tense—and temporally opposed to *i te kwê* 'he believed' and *i te mãje* 'he had eaten', which are noncontinuative past tense.

From the point of view of aspect, Eng. *I know* (*now*), which we might label (*a*) in the foregoing tabulation, corresponds to (*b*) *I once ate* or (*c*) *I have eaten*, rather than to (*aa*) *I eat* (*frequently*); and Eng. *I knew* (*then*), which we might label (*bbb*), corresponds to (*d*) *I had eaten* rather than to (*b*) *I once ate* or to (*bb*) *I ate* (*frequently*). And the same is true of Fr. *je sais* vs. *je mange, je savais* vs. *je mangeais*, etc. As for the progressive sense of such creole forms as continuative LA *mwẽ ka sav* and SN *mi e-sábi*, or pursuant HC *m'ap-kõnẽ*, these can be expressed only by paraphrase in either French or in English: *je suis en train de savoir, I'm getting to know*, and so forth.

Negation in these creoles is expressed by LC, HC, LA, and CC *pa* or *p'*, SN and JC *no* or *n'*, placed after the subject but before all else in the predicate: LA *nu ka mãje hwecẽ le-cek fwa; mẽ nu pa te ke ka mãje-y jamẽ si nu tuju te sa twape dot kalite pwesõ* 'we eat shark sometimes; but we should not ever eat it if we could always get other kinds of fish'; HC *mun k'a mãde padõ yo p'ap-neye-l* 'the person who asks pardon, they will not drown him'; SN *ef óto no ben-de, m ben-sa-e-waka te m n'â fútu móro* 'if there weren't any motorcars, I should be walking until I had no more feet'; JC *mi no kja we im waan du wais in no báda mi* 'I don't care what she does so long as she doesn't bother me'.

It should be observed here that the Haitian modal marker *ava- ~ av- ~ va- ~ a-* is automatically replaced after a negation by the aspectual marker *ap-*, etc. so, HC *y'ava-neye-l* 'they will drown him', but *yo p'ap-neye-l* 'they will not drown him' (or, according to context or situation, 'they are not drowning him'). This does not happen in Lesser Antillean nor, so far as I know, in Sranan; but the same restriction on the use of the Saramaccan modal marker *sa-* (to be distinguished from SM *sá* 'can, be able to, may'; see n. 2 above) has been reported by Voorhoeve (1961*b*, p. 159, n. 19), and occurs in the case of JC *wi-* and in that of CC *wa-* (Saint Quentin 1872, p. 131), though not in the case of modern CC *ke*.

DOUBLE PREDICATION

A construction common to most if not all West Indian creoles is that in which a statement in the usual order (subject + predicate) is preceded by the head of the predicate without any grammatical determinant other than (often though not always) a word meaning 'it is'. So, LA *(se) tõbe mwẽ tõbe; (se) kuhwi mwẽ te ka kuhwi; (se) las u las;* and *(se) sot i sot* may be translated literally as "(it's) fall I fell;" "(it's) run I was running;" "(it's) tired you're tired;" and "(it's) stupid he's stupid." The prominence thus given to the concept expressed by the predicate may be simply emphatic, but is more often explanatory: 'I *fell*', 'I've *fallen*', or '(what happened is that) I fell'; '(it's because) I was running' or 'I was *running*'; '(it's because) you're tired'; '(it's just that) he's so stupid'. Examples from other creoles are HC *lò m'a hwive se kusje m'a kusje* 'when I arrive I shall go straight to bed' (lit., "it's lie down I shall lie down"), SN *(a) lon mi wáni lon gowé* 'what I want to do is to run away', JC *a kom ju waan kom saida mi* 'it's just that you want to come beside me', PP *ta kôre e ta kôre baj* 'he's running away' (lit., "is run he's running go"; cf. LA *se kuhwi i ka kuhwi ale*, with the same meaning). Nor are similar constructions confined to the West Indies, for we find them also in Krio of Sierra Leone: *na wáka a bin de wáka*, lit., "it's walk I was walking," which likewise may be either emphatic or explanatory. And so naturally do such forms come to the lips of creole speakers that high-school students in the West Indies frequently carry them over into their French or English, as, for example, "C'est tomber que je suis tombé" or "It's fall I fell down," "C'est courir que je courais" or "It's run I was running."

A somewhat similar construction, which I have found attested only for Lesser Antillean and Jamaican creoles, serves to form concessive or oppositive subordinate clauses, as in LA *tut kuhwi mwẽ kuhwi*, (*mwẽ pa te sa jwẽn yo* "(despite) all running (that) I ran" = 'run as I might, (I was not able to overtake them)', and JC *aal di lie dem foul-ya lie*, (*dem no kaal fi set*) "(despite) all laying (that) these fowl lay" = 'however much these hens lay, (they don't stop to sit)'. Here the nominal status of the first occurrence of LA *kuhwi* and of JC *lie* is made evident by the preceding indefinite determinants, LA *tut* and JC *aal* 'all; every', as well as by the definite article *di* 'the' of the latter creole.

CREOLE EXPRESSIONS OF THE VERB "TO BE"

In most creoles, the expression or nonexpression of our verb *to be* depends upon function and context, though Papiamentu appears to be something of an exception in this respect. Compare

SM	PP	Gloss
de tá kulé	nang ta kôre	they are running; they run (recurrently)
de dê na wósu	nang ta na kas	they are at home
mi da hên máti	mi ta su amígu	I am his friend
mi pená	mi ta póbər	I am poor

From these examples we see that whereas SM *tá* (like LA and CC *ka*, LC and HC *ape-*, etc.) is an aspect marker pure and simple, PP *ta* functions also as a "copula" and as the "substantive verb." These latter functions are not expressed in all Saramaccan contexts, but when expressed, they are distinguished: *a da nêngè* 'he is (a) Negro', *a ná nêngè* 'he (is) not (a) Negro', but *a saí dê* 'he is there', *a saí akí* 'he is here', *a ná akí* 'he (is) not here'.

Sranan *de* 'be' serves not only as "substantive verb" (as does SM *dê* in some contexts), but also as "copula"—*mi no de wan témreman* 'I am not a carpenter', besides *pe Srnaman (e-)de j'a moro prisíri* 'where Surinamers (ever) are you have more fun'—although the "pronominal copula," (*n*)*a*, appears to be more common in the former function: *mi brâd a no mi ρa* 'my brother is not my father', *na so a de* 'that's the way it is' (Voorhoeve 1962, p. 37, and 1957, p. 378). And in a footnote (1957, p. 376), Voorhoeve warns: "The prefix *e*- [i.e., the aspect marker] is often confused in the literature on the subject with the independent verb *de* (to be), because in emphatic speech this prefix may assume the form *de*-. In a synchronic description we should take care to keep the prefix *e*- (occasionally *de*-) clearly apart from the verb *de*." Nevertheless, this does not exclude the possibility that SM *dê* and SN *de* 'occupy such a position' were originally one with SM *dê* and SN *de* 'there', as well as with the aspect marker SN (*d*)*e*-. As we have seen in the case of SN *wéri* 'tired; tire', qualities attributed to a subject are treated syntactically as verbs. As Voorhoeve puts it (1957, p. 377): "Hence *siki* can be a noun (meaning: sickness), an adjective (meaning: sick), an intransitive verb (meaning: to be sick or ill), and a transitive verb (meaning: to make ill)."

In Jamaican Creole, according to Bailey, "*de* expresses the location of someone or something, as in: *im de a yaad* 'she is at home', *dem de a di wedn* 'they are at the wedding'. It is often omitted, however, as in *dem outa shap* 'they (are) out at the shop'." JC "*a* is used with predicate-noun constructions, as: *di buk a fi-mi* 'the book is mine', *dat a fi-mi buk* 'that is my book'." It may or may not be significant that both these forms are homophonous with one or another variant of the Jamaican aspect marker, for which, "in some parts of the island one hears not *a*, but *da*, or *de*, or even *di*." And also in Jamaican Creole, qualitative attri-butes of the subject are predicative without any copula (Bailey 1962, pp. 11–17).

In the English creole of Sierra Leone known as Krio (studied by Alleyne in Wilson et al. 1964), "*de* (high tone, stress) is roughly equivalent to Spanish *estar*, i.e. 'to be (positionally)', and is followed as a rule by an adverbial phrase indicating location: *i de na os* 'he is in the house', *i bin de na di tabul* 'it was on the table', *di tjen nò bin de na usaj i kin de* 'the chain wasn't where it usually is'." Krio *de* also occurs, as in *bia de* 'there's beer', with "an elliptical 'in this (that) place' understood", "is omitted in the expression *we* + *NP* 'where is (are) NP?'," and like SM *dê*, SN *de*, and JC *de* is homophonous with the word meaning 'there'. It is also homophonous with the Krio aspect marker *de*, as in *a de waka* 'I'm walking' or *a bin de fat* 'I was getting fat', *a go de waka* 'I'll be walking' or *a go de fat* 'I'll be getting fat', and *a bin go de waka, if* . . . 'I should/ would have been walking, if . . .'. (Without the aspect marker, the fore-going would read *a waka* 'I have walked' or 'I walked' and *a fat* 'I'm fat', *a bin waka* 'I walked [previously]' *a bin fat* 'I was fat', *a go waka* 'I'll walk' and *a go fat* 'I'll be fat', *a bin go waka, if* . . . 'I should/would have walked, if . . .'.). Krio *na*

is the Krio copula and almost always takes a nominal construction after it: *im dadi na djèntri man* 'his father is (a) rich man'. But on the other hand there exists: *dis stori na bòt wan spayda* 'this story is about a spider'. It takes the particle *bin* postposed for Past Tense: *mi dadi na bin titja* 'my father was a teacher'. *Na*, as a copula, always has low tone and inferior stress. It is replaced by *bi* (high tone and stress) when preceded by the particle *go: mi dadi go bi titja* 'my father will be a teacher'. (Wilson et al. 1964, pp. 12–22)

In Lesser Antillean and Haitian creoles, *ye* 'be' is often employed in the sense of 'occupy such a position', and less often in that of 'experience such a condition', or as copula; but it occurs only where an adverbial complement or a predicative noun, pronoun, or adjective *precedes* the subject of an utterance—an order that is usual in some constructions, employed only for the sake of emphasis in others, and impossible in yet others where French and English require the copula.

This order is usual in utterances (whether questions or statements) containing a potentially interrogative word or expression, such as LA *o-la* or *ki kote* 'where', *ki lê* 'when' or 'what time', *kumã* 'how', *ki jã* (lit., "which folk") 'of what place' or 'of what nationality', *ki yõn* 'which one', (*ki*) *sa* 'what'. Thus, *o-la yo ye?* 'where are they?' and *mwẽ pa sav o-la yo ye* 'I don't know where they are', *ki lê i te ye?* 'what time was it?' (cf. *i te ki lê?* 'it was what time?') and *yo pa di mwẽ ki lê i te ye* 'they didn't tell me what time it was', *kumã u ye?* (or *ki nuvel u* 'what news of you?') 'how are you?', *doktê-a mãde u iyê kumã u te ye* 'the doctor asked you yesterday how you were', *mwẽ pa sav ki jã u ye* 'I don't know where you come from', *ki yõn sa te ke ye?* 'which one would that be?' (cf. *sa te ke ki yõn?* 'that would be which one?'), (*ki*) *sa sa ye?* 'what is that?' (cf. *sa se ki sa?* 'that is what?').[3]

It is also common in adverbial clauses introduced by *la* 'there; where' or by *kõ* 'as; like': *i te ka fê fwet la nu te ye* 'it was cold where we were', *kõ nõm-la ye, i pa ke devihwe sẽp* 'the way the man is, he won't come back sober', *malad kõ u ye, u pa ke sa fê thwavay-la* 'sick as you are, you won't be able to do the work'. It also occurs with an adjectival predicate as the second term of a comparison: *pa di mwẽ malad pase sa mwẽ ye* 'don't say that I'm sicker than I am' (lit., "don't day I sick beyond what I am").

In other constructions (including some with *la* or *kõ*) this type of inversion is emphatic: *ã jâdẽ mwẽ te ye* 'in (the) garden I was' vs. usual *mwẽ te ã jâdẽ* 'I was in (the) garden', *se la mwẽ ka ye le-swê* 'it's there (that)

---

[3] Except when uttered in isolation, or when removed for stylistic reasons to the end of a question (more exactly, to a position after the verb or copula), LA *ki sa?* 'what?' is contracted to *ka* in Guadeloupe (cf. AB *ke kua?* "which thing?" = 'what?', contracted to *ka*) and to *sa* in the islands south thereof: LA-G *ka i di u?* = LA-D and LA-M *sa i di u?* 'what did he say to you?', LA-G, LA-D, and LA-M *i di u ki sa?* 'he told you what?', LA-G *ka u tini* = LA-D and LA-M *sa u ni?* (LC *ki sa to gẽ?* HC *ki sa u gẽ?* CC *a ki sa to gẽ?*) 'what have you?' or 'what is the matter with you?'. Cf. also LA-G *ka sa ye?* = LA-D and LA-M *sa sa ye?* (LC and HC *ki sa sa ye?* CC *a ki sa sa?*) 'what is it?' or 'what is that?', but LA-G/D/M *sa se ki sa?* 'that is what?'.

I habitually am of an evening' vs. usual *mwẽ ka la le-swê* 'I go there of an evening' (lit., "I continuative there of an evening"), *se kõ sa u tuju te ye* 'it's like that you always were' vs. *u te tuju kõ sa* 'you were always like that', *(se) sjêpãtye nõm-la ye* '(it's) a carpenter the man is' vs. *nõm-la se sjêpãtye* 'the man is a carpenter'.

But emphasis cannot be given in this way to adjectival predicates, which are constructed with *ye* only as described above (*malad kõ u ye . . .; pa fê mwẽ malad pase sa mwẽ ye;* and analogous constructions), and otherwise behave exactly like verbal predicatives: *u malad* 'you (are) sick', *(se) malad u malad* '(it's) sick you sick' (emphatic or explanatory; see above), *u ka malad* 'you get sick' or 'you are getting sick', *u te ke malad* 'you would be sick', etc., like *u tõbe* 'you fell', *se tõbe u tõbe* 'you *fell*' (emphatic or explanatory), *u ka tõbe* 'you fall' or 'you are falling', *u te ke tõbe* 'you would fall', etc.

We may distinguish two usages of HC and LA *se*, which I shall call the pronominal copula, (1) as in *mwẽ se neg* 'I am (a) Negro', and (2) as in *se mwẽ* 'it's I/me'. The former contains neither more nor less emphasis than its negative counterpart, *mwẽ pa neg* 'I (am) not (a) Negro', though its transform, *neg mwẽ ye* 'Negro I am', does give prominence to the word for 'Negro'. It therefore seems justified to say that here *se* has the function of positive present tense copula. This function overlaps with— but is not equivalent to—that of *ye;* for if *sa se ki yõn?* 'that is which one?' may be regarded as a transform of *ki yõn sa ye?* 'which one is that?' (cf. *u pwã ki yõn?* 'you took which one?' vs. *ki yõn u pwã?* 'which one did you take?'), so also *sa te ke ki yõn?* 'that would be which one?' may be regarded as a transform of *ki yõn sa te ke ye?* 'which one would that be?', although it lacks any substitute for *ye* of the latter form. And whereas LA *se la nu te ye* 'that's where we were' requires both *se* and *ye*, LA *nu te la* 'we were there' allows neither.

On the other hand, in constructions where there is no preceding subject, like LA *se mwẽ* 'it's I/me', *se* does have some pronominal value, as is evident from its possible or necessary replacement by *sa* 'that' in *sa/se a mwẽ* 'it isn't I/me', *sa/se te mwẽ* 'it was I/me', *sa pa te mwẽ* 'it wasn't I/me', *sa pa te ke mwẽ* 'it wouldn't be me', *sa ke mwẽ* 'it will be me', etc. And at least so far as the Dominican dialect is concerned, a comparison of *se mwẽ* 'it's me' with the pronominal expression *sa mwẽ* 'mine' (cf. *se sa mwẽ* 'it's mine', but *sa se mwẽ* and *se mwẽ sa* 'that's me') makes it clear that *se* in this position does not lose its copular function, and that where it is replaced by *sa*, this function is taken over by *pa, te, pa te,* etc.

The same distinction appears to be reflected more clearly in Cayenne Creole, which has, however, neither *se* nor *ye* for our verb *to be*. Insofar as HC and LA *ye* translate our substantive verb, this is expressed by CC *fika* (cf. Ptg. *ficar*): thus, CC *kumã to fika?* = HC and LA *kumã u ye?*

'how are you?'. But as copula, *se* and *ye* of the other French creoles are replaced by CC *a* or *sa* (the latter apparently distinct from the homophonous demonstrative pronoun), as in *ye sa mun ki modi* 'they are bad people' (lit., "they are people who accursed"), *a ki sa sa?* 'what is it/ that?' (lit., "it's what that?"), *ye rakõte sa ba N.*, *ki sa tõtõ di kõpê Fifi* 'they told that to N., who is uncle to (the) co-sponsor of Fifi', *to pa sa* (*w*)*un bõ wõm* 'you are not a good man', *a pa mo* 'it's not me'. In the last example, the negation follows the pronominal copula, which here includes the subject; but in that preceding it, which has *to* 'you' as subject, the pronominal copula follows the negation *pa*, as do all predicative morphemes in this and other creoles. (Whether CC *a* and *sa* are allomorphs, as is sometimes assumed, or distinct morphemes cannot be established from the few texts in this creole that are available to me.) See Fauquenoy 1972, pp. 105–8.

I conclude that HC and LA *se* is a pronominal copula, as I have called it, and not a mere variant of the pronoun *sa* 'that', even though the latter may replace it in some constructions and must do so in others (somewhat as, in English, *any* usually replaces *some* after a negation). That its employment following an independent subject and before a nominal (or pronominal) predicate is obligatory only in the absence of negative, temporal, and modal markers may be explained by the fact that any of these may or does take over its copular function, as in the following Lesser Antillean sentences:

1. u se		you are		
2. u (± se) pa		you are not		
3. u (± se) te	yõ bõ nõm	you were	a good man
4. u pa te		you were not		
5. u (pa) ke		you will (not) be		
6. u (pa) te ke		you would (not) be		

In sentence 1, the presence of *se* is as necessary as is that of *are* in the English translation; in 2 and 3 it is permissible (perhaps only in Dominica) but unnecessary; in sentences 4, 5, and 6 it is excluded— from positive as well as negative forms of the last two.

As for the anomalous ordering of HC and LA *se* before instead of after the negation, which appears to be a direct consequence of its employment as subject + copula (*se mwẽ* 'it's I', etc.), I regard this as a gallicism of no more grammatical significance than have the equally anomalous "plural" and "partitive" forms of the trio LA (*yõ*) *lot* '(one/an-)other', (*de*) *lezot* '(two) others', (*mwẽ pa ni*) *dot* '(I have no) more/others'—to which, nevertheless, we can hardly deny a common bound morpheme, *-ot!*

Table 15 offers an overall view of forms which may be translatable by or with the help of our verb *to be* in nine West Indian and three African

Table 15. Expression of *To Be* in Twelve Creoles

	1	2	3	4	5	6	7
	Past tense marker	Future tense marker	Aspect marker	Copula	Substantive verb	'there'	Locative particle
HC	te	(v)a- ~ av(a)-	∅ ap(e)-	se; ye	ye	la	lã ~ nã
LA	te	ke	ka	se; ye	ye	la	ã; na
CC	te	ke; wa	ka	sa; a	fika	la	la
JC	ben	wi-; go	∅ (d)a-; de	a	de	de	iina
BH	mi	(w)ã	∅ a-	da; na	de	de	na
KR	bin	go	kin de	na; bi	de	de	na
SN	ben	sa-; go	(d)e-	(n)a-; de	de	de	(n)a
SM	bi	sa-; ó (< gó)	tá-	da (< na)	dê; saí	dê; alá	(n)a
PP	tába-; a	lo	ta	ta	ta	ej; ajá	na
PGC	-ba	ta	ta na	i	sta; la	ala	na
ST	ta(va)	ka	ka ska	sa	sa	la	na ~ ni
ND	ka; ha	lo	lo; le	bi (?)	bi (?)	da	na

creoles. *Very roughly* (exact equivalents do not exist) columns 1 and 2 give, respectively, past and future tense markers (LA *mwẽ te las* 'I was tired', *u ke malad* 'you'll be sick'), and column 3, the aspect markers. When only one form of the latter is listed, this has both iterative and progressive functions; otherwise the first form (including ∅ = zero or absence of marker) is iterative and the second progressive (HC *m'ap-mãje* 'I am eating'). Columns 4 and 5 list, respectively, forms employed as copula (particularly with nominal or pronominal predicates) and as substantive verb (SM *mi da nêngè* 'I am a Negro' vs. *mi dê na wósu* 'I am in the house'); but it must be remembered that usage differs from one creole (or other language) to another. Column 6, which gives the words for 'there', and 7, which gives the locative particle, have been added for the sake of comparison with other homophonous forms in this table. Some of these, such as PGC *ta* in columns 2 and 3, represent the same morphemes in different functions; others, such as PGC *na* in columns 3 and 7, or SN *de* in 5 and 6, today represent different morphemes, which may or may not have had a common origin.

In only one of these twelve languages—Krio—does the iterative function give rise to a distinct grammatical category. In Haitian, Jamaican, and British Honduran it is merged with the "achieved" or "nonpursuant" aspect: HC *m'mãje* and JC *mi njam* 'I eat (recurrently)' or 'I ate' or 'I have eaten'. In Lesser Antillean, Cayenne Creole, Sranan, Saramaccan, and Papiamentu (in the last of which it also coincides with the copula) it is merged with the progressive function in one category: LA *mwẽ ka mãje* and SN *mi e-njam* 'I eat (recurrently)' or 'I am eating'. In Portuguese Guinea Creole and Sãotomense (and perhaps also in Negro Dutch, although here the record is not clear) it is merged with the future or prospective mood: PGC *i ta dúrmi* and ST *i ka dumíni* 'he sleeps (every afternoon)' or 'he will sleep (later)'. For the progressive function, on the other hand, there is a distinct category in six of these creoles, although in the cases of Jamaican, Krio, and Portuguese Guinea Creole we may suspect that the morpheme by which it is represented had a common origin with those given in columns 5 and 6 or—in the case of Portuguese Guinea Creole—column 7, while ST *ska* may perhaps be analysed as *sa + ka*. Nevertheless, here as in the phonology, it is Saramaccan, the creole that has undergone the least external pressure, which shows the greatest number of distinctions.

SUMMARY AND CONCLUSIONS

In this chapter we have listed the West Indian creoles and compared a number of them one with another or with an African creole, taking into consideration some lexical, some phonological, and some grammatical features. Regrettable as our need thus to repeat the qualification "some" may be, this limited comparison does help to bring out certain facts in full relief.

Saramaccan is unique in having a basic vocabulary more than 73 percent of which is derived, in nearly equal proportions, from two clearly distinct languages, English and Portuguese; the remainder appears to come from African, Dutch, and other sources. This circumstance has made possible its comparison not only with the basic vocabulary of neighboring Sranan, but also with the vocabularies of Papiamentu and of the African Portuguese creoles: cf. SM *búnu*, SN *bun*, PP *bòng*, ST *bõ*, PGC *bòng* 'good'; SM *sábi*, SN *sábi*, PP *sábi*, ST *sebé*, PGC *síbi* 'know'; and such shared semantic deviations from a common model as are seen in SM *fan*, ST *fla*, and PGC *fála* vs. Ptg. *dizer* 'say'; PP *papía* and PGC *papía* vs. Ptg. *falar* 'speak, talk'; PP *katjó*, ST *kasó*, and PGC *katjúur* vs. Ptg. *cão* 'dog'; SM *pa(l)í*, ND *parí*, and PGC *pádi*, with three meanings, 'give birth to', 'be born', or 'beget', for which Portuguese has three words, *parir, nascer*, and *gerar*.

But without the aid of phonology, lexical comparison is inconclusive. Orthographic Fr./Ptg./Sp. *dormir* 'sleep' cannot justify the attribution of HC *drumi* > *dômi* and MC *durmi* > *dômi* to French; of SM *drumí* > *duumí*, ST *dumíni*, and PGC *dúrmi* to Portuguese; and of PP. *drûmi* to Spanish. Metathesis of the /r/ (as also in CC *drõmi*) is too common a phenomenon to be of any help here; but /u/ in the first syllable of the creole forms does point to Ptg. /dur'mir/ rather than to Fr. or Sp. /dor'mir/, French and Spanish having maintained the opposition *o ≠ u* in unstressed as in stressed syllables. If PP *kɔ̂re* 'run' comes from Sp. *correr*, can PP *mûri* 'die' come from Sp. *morir* (unless it be shown that the different contexts, /k——rr/ vs. /m——r/, are responsible for the different vowels in the first syllables)? If LA *kuhwi* 'run', with weak labio-velar spirant /hw/ (often reduced to plain /w/), comes from Fr. *courir*, can LA *muri* 'die', a somewhat archaic word with an apical flapped or trilled /r/, come from Fr. *mourir?* And if ST *kólo* 'color' comes from Ptg. *côr*, does ST *flôli* (cf. earlier SM *floli*) 'flower' come from Ptg. *flôr* (OPtg. *frol*), or from something more like *flore?*

We would like to derive HC and LA *pê* 'father' and *mwẽ* 'me; my' from Fr. *père* and *moi*, and ST *pê* and *mũ*, with the same meanings, from Ptg. *pai* and *mim;* but should we be justified in doing so without any more solid reason? In Haitian and Lesser Antillean creoles, the personal pronoun *mwẽ* is the only instance of intrusive nasalization (if it be that) following the group *mw-* or *nw-* (cf. *mwa* 'mois', *mwesõ* 'moisson', *nwa* 'noix', *nwê* 'noir', etc.); and it does not occur in the exclamation *ãmwe!* 'help!', which clearly comes from Fr. *á moi!* It would therefore seem plausible to suggest that LC, HC, LA, and Réunion Creole *mwẽ*, as well as ST *mũ*, might come from Ptg. *mim* by way of some intermediary such as **mwī* or **muī.*

It may be that /u/ (instead of /o/ or /õ/) in LA *kumã* 'comment', *kumãde* 'commander', *kumãse* 'commencer', and *makumê* '(ma) commère' reflect only models belonging to a French dialect other than that from which came LA *kõ* 'comme' and *kõmkwe* 'comme quoi', *kõmês* 'commerce', *kõmẽ* 'commun' and *kõmmê* 'combien', *kõmisyõ* 'commission', and *kõmod* 'commode'. Nevertheless, it is interesting to compare the first of these words, LA *kumã* (the /u/ of PGC *kúmsa* 'começar' and of ST *kumê* 'comãe' is normal since it comes from an unstressed vowel of the model) with ST and PGC *kúma* 'how' and SM *kumá* 'just as' (contrast SM *kòmê* 'eat', where ST has *kumê* and PGC has *kúme*), both of which may stem from *coma* of Old Portuguese and Provençal. This and some other words—such as SM *búka* 'mouth', *búnu* (and SN *bun*) 'good', PP *dũna* 'give', LA *asid* 'sit', CC *wey* and ST *we* 'eye(s)', HC, LA, and MC *asu* (prep.) 'on', *adã* (prep. and adv.) 'in; inside, within'—suggest Romance models that were neither Portuguese, Spanish, nor French, but which, whatever their home, may well have found shelter in the old Afro-Portuguese lingua franca. (And can PP *lânda*, ST *lãda*, both 'swim', be adequately explained as showing no more than parallel development from Ptg./Sp. *nadar?*)

All the creoles discussed here show a number of grammatical traits which, while foreign to the reputed European parent, are shared by at least one other creole of a different lexical group. These may be summarized and their distribution shown as follows:

1. The personal pronoun of third plural serves as nominal pluralizer (e.g., HC *pitit-la* 'the child', *pitit-yo* 'the children'; ST *mína sê* 'the/this

child', *uné mína* 'the children'): LC, HC, CC, ND, JC, SN, SM, PP, ST, KR.

2. The creole equivalent of 'give' is employed with the prepositional functions of our dative 'to' and 'for' (e.g., LA *yõ mun ka balye kay-la ba mwẽ,* ST *ũa nge ka balí kê sê da mũ* 'somebody sweeps the house for me'): LC, HC, LA, CC, ND, JC, SN, SM, ST.

3. An interrogative determinant (adjective) followed by a noun or pronoun is employed where a simple interrogative pronoun or adverb would be used in the European parent language, i.e., 'which thing?' for 'what?', etc. (e.g., PP *kí-ko bo ta kôme?* ST *ke kwa bo ka kumê?* 'what do you eat?', LA *ki mun ki wê-y?* ST *ke nge ku be le?* 'who saw him?'): LC, HC, LA, CC, SN, SM, PP, ST, KR.

4. A combination of the markers of past tense and prospective mood (or whatever serves to indicate futurity) is employed to express the conditional (e.g., SN *a ben-sa-sábi ef* . . ., PGC *i ta síbi ba si* . . . 'he would know if . . .'): LC, HC, LA, CC, SN, SM, PP, PGC, MC.

5. The demonstrative pronoun is postposed to the word that it determines (e.g., LA *kay sa ghwã* ST *kê sê glãdji* 'this house is big'): LC, HC, LA, SN, SM, PP, ST.

6. The pronominal (possessive) as well as the nominal determinant is postposed to that which it determines (e.g., HC *pôt kay papa-m,* ST *pôtu kê papá-m* (or *pê mũ*) 'the door of my father's house'; PQ *mailo mi,* LA *mahwi mwẽ* 'my husband'; PQ *moná si,* LA *isj u* 'your child (son or daughter)'): HC, LA, PQ, ST.

Other features might serve to group the creoles into two or more grammatical classes. Thus, only Réunion Creole has the exact equivalent of our possessive absolute pronouns. In other creoles:

7. Our possessive absolute pronouns are replaced by

   a) nominal or pronominal phrases such as HC *pa-m* 'share (of) me', CC *mo pa* 'my share', LA *sa mwẽ* 'that (of) me', which are equivalent to 'mine', etc.: LC, HC, LA, CC, KR; or by

   b) prepositional phrases meaning literally 'for me', etc., in JC, ND, SN, SM, and MC, or 'of me', etc., in PP, PQ, PGC, and ST. (See Tables 11 and 12).

8. Except in Palenquero and Krio, where it is distinguished, the iterative function is included in

   a) the unmarked (achieved or nonpursuant) aspect of the predicate, as in HC *m(wẽ) mãje rekẽ* 'I eat shark; I have eaten shark; I ate shark' (according to context): LC, HC, JC. Or,

   b) in the marked (incompletive or continuative) aspect, as in SN *mi nee-* (< *no* + *e-*) *dring bíri* 'I don't drink beer; I'm not drinking beer' (according to context): LA, CC, SN, SM, PP. Or,

c) together with the future, as in PGC *i ta bing* 'he (often) comes; he will come (tomorrow)', *i ta gráandi* 'it is (habitually) big; it will be big': PGC, ST, and (doubtfully) ND (cf. ND *mi lo ki am da* 'I see him there; I'll see him there', the first of which translations could be progressive rather than iterative in its sense).

Postposition of the definite article of those creoles which have one appears to be confined to the French group (Louisiana, Haitian, Lesser Antillean, Cayenne, and Mauritian creoles); but in Sãotomense, which has none, the demonstrative *sê* (cognate with AB *say*, which probably comes from a contraction of Ptg. *essa aqui*) must often be so translated: ST *lívlu sê sa lá* 'the book is there'.

SM *mi ó tjá í gó* 'I'll take you away', PP *e a kɔ̃re baj* 'she has run away', ND *am ha flig lo* 'it has flown off' (*gó, baj,* and *lo* meaning 'go')—like LA *pôte ale* "carry go" = 'take away' (Fr. *emporter*), *pôte vini* "carry come" = 'bring' (Fr. *apporter*), *pôte vihwe* "carry turn" = 'bring/take back' (Fr. *rapporter*)—all exemplify constructions typical of both creole and West African languages.

Typically West African also are the traits listed above, with the apparent exception of that numbered 4. The latter is certainly reminiscent of the original formation of the Romance conditional mood and of our English clauses in *should* and *would;* yet only linguistic analysts, such as those who evolved the creole forms assuredly were not, could have based them upon the European languages.

The wide distribution of creole forms in *na* and *de* (see Table 15) is remarkable enough to warrant some speculation as to its cause. In Table 15 the former appears ten times as locative particle (column 7), four times as copula, and once as aspect marker; while the latter appears five times in the sense of 'there' (which English word may well be its etymon), five times as substantive verb, three times as aspect marker, and once as copula. (Cf. Igbo *na* and *de,* which would appear in columns 3, 7 and 4, 5, respectively.)

Yet Schumann (1778) does not list either SM *da* or *dê;* and for his time, the Saramaccan forms in columns 4–7 apparently would read *na, saí, alá, na.* It could have been the introduction of SM *dê* (probably borrowed from Sranan) and the rise of a need to distinguish the copula from the locative particle that led to the former's remodeling as *da*—perhaps as a contraction of *dê* + (*n*)*a.* But such homophony has brought about no like change in Sranan (which has *na* in two functions and *de* in four), in Krio (which has *na* in two functions and *de* in three), nor yet in Portuguese Guinea Creole or in Igbo (which have *na* both as aspect marker and as locative particle; see above, the second section of this chapter. On the other hand, the common occurrence of *tá nán-go*—as in SM *m'á bi nán-go a sikôò, ma mi kó tá nán-gó* '(for a time) I didn't go to school, but now I do go' (lit., "but I have come to be going")—suggests than *tá-nán* (or *tá-ná* if nasalization of the last /á/ should be secondary) might have been employed at one time as a copula, which was contracted to **t'na*, then coalesced as *da*.

But whatever may be the present status of these homophonous morphemes, it is not implausible to suggest that they might have had the same origin. I may perhaps be able to show this from one type of construction in Scottish Gaelic, a language far removed from any creole. So, compare:

> *tha e 'na ruith* 'he is running' (lit., "he is in his running"),
> *tha e 'na dhuine math* 'he is a good man' (lit., "he is in his man good"),
> *tha e 'na thaigh* 'he is in his house'.

Here *tha* (pronounced *ha*) is the substantive verb, while *'na* is a contraction of the preposition *an(n)* 'in' with the possessive pronoun *a* 'his or her' (cf. *'nam* 'in my', *'nan* 'in their', etc.). But pidginization and creolization might well result in the loss of *tha* from these constructions, with reduction of the contracted forms to one, which would then assume new and different functions. But neither Dutch, English, French, Portuguese, nor Spanish has, so far as I know, anything analogous to the first two Gaelic constructions cited above; and it may well be that the divergent functions of creole *na* and *de*, if not their models, stem from Africa. (Cf. Igbo *mgbɛ ɔ de na nwata* 'while he is a child', but lit., "time he be in child.")

All this is not to say that creole grammars have nothing in common with those of the European languages. Adjectives other than demonstrative, when employed as determinants rather than predicatively (*ghwã kay-la* 'the big house' vs. *kay-la ghwã* 'the house is big'), usually follow the same order as does the European model: e.g., SN *wan tra moi bláka spanjóro úma* 'another beautiful black Spanish woman', which might be rendered as LA *yõ lot bel fãm spanyol nwẽ*, though this last word would more usually be replaced by the clause *ki nwê* 'who is black'.

The alternative 'either . . . or' is expressed in Haitian and Lesser Antillean creoles by *swe . . . swe*, which clearly echoes Fr. *soit . . . soit*. 'Whether . . . or (not)', indicating some degree of indifference, is rendered by *ke . . . ke* in Haitian Creole and by *ki . . . ki* in Lesser Antillean, as in LA *ki jôdi ki demẽ, (yo oblije vini)* 'whether today or tomorrow, (they're bound to come)', or *ki yo vini ki yo pa vini, (mwẽ k'ay supe talê)* 'whether they come or not, (I'm going to have dinner soon)'. Here there may be some doubt as to whether the model was Fr. *que . . . que* or Ptg. *quer . . . quer* (cf. Fr. *que ce soit aujourd'hui, que ce soit demain*, with Ptg. *quer hoje, quer amanhã;* and likewise in the case of the second example).

In most if not all creoles, a pronominal object follows the predicative word in positive or negative statements, questions, and commands. Where two such objects may occur without a preposition, the indirect always precedes the direct object. So, 'he gave/has given it to me' becomes LA *i ba mwẽ-y*, SN *a gi mi en*, SM *a dá mi ên*, PP *e a duná mi e* (usually contracted to *e a 'na m'e*), like Ptg. (*êle*) *deu-mo* (< *deu-me-o*), but unlike Fr. *il me l'a donné* and Sp. (*él*) *me le dió*. In the negative, LA *mwẽ pa ka ba-y-li* and PP *mi no ta dun'-e-le* 'I'm not giving it to him', the same order (lit., "I not am-giving to-him it") differs from that of all three Romance languages: Fr. *je ne le lui donne pas*, Sp. (*yo*) *no se lo doy*, Ptg. (*eu*) *no lho dou*. Here it seems impossible to decide between Afro-Portuguese influence and plain simplification.

Other structural resemblances between the creoles and their European "parents" consist mainly in set phrases and calques—such as, for example, LA *i ni* "he/she/it has" = 'there is/are', based on Fr. *il* (*y*) *a;* LA *lezot*, *dot*, and *lot* from Fr. *les autres*, *d'autre*(*s*), and *l'autre;* and postposition of the negation *pa* when it is constructed with the pronominal copula *se* (from Fr. *c'est*), as in *se pa mwẽ* 'It is not I'.

If we now try to answer the questions raised at the end of Chapter 7, it appears that the creoles' relationship to their European "parents" is in most cases clear and close but of an almost exclusively lexical nature, although there is much in Papiamentu, in Sranan, and especially in Saramaccan to suggest that such lexical affiliation may be, under certain circumstances, subject to change. Certainly, similarities and differences between the basic vocabularies of these last two creoles are of such magnitude that one or both languages must have changed more than hitherto has been thought possible in the space of three hundred years.

In their phonologies and especially in their grammars, the various creoles have more positive as well as negative features in common than has any one of them (with the possible exception of Jamaican and the probable exception of Réunionnais) with its European "parent"; and such groupings among them as could be made on the basis of structural criteria would often cut across those based only or principally on vocabulary.

In my opinion it is this Janus-like characteristic that distinguishes the creoles from other languages.

APPENDIX TO CHAPTER 9:
A NOTE ON MAURITIAN CREOLE

I should have liked to include in this chapter comparative material from an Afro-French creole. Unfortunately, the only description of one that I have seen, an unpublished thesis on Mauritian Creole by M. Kiamtia (a native speaker), suffers from inadequate phonological and grammatical analysis; and I therefore think it better to confine my remarks on the subject to this note, in which I attempt to give a brief and tentative outline of the Mauritian predicative system based on a reanalysis of Kiamtia's data.

The minimum complete utterance in Mauritian Creole (except for the injunctive, in which the subject is usually omitted) consists of subject plus predicate, in that order; by *predicate* I mean the predicative word alone or accompanied only by grammatical determinants. Apart from the negation *pa*, which immediately follows the subject, there appear to be six such possible determinants—*ti* [či], *va*, *pu*, *fek*, *apre*, and *fin*—none, one, two, or three (but no more) of which may occur, in that order, before the predicative word. So, *ti* may be followed by *va, pu, fek, apre*, or *fin*; *va* may be followed by *pu, fek, apre*, or *fin; pu* or *fek* may be followed by *apre* or *fin;* and *fin*, in turn, only by the "verb" or other predicative word. If I am right in believing that *pu* and *fek* on the one hand, *apre* and *fin(i)* on the other, are mutually exclusive, it seems clear that either pair constitutes one grammatical category or paradigm. What the former pair should be labeled I do not know; but *apre* and *fin* clearly mark, respectively, what we may call progressive and completive aspects; while a third, unmarked or neutral aspect indicates, inter alia, the iterative function.

Progressive	*Completive*	*Unmarked aspect*
1. mo apre mãze	1. mo fin mãze	1. mo mãze
2. mo ti apre m.	2. mo ti fin m.	2. mo ti m.
3. mo va apre m.	3. mo va fin m.	3. mo va m.
4. mo pu apre m.	4. —	4. mo pu m.
5. mo fek apre m.	5. —	5. mo fek m.
6. mo ti va apre m.	6. mo ti va fin m.	6. mo ti va m.
7. —	7. mo va pu fin m.	7. mo va pu m.
8. mo ti pu apre m.	8. —	8. mo ti pu m.
9. mo ti fek apre m.	9. mo ti fek fin m.	9. —
		10. mo ti va fek m.

Glosses	*Glosses*	*Glosses*
1. I am eating	1. I've eaten, I ate	1. I eat
2. I was eating	2. I had eaten	2. I ate
3. I shall be eating	3. I shall have eaten	3. I shall eat
4. I have to be eating	4. —	4. I have/am about to eat
5. I've just been eating	5. —	5. I've just eaten
6. I'd be eating (if)	6. I'd have eaten (if)	6. I'd eat (if)
7. —	7. I'll have almost finished eating	7. I'm just about to eat
8. I should be eating	8. —	8. I had to eat
9. I had just been eating	9. Just as I'd finished eating	9. —
		10. I should just have eaten

Only twenty-three out of a theoretically possible thirty-two combinations seem to be attested in Kiamtia's examples; and probably at least some of the other nine never occur because they would make semantic (rather than grammatical) nonsense. The particle *ti* seems to mark past tense, and *va* the future; but the combination *ti va* (see 6 and 10 in the above table) suggests that the latter might better be classed as modal. And similarly, the combinations *va pu* and *va fek* (7 and 10) make it impossible to place *va* and *pu* in the same paradigm. On the other hand, *fek* 'have just' and *pu* 'be about to; have to' are clearly commutable, as are also *apre* and *fin*. In addition to the five lacunae indicated in the table, the following combinations are also missing: **va fek* (but cf. *ti va fek* in 10), **va fek apre*, **va fek fin*, and **ti va pu*.

Since writing the above, I have been able to consult Corne's grammatical sketch of Mauritian (Corne 1970). This author's analysis of the predicative system, based on his own data, differs in several respects from that given above, which is based on Kiamtia's material.

Corne regards *fek* as an auxiliary verb, not to be included among the verbal particles (grammatical determinants), to which, on the other hand, he adds *a*, occurring before *va*, before *pu*, or alone before the predicate center with future tense function (*li a mãze, li a pu mãze, li a va mãze*, all 'il mangera'). Up to four such particles may occur before the verb: *mo ti a va fin travaj pli dir, si li ti fin pej mua pli ser* 'j'aurais travaillé plus dur s'il m'avait payé plus'. Moreover, according to Corne, *pe* and *fin* (*pe ~ ape* and *fin ~ in ~ n* in place of Kiamtia's *apre* and *fin*) are not mutually exclusive: *li ti pu pe fin mãze* 'il aurait été en train de manger'.

But Dr. Corne himself comments: "L'emploi de ces morphèmes, et de leurs diverses combinaisons, accuse un certain flottement. L'exposé que nous en donnons ici comprend toutes les formes que nous avons relevées, mais reste néanmoins sujet à caution." And again: "Mais le fait le plus saillant est la facilité dont le créole se passe des expressions de temps et d'aspect complexes. Les combinaisons de morphèmes les plus employées sont *ti pu, ti a, ti a fin, ti pe, ti fin.*" This being so, it might seem that the grammar of Mauritian Creole is in need of further investigation; and I have therefore thought it best to add to—rather than to revise—the earlier part of this note.

TEN

OUTLINE
OF DOMINICAN
CREOLE

❈

BACKGROUND

Lying midway between the French islands of Guadeloupe (to the north) and Martinique (to the south), Dominica (15°30′ N × 61°20′ W), though smaller (295 sq. mi.) and less populous (60,000 inhabitants in 1960) than its neighbors, is like them a mountainous volcanic island whose tropical climate is tempered throughout most of the year by the northeast trade winds. Discovered by Columbus on his second voyage (3 November 1493), it remained, at least officially, in the possession of the native Island-Carib Indians until, by the Treaty of Paris of 1763, it was annexed by Great Britain. Subsequently, the island was on several occasions captured by the French, but has remained in British hands since 1814.

Even before 1763, however, a number of Englishmen and especially Frenchmen had settled in Dominica together with their slaves; and it was these latter who introduced the French creole patois which has become the mother tongue and first language of almost all the present population. Though mutually intelligible with the creoles of Guadeloupe, Martinique, St. Lucia, Grenada, and Trinidad, it is identical with none of them and may itself be subdivided into an indefinite number of local varieties differing chiefly in the distributions of certain phonemes and in the total number of these distinctive units.

While Dominica has its tradesmen, professional class, and a few owners of large estates, it is essentially a land of peasant culture. Racial mixture (Negro, white, and to a lesser extent, Amerindian) has proceeded further there than in Guadeloupe, Antigua, and Barbados, though not as far as in Martinique. Of the two or three hundred white people who live there

This chapter was originally published as "Le créole de la Dominique," in *Encyclopédie de la Pléiade: Le langage* (Paris: Gallimard, 1962), pp. 1022–49, and is here reprinted, in revised and translated form, by permission of the original publishers.

today, none of the adults was born on the island. And since the local creole has been unable for the past 150 years to renew itself except by borrowing from English, it differs from the creoles of the French islands in lacking social varieties while retaining those of a local character, some of the latter being very conservative, while others have been more or less strongly influenced (mainly in vocabulary, but also to some extent in syntax) by English, the island's only official language.

PHONOLOGY

Dominican Creole is not a tone language; and while the range of intonation commonly employed is greater than that found in most European languages, stress, employed for emphasis, is largely free.

Its phonemes include, depending on the variety, from seven to nine oral vowels with four degrees of aperture, three nasal vowels, two semi-vowels (which behave like consonants in the morphology), and from twenty to twenty-two consonants forming five series and four principal orders. In the following table, phonemes which do not belong to all varieties of this creole have been placed in parentheses.

m	n	(ɲ)	ŋ			
p	t	č	k	i	(ɨ)	u
b	d	ǧ	g	ẹ		ọ
						ẽ õ
f	s	š		h	ę	ǫ
v	z	ž	(γ^ω)		a (α)	ã
	l, r					
w	y					

In what follows, some of these symbols will be replaced orthographically: the palatal and velar nasals, /ɲ/ and /ŋ/, by ny and ng (/ŋg/ will be written ngg); the voiced and voiceless hushing affricates, /ǧ/ and /č/, by dj and c; the voiced and voiceless hushing sibilants, /ž/ and /š/, by j and sj; the labiovelar spirant, /γ^ω/ (voiced except when following a voiceless consonant), by hw; the lower mid and back open vowels, /ę/, /ǫ/, and /α/, by ê, ô, and â; the higher mid vowels, /ẹ/ and /ọ/, by e and o.

In free syllables and in those checked by one of the semivowels (y, w), the oppositions of the ten vowels not in parentheses are common to every variety of this creole. Examples: pi 'puis; puits' and bi 'bille'; pe 'paix (be quiet)', pê 'avoir peur (be afraid); Père (Father = priest)', and bê 'beurre (butter)'; pẽ 'pain (bread)' and bẽ 'bain (bath)'; pa 'pas (not; step)' and ba 'bas (low; stocking)'; pã 'paon (peacock)' and bã 'banc (bench)'; bô 'bord (edge; beside)', bo 'kiss (v. or n.)', and po 'pot (measure of capacity)'; *bõ* 'bon (good)' and *põ* 'pont (bridge)'; *bu* 'bourre (wad, wadding)' and *pu* 'pour; pou (for; louse)'; *i le-y* 'il le veut (he wants it)' and *i le-w* 'il te veut (he wants you)', but *i lê-y* [ilɛị] 'il est son heure (it is his time)' and *i lê-w* [ilɛų] 'il est ton heure (it is your time)'; *lo-y* [loị] 'son lot (his portion)' and *lo-w* [loų] 'ton lot (your portion), but *lô-y* [lɔị] 'son or (his gold)' and *lô-w* [lɔų] 'ton or (your gold)'.

In syllables checked by a consonant, the vowels *i, u, e,* and *o* are more open and less tense, and the opposition of higher to lower mid (*e* ≠ *ê*, *o* ≠ *ô*) is neutralized except in a very few conservative varieties, in which one may hear, e.g., *nef* [nɛ̌f] 'neuf (nine; new)' but *nêf* [nɛ̄f] 'nerf (nerve; tendon)', *sot* [sɔ̌t] 'sot (foolish)' but *sôt* [sɔ̄t] 'sorte (sort)', *pot* [pɔ̌t] 'pot (recipient)' but *lapôt* [lapɔ̄t] 'porte (door)'. Here the vowels of *nef* and *sot* are laxer and more open than those of *ne* 'noeud (knot)' and *so* 'saut (fall)', without being confused (in such conservative varieties) with the vowels of *nêf* and *sôt*, which are phonetically and phonemically the same as those of *nê* 'hour (period of time)' and *sô* 'saur (dried and salted)'. But for most if not all those of the younger generation, *nef* and *nêf, sot* and *sôt* have the same vowel. (See Diagram 1.)

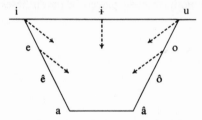

DIAGRAM I.   Dispersion of the close and higher mid vowels.

Most varieties of this creole have a close, unrounded central vowel, here written *i,* as in *fijê* 'fern' (fr. dial. Fr. *feugère*), *hwipõn* 'repondre (to lay again)', *hwisivwê* 'recevoir (receive)', *sime* 'semer (sow)'. Although rather infrequent and virtually without functional load, it seems impossible to identify this sound with a variant of another phoneme because one finds in the speech of those who employ it as above such nearly minimal oppositions as are seen in *hwujê* 'rougeur (redness)' and *lizyê* 'lisière (edge)', *hwepõn* 'répondre (reply)', *hwusi* 'roussir (to brown)' and *hwisi* 'reçu (receipt)', *gume* 'se battre (to fight)' and *fime* 'fumer (to smoke)'. Moreover, in varieties lacking this sound, its replacement is not uniform, for one hears *fujê, fwijê,* and *fijê* for what with perhaps most speakers is *fijê.*

In conservative varieties having two open oral vowels, front *a* is opposed to back *â* both in free syllables and in those checked by a consonant: *la* 'là (there)' but *lâ* 'lard (bacon)', *pak* 'Pâques (Easter)' but *pâk* 'parc (enclosure for animals)', *mas* 'mascarade (carnival)' but *mâs* 'mars (March)', *kat kât* 'quatre cartes (four cards)'. In those varieties (the majority) which have only one open oral vowel, this may be retracted before a pause (*elâ!* 'alas!') but is a front *a* elsewhere.

In syllables checked by a nasal consonant (*m, n, ny,* or *ng*), the higher mid and front open vowels (*e, o,* and *a*) maintain either their opposition to the lower mid and back open vowels (*ê, ô,* and *â*) or—for varieties in which *nêf, sôt, kât* fall together with *nef, sot, kat*—their opposition to the nasal vowels (*ẽ, õ,* and *ã*), but not both of these. Thus, *têm* 'terme (term)', *bôn* 'borne (boundary)', and *sjâm* 'charme (charm)' are never confused with *tẽm* 'timbre (stamp)', *bõn* 'bonde (bung)', and *sjãm* 'chambre (bedroom)'; although these oppositions may be realized (depending on the variety of this creole) in different ways: e.g., *sjâm* [šɑm] 'charm' vs. *sjãm* [šam] 'bedroom', or else, more often, *sjâm* [šam] 'charm' vs. *sjãm* [šãm] 'bedroom'.

Vocalic groups are limited to two vowels and are always dissylabic: *au* or *aut* 'août (August)', *hai* 'haïr, hait (hate)', *kai* 'sprat' (cf. *kay* 'house'). Some but not all of them (not *au*) may be interrupted by a semivowel, freely introduced or omitted: *pe(y)i* 'pays (country)', *pwi(y)e* 'prier (pray)', *i(y)ê* 'hier (yesterday), *klo(w)izõ* 'cloison (partition)', *no(w)el* (sometimes reduced to *nwel*) 'Noël (Christmas)'.

The phonological status of the semivowels *y* and *w* appears clearly in the following oppositions: *cwi* [tšy̨i] 'cuir; ceinture (leather; belt)', *cu-y* [tšu̧i] 'son cul (his bottom)' and *cwiyi* [tšwiyi] ~ *cuyi* [tšu̧i̧i] 'cueillir (gather)'.

DISTRIBUTION OF PHONEMES

Any consonant or semivowel except *ny* and *ng* may occur before any vowel as syllable-initial; and any consonant or semivowel except *h, hw,* and *r* may occur after any oral vowel as syllable-final.

The distinctively voiced occlusives do not occur as syllable-final after a nasal vowel. Thus—besides *sãble* 'assemble, gather together', *cu-sãdhwõ* 'Cinderella (lit., "ash bottom")', *sãgle* 'gird, girded', and *lãgaj* 'language'—we find *sãm* 'sembler; ressembler (seem; resemble)', *sãn* 'ashes', *sãng* 'sangle (girth; belt)', and *lãng* 'langue (tongue)', in which the labial and apical nasals result from the neutralization, after a nasal vowel, of the *b ≠ m* and *d ≠ n* oppositions: cf. *plẽn* '(se) plaindre (complain)' and *plẽn* 'pleine = gravide; féconder (pregnant; to impregnate)', which are homophonous. But the dorsovelar nasal *ng* cannot be regarded as a combinatory variant of *g;* for it occurs not only after the nasal vowels *ẽ, õ,* and *ã,* but also after *i* and *y,* which are never distinctively nasal: *ling* 'ligne (line, cord)', *ti-zing* 'a very little', *linggwez* '(kind of) whip', *maynggwẽ* 'maringouin (mosquito)'.

Nor does either of the affricates, *c* or *dj*, occur after a nasal vowel, though this may be explained by the fact that these phonemes do not occur at all as syllable-final except in words borrowed from English, such as *pic* 'tarred (pitched) road' and *badj* 'badge'.

The palatal nasal (*ny*) and the labiovelar spirant (*hw*) now belong only to very conservative varieties of Dominican Creole. So, the first may serve to distinguish *pẽny* 'peigne (comb)' from *pẽ-y* 'son pain (his bread)', the second to distinguish *hwahwa* 'crécelle (kind of rattle)' from *wawa* 'wild yam (Rajana cordata)' and *khwi* 'cru (raw)' from *kwi* 'coui (half calabash employed as dish)'. But these oppositions are today employed by no speaker for more than a very few pairs of words.

Loss of the palatal nasal is usually compensated for by nasalization of the following syllable, except where this is checked; so that *pẽny* 'comb', *pẽnye* 'to comb', *pãnye* 'panier (basket)', *põnyet* 'poignet (wrist)', *ghwafinye* 'grafigner (to scratch)', *ghwinye* 'grigner (to make a wry face)', and *ghwinyote* 'grignoter (to nibble)' then become *pẽy* (homophonous with *pẽ-y* 'his bread'; but cf. *pẽy-li* 'his comb'), *pẽyẽ*, *pãyẽ*, *põyet*, *ghwafiyẽ*, *ghwiyẽ*, and *ghwiyõte*. Exceptionally, *sinye* 'signer (to sign)' and *linye* 'aligner (to align)' have given *si(y)e* (homophonous with the word meaning 'to saw', from Fr. *scier*) and *li(y)e;* and since this creole has no close nasal vowel, *n* or *ng* takes the place of *ny* in forms such as *ling* 'ligne (line, cord)' and *sin* 'signe (sign)'. (It should be noted, however, that in older French, *signe* was pronounced /sin/.)

In the case of the labiovelar spirant *hw* (whose model clearly was the velar *r* of northern French), loss takes the form of confusion with *w*, the velar element ceasing to be distinctive, so that many speakers pronounce indifferently *hwi* or *wi* for 'oui (yes)' as well as for 'rire, rit (laugh)', and *dhwet* or *dwet* for 'doigt (finger)' as well as for 'droite (straight)'. But the phoneme /hw/, which seems to be in process of elimination, is never confused with apical /r/: so, *bhwav* or *bwav* 'brave' but *braf* 'broth made with fish', *hwãm* or *wãm* 'rame (oar)' but *rãm* 'ram (tool); to ram', *hwul* or *wul* 'roue (wheel)' but *rul* 'custom (rule)', *hwive* or *wive* 'arriver (arrive)' but *ribote* 'riboter (to feast)'.

The phoneme /h/, which, like /hw/ and /r/, never occurs as syllable-final or before another consonant, is always aspirated, and generally corresponds to the so-called aspirate *h* of French, as in *dehô* 'dehors (outside)', *hâd* 'hardes (clothes)', *hai* 'haïr (to hate)', *hahwã* 'hareng (herring)', *hasj* 'hache (ax)', *hazã* 'hazard', *hazye* 'bushes; weeds' (fr. dial. Fr. *hasier*, mod. *hallier*), *hãni* 'henir (to neigh)', *hãsj* 'hanche (hip)', *hãyõ* 'haillons (rags)', *hele* 'crier, héler (call, yell)', *ho* 'haut (high)', *hõt* 'honte (shame)', *humâ* 'hommard (lobster)', *lahal* 'halle (market hall)', *lahẽn* 'haine (hatred)'. But in a few cases, its presence cannot be so explained: *legohin* (also, in other varieties, *legovin* and *legojin*) 'egohine, égoïne (handsaw)', *halēn* 'haleine (breath)'—with which compare *alēn* (as well as *zalēn*) 'alène (awl)'.

Any consonant occurring as syllable-initial except *h*, *hw*, and *r* may be followed in this position by *w* (see Table 16). Of these seventeen consonants, eleven may be followed by *y;* eight by *hw* or *r;* one (*s*) by *p*, *t*, or *k*. It should be noted that *y* can follow neither *m* nor *n* (which is why the palatal nasal /ɲ/ can be written *ny*); so that *miet* 'miette (crumb)' has two syllables whereas *tyed* 'tiède (tepid)' has only one, and *maniê* 'manière (manner)' has three syllables whereas *matyê* 'matière (matter)' has only two. The initial group *sl-* is probably to be found only in words borrowed from English, such as *slup* 'sloop' and *slak* 'to dismiss, discharge (workman)' (from a confusion of Eng. *sack* and *slack?*). And the same may be said of the three initial consonantal groups constituted of *sp- st-*, or *sk-* plus *r*, as in *spre* 'to spray (plants)', *strik* 'strict', and *skrip* 'any written communication (script)'. Finally, *w* may follow initial *y* (but not the reverse), though *ywit* 'huit (eight)' seems to be the unique example of this group.

TABLE 16. Occurrence of Consonant Clusters in Dominican Creole

First element of group	Second element of group
s p, b; t, d; k, g⎱ f, v⎰ z l sj, j; c, dj m, n	p, t, k⎱ ⎰l hw, r⎰ ⎰y ⎰w

In syllable-final position the only permitted groups are those of consonant plus *s* (but not *z*) and of semivowel plus consonant: *mêls* 'merle(s) (blackbird)', *bins* 'bean(s)', *bowl* 'ball', *keys* 'lawsuit (case)', *cayk* 'girlfriend; boyfriend', *ciwp* (the implosive sound by which West Indians express incredulity or scorn). Other final consonantal groups of the model are changed or reduced: *deks* 'desk', *flim* 'film', *hwis* 'risque (risk)', *kataplām* 'cataplasme'.

Internal consonantal groups that occur between two vowels belonging to the same lexeme are always analyzable as a sequence of final phoneme or group and initial phoneme or group, though by no means are all such combinations found. So, *-p* (*tap* Fr. 'tape') plus *lw-* (*lwil* Fr. 'huile') is reduced to *-pl-* (*lapli* Fr. 'pluie'), while *-d* or *-t* is replaced by *-l* before *b-* or *p-* (*kat* Fr. 'quatre' .. *pat* Fr. 'patte' → *kalpat* Fr. 'à quatre pattes').

Examples: *e(k)sthwôdinê* 'extraordinaire (extraordinary)', *maynggwẽ* 'maringouin (mosquito)', *linggwez* 'rigoise (whip)', *esplice* 'expliquer (explain)', *lesklavaj* or *lestravaj* 'esclavage (slavery)', *ceksyõ* 'question', *kudzye* 'coup d'oeil (eye = glance)', *pulbwa* 'pou de bois (wood-ant, termite)', *malpwopte* 'malpropreté (dirtiness)', *takte* 'tacheté (spotted)', *hwivesjte* 'to speak harshly to' (cf. Fr. *revêche*), *jãntõ* 'hanneton (cock-chafer)', *hwõnmã* 'persistently' (cf. Fr. *rondement*), *glinse* 'glisser (to slip)', *lajle* 'gelée (jelly)', *pishet* 'pisquette (a sort of very small fish, whitebait)', *gulhowp* 'Good Hope' (toponym), *kalvê* 'Cap Vert' (appellation at first applied to Cape Verde Negroes, and later to any particularly black ones).

Geminate consonants, though not very frequent, originate in three ways: they may be expressive as in *ẽmme* 'aimer (to love)', assimilative as in *kõmmẽ* 'combien (how much/many)', or combinative as in *hwob blã* 'robe blanche (white dress)'. So, *yõ liv vyãn* 'une livre (de) viande (a pound of meat)' and *yõ liv yãn* 'un livre (de) Yann (a book of Yann's)' are distinguished only by the length of the *v*.

One might wish to regard the affricates, *c* and *dj*, as groups composed of an apical stop (*t, d*) plus a hushing sibilant (*sj, j*); or, perhaps as groups composed of an apical or a dorsal stop (*t, d,* or *k, g*) plus the semivowel *y*. The former solution seems to be excluded by the fact that, except for these cases, no hushing sibilant and no distinctively voiced consonant occurs as second element of an initial group. The latter solution, if it were possible, would be attractive because of the existence of variants and alternations which appear to support it: *cwizin* or *twizin* 'cuisine (kitchen)', *zedjwi* or *zedwi* 'aiguille (needle)', *puci* or *puki* 'pourquoi (why)', *bece* or *beke* 'white person', *pice* 'piquer (to prick)' besides *pikã* 'piquant (thorn)'. Were this solution adopted, *twizin* would then result from the reduction of an initial group **tyw-* present in [tšųizin] (cf. *yw-* in *ywit* 'eight'). But this approach is rendered impossible by the existence of groups composed of these same stops followed, phonetically as well as phonologically, by the palatal semivowel: *kyap* 'cap', *kyãn* 'tin can', *kyasj* 'cash' besides *cak*, a disease of poultry, *tyed* 'tiède (tepid)' besides *(la)cet* 'quête (collection)', *gyal* 'girl' and *gogyo* 'girlfriend' besides *djel* or *djol* 'gueule (animal's mouth)', *dyẽt!* 'diantre! (damn!)' and *dye* 'Dieu (God)' besides *dje* 'gai (gay)'.

THE SIGNIFICANT UNITS:
SENTENCE STRUCTURE

The minimum complete utterance (except for the command construction, in which the subject is rarely expressed) must contain, in that order, a subject and a predicate, each of which may be reduced to a single morpheme (significant unit) or else may be accompanied by one or more grammatical determinants. The predicate of such an utterance, if unaccompanied by any grammatical determinant other than the subject, indicates that the latter has, at the moment of speaking, reached the state, acquired the quality, or accomplished the process designated. The lexical subject when unaccompanied by any grammatical determinant has a general or a partitive sense. For example, *soley kusje* 'the sun has set', *lapli pase* 'the rain has passed', *zetwel dehô* 'the stars are out (have appeared)', *mun sot* 'people (in general) are stupid'; or, with a nonlexical subject, *mwẽ las* 'I am tired', *nu la* 'we are there', *u thwavay* 'you (have) worked', *zot hwive* 'you (pl.) have arrived', *i lê (pu nu ale)* 'it is time (for us to go)', *yo swef (fẽ, pê, hõt, sõmey)* 'they are thirsty (hungry, afraid, ashamed, sleepy)', *yõn (di nu) kuhwi* 'one (of us) ran', *adã (di yo) dakô* 'some (of them) have agreed'. Moreover, many autonomous phrases (i.e., phrases whose function does not depend on their position in the sentence) may also serve as predicate: *yo lakay* 'they (are) at home' (cf. *kay* 'house'), *yo ã jâdẽ* 'they (are) in the garden', *nu asu tab* 'we (are) at table', *tut mun kõ sa* 'everybody (is) like that'.

In positive statements where the predicate only identifies the subject, predication is transferred, in the absence of any other grammatical determinant, to a copula, *se* (from Fr. *c'est*): *neg se mun* 'Negroes are people', *kopye se vole* 'copying is stealing', *mwẽ se yõ nõm* 'I am a man', *u se yõ fãm* 'you are a woman', *i se fwê mwẽ* 'he is my brother' (cf. *i kõnet fwê mwẽ* 'he knows my brother'), *sa se kay-la* 'that is the house'. In negative statements of this kind, however, *se* may be omitted—*thwoce (se) pa vole* 'to exchange (is) not to steal'—and it cannot be employed in those statements where tense or mood is determined otherwise: *mwẽ te yõ nõm* 'I was a man', *u ke yõ fãm* 'you will be a woman', *i te ke fwê mwẽ* 'he would be my brother'.

A lexeme (compound, derivative, or simple morpheme) belongs to the nominal class if, in a minimum complete utterance, it may be preceded by the indefinite determinant *yõ* 'a(n)', or by *cek* 'some', which implies it: *yõ lapli pase* 'a shower of rain passed', *yõ zetwel dehô* 'a star is out', *cek mun vini* 'some person/people has/have come', *yõ kay pwi dife* 'a house has caught fire', *yõ lafime mõte* 'a smoke arose', *mi yõ nwit ki long* 'what a long night'.

A lexeme, or what elsewhere is an autonomous phrase, belongs to the predicative class if it alone takes the place of predicate in a minimum complete utterance: *i fime (pip-li)* 'he smoked (his pipe)', *i pê (lamô)* 'he is afraid (of death)', *i mô (lapêhwez)* 'he is dead; he died (of fear)', *i las (mwẽ)* 'he is tired (of me)', *i lasi mwẽ* 'he tired me', *i ã cwizin* 'he is in the kitchen', *i esit* (or *isi*) 'he is here', *i ni tô (hwezõ, laj)* 'he is (lit., "has") wrong (right, old enough)'. There is no formal difference between *i ni* 'he (she, it) has' and *i ni* 'there is (are)' employed as an actualizer: *i ni zõbi* 'there are demons', *i pa ni zõbi* 'there are no demons', *i ni lajã* 'he/ she/it has money' or 'there is money'. But *mi* 'voici, voilà', which is employed as an actualizer to draw attention to the presence of something or of somebody, is not predicative: *mi mwẽ* 'here I am'.

There is also a class of adverbial lexemes whose only function is to expand the predicate. Such are, for example, *ãkô* 'again; yet, still', *acwelmã* 'now', *dabô* 'at first', *espwe* 'on purpose', *hwõnmã* 'persistently, constantly', *jamẽ* 'never; ever', *osi* and *tu* 'also; too', *pitet* 'perhaps', *siltâ* 'sur le tard (late in the afternoon, early evening)', *suvã* 'often', *talê* 'tout à l'heure (just now)', *tuju* 'always', *tãzãtã* 'de temps en temps (now and again)'.

In most cases, a lexeme cannot belong to both the first two classes; thus, *lapli, mun, kay, lãvi,* and *lafime* are always nominal; *kuhwi, pê, lasi, ãvi,* and *fime* are always predicative. But there are many exceptions; and the same lexeme may then appear in different classes, according to context. For example, *lê* (from Fr. *l'heure*) is a governed noun in *yõ lê pu i vini pâkô fikse* 'a time for him to come has not yet been fixed', and in *lê pu i vini ja pase* 'the time for him to come has already passed'; but it is predicative in *i lê pu i vini* 'it is time for him to come', functional in *lê i vini (mwẽ pa te la)* 'when he came (I was not there)', and together with *yõ* (indefinite determinant) it constitutes an autonomous phrase in *tut mun ni pu mô yõ lê* 'everybody has to die sometime'. And similarly, *labitil* is a governed noun in *i ni yõ move labitil* 'he has a bad habit', an autonomous morpheme in *i pa ka fê sa labitil* 'he doesn't do that usually'; *ba* is employed first as a predicative lexeme and then as a functional morpheme in *ba mwẽ pôte-y ba-w* 'let (lit., "give") me carry it for (lit., "give") you'.

Or else it may be a question of different homophonous units whose meanings are related. So, *lakle* 'key' and *lakle* 'to lock', *mãje* 'food' and *mãje* 'to eat' appear to be confused in *lakle-y ã didã* 'his key is inside' or 'lock him in', *mãje yo fwet* 'their food is cold' or 'eat them cold'; but negation suffices to bring out the distinction: *lakle-y pa ã didã* 'his key is not inside' and *pa lakle-y ã didã* 'don't lock him in', *mãje yo pa fwet* 'their food is not cold' and *pa mãje yo fwet* 'don't eat them cold'. The noun *lakle* is commutable only with another noun, such as *lafime* 'smoke (n.)'; the predicative *lakle* only with another predicative, such as *fime* 'to smoke'.

Apart from elliptic expressions like *nuvo lãne, nuvo lwa* '(a) new year (brings, justifies) (a) new law', the predicate must contain a predicative lexeme. But the subject is not necessarily nominal or pronominal, for a predicative lexeme may also fulfill this function: *la ni yõ layvyê* 'there is a river there', *thwo pwese pa ka fê ju uvê* 'to be in too much of a hurry does not make day open', *hwãn sêvis ka bay mal do* 'to render (somebody a) service gives (one) a backache'.

One of the functions of the noninterrogative complement is marked by its constant postposition, whatever may be the determinatum: *zãfã ẽmme mãje thwop ghwẽn balata* 'children like to eat too many balata (*Manilkara nitida*) fruits', where *mãje* 'eat', *thwop* 'too many', and *ghwẽn* 'berries, fruits' both determine the preceding word and are determined by that which follows. This "direct" function may be fulfilled by a noun (*ghwẽn, balata*), by a predicative (*mãje, thwop*), or by a pronoun: *zãfã ẽmme yo* 'children love them', *yo ẽmme zãfã yo* 'they love their children'.

Another function is marked by postposition alternating with the employment of functional *ba* 'to; for', and by the first position in the case of two complements without a functional morpheme. This "attributive" function may be fulfilled by a noun or by a pronoun: *i ba fwê-y bef-la* 'he has given the cow to his brother', *yo ba mwẽ (fê)-y* 'they have given it to me (to do)', *i ba yo-i* 'he has given it to them', *i di mwẽ sa* 'he told me that', *i mãde mwẽ kesjôy* 'he asked me something'; but *i vãn bef-la ba fwê-y* 'he sold/has sold the cow to his brother', *yo fê-y ba mwẽ* 'they did (have done) it for me' or, with change of emphasis, *ba mwẽ yo fê-y* 'for me they did (have done) it'.

Other complements consist of autonomous lexemes or phrases (with or without a functional morpheme), which indicate their function by themselves (although most of them are normally postposed). Examples (of which several include more than one kind of complement) are *yo ka jwe epi zo* 'they play' or 'they are playing with bones' (cf. *yo ka jwe zo* 'they play' or 'they are playing knucklebones'), *mwẽ tãn pâle di-y* 'I've heard (lit., "heard speak") of him', *i pôte plẽt kõt madãm-li* 'he's brought a charge against his wife', *i di sa asu mwẽ* 'he said that about me', *yo mô laswef* 'they died of thirst', *mwẽ fê-y bõ cê* 'I did it gladly', *i vini lãnwit* 'he came at nighttime', *mwẽ pa ke fê-y ãkô* 'I'll not do it again', *mwẽ pôkô ke fê-y* 'I'll not do it yet', *yo suvã vini lakay nu yõ dimãsj bõmatẽ* 'they have often come to our house on a Sunday morning', *mwẽ te k'ay ba-w pôte yo vihwe lakay-li* 'I was going to give them to you to take back to his home' (cf. *pôte ... vini* 'bring', *pôte ... ale* 'take away', *kuhwi ale* 'to run away', etc.).

The predicate has but one orientation in the sense that the agent can be expressed only in the subject. So, 'he is liked by everybody' becomes *tut mun ẽmme-y* 'everybody likes him'. But where there is no agent, the subject may indicate a patient: *mwẽ oblije fê-y* 'I'm obliged to do it' and *dite-a ja dusi* 'the tea has already been sweetened', as well as *i oblije mwẽ fê-y* 'he obliged me to do it' and *mwẽ ja dusi dite-a* 'I've already sweetened the tea'. Some predicatives, like *di* 'say', *fê* 'do', and *sjofe* 'to heat (v.t.)', do not normally occur without a direct object; and some others, like *fet* 'to be done; to be born' and *sjo* 'to heat (v.i.); to be hot', can govern only autonomous complements: *sa pa ka fet (ã de minit)* 'that is not done (in two minutes)', (*acwelmã*) *dlo ka sjo* '(now) the water is heating'.

When the agent and the patient are identical, the latter is expressed by the noun *kô* 'body' followed by the appropriate personal pronoun: *es u fê kô-w mal?* 'did you hurt yourself?', *mwẽ k'ay lave kô mwẽ* 'I'm going to wash myself' (cf. *mwẽ k'ay lave* 'I'm going to wash'—'clothes' being understood). But often a predicate without direct object implies the reflexive nature of the action: *bõmatẽ mwẽ bẽyẽ* 'this morning I bathed', *mwẽ leve bõnê* 'I got up early'.

Apposition is seldom employed, although one may cite such examples as *mwẽ, zãfã de mun!* 'I, the child of two people!' (expressing emphatic or surprised protest), *mwẽ, Odjis Fwãswa, sjef Khwaib,* ... 'I, Auguste François, Chief of Caribs, ...'.

We may distinguish (A) a class of "qualitative" predicatives, susceptible of taking one of the determinants of degree—*mwẽ* 'less', *pli* 'more', *thwo* 'too'—preposed as modifiers, and (B) the other predicatives, which take only the lexical counterparts of these modifiers—*mwẽs, plis, thwop* ('too much, too many')—postposed as complements and which may themselves have predicative functions. So, *i thwo led* or *i led thwop* 'he's too ugly', *i thwo ẽmme jwe* or *i ẽmme jwe thwop* 'he's too fond of playing'; but only *i pâle thwop* 'he spoke too much' and *i ni thwop* 'he has too many'. With a very few exceptions, only (but not all) predicatives belonging to the first class may function as attributive adjectives.

There are three kinds of attributive adjectives: those which usually follow the word governed (e.g., *ãgle, fwãse, blã, nwê, sjo, fwet, malad, pôtã, hwõ, kahwe*), those which usually precede it (e.g., *bõ, move, bel, led, jẽn, vye, ghwo, ghwã, piti*), and those which may, with or without change of meaning, either follow or precede it (*yõ mun sot* or *yõ sot mun* 'a stupid person', *yõ nõm pov* 'a poor (impecunious) man' and *yõ pov nõm* 'a poor [pitiable] man'). Besides their predicative and attributive functions, all of them may be employed as complements—*i ka fê* (*mwẽ*) *sjo* 'it (the weather) is less hot', *i ka gâde* (*thwo*) *led* 'it looks (too) ugly/bad', *i vini* (*pli*) *pov* 'he has become poorer'—but only a few of them may serve as nouns— *yõ piti ke ase* 'a small (one) will suffice', *yõ blã debace* 'a white man has landed'. And since *yõ sjo, yõ fwet, yõ bõ, yõ move*, etc., are felt as an unusual employment of ellipsis, such a construction as *yõ move labitil* must, it would seem, be regarded as belonging to the type determinans-determinatum. On the other hand, *piti* is rarely attributive (perhaps because it is often replaced by the diminutive prefix *ti-*): *piti hasj ka bat ghwo bwa* 'small axes fell big trees', *piti maniê* 'stingy, mean'.

The only relative pronoun, *ki* 'which, who', is always subject of the clause that it introduces and is never absolute: *sa ki ke viv ke vwẽ* 'those who live will see'. The relative clause that does not refer to the subject is marked only by its place in the sentence, as often also in English: *se ba u mwẽ ka pâle* 'it's to you (that) I'm speaking', *tut sa mwẽ te (v)wê te malad* 'all those (whom) I saw were sick', but *mwẽ (v)wê tut sa ki te malad* 'I saw all those who were sick'. The subordinate clause may be introduced by a conjunction, or else marked only by its place in the sentence: *mwẽ ke vini sãmdi si se pa lapli* 'I'll come on Saturday unless it rains', *u te ka dõmi lê mwẽ hwive* 'you were sleeping when I arrived', *mwẽ (v)le yo vini* 'I want them to come' (lit., "I want they come"), and—with or without *kõmkwe* (Fr. *comme quoi*) 'that'—*i di mwẽ (kõmkwe) u ka dwe-y* 'he told me (that) you owe him (money)'.

Sentences containing a subordinate clause—such as *mwẽ sav i ka etidye* 'I know (that) he is studying' (or, according to context, 'that he studies') and *mwẽ tãn i ka jwe flit* 'I've heard (that) he plays the flute'—are distinguished from those containing a "progressive" direct complement—such as *mwẽ jwẽn-li ka etidye* 'I found him studying' and *mwẽ tãn-li ka jwe flit* 'I heard him playing the flute'—for enclitic *-li* is never subject (with other persons this distinction is marked only on the prosodic level). A complement in *ka* always has the progressive sense of our present participles in *-ing;* and if it follows upon a predicate center also in *ka*, this latter can only have the iterative sense ('usually, often, sometimes') of our so-called present tense: *cek fwa nu ka jwẽn-li ka thwavay* 'sometimes we find him working', *yo ka asid ã cwizin ka pâle* 'they sit in the kitchen talking'. This allows us to distinguish two other classes of predicatives: (1) those which combine with *ka* only in such contexts and situations as require the iterative sense, like *ãvi* 'to desire to', *ẽmme* 'to love; to like', *la* 'to be there' (and all other predicatives of place), *ni* 'have', *sav* 'know', *(v)le* 'wish', and *ye* 'be'; and (2) those which combine freely with *ka*, taking, according to context, either an iterative or a progressive sense, like *bay* 'to give', *fê* 'do; make', *las* 'be tired', *mô* 'die', *sjo* 'be hot; heat (v.i.)', and *(v)wê* 'see'. The progressive complement occurs only with predicatives of the second class; but it should be noticed that these two classes, 1 and 2, do not coincide with those, A and B, described above; so, *ãvi* and *ẽmme* are A1, *bay* and *fê* B2, *las* and *sjo* A2, *ni* and *sav* B1.

Most of the coordinative conjunctions have the same functions as their French models: *mwẽ pa te ni tã fê-y, pis mwẽ te malad* 'I didn't have time to do it because I was sick', *mwẽ te ke vudhwe fê-y, mẽ mwẽ pa pe* 'I'd like to do it, but I can't', *yõn o lot* 'one or the other', *bwê-y, o-sinõ u ke malad* 'drink it, or else you'll be sick', *ni yõn ni lot pa vini* 'neither one nor the other came'. But without the negation *pa, ni . . . ni* has the positive meaning of 'both': *ni yõn ni lot vini* 'one and the other came, both came'. The phrase *kõ sa* 'like that' may be conjunctive with the sense of 'therefore, so that': *i gãyẽ, kõ sa i kõtã* 'he has won, so he's happy'. The The commonest of all the coordinatives, *epi* 'then, and' (or, as a functional morpheme, 'with' = 'in company of'), may express the aggregation of two members of a clause, of two clauses, or of two sentences: *u epi mwẽ* 'you and I' (or, according to context, 'you are with me'), *mwẽ sãti-y epi mwẽ tãn-li* 'I felt it and I heard it', *sete yõ vye-kô ki pa te ni zãfã; epi madãm-li vini mô* 'it was (about) an old fellow who had no children; and his wife came to die'.

Under the conditions in which this language is now used, new units created by composition and by derivation would have but small chance of surviving, spreading, and ousting their equivalents borrowed from English. Analogy, however, seems to have played a part in the past; and it is unlikely that the following go back to French models: *hal-ho* and *hal-ba* (*hale* 'hawl; pull', *ho* 'high', *ba* 'low'), which designate the respective positions taken up by two crosscut sawyers at work, *lõngvie* 'to look through a telescope; to screw up the eyes in looking, as short-sighted people do', *hwivesjte* (cf. Fr. *revêche*) 'to speak harshly to', *rofte* 'to treat roughly' (presumably an Anglo-French blend), *sipe* 'to sip' (also Anglo-French?), *hos-tottot* (cf. *hose* 'to raise, lift', *tottot* 'breast [in children's speech]') 'brassiere' (cf. Fr. *soutien-gorge*)—this last of fairly recent creation.

The meaning of *blã-balẽn* 'candle', which cannot be explained by the combination of its elements, *blã* 'white' and *balẽn* 'whale', obliges us to regard it as a compound, although its model clearly was Fr. *blanc de baleine* 'spermaceti', from which candles once were made. But elsewhere, composition is often indicated by the occurrence of variants found only in compounds. And since the creole speaker recognizes *cek* 'some' and *sjôy* 'thing' in *kesjôy* 'something', *kat* 'four' and *pat* 'paw' in *kalpat* 'on all fours', it is not surprising if he sees variants of *avã* 'avant (before)', *ã* 'en (in)', *bô* 'side; beside', *bwa* 'wood; tree', *ku* 'coup (stroke)', *lãmẽ* 'hand', *lãmê* 'sea', *mal* 'mal (pain)', *-mê* (only in composition) 'mère (mother)', *pu* 'pou (louse)', *vã* 'wind', *zafê* 'affair; business', and *zye* 'eye' in the following compounds: *ãnafê* 'inquisitive; prying into others' business', *ãnavã* 'forwards', *bôdlãmê* 'on the seafront', *kudmẽ* 'coup de main (a helping hand; voluntary free help)', *kudzye* 'coup d'oeil (glance; watchful eye)', *kudvã* 'coup de vent (hurricane)', *maldimê* 'mal de mère (uterine pains)', and *pulbwa* 'poux de bois (wood-ants)'. But it is improbable that *kõmkwe* 'comme quoi (that [conj.])' should still share a member with *dukwe* (cf. Fr. *de quoi*) 'comfortable financial means', although *kõm-* is recognized as a variant of *kõ* 'comme (as)'.

Apart from some peculiarities of its own, the creole derivation follows its French models (though not always the standard language) rather faithfully. Thus, for example, *sjo* 'to heat (v.i.); to be hot', *sjofe* 'to heat (v.t.)', *sjofê* 'chauffeur', *sjode* 'to scald' (but also 'to burn'), *sjodyê* 'caldron, cook-pot', *sjalê* 'heat', *so* 'saut (n.) (fall [n.])', *sote* 'to jump', *sotê* 'jumper (one who jumps)', *vol* 'flight; theft', *vole* 'to fly; to steal', *volê* 'thief', *du* 'sweet', *dusi* 'to sweeten', *dusê* 'sweetness', *dusmã* 'softly, gently', *su* 'drunk; to be or to get drunk', *sule* 'to make drunk', *sulâ* 'drunkard', *sulezõ* 'drunkenness', *sale* 'salted; to salt', *salezõ* 'saltiness; brine, marinade', *fule* 'to sprain', *fulezõ* 'sprain (n.)', *gume* 'to fight', *gumezõ* 'fight (n.)', *bel* 'beautiful', *belte* 'beauty', *ãbeli* 'embellie (a temporary improvement in the state of the weather or of the sea)', *nuvo* 'new', *nuvelté* 'novelty', *nuvelmã* 'newly', *move* 'bad', *movezte* 'badness', *mesjã* 'unkind', *mesjãste* 'unkindness', *bwê* 'to drink; (something) to drink', *bwesõ* 'beverage, drink (n.)', *pise* 'to piss', *pisa* 'piss (n.)', *kakatwê* 'latrines' (cf. Fr. *caca*), *pase* 'to pass', *pasay* 'passage', *guvêne* 'to steer; to govern', *guvênaj* 'gouvernail (rudder; tiller)', *guvêlmã* 'government'.

Analogic formations are comparatively rare, though one may cite *lusê* 'heaviness' and *lasi* 'to tire' (cf. Fr. *lourdeur* and *lasser*), from *lu* 'heavy' and *las* 'tired, weary', the latter derivative avoiding a possible confusion with *lase* 'to lace' (Fr. *lacer*). We may also mention *cĕbe* 'to take hold of', which many speakers say derives from *cĕn* 'to hold'. The productivity of the suffix *-mã* (from Fr. *-ment*) seems to be assured by the existence of a creation like *malmã* 'poorly, indifferently, "any old how"' (cf. colloquial Fr. *vitement* 'in a hurried manner', which also exists as creole *vitmã* with the same meaning) from *mal* 'badly'; but *acwel-* does not occur except in *acwelmã* 'now', and *hwõnmã* 'persistently, constantly' (cf. Fr. *rondement*) has no clear semantic connexion with *hwõ* 'round'.

From the qualitative predicative *piti* comes a diminutive prefix *ti-*, whose use is widespread: *tikay* 'little house', *tibef* 'calf', *tipul* 'chicken', *timun* 'child' (*yõ ghwã timun* 'a big child'; but in reference to a small person, *yõ mun ki piti* 'a small person [lit., "a person who is small"]' is employed). Another prefix, *l(a)-*, which should not be confused with the homophonous functional prefix of *lakay* 'at home' or 'at the house of', is combined with certain predicatives to form nouns: *lãvi* 'desire', *lafime* 'smoke', *lafĕ* 'hunger', *laswef* 'thirst', etc., from *ãvi* 'to desire', *fime* 'to smoke', *fĕ* 'to be hungry', *swef* 'to be thirsty', etc.

THE SIGNIFICANT UNITS:
FORMS

Several French phrases have been taken over as simple forms by the Dominican creole. Thus, *pitet* 'peut-être (perhaps)', *siltâ* 'sur le tard (toward evening)', *suple* 's'il te/vous plaît', *eti?* 'plaît-il? (what did you say?)', and *talê* 'tout à l'heure (just now)' are autonomous simple forms in the same way as are *demĕ* 'tomorrow', *i(y)ê* 'yesterday', *jôdi* 'today', and *tãto* 'later (in the day)'. Many complex nouns and nominal phrases, most of which refer to a time or a place, also have autonomous functions: *bõmatẽ* '(this) morning', *labitil* 'habit; habitually', *lãdemẽ* 'the following day', *lãnwit* '(at) night', *laplas* '(at the) market', *layvyê* '(at the) river', *lekol* '(at/to) school', *Hwozo* '(at/to) Roseau', *Alõn* (from Fr. *à Londres* 'in London') '(in) England', *lot bô* '(on) the other side (of a river)', *bõ cê* '(de) bon coeur (good heart; gladly)', *fwa sa* 'this time', *yõ ju* 'one day'. Examples: *mwẽ jwẽn-li laplas* 'I met him at the market', *mwẽ khwẽn voye-y lekol (pâ kô-y yõn)* 'I'm afraid to send him to school (by himself alone)', *mwẽ ka ba-w-li bõ cê* 'I give it to you gladly' (cf. *se bõ cê khwab ki fê i pa ni tet* 'it's the crab's good heart which is the reason that he has no head', in which *bõ cê* is dependent).

The subject precedes and the noninterrogative dependent complement follows the predicate center: *i fukã ale jwẽn mõnõk madãm frẽn-li* 'he cleared out to go and join the uncle of his friend's wife', in which *fukã* is the predicate center.

This creole employs some fifty functional morphemes (prepositions, quasi-prepositions, subordinative conjunctions, and one relative pronoun), some of which have a very restricted and others a very extensive use by comparison with their French models.

So, *a* 'à (to, at, etc.)' enters into the conjunctive phrase *a-koz* 'because of', as well as into some adverbial phrases, such as *a-dhwet* 'to the right', *a-gosj* 'to the left', *a kote* 'to the side of; beside', *a-lãdhwet* 'on the right side', *a-lãvê* 'on the reverse side', *a-pye* 'on foot', *a-tê* 'on land; on the ground', and is rather regularly employed to express a temporal relationship: *a-pwezã* 'at present', *a-sizê* 'at six o'clock', *a-tã* 'in time' (cf. *nẽpôt ki tã* 'no matter what time'). And similarly, *di* 'de (of, etc.)' is hardly employed except in selective locutions—such as *yõn di nu* 'one of us', *adã di yo* 'some of them', *de nê di tã* 'two hours (of) time'—and after the predicative *pâle* 'to speak', where it has the sense of 'about; concerning' and may be replaced without change of meaning by *kõt* (cf. Fr. *compte*). In a petrified state, it also subsists in a few compounds, as in *labâ-di-ju (kase)* 'day (lit., "the bar of day") has broken', and in the name of a tree, *lohwie bô-di-mê* 'laurier (du) bord de mer (seaside laurel)'.

On the other hand, this creole makes an extensive use of *ã* 'en (in)' and *pu* 'pour (for)'. So, with *ã:* *i fê-y ã de ju* 'she did it in two days', *i fê-y ã cwizin* 'she did it in the kitchen', *i ale ãjâdẽ* 'she has gone to the garden', *i sôti ã jâdẽ* 'she has come from the garden', *mãje-w ã dife ka sjo* 'your food is on the fire heating'; and with *pu:* *mi hâd pu lave* 'here are clothes to be washed', *thwavay sa mal pu fê* 'this work is hard to do', *tut mãje bõ pu mãje, mẽ tut pahwol pa bõ pu di* 'all food is good to eat, but all words are not good to say', *i kõnet maniê pu fê-y* 'she knows the way to do it', *i hõt pu-w* 'she is ashamed of you'. Moreover, just like *lakay* 'at home' or 'at the house of', so also such phrases in *ã* as *ã-ba, ã-ho, ã-dehô, ã-didã, ã-fas, ã-lê,* and *ã-mitã* ('under(neath)', 'up above', 'outside', 'inside', 'opposite', 'over; above', 'in the middle; between') have both adverbial and prepositive functions: *i pase ã-lê kay nu* 'it passed over our house' (lit., *en l'air* 'in the air'), *i ã-ba tab-la* 'it is under the table'.

Five nouns and five predicatives have functional uses. The former are *bô* 'border, side' or 'beside, near (something)', *kote* 'side; place' or 'beside (someone'; *a-kote* is adverbial, never prepositive), *kõt* 'account' or 'concerning', *lê* 'time of day, o'clock' or 'when', *tã* 'time; weather' or 'at the time of, when'. The latter are *ba(y)* 'to give' or 'to, for', *essepte* 'to except' or 'except', *hwive* to arrive' or 'as far as', *pase* 'to pass' or 'beyond; more than', *sipoze* 'to suppose' or 'supposing that'.

Some prepositives have a very restricted use. *Dã* 'in' expresses only a temporal relationship (*dã de ju* 'in [= after] two days'); *êvê(k)* 'with, with regard to, by means of, (by comparison) with' is most often replaced by *epi* in the sense of 'with; accompanied by'. *La-* 'at' is found only in a few complex forms like *lakay* 'home; at the home of', *lasjas* 'hunting (for)' (cf. *ã-sjas* 'on heat'); *la* and *li* 'by the (unit)' as in *kõmmê la liv/li pye?* 'how much a pound/the foot?' and (*li* only) in dates, as in *li cẽz aut* 'the fifteenth of August'. *Le* (from Fr. *les*) is found in a few locutions denoting a temporal relationship, where it expresses generality: *le cek fwa* 'sometimes', *le swê* 'of an evening, in the evening (generally)', *le momã* 'at certain moments'; and *o-* occurs only in (*iyê*) *o-swê* '(yesterday) in the evening' and in *o-swê-a* 'this evening'.

Two functional morphemes are specifically creole. One, *o* 'to fetch, to get', clearly had as its model Fr. *au(x)*, only one of whose marginal senses (as in *aller aux provisions* 'to go for supplies') has passed into creole: *mwẽ sôti o dlo, epi a pwezã mwẽ ni pu ale o bwa* 'I've just come from fetching water, and now I have to go for wood'. The other, *oti* (cf. Fr. *où est-il*), is employed only in the sense of appealing or addressing oneself 'to' somebody: *i vini oti mwẽ* 'he came to me, he appealed to me, he addressed himself to me'.

The following list contains most of the other functionals: *apwe* 'after', *avã* 'before', *depi* 'since', which are conjunctive, prepositive, and adverbial; *adã* 'in; inside', *dêyê* 'behind', *duvã* 'in front of; before', *hwõ* 'around' *lwẽ* 'far (from)', *otu* 'surrounding', *pwe* 'near (to)', *silõ* 'according to; accordingly', *vizavi* 'opposite', which are prepositive and adverbial; *kõ* 'like; as' and *puki* or *puci* 'why', which are conjunctive and adverbial; *maghwe* 'despite', *pãdã* 'while; during', *pu* 'for', *sã* 'without', which are conjunctive and prepositive; *asu* or *asi* 'on; at; concerning', *hôd* 'outside of; except for', *jik* or *jis* 'until; to (as far as)', *kõt* 'against', *pâ* 'by', *pâmi* 'among', *sof* 'except for, apart from', which are prepositive; *a-koz* 'because', *aselfẽ* 'so (in order) that', *kãmẽm* 'even though/if', *kõmkwe* '(in effect) that', *olye* 'instead of', *osito* 'as soon as', *pâs* and *pâs puci koz* 'because', *pis* 'since, because', *si* 'if', *swe* 'either that', which are conjunctive; *ki* 'than' (correlative: *u pli hwisj ki mwẽ* = *u hwisj pase mwẽ* 'you are richer than I'), *ki* 'who; which' (relative pronoun). Creole *ki . . . ki*—indicating an alternative, as in *ki ã jâdẽ, ki ã laku* 'either in the garden, or else in the yard'—resembles, as a construction, Ptg. *quer . . . quer* rather than Fr. *que ce soit . . . ou bien.*

The personal pronouns are sg. I *mwẽ*, 2 *u* or *-w*, 3 *li, ni, i,* or *-y;* and pl. I *nu*, 2 *zot* or *zô*, 3 *yo*. Except for *li* (or its variant, *ni*), which never occurs as subject, all these forms may serve either as pronominal subject before a word or a phrase having the function of predicate, or as direct or attributive complement after certain predicative words and phrases, after a noun or a nominal group, or after the demonstrative pronoun *sa*. The semivocalic forms *w* and *y* occur only after a preceding vowel, with which they form a diphthong, and are optional variants except where the use of the vocalic form, *u* or *i*, would result in a group of three vowels, inadmissible in this language. As complement, *-li* (often *-ni* after preceding *n*) replaces *i* or *-y* after a consonant or a semivowel. Examples: *u ale* 'you went', *lê w ale* 'when you went', *i ale* 'he/she/it went/has gone', *lê y ale* 'when he went', *mwẽ tãn u* 'I heard you', *mwẽ (v)wê w/u* (phonemes in parentheses may be omitted; the symbol '-/-' indicates optional employment of one or the other alternative) 'I've seen you; I saw you', *mwẽ tãn-ni/-li* 'I (have) heard him', *mwẽ (v)le-y* 'I want it', *tet-li* 'his/her head', *zôhwey-li* 'his/her ears', *pye-y/i* 'his/her feet', *tet u-a* 'your head (in particular), that head of yours', *pye-w-la* 'those feet of yours', *i ba nu-y/i* 'he gave/has given it to us', *nu ba-y-li* 'we gave it to him', *nu ba-w-li* 'we've given it to you'.

The only demonstrative pronoun, *sa* 'this; that', has the same functions as the personal pronouns: *sa hwive* 'that (has) happened', *u ke pwã sa* 'you will take this', *nõm sa-a* 'this/that man', *sa nõm-la* 'that of (which belongs to) the man (in question)', *sa mwẽ* 'mine' (lit., "that of me"), *sa lezot* 'others' (property)', *sa kuzẽ mwẽ* 'that (belonging to) my cousin'.

There are two interrogative pronouns, *kiles* and *sa* (the latter replaceable by the phrase *ki sa;* see below). These normally are sentence-initial and are followed by the subject or by the relative pronoun *ki: kiles ki hwive?* 'who has arrived?', *sa ki hwive?* 'what has happened?', *kiles u ke pwã?* 'which will you take?', *sa u ke pwã?* 'what will you take?', *kiles* (or *sa*) *ki di-w sa?* 'who told you that?'; but *kiles* may, nevertheless, follow the predicate as complement: *u ke pwã kiles?* 'you will take which?'.

We must distinguish *yõ* 'one; a(n)', numeral and indefinite determinant, *yõn* 'one', numeral and indefinite pronoun, and *yõn* 'unaccompanied; (be) alone', qualitative determinant and predicative lexeme. (The other numerals, such as *de* 'two' and *dezyẽm* 'second', function either as pronominals or as determinants.) Quite exceptional are (*yõ*) *lot* '(an)other', (*de*) *lezot* '(two) others', and (*mwẽ pa ni*) *dot* '(I haven't) any more/any others'. And in constructions such as the following, they could be regarded either as determining or as determined: *yõ lot fwa* 'another time', *lezot fwa* 'at other times; former times' (*yõ fi lezot fwa* 'a girl of former times'), *mwẽ pa ni dot sigahwet* 'I haven't any more/any other cigarettes'. Other indefinite pronouns are *adã* 'some', *tut* 'all', *pêsõn* 'nobody', *ocẽn* 'none', *pyes* '(not) at all', *ãyẽ* and *hak* 'nothing'.

The interrogative determinant *ki* 'which' has extensive functions: *ki initil?* 'what's the use?', *ki kote?* (or *o-la?*) 'where?', *ki lê?* 'what time?' or 'when?', *ki mun?* 'who?' (lit., "which person?"), *ki sa?* 'what?' (cf. *pu ki sa?* 'why?'), *ki tã?* 'when?', *ki yõn?* 'which one?' (*ki yõn u ke sjwezi?* 'which one will you choose?').

The indefinite determinants are *yõ* 'a(n)', *cek* 'some' (cf. *cek fwa* 'sometimes' but *kesjôy* 'something'), *sjak* 'each' (*sjak yõn* 'each one'), *tut* 'all; every', *ocẽn* and *pyes* 'no'—the last two, used as follows: (*mwẽ pa ale*) *ocẽn pâ* '(I didn't go) anywhere', (*mwẽ pa wê*) *pyes mun* (or *mwẽ pa wê pêsõn*) '(I didn't see) anybody'.

The definite determinant *la* (or *nã* if *n* precedes) after a consonant or a semivowel, *a* after a vowel, is enclitic. Indifferent as to number and gender, and incompatible with the indefinite determinants *yõ*, *cek*, and *sjak*, it is employed only to particularize the word or phrase it determines: *kay-la* 'the house(s) (in question)', *mun-nã* 'the person(s) (referred to)', *jôdi-a* 'this very day', *mwẽ-a* 'I myself', *yõn sa-a* 'this/that (very) one'. The plurality of reference of a noun so determined may be indicated by preposing *se* (from Fr. *ces*), which is often translatable by 'these' or 'those', but which lacks the force of a demonstrative: (*tut*) *se kay-la* '(all) the/those houses', *se kay sa mwẽ-a* 'those houses of mine', *se sjimiz nõm-la* 'these men's shirts (ces chemises d'homme)', and *sjimiz se nõm-la* 'the shirts of these men (les chemises de ces hommes)'. And since the nominal phrase cannot include more than one definite determinant, which is always final, such a construction as *sjimiz nõm-la* 'this man's shirt' ('la chemise de cet homme' or 'cette chemise d'homme') is ambiguous apart from context.

Of the graduating modifiers—*ase* 'sufficiently', *mwẽ* 'less', *pli* 'more', *thwo* 'too', and *tu* 'altogether; quite'—which determine qualitative predicatives, only the first has the same form as its lexical counterpart (cf. *mwẽs* 'less', *plis* 'more', *thwop* 'too much/many', and *tut* 'everything; all').

Modifications of aspect, mood, and tense are marked by the presence— or indicated negatively by the absence—of three morphemes *ka*, *ke*, and *te*, placed alone or in combination before the predicative (predicate center). There are, therefore, eight possibilities:

		aspect			
		noncontinuative	continuative		
m		(zero)	*ka*	nonpast	
	nonprospective				t
o		*te*	*te ka*	past	e
					n
o		*ke*	*ke ka*	nonpast	s
	prospective				e
d		*te ke*	*te ke ka*	past	

The continuative aspect indicates, according to context, either progression or iteration. The prospective mood indicates futurity, contingence, intention, or will. Examples: *mwẽ kuhwi, mwẽ las* 'I ran, I'm tired', *mwẽ pê-y* 'I'm afraid of him', *mwẽ khwie-y pu i vini jwẽn mwẽ* 'I've called him for him to come and join me' (he's still expected), *mwẽ te kuhwi, mwẽ te las* 'I had run, I was tired', *mwẽ te pê-y* 'I was afraid of him', *mwẽ khwie-y pu i te vini jwẽn mwẽ* 'I called him for him to come and join me' (he was expected in the past), *si mwẽ kuhwi, mwẽ ke las* 'if I run, I'll be tired', *si mwẽ pa las, mwẽ ke kuhwi* 'if I'm not tired, I'll run', *si mwẽ pa te las, mwẽ te ke kuhwi* 'if I weren't tired, I'd run', *si mwẽ te kuhwi, mwẽ te ke las* 'if I had run, I'd be tired', *lê mwẽ ka kuhwi, mwẽ ka las* 'when I run, I get tired', *mwẽ ka pê se mun-la* 'I'm beginning to be afraid of those people' or, according to context, 'I get afraid of those people', *lê mwẽ te ka kuhwi, mwẽ te ka las* 'when I ran (= used to run), I got tired', *yõ lê kõ sa demẽ, mwẽ ke ka thwavay ã jâdẽ mwẽ* 'at this time tomorrow, I shall be working in my garden', *si mwẽ pa te oblije, mwẽ pa te ke ka thwavay jôdi-a* 'if I were not obliged (to do so), I should not be working today'.

With some predicatives such as *bel* 'to be beautiful, fine', *bõ* 'to be good', *lê* 'to be time', etc., the continuative aspect is rarely or never used. And with others (including all predicatives of place) this aspect can have only its iterative sense: (*labitil*) *mwẽ ka ni-y* '(usually) I have it' and *mwẽ ka la* (*le swê*) 'I'm there (in the evenings)', but *mwẽ ni-y* 'I have it (now)' and *mwẽ la* 'I am there (at this moment)'. On the other hand, predicatives preceded by *ke ka* are rather uncommon, being often replaced by a predicate in *ke* followed by a complement in *ka*, as in *mwẽ ke ã jâdẽ-mwẽ ka thwavay* 'I'll be in my garden, working'.

Several predicatives have, beside their ordinary uses, a special value as auxiliaries of aspect—for example, *mwẽ k'ay* (fr. *ka* + *ay* fr. *ale* 'go') *di-w kesjôy* 'I'm going to tell you something', *mwẽ sôti hwive* 'I've just arrived' (with *sôti* 'come/go out [from]'), *i mãce tõbe* 'he almost fell' (with *mãce* 'to lack'), *i te vini hai mwẽ* 'he came to hate me' (with *vini* 'come'), *i pwã plehwe* 'she began to cry' (with *pwã* 'take'), *i mete kuhwi* 'he took to his heels' (with *mete* 'put', which, as an auxiliary, implies great effort), *i sa mâsje* 'he may walk' (with which compare *i sav mâsje* 'he can [knows how to] walk', *sa*, as opposed to *sav* 'know', being employed only as an auxiliary indicating possibility or uncertainty).

The interrogative morpheme *es* (from Fr. *est-ce que*), which may be replaced by a rising intonation, is always placed before the corresponding affirmative sentence: *es u di sa?* 'did you say that?' (cf. *u di sa* 'you said that'), *es i vini?* 'did he come?', *es u ke la?* 'will you be there?', *es i te lê?* 'was it time?', *es se sa?* 'is it that?', *es se mwẽ?* 'is it I?', *es se sa mwẽ?* 'is it mine?', *es sa se yõn?* 'is that one?', *es u byẽ?* 'are you well/all right?', *es u se jã Vye Kaz?* 'are you from Vieille Case?' (*jã* probably comes from Fr. *gent* rather than from the plural *gens*).

Specific interrogatives are usually (but not necessarily) placed at the head of the question: *kumã u vini?* 'how did you come?', *puci yo las/pê?* 'why are they tired/afraid?', (*a*) *ki lê i vini?* '(at) what time did he come?', *kõmmẽ i mãde?* 'how much did he ask?', *o-la u ke ale?* 'where will you go?', *sa* (= *ki sa*) *u di?* 'what did you say?' (cf. *u di ki sa?* 'you said what?', in which order *ki* cannot be omitted). In the case of most predicatives, this order involves no change in the rest of the sentence; but an interrogative in this position cannot itself be predicative (as, for example, are *ki lê* 'what time' and *o-la* 'where' in *i te ki lê?* 'it was what time?' and *u ke o-la?* 'you'll be where?'); and predication is then transferred to the predicative morpheme *ye* 'to be', which, under the same conditions, replaces the copula *se: ki lê i te ye?* 'what time was it?', *o-la u ke ye?* 'where will you be?', *kumã u ye?* 'how are you?', *ki yõn sa ye?* 'which one is that?' (cf. *sa se ki yõn?* 'that is which one?'), *sa sa ye (sa)?* 'what is that?' (cf. *sa se ki sa?* 'that is what?'), *ki jã u ye?* 'where are you from?' or, more literally, 'what "nationality" are you?' (cf. *mwẽ se fwã Khwaib* 'I am a pure Carib').

For expressive, explanatory, or other purposes, prominence may be given to the predicate by preposing *se* followed by the predicative lexeme to normal subject-predicate construction. So: *se kuhwi mwẽ kuhwi* (from *mwẽ kuhwi* 'I ran') 'it's because I ran' or 'I *ran*' (lit., "it's run I've run"), *se mô i ka mô* 'he's *dying*', *se su u ke su* 'you'll be *drunk*', *se las mwẽ te las* 'it's because I was tired'. But a predicate of place, time, or manner of being, instead of being repeated, is replaced by *ye* 'be' in the relative or subordinate clause: *se la mwẽ ka ye le swẽ* 'it's there that I am (am wont to be) in the evening', *se lê sa i te ye* 'that's the time it was', *se kõ sa u tuju te ye* 'that's how you always were' (cf. *u te tuju kõ sa* 'you were always like that'), *se fwã Khwaib mwẽ ye* 'pure Carib I am' (and not something else). Sometimes, by ellipsis, *se* may be omitted: *bô funet i ke ye* 'by the window it must be'. Wherever it occurs, *ye* serves to attach the subject to a preposed "attribute", which may or may not itself be predicative.

But it has no lexical value; and the closest approximation, in this creole, to Descartes's "Je pense, donc je suis" would be *mwẽ ka sjõje, kõ sa mwẽ la* 'I think, therefore I'm there'.

If we replace *se* by *tut* 'all' in such a construction as *se kuhwi mwẽ kuhwi*, we obtain a subordinate clause, *tut kuhwi mwẽ kuhwi*, (*mwẽ hwive thwo tâ*), translatable by 'run as I might, (I arrived too late)'; but grammatically, the first part of this utterance (out of parentheses) is equivalent to 'all running (that) I ran'.

In utterances of the type *se mwẽ* 'it's I', where subject and predicate are confused, *se* remains in the negative (*se pa mwẽ*) and combines with *te* to form a past positive, *sete mwẽ* 'it was I'. But in the past negative, as well as before *te*, *ke*, or *te ke* (identificative sentences in the continuative aspect do not occur), *sa* 'that' resumes the place of subject: *sa pa te mwẽ* 'it was not I', *sa te ke mwẽ* 'it would be I'. Postposition of the negation *pa* to a predicative is exceptional; but *se* and *sa* are clearly distinguished, as in *sa se mwẽ* 'that is I/me' (as when showing a photograph), as against *se sa mwẽ* 'it is mine' (lit., "it's that of me"), while the predicative character of *se* seems to be shown by its alternation with *ye*.

Apart from its combination with *se*, the negation *pa* 'not' always heads the predicate: *mwẽ pa te ke fê sa* 'I shouldn't do that'. But *jamẽ* 'ever' (or, in the positive, *tuju* 'always', *suvã* 'often') may occur in any one of the positions marked X in the following: *X mwẽ pa X te X ke X fê sa X* 'I shouldn't ever do that'—that is to say, anywhere except between the subject and the negation *pa*, or between the predicative and a dependent complement. Creole *ãni* (cf. Eng. *only* and Igbo *nane*, which have the same meaning) often replaces *selmã* 'only' in the sense of 'nothing but; none but': *ãni nõm* 'only men', *se ãni mwẽ i ni pu cẽn-li kõpãni* 'it's only me he has to keep him company'. It also occurs in the conjunctive locution, *ãni pu di*, lit. "only to say," which has the same force as 'except that'.

In the command construction, the subject is not usually expressed: *kuhwi!* 'run!', *las fê thwẽ!* 'enough noise!', *pe la!* or *pe busj u!* 'be quiet!' or 'shut up!', *pa pê!* 'don't be afraid!', *ni labôte!* 'have the goodness; be so kind!', *ale!* 'go!' but *ãnu* 'let's go!'. By preposing *ãnu* to other predicatives, we obtain other command constructions in the first person plural: *ãnu mãje* 'let's go and eat', and even *ãnu ale* 'let's go'. Several predicatives —such as *pe* 'be able', *sa* 'may', *sav* 'know', and *ye* 'be'—do not occur in the command construction, whose function is then fulfilled by paraphrase: *u ni pu sav* 'you have to know', *cẽbe cê!* 'take heart!' (in place of 'be brave!'), *pa fê cê-w sote!* 'don't make your heart jump!' (in place of 'don't be astonished!') *kõpôte kô-w byẽ* 'conduct yourself well' or *bihev!* 'behave!' (in place of 'be good!').

The warning *abõnê* (*u k'ay tõbe*), which is more or less equivalent to 'I bet (you'll fall)', contains a curious form, *abõnê*, which may have had as its model an archaic French phrase, *il y a bon heur que* ..., in which *heur* had kept the old sense of 'omen, augury'. The challenge *latẽ* (*u fê-y*) 'I dare (you to do it)' clearly comes from Fr. (*tu y perdrais ton*) *latin*.

The significant units of creole are for the most part distinct segments, unique and identical to themselves; but there are some exceptions, of which the most striking are the case of *lot, lezot, dot* (see above) and that of the semantic distinction made between the compound *pôkô* (from Fr. *pas encore*) 'not yet' and discontinuous *pa* ... *ãkô* 'not again; not any more'.

The predicative *bay* 'give' becomes *ba* before an attributive complement, including all those cases in which it is employed as a functional morpheme. The predicative *ale* 'go' has a variant *ay*, employed principally (though not only) in combination with *ka* to form *k'ay* 'going to' as an auxiliary, *mwẽ k'ay mãje* 'I'm going to eat'. Also compare *o-la u k'ay?* 'where are you going?', *i ay lapesj* 'he's gone fishing'. The parenthetic consonant of (*v*)*wê* 'see' and (*v*)*le* 'wish, want to' is often (perhaps usually) omitted. Moreover, the latter form, (*v*)*le*, has a variant *vudhwe* (from Fr. *voudrait*) which occurs only after *te ke* and is usually auxiliary: *mwẽ te ke vudhwe dômi* 'I'd like to sleep'.

The following should be distinguished: *mete* 'to put' and *met-ba* 'to give birth', *môde* 'to bite' and *môd* 'take the bait', *sav* 'to know' and *sa* 'may' (auxiliary) (which do not necessarily have the same origin), *pwã* 'to take' and *pwi* 'to be taken; to catch (fire); to light' (*mwẽ pwã lãp-la* 'I've taken the lamps' vs. *mwẽ pwi lãp-la* 'I've lit the lamp[s]'). Local variants found in Dominican Creole may be exemplified by *asid* and *asiz* 'to sit'; *jâdẽ* and *hâdẽ* 'garden (provision ground)'; *legohin, legojin,* and *legovin* 'hand-saw'.

The numerals, *yõ* (or *yõn;* see above), *de, thwa, kat, sẽk, sis, set, ywit, nef, dis, wõz, duz, thwez, katôz, cẽz,* ..., *vẽ,* ..., *sã,* are generally invariable, whatever the initial phoneme of the following determinatum, although for some speakers *sẽk, sis, ywit,* and *dis* lose their final consonants before *fwa* 'times', *ju* 'days', or *mwa* 'months': thus, *yõ* (*bõ*) *avi* 'a (good) counsel' like *yõ* (*bõ*) *kay* 'a (good) house', *vẽ ak* 'twenty acres' like *vẽ kay* 'twenty houses'. But with *lê* 'time of day (or night)' (contrast *nê* 'hour [= twenty-fourth part of a day]') they combine to form the following compounds: *yõnê* 'one o'clock', *dezê* 'two o'clock' (contrast *de nê* 'two hours'), *thwazê, kathwê, sẽcê, sizê, setê, ywitê, nevê, dizê, wõzê, duzê* = *midi* or *mẽnwit*. And the same numeral variants (except for *sẽc-*) enter into composition with *-ã*, which may be regarded as a variant of *lãne* 'year(s)', as do some other numeral variants not occurring with *-ê* 'o'clock'; so, *dezã* 'two years', *kathwã* 'four years', *sẽkã* 'five years', *vẽtã* 'twenty years', *vẽteyẽnã* 'twenty-one years' (*vẽteyẽ* 'twenty-one' is itself a compound), and *sãtã* 'a hundred years'.

ELEVEN

SOME SOCIAL
ASPECTS OF THE
CREOLE LANGUAGES

❄

LINGUISTS ARE FOND of saying that "anything can be expressed in any language"; and there certainly is nothing about the structure of those creoles with which I am acquainted that could render them less fit than another language for whatsoever purpose. (I do not refer to vocabulary, which all languages can and do adapt to changing cultural conditions.) But languages, like people, usually are rated according to what they do or have done, rather than according to that of which they are capable. So, while some (like Swahili) serve as a means of communication among considerable segments of the world's population, and others (like Italian) form the basis of a great literature, some do both and yet others neither. To this last category belong, together with the vast majority of 'normal' languages spoken on earth today, all the creoles. And most of the creoles suffer yet another social disadvantage in that they began as languages employed only among slaves and between slave and master. As a cause determining use or disuse of a creole and its replacement by another language, however, this last consideration seems to be no more than a particular case of a more general principle: any language prospers or declines accordingly as circumstances facilitate or impede its employment throughout the economic community. Let us look at some examples.

Following the Norman Conquest, English gave way to French as the everyday speech of all but churls, because the country's entire economy was then reorganized and controlled by the conquerors. The situation in fourteenth-century England is described as follows in Trevisa's translation of Ranulph Higden's Latin (as cited by Barber 1964, p. 158):

Þis apeyring of þe burþtonge ys bycause of twey þinges. On ys for chyldern in scole, ayenes þe vsage and maner of al oþer nacions, buþ compelled for to leue here oune longage, and for to construe here lessons and here þinges a Freynsh, and habbeþ suþthe þe Normans come furst into Engelond. Also gentil men children buþ ytaught for to speke Freynsh fram tyme þat a buþ yrokked in here cradel, and conneþ speke and playe wiþ a child hys brouch; and oplondysch men wol lykne hamsylf to gentil men, and fondeþ wiþ gret bysynes for to speke Freynsh, for to be more ytold of.

And in 1340, a decree issued by the University of Oxford bade students use either French or Latin in conversation—much as, at the present time, schoolboys and girls in the creole-speaking islands of the former British West Indies are bidden (under pain of being thrashed) to use English, even during recreation.

But Norman–Saxon intermarriage and a new sense of solidarity occasioned by the Hundred Years' War restored English to the position of national language, as testified in the poems of Geoffrey Chaucer, some three centuries later. And after 1399, when Henry IV (himself a native speaker of English) seized the throne, Anglo-Norman quickly died out as a spoken language, although legal documents continued to be written in it until 1731 and even today, royal assent to a parliamentary bill takes the form "Le Roy (or la Royne) le veult."

The prehistoric Karina (Carib) Conquest of the Lesser Antilles had a similar, though somewhat different, linguistic consequence. Here, the language of the conquerors came to be known as the "men's speech" and was learned with diminishing success by subsequent generations of Island-Carib youths, while that of the conquered, Arawakan-speaking indigenes subsisted as the "women's speech" and continued to be, in fact, the mother tongue and first language of all. Today, although traces of this linguistic apartheid may still be found among the Black Carib of Central America, such differences now amount to little more than would, in English, those between *endure* and *bear*, *beverage* and *drink*, *feeble* and *weak*, were the members of these pairs but synonyms belonging, respectively, to the speech of men and to that of women.

At the time of the French Revolution and later, when slavery was abolished, the local creole dialects or patois came to enjoy a considerable vogue in the Lesser Antilles. Thus, the historian Breen (as cited by Alleyne 1961), writing of the situation on St. Lucia during the early part of the nineteenth century, regrets that "patois has superseded the use of the beautiful French language even in the highest circles of French colonial society," one reason allegedly being a desire on the part of the colonists, then hostile to the metropolitan government, to mark their independence from the latter. And at about the same time, the Island-Carib remnant on Dominica, reduced to some three hundred souls, began to relinquish its own (Arawakan) language for the local French Creole.

And now, according to Professor R. B. Le Page (1967), "The processes of change in linguistic habits can be studied admirably at the present time in the Windward Islands of St. Vincent, Dominica, St. Lucia and Grenada, and in Trinidad, each of which has had a Creole French past and is moving or has moved towards a Creole English future"; and "the particular case of the Windward Islands . . . is similar to that of Saramaccan and Sranan dialects in Surinam."

In Surinam, whose very heterogeneous population then numbered some 330,000, a survey made in 1950 among those of eighteen or more years of age showed that 85–90 percent knew Sranan (also called Negro English and Taki-Taki), 50–55 percent knew Dutch, 30–35 percent Hindi, and 15–20 percent Javanese. And while it is true that Sranan and especially Dutch are still a second or a third language for the majority of those Surinamers who employ them (the former being native to some 30 percent and the latter to some 3 percent of the population), the first is gaining native speakers at the expense not only of Hindi and Javanese, but also at that of the Bush Negroes' creoles (Djuka and Saramaccan) and of the Amerindian vernaculars (Arawak, Carib, Trio, Wayana), though the ethnic groups represented by these languages are, for the most part, increasing.

This trend would almost certainly become clear should another linguistic survey be made at the present time—especially if children of school age were to be included. "I don't like my language," said an Arawak youth when I reproached him for speaking Sranan to his sister and brothers; and he explained, in English, by saying that while a knowledge of Dutch was necessary in order to acquire an education and the chance of congenial employment, Sranan was the only acceptable language of social intercourse among his companions at work and at play. (The local football team plays a considerable part in the process of linguistic acculturation.) English also had its merits if one were to work for the American-owned SURALCO (Surinam Aluminum Company). But Arawak served only as a link with the past and with a way of life in which he wanted no part.

The case of this young man may not yet be typical, but neither is it exceptional. He lives some twenty-five kilometers from the capital of Surinam, Paramaribo, in an Indian village that is partly Arawak and partly Carib. Social intercourse between members of the two communities is minimal, and Sranan is their only common language. The local Arawaks include his father's parents (who speak virtually nothing but Arawak) and eight brothers and sisters, together with the latter's wives, husbands, and children (some already adult)—well over sixty persons in all. For the most part, those of his father's generation always speak Arawak to one another, though all know Sranan and some, a little Dutch. But his own mother and two other of the wives come from Orealla in former British Guiana; and although they understand and speak some Arawak, they are more fluent in English, which they have taught their husbands and, to some extent, their children. Yet while these women hardly ever venture to employ Arawak except when speaking to their parents-in-law, they have had to learn Sranan, which is their own children's everyday language. And although those of this village's younger generation both of whose parents habitually speak Arawak (or Carib) still employ the old language when addressing their elders, most of them now resort to Sranan among themselves.

In this and similar ways, Sranan is gaining and other languages are losing native speakers throughout the country, though at different rates according to the accessibility of a particular community to outside influence. And while knowledge and use of Dutch are also on the increase, thanks to the spread of education, this is mainly as a second language. For unlike Sranan, Dutch is rarely employed in familiar conversation between Surinamers of equal status, but is reserved for formal occasions and for those in which it is desired to mark social distance or to show respect.

In those of the Lesser Antilles where a creole language is spoken concurrently with French or English, the two languages also fulfill different functions—in rather the same way as do French *tu* and *vous* and their equivalents in other European languages (Brown and Gilman [1960] call these, respectively, the pronouns of solidarity and of power). Among the growing numbers of these islands' inhabitants who use both, the creole is the language of familiarity, relaxation, or condescension; French or English, that of politeness, formality, or formalization. And as was the case in older European usage of the two pronouns of address, so the modern creole speaker who is bilingual frequently switches from one language to the other in order to convey a transient shift of mood, attitude, or subject matter. Such bilinguals have now come to constitute a considerable proportion of these islands' inhabitants; for, as in the case of Dutch in Surinam, a reasonably good knowledge of French or English is requisite for those who would attain to a fair degree of comfort and security in the modern world.

But in other respects, the linguistic situation on the creole-speaking islands of the Caribbean differs from that found in Surinam. On the islands, with the partial exception of Trinidad, and despite—or just because of—the many and various degrees of racial intermixture, there are no longer any clear-cut groups based on the threefold distinction of race, language, and culture; and almost all those who use the local creole speak it as their mother tongue.

On the other hand, links between the ex-British colonies of the Eastern Caribbean have been strengthened by the abortive Federation and the attainment of internal self-government, while those between neighboring French and British islands have been weakened by the former's assimilation as *départements d'outre mer*. The creoles of Guadeloupe, Dominica,

Martinique, and St. Lucia are still sufficiently alike to be mutually intelligible; but as their vocabularies become adapted to changing cultural conditions by borrowing from two different sources, they are growing apart with each succeeding generation. And intercourse (commercial, social, or other) between the French and British islands, though constant, is now slight in comparison with that which takes place among the latter, in many of which (e.g., Antigua, Barbados, Montserrat, Nevis, St. Kitt's, and St. Vincent) a French creole is not or no longer spoken; so that even the enthusiasm aroused by interisland cricket matches (in which the French islands do not participate) does something to extend the use and knowledge of English.

Of English? Le Page thinks that the islands he names are moving or have moved from "a Creole French past" toward "a Creole English future." If by these terms he refers to regional dialects comparable to Southern French and Northern (British) English, I agree that the emergent English he has in mind is likely to be more or less heavily tinged with creolisms, but I object to the use of "Creole French" to designate an idiom as structurally different from French as is the language said to be in process of replacement. And if by "Creole English" he means a language as structurally different from English as are Sranan and Saramaccan—which I should call, for want of a better name, "English creoles"—I very much doubt whether any such language will ever evolve in the Lesser Antilles; for, understandably, the literate West Indian does not ask, "What can I do for my language?" but "What can my—or another's—language do for me?" And of the French islands, where the linguistic situation is no more static than in those considered by Le Page, the only significant statement could be to say that they are moving from "a French Creole past" toward "a Creole French future."

And although Le Page appears to find this distinction superfluous, as expressing a difference in degree, not kind, yet it seems legitimate to distinguish between, for example, "French Creole" /kumã u ye?/ 'comment vous est?' and "Creole French" /kumã èt-vu?/ 'comment êtes-vous?', both meaning 'how are you?', where standard French has *comment allez-vous?* or *comment vas-tu?* or *comment ça va?* For here, the second form (but not the first) employs the French inflection of the verb, with inversion; and though unidiomatic, is probably intelligible to most Frenchmen from the mother country. Similarly, "Creole English" /hwat abowt yu?/ 'what about you?', which also means 'how are you?' (and may be so used to initiate a conversation), though unidiomatic in this sense, is more intelligible to a stranger than is either its "English Creole" equivalent, SN /fa fu yu?/ "how for you?" or /fa yu tan?/ "how you stand?", or its "French Creole" equivalent, LA /sa kõt u?/ 'ça compte vous?'—literally, "what concerning you?" Moreover, whereas Creole

French and Creole English are usually closer to the standard than the above examples might lead one to suppose, this is not true of French and English creoles.

Le Page (1967) argues—brilliantly, I think—that "there is no such thing as a language except insofar as the idiolects of two or more people overlap"; and he goes on to say that "nearly all linguistic change results from either contact or from a shift in the functional loading of the structures of an idiolect due to environmental change; each contact, each shift results in a newly modified system." Obviously, the creoles owe their very existence to contact; and as we have seen in preceding chapters, there has often been some overlap of an accidental nature between the presumably unrelated languages in contact, enhanced in perhaps most cases by the common conditions of enslavement and transportation. And today, bilingualism, which is contact in its most "contagious" form, combines with cultural change to modify the structures of most creole idiolects. We can examine a small sample of this process.

When I first visited the island of Dominica, I was intrigued by the creole way of counting money, which included such apparently un-explainable terms as *pwedyal* "predial" = 'three halfpence', *sẽ nwè* "five blacks" = 'threepence', *dis nwè* "ten blacks" = 'sixpence', *sẽ ti-pyes* "five little bits" = 'ninepence', and *sẽk eskalẽ* "five *escalins*" (Fr., from Du. *schelling*) = 'one shilling and sixpence'—*nwè, ti-pyes,* and *eskalẽ* being otherwise unknown as names for coin or for money of account. But I then found out that Dominica had had, until about one hundred years ago, a pounds, shillings, and pence currency of its own, whose value at the time that it was converted into sterling was three-fifths that of the latter (one Dominican pound of twenty shillings then being worth twelve shillings sterling). So that

yo nwè 'one penny'	became obsolete
yõ pwedyal 'twopence halfpenny'	became 'three halfpence'
yõ ti-pyes 'a threepenny bit'	became obsolete
sẽ nwè 'fivepence'	became 'threepence'
yõ eskalẽ 'a sixpenny bit'	became obsolete
dis nwè 'tenpence'	became 'sixpence'
sẽ ti-pyes 'five threepenny bits (1s/3d)'	became 'ninepence'
sẽk eskalẽ 'five sixpenny bits (2s/6d)'	became 'eighteen pence'.

Clearly, the old terms were transferred to their exact equivalents in the new currency when such existed, and otherwise forgotten; so that those which survived ceased to have "meaning" though they continued to have "reference." Strangely, I think, none of them has been adapted to the new decimal currency, so that *dis nwè* continues to refer to 'twelve cents', while 'ten cents' is *tensens*. Such conservatism may well lead to the disappearance of the old terms, for prices such as 3, 6, 12, 18, and 36 cents are uncommon in countries having a decimal coinage. But one still may hear *sẽ pwedyal* employed for '15 cents'; and I am still unable to find the connection between Eng. *predial* and this creole word.

Any living language must be adapted to the changing needs of its speakers or else perish; and there can be no doubt that Sranan, the coastal creole of Surinam, has won enhanced prestige and a new lease on life through the efforts over the past fifteen years of native poets and writers, themselves stimulated, more often than not, by contacts made outside their own country. See Voorhoeve and Lichtveld 1975. And the same is said to be true of Papiamentu, the creole of the Dutch Antilles. On the other hand, the creoles (or one-time creoles) of Barbados, Antigua, Jamaica, and British Honduras appear to be in the process of reabsorption by English and to have the status of what David DeCamp has called "post-creole continua." Some may be tempted to attribute this difference to the absence or continuation of pressure from the model language, but such a hypothesis is not supported by a glance at the French-based creoles, those spoken in the French départements d'outre mer being just as distinct from French as are those spoken in islands where English is the official language. And in neither of these two groups of French-based creoles has much effort been made to produce a worthwhile literature in the native creole.

It seems at least possible that an explanation may be found in the divergent attitudes, in recent times, of the colonial or excolonial powers toward the inhabitants of their colonies or excolonies. The Dutch are and long have been used to other peoples' ignorance of their language and have themselves shown great aptitude for learning foreign tongues. Not until after the abolition of slavery in 1863 were the slaves in Surinam even allowed to learn the masters' language; and although compulsory education has since then brought some knowledge of Dutch to an ever-increasing number, proficiency in that language is achieved only by those having more than ordinary ambition. As Christian Eersel (1971, p. 319) puts it:

For some Surinamers, who have rejected Sranan, the situation is hopeless, for they have no language of their own. An open acceptance of Dutch as one's mother tongue is considered a betrayal of the growing national consciousness. A Surinamer does not want to be called a Dutchman. Consequently, Dutch is not his language, although he will not go so far as to say that Sranan is. His pragmatic attitude leads him to learn Dutch in order to study at a Dutch university, to be able to carry on business and politics and by doing so to gain prestige in the society. This ambivalence is certainly one of the causes of the lack of substantive creative writing in Dutch. In the end, the nationalistic attitude and the linguistic ambivalence produce the same result: weakening of the prestige position of the Dutch language.

Yet this national consciousness seeking a national language owes its growth to the privileged few who, in Holland and elsewhere abroad, have learned that Dutch is not a world language and that Western European culture and society are not the only—nor necessarily the best—models for all the world to follow.

The situation in the French départements d'outre mer is quite different, especially since the assimilation of 1946. But since long before then the French, who themselves learn foreign languages with reluctance, have put a premium on a good knowledge of their language and culture; and wherever they have gone, they have sought to train an élite that thought and felt itself to be French and was able to assume the highest positions. In this they have had considerable success; and when, some years ago, de Gaulle asked the Martiniquais whether they had rather continue as part of the glorious French *communauté* or become independent as a particle of dust in the Atlantic Ocean, there were few who would have chosen the latter alternative. Black and white, communist and royalist alike, the vast majority of Martiniquais consider themselves to be Frenchmen; and the same is true of nearly all the inhabitants of the other "assimilated" French territories, like Guadeloupe, French Guiana, and Réunion.

As a result of this attitude, itself the consequence of good modern educational facilities within the country, the average Martiniquais today speaks much better French than his counterpart in such formerly British islands as Dominica and St. Lucia speaks English. And he has achieved this without relinquishing or being asked to relinquish his native creole patois. But feeling that French is or should be his own language just as much as creole, he now restricts the latter's functions to the more informal kinds of social intercourse, while local writers and poets like Aimé Césaire understandably prefer to address a wider public in what, after all, is still a world language.

Speakers of a French creole belonging to islands where English is the official language are in a more difficult situation. For more than a hundred years their patois has been decried as "a monkey language" or as no language at all, while assiduous though ineffectual attempts have been made to eradicate it by the importation of elementary school teachers from Barbados and Antigua, and by teaching small children that the use of their mother tongue was degrading.

But opportunities for hearing—and especially for using—what might pass for standard English have been and still are rare in small islands like Dominica (295 sq. mi., 70,000 inhabitants) and St. Lucia (240 sq. mi., 100,000 inhabitants); and the English have never encouraged their subject peoples to regard themselves as Englishmen. Under these circumstances it is hardly surprising that the use of creole among the better-educated town dwellers has diminished and that no native writer or poet has yet attempted a "Défense et Illustration" of the creole language. For, as Auguste de Saint Quentin wrote a hundred years ago, with special reference to the creoles of Cayenne, the Lesser Antilles, and Haiti:

idiome qui pourrait devenir une langue [nationale] un jour, si la population d'Haïti, acquérant la sève et la vigueur nécessaires pour être plus tard un peuple civilisé, trouvait en elle-même quelques génies organisateurs qui sussent manier le créole, le développer et le fixer par des monuments littéraires sérieux. Eventualité peu probable, car les Haïtiens paraissent plus jaloux, tout en parlant créole, d'écrire un détestable français, que de fonder une langue nationale.

TWELVE

CREOLE TEXTS AND
WORDLISTS

❖

TEXTS

Sranan. *Basja Pataka*

0. a ningi ningi ba busara,
ningi ningi ba busara,
how a how, ningi ningi ba busara-o.
a ningi ningi ba ningi ningi ba ningi ningi ba busara-o.
a how a how, ningi ningi ba busara.
di moni no de, s'sa Akuba lowe,
ma ningi ningi ba busara,
hej a hej, ningi ningi ba busara.
a ningi ningi ba busara,
ningi ningi ba busara,
how a how, ningi ningi ba busara-o.

1. Tje!
we i si, a tor disi, di i jere e singi de—"a ningi ningi ba busara, ningi ningi ba busara"—a no now a un w'wan uma e gowe libi man. 2. sens a fosi ten i be a wan basja, di e kari basja Pataka. 3. a pranasi kom broko now, na biro Kawna; now skowtupost kom dape de—a Kunofru.

4. We dape ben de a moro hogri presi, pe den ben e tjari srafu gowe go makti. 5. ef i de wan hogri srafu, dan den tja i gowe go makt a Kunofru. 6. uma den ben e poti ton a den mofo hari ken-pondo. 7. dat wan taki den e prej buriki fu hari ken-pondo.

8. We a ningi ningi ba busara.

9. We, a basja fu dape, hen nen ben de basja Pataka. 10. We basja Pataka—pataka a wan sani, a de a libi, ef i mek krapi nanga hen, a e bet tumsi takru. 11. a dede, tok a e beti. 12. biká, ef i ab a drej pataka, kabá i anu misi go na hen tifi sej, a sut i kabá.

13. j'e njam hen srefi, tok a e bet ju. 14. *dùs* pataka na wan hogri sani 15. *want* a man ben de wan hogri nengre, ne a tek hen nen fu pataka. 16. dan a ben kon de basja. 17. dan ala suma e kar hen taki Basja Pataka.
18. we te a kon na oso, ala dej a mu njam dri sortu tonton. 19. den tonton ben tan na ini baki ini. 20. wan sej weti kasaba tonton, wan sej baana tonton, wan sej kokorí tonton.
21. dat wan taki: dri sortu tonton e de na a pikin baki fu hen, pe a e njam 22. komki no ben de a ten dati: na ini bigi krabasi nanga krabasi spun. 23. dan na okro brafu de na ini wan krabasi, dan a kap-kapu jarabaka ede nanga katfisi, stimofo, bonjo-bonjo sowtu meti de na a wan krabasi.
24. *dùs* ala dej s'sa Abeni, na hen ben e bor tonton. 25. ef a dej dia kom, s'sa Abeni bor bana, a e kis s'sa Abeni, a e fom hen. 26. no fom hen prej-prej fom-fom, a e fom hen bun fom-fom. 27. s'sa Abeni no kan tjar hen go a fes-sej go kragi a granmasra, biká a gran-basja kabá.
28. we, s'sa Abeni no si wan fasi fu du, di a fom-fom kon sar hen skin. 29. ne s'sa Abeni tagi wan fu den trawan, a taki: "basja e fom mi tumusi!"
30. a tak: "we sisa fa j o du?"
31. a tak: "baja, mi no a wan weni, noso mi sa dede sref-srefi!"
32. we now, ala basja moni, a s'sa Abeni ben e hor hen. 33. ma nomo basja tan te wan pisi.
34. ala sonde pagara ben e go pranasi. 35. now un jere a singi disi. 36. den fosten suma ben e singi hen taki:

37.   a kor mi-o, baja Kwami kor mi-o!
       a kor mi, fa m baja Jaw kor mi!
       a taki: Pagara kon, a e go baj wan koto,
       pagara kon, a e go baj jaki!
       now di pagara kon, m baja go a mangro.
       a go a mangro, a go a mangro.
       pagara kon, m baja go a mangro,
       a go a mangro, a go a mangro,
       pagara kon, m baja go a mangro.

38. ma basja Pataka dati no ben go a mangro. 39. dati wan tak a singi. 40. biká te den pramisi den uma den sani, tak te pagara kom...
41. biká ala sonde pagara ben e kon na ini pranasi. 42. krara e kon, koto e kon, angisa e kon! 43. gowtu keti no ben de, buj no ben de. 44. a krara ben e taj na anu—unge, sabi diri—na den krara dat ben de, a dat den ben e taj na anu.
45. dosu te pagara kom, te a baja no man baj, dan a e gowe fu hen a jur dati. 46. dan a sab tak pagara e kom, dan a e gwe fu hen a mangro, tak a o kis krabu. 47. na hen na a singi.
48. We ma basja Pataka dati no ben go a mangro, leki...

49. a s'sa tagi wan fu den trawan, a taki: "baja, mi no kan man anga a fom-fom fu basja moro."
50. a tak: "we sisa, dan a gowe i mu gowe lib hen."
51. a tak: "we a somen ten di mi tan katibo gi basja, tek somen fom-fom. 52. dan basja abi somen moni."
53. a tak: "we sisa, dan i mu e begi hen hala juru, mek a e baj wan sani gi ju. 54. dan te a moni kabá, dan i mu gowe!"
55. a tak: "haj! i gi mi wan bun laj!"
56. basja prit hen skin. 57. a jur di basja lib hen, hen ati kowru, a tak:
58. "basja, mi wan begi ju, te pagara kom, i no kan baj tu dobrusten koto gi mi?"
59. a tak: "aj, mi sa baj gi ju."
60. a so ala juru a e begi wan tra sani. 61. ma a no e kis fom-fom moro, biká a e fom a tonton now ala dej. 62. a no e tak hen gowé, te ala a moni fu basja kabá.
63. nomo a pak-pak ala den san fu hen na ini hen pagara, a floisi a go a wan tra pranasi.
64. a jur di basja komopo kom na oso, a o si a oso drej. 65. ne basja kon a mofo doro, ne basja bigin taki a tori. 66. dan ala suma fu pranasi sabi, tak s'sa Abeni gowé:
67. "baja, fa fu s'sa Abeni?"
68. ne basja no man taki. 69. ne basja taki bari:

70.   a ningi ningi ba busara,
     ningi ningi ba busara,
     hej a how, ningi ningi ba busara.
     moni no de, na uma lowé,
     ma ningi ningi ba busara,
     a how a how, a ningi ningi ba busara-o.
     a ningi ningi ba busara-o,
     a ningi ningi ba busara,
     a hej a how, ningi ningi ba busara.
     moni kabá, na uma lowé,
     ma ningi ningi ba busara,
     hej a hej, ningi ningi ba busara-o.

71. dosu lowé fu uma nanga takru du fu umasuma, a no now a ben de, a kon. 72. sensi grontapu seti a ben de.

(told by Alex de Drie)

Translation. Basha Pataka
0. [The much repeated "ningi ningi ba busara" is thought to mean "Negroes are ungrateful," but only the sixth line is in straightforward language, meaning "When there was no money, Sis(ter) Akuba ran away."]

1. Listen!

Well, you see, this story that you just now heard being sung—*a ningi ningi ba busara, ningi ningi ba busara*—it is not just nowadays or only among us that women go away and leave men. 2. There was, long since, an overseer called Pataka. 3. The plantation, on the lower Commewyn, is now in ruin; now it's a police station—Kunofru.

4. Well, that was the worst place, where they took slaves to be tamed. 5. If you were a bad slave, then they took you to be tamed at Kunofru. 6. With women, they used to put a bit in their mouth to haul the sugarcane pontoons. 7. That means they served as donkeys to haul the cane pontoons.

8. Well, that is *ningi ningi ba busara*.

9. Well, the overseer there was called Basha [overseer] Pataka. 10. Well, Basha Pataka—*pataka* is something, if it is alive and you are careless with it, it'll bite you very badly. 11. And if it's dead, it still bites you. 12. Because, if you take a dried pataka, your hand has no sooner chanced to go near his teeth than he has already stabbed you.

13. Even when you eat him he will bite you. 14. So pataka is a bad thing. 15. Because the man was a bad negro, that is why he took his name from the pataka. 16. And then he became overseer. 17. Then everybody called him Basha Pataka.

18. Well, when he came home, every day he must have three kinds of *tonton* to eat. 19. These were placed on a tray. 20. On one side was tonton of sweet manioc, on another was tonton of plantain, and on yet another was tonton of bitter manioc meal.

21. That means there were three kinds of tonton on the little tray from which he ate 22. (bowls did not exist at that time), in big calabashes with a calabash spoon. 23. Then the okra was in one calabash, and the chopped *yarabaka* heads, together with catfish, tidbits, and salted meat with bones in another.

24. And so every day Sis' Abeni, it was she who made tonton. 25. If one day when he came home, Sis' Abeni had cooked plantains, he would take hold of Sis' Abeni and beat her. 26. Not beat her playfully, but give her a sound thrashing. 27. Sis' Abeni could not take him to the front side and make a complaint to the owner, because he was already the head overseer.

28. Well, Sis' Abeni didn't see what she could do when the beatings became more than she could bear. 29. So Sis' Abeni said to one of the others, she said: "Basha beats me too much!"

30. He said: "Well, sister, what are you going to do?"

31. She said: "Friend, I see no way out until I myself shall be dead."

32. Well, now, all the overseer's money, it was Sis' Abeni who took care of it. 33. But no more about the overseer for a while.

34. Every Sunday a huckster used to visit the plantation. 35. Now listen to this song. 36. The old-time people used to sing it like this:

37.   He cheated me, friend Kwami cheated me!
He cheated me, and how friend Yao cheated me!
He said: When the huckster comes he'll buy [me] a skirt,
when the huckster comes, he'll buy a jacket.
Now when the huckster came, my friend went to the mangrove
swamp,
He went to the mangrove, he went to the mangrove.
The huckster came, my friend went to the mangrove swamp,
he went to the mangrove, he went to the mangrove,
the huckster came, my friend went to the swamp.

38. But as for Basha Pataka, he didn't go to the mangrove swamp. 39. That's the meaning of the song. 40. Because when they promise women things, when the huckster comes, ...

41. Because every Sunday the huckster used to come to the plantation. 42. He brought beads, he brought skirts, he brought kerchiefs. 43. He did not bring gold chains, he did not bring bracelets. 44. Beads were tied around the arm—[those called] *unge, sabi diri*—whatever beads there might be were tied on the arm.

45. So, when the huckster came and the boyfriend couldn't buy, then he would go away at that time. 46. Since he knew that the huckster was coming, he would go to the mangrove swamp and say that he was going to catch crabs. 47. That is the song.

48. But as for Basha Pataka, he didn't go to the swamp, like ...

49. Sis' said to one of the others, she said: "Friend, I can't put up with Basha's beatings any more."

50. He said: "Well, Sister, then you'll just have to leave him."

51. She said: "Well, I've been slaving for Basha so long, and taken so many beatings. 52. Besides, Basha has so much money."

53. He said: "Well, Sister, then you must be at him all the time for him to buy something for you. 54. Then when the money is finished, then you must go away!"

55. She said: "Fine! You've given me good advice!"

56. Basha gave her a hiding. 57. When Basha left her and had cooled down, she said: 58. "Basha, I want to ask you, when the huckster comes, won't you buy two diced skirts for me?"

59. He said: "Yes, I'll buy them for you."

60. And so all the time she kept asking for something or other. 61. But she didn't get beaten any more, because now she pounded tonton every day. 62. She says nothing about going away until all Basha's money is finished.

63. Then she packed all her things in her basket and flitted to another plantation.

64. When Basha quit work and came home, he finds the house empty.
65. So Basha comes to his doorstep and begins his lamentation. 66. Then all the plantation knew that Sis' Abeni had gone:
67. "Friend, how is Sis' Abeni?"
68. So Basha cannot answer. 69. So Basha shouted:

70.   *a ningi ningi ba busara,*
ningi ningi ba busara,
hey a how, ningi ningi ba busara.
There's no money, the woman's run away,
but *ningi ningi ba busara,*
a how a how, a ningi ningi ba busara-o.
a ningi ningi ba busara-o,
a ningi ningi ba busara,
a hey a how, ningi ningi ba busara.
The money has finished, the woman has run away,
but *ningi ningi ba busara,*
hey a hey, ningi ningi ba busara-o.

71. And so women's running away and women's misdeeds are not something that has come about in our own time. 72. They have existed since the world came into being.

Commentary

This story probably dates from the time shortly before or shortly after the abolition of slavery in Surinam (1863), for its heroine, Sister Abeni, apparently was free to leave one plantation for another.

The word *basha* comes from Eng. *overseer*, to which the Jamaican equivalent, *obasia*, is one step nearer. The *pataka* is a fish resembling the snook, with very sharp teeth.

One of the traditional openings in telling a story is by the formula *Cric! Crac!;* another is the singing of a song, the meaning of whose words is sometimes, as here, quite obscure.

The words *dùs* 'thus; so' (14, 24) and *want* 'because' (15) have been italicized in the text because they are unassimilated Dutch loanwords. Elsewhere in the same text we find their Sranan equivalents, *dosu* (45) and *biká* (passim).

Some words have been left untranslated. Thus, *tonton* (18 and passim) is a dish made by boiling, then pounding, green plantains, breadfruit, etc.; *yarabaka* (23) and *pataka* (passim) are species of fish; *unge* and *sabi diri* (lit., "knowledge is precious") are names given to different kinds of beads. SN *baja*, here rendered 'friend', may come from Ptg. *compai*.

The word *pagara* is a Karina loanword which refers primarily to a type of Amerindian basket widely used for storing and transporting clothes, etc. Here it refers to the huckster with his pagara full of things he hopes to sell on the plantations; and I have therefore translated it by 'the huckster', except in 63, where the word 'basket' is applicable. In 27, "the front side" refers to that part of the plantation where the owner or director lives. In translating *floisi* 'to change dwelling place' (63), I have employed the Yorkshire term 'flit', but 'move' would do just as well. The meaning of *weni* in 31 (*mi no a wan weni* 'I haven't one X') is doubtful, but probably is 'refuge' or 'way out (of a difficulty)'.

Finally, the word *stimofo* in 23 deserves some explanation. It is a contraction of *switi mofo*, literally "sweet mouth," but referring to anything to eat that is especially agreeable to the taste. It is interesting to note that CC *sjwit* (from Eng. *sweet*) and LA *du* (from Fr. *doux*) are also employed with this meaning ('agreeable to the taste').

Lesser Antillean, Dominican dialect. Listwê Karuhú

1. tã lõtã i pa te ni pyes sjimẽ Ladominik—ãni thwas tu sel. 2. epi se asu se thwas kõ sa yo fê pwemie sjimẽ.

3. ebẽ, yõ pâti se vye Khwaib sôti ãsãm pu yo desãn Wozo. 4. tã sa-a, se pâ letã Bweri mun te ka pase. 5. kõ yo te ka ale, yo te ka sjãte, epi, silõ lakutim, yo te ka bat lamẽ epi kõye asi fes yo:

> hĩyara hĩya, sosori so!
> tefẽ fwê mwẽ te ka tãse
> pli meyê pase mwẽ.
> nu ka tesãn Woso,
> tã pu pêlê, fê kõ feke.

6. lê yo ãbâce ã-lê môn, hwive pwe letã Bweri, yõ fãm mãde mahwi-y pêmi pu i sa kite, pu i te pe ale fê kesjôy pu lavi-y. 7. se lezot epi mahwi-a fê sjimẽ yo. 8. lê i fini, tã i te ka gâde bô letã pu se ti kokiyaj hwuj u ka jwẽn la, madãm-la hwimâce cek bel ti mas kohway. 9. i hwamase yõn, epi i pwese kô-y pu i jwẽn lezot. 10. i ale, i ale, mẽ apwe i mâsje cek tã, i thuve i te devihwe asu mẽm plas la i te ye bô letã-a. 11. i pati ãkô, epi yõ lot fwa i ãni devihwe asu mẽm plas la i te sôti. 12. i hwipati, mẽ lê i thuve i te mâsje ã-hwõ pu twazyẽm fwa, i jete ti mas kohway-la, epi i sôti yõ kathwiyẽm fwa. 13. i ale, i ale—jik tã i hwive ã-lê yõ ghwã plat. 14. soley te ka kusje, mẽ i pa te sa wê pyes mun. 15. i twavêse plat-la, epi i mõte, i mõte. 16. lê i te hwive õ bõ distãs ã-lê plat-la, i wê yõ ti kay duvã-y. 17. i hele, mẽ i pa tãn pyes hwepõs. 18. lê i vini pli pwe, i vwê cwizin-la te vid epi lapôt kay-la te fême. 19. kãmẽm, yõ funet te uvê: si-y hose kô-y asi lapwẽt zôtey-li, i hwive jis pu i te sa vwê ã-didã. 20. pyes mun pa te la— ãni yõ kãtite kasav ki te palâce ã-lê yõ ling pu i sjes.

21. ebẽ, i te pêd, i te las, i te fẽ. 22. kõ sa i hale kô-y mõte, epi y sote

hwãthwe adã kay-la. 23. i mãje yõn se kasav-la, epi i kusje pu poze. 24. cek tã pase, epi y wê yõ ti nõm êvê yõ khwey pwesõ ã lamê-y ka vini piti pa piti pa, kõ si di i te pê. 25. i khwie-y: "misyê-oy! pa pê; mwê se yõ mun kõ u-mêm. 26. ãni pu di mwê egahwe, epi, kõ mwê te las epi mwê te fê, mwê hwãthwe esit pu mwê poze, epi mwê mãje yõn se kasav-u-a. 27. me mwê se yõ mun kõ u-mêm, pa pê!" 28. piti nõm-la pa di hak. 29. i ale ã cwizin, i netye pwesõ-y, i pahwe supe. 30. lê tut bitê te pahwe, i sepahwe mãje epi lõje sa madãm-la ba-y a-distãs, yõ maniê kuca, kõ si i te pê-y. 31. epi apwe yo fini mãje, i mõthwe-y la pu i dômi. 32. tut tã sa i pa te di yõ sel pahwol ba-y. 33. kãmêm, lê lãnwit vini, i jwên-li dusmã, epi kusje pwe-y pu dômi. 34. lãdmê bõmatê, tuju sã i di ãyê, ti nõm-la pwã golet-li epi i ay lapesj (pis sa te leta-y). 35. pu devihwe yõ ti mumã avã soley hwãthwe kõ pwemie ju-a.

36. cek tã pase kõ sa, jis fãm-la vini fê yõ zãfã ba nõm-la.

37. mahwi madãm-la, a-pwezã, te hwive Wozo êvê hwestã se Khwaib-la. 38. yo fê zafê yo epi yo devihwe o-vã sã yo tãn ãyê kõt madãm-la. 39. tut sjasje i te sjasje, pov mahwi-a pa te sa jwên êvê pyes lapahwãs madãm-li. 40. yõ ju, vye Wanuhí—ki, natihwelmã, te sav tut sa ki fet—vini thuve mahwi-a. 41. i di-y: "initil u sjasje pli lwê pu madãm-u; u pa te ke jwên-li. 42. yõ lot maniê, mwê sa di-w o-la i ye. 43. i ka viv ãsãm êvê yõ zõbi yo ka khwie Karuhú adã kay-li ã-lê letã Bweri. 44. i jis fê yõ zãfã ba-y. 45. si lide-u di-u pwã-y vihwe, u ke jwên-li la i yõn (pis Karuhú ka pase tut lajunê dehô ka pesje), epi i ke swiv-u. 46. mê, avã u mene-y ale, pwã titak kotõ, kade-y, epi fê yõ ti ling êvê-y. 47. epi khwasje ã lasal, epi khwasje ã sjãm-la, epi khwasje tu hwõ kay-la, epi khwasje adã cwizin, epi pwã ling epi mete-y hwõ ku zãfã-a, epi pwã madãm-u epi ale."

48. ebê, mahwi-a pwã sjimê-y; i ale, i ale. 49. ãfê i hwive duvã kay zõbi-a. 50. lê madãm-li vwê i ka vini, i kumãse pê. 51. i pwã plên: "mahwi mwê oy! se pa pu u sevê êvê mwê, pis se u-mêm ki kite mwê pêd. 52. epi sa ki hwive mwê se pa pã pyes fot-mwê." 53. "mwê pa vini pu pale sa," nõm-la di-y; "tu sa mwê le se pu mwê mene u vihwe a-kay." 54. pi, kõ i sjõje sa Wanuhí te di-y, i pwã titak kotõ, i kâde-y, epy i têd-li pu fê yõ ti ling. 55. apwe sa, i khwasje ã lasal, i khwasje ã sjãm-la, i khwasje tu hwõ kay-la, i khwasje ã cwizin, i mete ling-li hwõ ku zãfã-a, pwã madãm-li epi ale sjimê-i.

56. yõ ti tã apwe sa Kuruhú hwive êvê ti khwey pwesõ ã lamê-y, kõ lakutim. 57. i ale dwet ã cwizin epi i khwie fãm-la. 58. lavwa-y hwepõn jik ã-didã kay, mê lê Karuhú ale la, i pa te sa wê-y pyes kote. 59. i khwie-y ãkô; fwa sa-la, vwa-y hwepõn deyê kay. 60. i sôti ã laku, mê lê i pa wê-y i khwie ãkô. 61. voyay-sa, lavwa-y hwepõn ã cwizin. 62. sa kõtinnê kõ sa jik tã Karuhú vini si-telmã kolê, i pwã zãfã-a, i voltije-y ã lê, epi y sufle ã bõda-y. 63. mêm mumã zãfã tunê kalbas-plõ epi vole ale.

(told by Ma' Bernard)

Translation. *The Child of Karuhú*

1. In olden times there were no roads in Dominica, but only trails. 2. And it was upon such trails that the first roads were built.

3. Well, a band of old-time Caribs set out together to go down to Roseau. 4. At that time people used to pass by way of the Boeri Lake. 5. They used to sing as they went, clapping their hands and slapping their buttocks as was the custom:

> Hingyara hingya, so sorry so!
> my late brother coult tance
> better than myself.
> We're koing town to Rosseau,
> time for Pelair, chust like féké!

6. When they got to the top of the hill, near to the Boeri Lake, a woman asked her husband's leave to drop behind in order that she might relieve herself. 7. The others, together with the husband, went on their way. 8. When she had done, and while looking on the lakeside for those little red shells you find there, the woman noticed some pretty little branches of coral. 9. She picked one up, and hastened to overtake the others. 10. She went on and on; but after walking some time, she found she had returned to the same spot by the lake. 11. She set out again, and once more she only returned to her starting point. 12. She made a fresh start; but when she found that she had been walking in a circle for the third time, she threw away the little coral branch and set out a fourth time. 13. She went on and on until she came to a big plateau. 14. The sun was setting, but there was no one in sight. 15. She crossed the plateau and climbed up and up. 16. When she had gained a good height above the plateau, she saw a little house before her. 17. She called, but got no answer. 18. As she drew nearer, she saw that the kitchen was empty and the house door closed. 19. However, a window was open; and by raising herself on the point of her toes she was just able to see inside. 20. Nobody was there—only a lot of cassava bread hung up on a line to dry.

21. Well, she was lost and tired and hungry. 22. So she pulled herself up and jumped into the house. 23. She ate one of the cassavas and lay down to rest. 24. Some time passed; then she saw a little man with a string of fish in his hand approaching stealthily, as if afraid. 25. She hailed him: "O, Sir, don't be afraid! I'm just as human as yourself. 26. It's only that I went astray; and as I was tired and hungry, I came in here to rest and ate one of those cassavas of yours. 27. But I'm a human being like you, never fear!" 28. The little man said not a word. 29. He went into the kitchen, cleaned the fish, and prepared supper. 30. When everything was ready, he shared out the food and passed the woman hers at arm's length, shyly, as if afraid of her. 31. Then after they had finished eating,

he showed her where she was to sleep. 32. And all this time he had not said one word to her. 33. Nevertheless, when night came, he joined her softly and lay next to her to sleep. 34. The next morning, still without saying anything, the little man took his rod and tackle and went fishing (for such was his occupation), 35. to return a little before sunset as on the first day.

36. Some time passed like that, until the woman came to bear a child to this man.

37. Now the woman's husband had reached Roseau together with the rest of those Caribs. 38. They did their business and returned home to windward without hearing anything about the woman. 39. Search as he might, the poor husband was unable to find the slightest trace of his wife. 40. One day, old Wanuhí—who, naturally, knew everything that happened—came to see the husband. 41. He told him: "It's useless for you to search further for your wife; you wouldn't find her. 42. Besides, I can tell you where she is. 43. She's living together with a zombi called Karuhú in his house above the Boeri Lake. 44. She has even borne him a child. 45. If you are so minded to take her back, you will find her there alone, and she will follow you (for Karuhú spends all the day out fishing). 46. But before you go off with her, take some cotton, card it, and make a little cord of it. 47. Then spit in the living room, spit in the bedroom, spit all around the house, and spit in the kitchen; then take the cord and put it round the child's neck, and take your wife and go."

48. Well, the husband set out on his way: he went on and on. 49. At last he arrived before the zombi's house. 50. When his wife saw him coming, she began to be afraid. 51. She started to complain: "O, husband, you must not be hard on me, for it was yourself who let me get lost. 52. And what has happened to me was through no fault of mine." 53. "I have not come to talk of that," the man told her; "all I want is to take you back home." 54. Then, remembering what Wanuhí had said to him, he took some cotton, corded it, and twisted it into a little cord. 55. After that he spat in the living room and spat in the bedroom, he spat all around the house and spat in the kitchen; then he put the cord around the child's neck, took his wife and went his way.

56. Soon after that Karuhú arrived with a little string of fish in his hand as usual. 57. He went straight to the kitchen and called the woman. 58. Her voice answered from inside the house; but when Karuhú went there, she was nowhere to be seen. 59. He called her again; this time her voice answered from behind the house. 60. He went out into the yard, but not seeing her, he called again. 61. This time her voice answered from the kitchen. 62. And so it went on until Karuhú got so very angry that he took the child, flung it into the air, and blew into its buttocks. 63. In that instant the child turned into a kingfisher and flew away.

Commentary

Although the Island-Carib language has been extinct in Dominica for the past fifty years or more, some of the older people living in or near the reserve remember "old-time Caribs" whose native language it was; and the little song at the beginning of this story purports to imitate their mispronunciation of the local French creole patois: *tefẽ* for *defẽ* 'late (dead)', *tãse* for *dãse* 'dance', *tesãn* for *desãn* 'go down', *Woso* for *Wozo* 'Roseau', *pêlê* for *bêlê* 'belair (kind of dance)', and *feke* for *beke* 'white person/people'. Except for the last (which is unlikely), these changes are plausible; for the Dominican dialect of Island-Carib had only one sibilant and aspirated-unaspirated (instead of voiceless-voiced) oppositions of bilabial, apical, and dorsal stops.

The old soothsayer Wanuhí crops up in other Dominican tales, as does his female counterpart, Wanúi, in tales of the Black Carib of Central America. Although it is not clear what kind of zombi Karuhú is meant to represent (a bush spirit or a water spirit?), it should be noted that in the Lesser Antilles, the word *zombi* is applied to any and all spirits and has no implications of living dead such as has the same word in Haiti.

Lesser Antillean, Dominican dialect. *Khwaib epi sjiẽ-i*

1. ebẽ, sete yõ vye kô ki pa te ni zãfã, epi madãm-li vini mô. 2. i te ka hwete adã yõ ti kay pâ kô-y yõn, êvê ãni yõ fimel sjiẽ pu cẽn-li kõmpẽni. 3. lê i te kay ã jâdẽ, sjiẽ-a te ka tunẽ fãm, balye kay, gwaje mãyok, cwit kasav, bwiye mãje, ale o bwa, lave. 4. ãfẽ se i te ka fê tut bitẽ. 5. epi le-swê, lê nõm-la sôti ã jadẽ, se sjiẽ-a ki te ka vini jwẽn-li. 6. vye nõm-la di: "a, yõ bõ mun vini fê thwavay-la ba mwẽ!" 7. i ale di vwezinaj gwã-mêsi, mẽ yo tut di-y yo pa kõnet ãyẽ kõt sa.

8. sete yõ lot vye nõm a pwezã, ki te ka sjae pawol. 9. nõ-y te Wanuhí. 10. epi se i ki vini di vye kô-a: "tut fwa u sôti, sjiẽ u ka tunẽ fãm. 11. se i ka fê tut thwavay-la ba-w. 12. si u le i hwete fãm, pu u sa pwã-y fê mun-u, menê sjiẽ-a epi fê-y asiz ã kuwã laivyê. 13. epi pwã yõ pãye epi pase-y ã dlo ã lê sjiẽ-a pu sjifõnẽ pwesõ." 14. nõm-la fê sa Wanuhí te di-y. 15. lê y pase pãye-a ã dlo ã-ho la sjiẽ asiz, i fê yõ teta pase ã jãm sjiẽ-a, ki tunẽ fãm.

16. ebẽ, nõm-la pwã-y pu fê mun-li nõ! 17. yo dakô byẽ jis tã vye Wanuhí vini mãde nõm-la si y pa las pwã mẽm vye sjiẽ-y wõnmã. 18. i fê nõm-la pwã pãye-y epi menê fãm-la laivyê. 19. lê y sjapote dlo êvê pãye-a, ku sa-la i fê yõ losj pase ã jãm fãm, ki tunẽ ã mal sjiẽ. 20. i pa jamẽ vihwe tunẽ fãm.

(told by Ma' Bernard)

Translation. *The Carib and his dog*

1. Well, there was an old fellow who was childless, and his wife died. 2. He lived in a little house by himself, with only a bitch for company. 3.

When he went to the garden (provision ground), the dog would turn into a woman, sweep the house, grate manioc, bake cassava, cook food, go for wood, wash. 4. In short it was she who did everything. 5. And in the evening, when the man came from his garden, it was the dog that came to meet him. 6. The old man said: "Ah! some kind body has been and done the work for me!" 7. He went to thank his neighbors, but they all said they knew nothing about it.

8. Now there was another old man, who was a talebearer. 9. His name was Wanuhí. 10. And it was he who came and told the old fellow: "Whenever you go out, your dog turns into a woman. 11. It is she who does all that work for you. 12. If you want her to remain a woman, so that you may take her to be your mate, take the dog and make it sit in the current of the river. 13. Then take a basket and pass it in the stream above the dog so as to disturb the fish." 14. The man did as Wanuhí had told him. 15. When he passed the basket through the water upstream from where the dog was sitting, he caused a suckerfish to pass between the legs of the dog, which thereupon turned into a woman.

16. Well, the man took her as his mate, to be sure! 17. They got along well together until old Wanuhí came and asked the man whether he were not tired of taking ever that same old dog of his. 18. He prevailed upon the man to take his basket and lead the woman to the river. 19. When he splashed the water with the basket, at the same instant he caused a loach to pass between the legs of the woman, who turned into a male dog. 20. Never again did the dog turn back into a woman.

Commentary

Although the main theme of this little tale is the same as that told in Arawak and called "The Besoana Clan" (see above, Chapter 6), the details and especially the conclusion are very different. Here, the moral seems to be that while information given by know-it-alls like Wanuhí is always correct, their advice does not always lead to desirable results, and should not be followed blindly.

Lesser Antillean, Dominican dialect. Bakámu

1. yŏ fi lezot fwa ale ã hôtê adã yŏ tê mãyok, epi la i jwẽn êvê yŏ beke. 2. selmã, nŏm-la te sã cilot, epi i pa te ni bel nẽ kŏ beke. 3. yŏ lot sjoy a-pwezã, sa pa te yŏ nŏm tutafet nŏ pli, pis yŏ maniê i te yŏ tet-sjiẽ

4. zãfã fi-a fê ba-y te ni tet yŏ mun êvê kô yŏ tet-sjiẽ. 5. lê i kumãse pwofite, kalite dwa i pwã asu mãmã-y, pov fi-a te khwẽn zãfã-a te ke fini khwaze-y. 6. i te kay ã hazye deyê ti mãje-y (tel kŏ ti kuhwes); mẽ wŏnmã, lê y hwuvini a-kay, i te ka vihwe hwãnthwe ã sak mãmã-y.

7. yŏ ju, yŏ vye mãyetis yo khwie Wanuhí vini pase duvã kay mãmã zãfã tet-sjiẽ-a. 8. i vwê mizi budẽ pov fãm-la te gŏfle; epi y ba-y kŏsey pu

i debahwase zãfã-y, êvê maniê pu y fê. 9. nõm-la di-y sjasje yõ gwã zekal bwigo epi yõ pye balata. 10. i di se pu fi-a voye ti tet-sjiẽ deyê ghwẽn adã pye balata-a. 11. kõ i pwã mõte, se pu fi-a fuhwe tet zãfã-y adã zekal bwigo-a, khwasje tu hwõ pye bwa-a, epi fukã. 12. khwasja te ke hwepõn ã lavwa-y jik tã i vini sjes; 13. mẽ apwe sa, ti tet-sjiẽ te ke pwã deyê lôdê-y. 14. lê y tãn-li ka vini, se pu fi-a pise asu yõ môso sab.

15. ebẽ, fi-a fê tut sa divinê-a di-y pu fê. 16. lê ti tet-sjiẽ thuve yo kwiyõnẽ-y, kõ sa i mete deyê mãmã-y. 17. lê y vini sãti pisa mãmã-y, pisa-a tunẽ yõ gwã laivyê ki pôte-y ale ã lãmê. 18. acwelmã i se Bakámu. 19. lê yõ bel lanwit u sa wê-y ka lõje kô-y depi la ba asu lãmê jik ã-lê mõtãy pâ la. 20. i ni tet yõ mun, yõ gwo zye hwuj, epi kô yõ tet-sjiẽ.

Translation. Bakámu

1. A girl of former times went to a manioc field in the heights, and there she met a white man. 2. Only this man was without breeches; and he did not have a fine nose like white men. 3. Then again, he was not altogether a man either, for in a way he was a boa constrictor.

4. The child that this girl bore to him had a human head with the body of a boa. 5. As he began to grow, such demands did he make on his mother that the poor girl feared this child would completely destroy her. 6. It would go in search of its own food (such as little grass snakes) into the bush; but still, when it came home, it would go back into its mother's womb.

7. One day, an old magnetist called Wanuhí happened to pass before the house of the snake-child's mother. 8 He saw how distended the poor woman's belly was, advised her to get rid of her child, and told her what to do. 9. This man told her to look for a big burgau shell and a balata (*Manilkara nitida*) tree. 10. He said the girl must send the little boa up the tree for its fruit. 11. As he began to climb, the girl must stuff her child's head into the burgau shell, spit all around the tree, and run away. 12. The spittle would answer with her voice until it became dry; 13. but after that the little boa would follow her scent. 14. When she heard him coming, the girl should piss on some sand.

15. Well, the girl did everything that the diviner had told her to do. 16. When the little boa found that they had cheated him, he at once set out after his mother. 17. When he came to smell his mother's urine, it became a great river which carried him out to sea. 18. Now he is Bakámu. 19. On a clear night you may see him stretching himself from the sea down there to up over the mountain yonder. 20. He has a human head, a big red eye, and a boa's body.

Commentary

This story, despite all differences and reduction, is comparable to the Arawak tale given in Part I above and entitled "The Snake Children's

Mother" (see Chapter 6). In both we have a girl made pregnant by a snake-spirit whose child is sent up a balata tree to collect its fruit, and then suffers death and transformation at the hands of the mother's brother or—in the case of the creole version—by the agency of the mother herself. The name *Bakámu* also occurs in a Central American Island-Carib story in Chapter 6. According to Ahlbrinck (1931, p. 353 and passim), the constellation is named after the fish *Batrachoides Surinamensis* (*lomp* or *lompu* in Sranan creole), which has a peculiarly shaped head. The name (*pakamu* in Karina) may or may not contain the stem *paka-* 'come/go out; emerge; arise; awake'.

On the other hand, it seems reasonable to identify the Master Boa who sired Bakámu with the creature (or protecting spirit) to which the following refers: "They all say that their first Kallinago [Carib] father, having left the mainland accompanied by his family, settled in Dominica. He had a long posterity there, and saw the nephews of his nephews, who, in their extreme cruelty, killed him with poison. But he was changed into a fish of monstrous size, which they call Akáyuman, and is still quite full of life in their river" (Rennard 1929, p. 46).

Now *akáyuman* seems to be merely another form of K *okoyumo* or *okoyumbo* 'the great water spirit', which seems to contain K *okoyu* 'snake' (just as A *orio* 'water spirit' seems to contain *óri* 'snake'); and *-man* (possibly a contraction of *yuman* 'father; protector') occurs as word-final in many star-names. Dominica, however, has not (and probably never had) any water snakes; so that tribal legends of the Guianese anaconda may have been transformed into the Master Boa, still believed in, and of which Bouton (1640, p. 108) wrote:

They say that there is in Dominica a snake which makes itself now big, now small; that it has, in the middle of its forehead, a carbuncle or very brilliant stone which it removes when it wants to drink, and then puts back in place; and that nobody can or dare go to see in its cave unless he has previously fasted and abstained from his wife; otherwise he would not see it, or would be in danger of being "matté" by it, that is to say, killed.

At all events, the above citations tend to support my belief that the connection between the Arawak tale reproduced in Part I above and the modern Lesser Antillean creole story given here is an ancient one.

WORDLISTS

Saramaccan (*list A*): Surinam

1. I	mi
2. thou	ju ~ i
3. we	u
4. this	dísi
5. that	díde

6. who?	ambê ~ ámmè
7. what?	andí
8. not	ná ~ á
9. all	túu
10. many	hí(l)a
11. one	wán
12. two	tú
13. big	bígi; gaán
14. long	lánga
15. small	pikí
16. woman	mujêè
17. man	(w)ómi
18. person	sòmbè ~ sèmbè
19. fish	físi
20. bird	fou
21. dog	dágu
22. louse	lósu; piójo
23. tree	páu
24. seed	síi
25. leaf	wiwíi ~ uwíi
26. root	lútu
27. bark	kákísa (< kásika)
28. skin	sinkí(n)i
29. flesh	gbamba; mbéti
30. blood	buúu; sangá; nòngô; akóni, gadjabia
31. bone	bónu
32. fat	fátu
33. egg	(w)óbo
34. horn	tutú
35. tail	lábu
36. feather	puúma
37. hair	= 25
38. head	(h)édi
39. ear	jési
40. eye	(w)ójo
41. nose	núsu
42. mouth	búka
43. tooth	tánda
44. tongue	tôngò
45. claw	húnja
46. foot	fútu
47. knee	kiní
48. hand	máu
49. belly	bêè; baíka (arch.)
50. neck	gangáa
51. breast	bóbi
52. heart	(h)áti
53. liver	lêbèn
54. drink	bebé; diíngi
55. eat	nján; kòmê (arch.)
56. bite	nján
57. see	sí

58. hear	jéi
59. know	sábi (cf. *sá* 'can')
60. sleep	duumí
61. die	dêdè
62. kill	kíi
63. swim	sún
64. fly	buá
65. walk	wáka
66. come	kó
67. lie	kándi
68. sit	sindó (< sindá)
69. stand	tán-a-pê; taámpu
70. give	dá
71. say	fan
72. sun	sónu
73. moon	líba
74. star	teéa (< teréja)
75. water	wáta
76. rain	tjúba
77. stone	sitónu
78. sand	sándu
79. earth	dóti
80. cloud	líba(hoos); wóluku
81. smoke	súmúku
82. fire	fája; vêvê
83. ashes	síndja
84. burn	tjumá (< tjimá)
85. path	pási
86. mountain	kúnunu ~ kúuun
87. red	bè (cf. *guunsí* 'purple, wine-red')
88. green	giín ~ guún
89. yellow	donú; fòkò
90. white	wéti
91. black	baáka
92. night	ndéti
93. hot	kéndi
94. cold	kôtò
95. full	fúu
96. new	njú-njú
97. good	búnu
98. round	lóntu (< lulúntu; logo)
99. dry	dèê
100. name	nê

Saramaccan (*list B*): *Surinam*

101. ye	únu ~ un
102. he	a
103. they	de
104. how?	ún-fá
105. when?	ún-té; ún-júu
106. where?	ún-sê; ún-kamía

107.	here	akí
108.	there	alá
109.	other	óto
110.	three	dií
111.	four	fô
112.	five	féifi
113.	sky	= 80
114.	day	dáka
115.	wind	véntu
116.	flow	kulé
117.	river	lío
118.	wet	munjá
119.	wash	wási
120.	snake	sindéki
121.	worm	bítju
122.	back	báka
123.	arm	= 48
124.	wing	hánza
125.	navel	bíngo
126.	guts	tiípa
127.	saliva	tu(n)tá
128.	fruit	fuúta
129.	flower	foló (< floli)
130.	grass	gaási
131.	with	ku
132.	in	dándu; na
133.	at	na
134.	if	é
135.	mother	mamá
136.	father	tatá
137.	husband	mánu
138.	salt	sátu
139.	child	miíi (< miníni)
140.	dark	zugúu
141.	cut	kóti
142.	narrow	fitjá
143.	far	lóngi
144.	near	zúntu
145.	thick	dégi
146.	thin	fínu
147.	short	sáti
148.	heavy	híbi
149.	sharp	tjôni
150.	dirty	súndju
151.	bad	(w)ógi; taku
152.	rotten	póndi; lôtò
153.	smooth	línzo
154.	straight	léti
155.	correct	= 154
156.	old	gaándi
157.	rub	feegá
158.	throw	vínde

159. hit	fón; náki
160. split	fèn
161. pierce	fulá; tjòkô
162. dig	díki
163. tie	tái
164. sew	nái
165. fall	kaí
166. swell	sói
167. think	tínga, nínga
168. sing	kandá
169. smell	sumêè
170. puke	pío
171. suck	tjupá
172. blow	bóô
173. fear	fèêè
174. squeeze	peetá
175. hold	panjá; hói
176. down	básu
177. up	= 80
178. ripe	mandú
179. year	jáa

Segmental unit phonemes are *p kp t tj k; b gb d dj g; f s; v z; mb nd ndj ng* (prenasalized stops); *m n nj* (nasals); *w j* (semivowels); *l; h; i u, e o, è ò, a. kp* and *gb* are bilabial implosives; *tj* and *dj* are palatal affricates. Relevant vocalic length is shown as $VV(V)$. There are two relevant tonal heights, the lower unmarked, the higher shown by the acute accent except in the case of the lower mid vowels, *è* and *ò*, where it is shown by the circumflex, *ê* and *ô*. Vocalic nasalization is shown as *Vn* or (before a labial) *Vm*. All syllables end in a vowel (oral or nasal); and there are no consonant clusters.

Sranan (list A): Surinam

1. I	mi
2. thou	ju ~ i
3. we	únu ~ un ~ u ~ w
4. this	dísi
5. that	dáti
6. who?	súma ~ sma
7. what?	san
8. not	no
9. all	ála
10. many	fúru
11. one	wan
12. two	tu
13. big	bígi
14. long	lánga
15. small	ptjin ~ pikín
16. woman	úma
17. man	man

18. person   = 6
19. fish   físi
20. bird   fówru
21. dog   dágu
22. louse   lóso
23. tree   bon
24. seed   síri
25. leaf   wiwíri
26. root   lútu
27. bark   búba
28. skin   stjin
29. flesh   méti
30. blood   brúdu
31. bone   bonjó
32. fat   fátu
33. egg   éksi
34. horn   tutú
35. tail   tére
36. feather   = 25
37. hair   = 25
38. head   éde
39. ear   jési
40. eye   aj
41. nose   nóso
42. mouth   mófo
43. tooth   tífi
44. tongue   tóngo
45. claw   nángra
46. foot   fútu
47. knee   kindí
48. hand   ánu
49. belly   bére
50. neck   néki
51. breast   bóbi
52. heart   áti
53. liver   léfre
54. drink   dríngi
55. eat   njam
56. bite   béti
57. see   si ~ sji
58. hear   jére
59. know   sábi
60. sleep   sríbi
61. die   déde
62. kill   kíri
63. swim   swen
64. fly   frej
65. walk   wáka
66. come   kon
67. lie   didón, lidón
68. sit   sidón
69. stand   tanápu

70. give	gi
71. say	táki
72. sun	son
73. moon	mun
74. star	stári
75. water	wátra
76. rain	alén
77. stone	ston
78. sand	sánti
79. earth	dóti
80. cloud	wórku
81. smoke	smóko
82. fire	fája
83. ashes	asísi
84. burn	bron
85. path	pási
86. mountain	bérgi
87. red	rédi
88. green	grun
89. yellow	géri
90. white	wéti
91. black	bláka
92. night	néti
93. hot	áti; fája
94. cold	kówru
95. full	= 10
96. new	njun
97. good	bun
98. round	lóntu
99. dry	drej
100. name	nen

Sranan (*list B*): *Surinam*

101. ye	= 3
102. he	a
103. they	den
104. how?	o-fá(si)
105. when?	o-ten; o-júru
106. where?	o-pé
107. here	dja
108. there	drápe
109. other	tra
110. three	dri
111. four	fo
112. five	féjfi
113. sky	tápu
114. day	déj
115. wind	wínti
116. flow	lon
117. river	líba
118. wet	náti

119.	wash	wási
120.	snake	snéki
121.	worm	worón
122.	back	báka
123.	arm	= 48
124.	wing	= 64
125.	navel	kumbá
126.	guts	trípa
127.	saliva	spíti
128.	fruit	fróktu
129.	flower	brómki
130.	grass	grási
131.	with	nánga
132.	in	íni; na
133.	at	na
134.	if	éfi
135.	mother	mamá
136.	father	tatá, papá
137.	husband	másra
138.	salt	sówtu
139.	child	= 15
140.	dark	dúngru
141.	cut	kóti
142.	narrow	smára
143.	far	fára
144.	near	krosbéj
145.	thick	déki
146.	thin	fíni
147.	short	sjátu
148.	heavy	ébi
149.	sharp	srápu
150.	dirty	dóti; mórsu
151.	bad	ógri; tákru
152.	rotten	póri
153.	smooth	gráti
154.	straight	léti
155.	correct	= 154
156.	old	ówru
157.	rub	frífri
158.	throw	fríngi
159.	hit	fom; náki
160.	split	príti
161.	pierce	djúku; ólo
162.	dig	díki
163.	tie	taj
164.	sew	naj
165.	fall	fadón
166.	swell	swéri
167.	think	dénki
168.	sing	síngi
169.	smell	sméri
170.	puke	pió

171. suck	sójgi
172. blow	bro
173. fear	fréde
174. squeeze	kwínsi
175. hold	fási; óri
176. down	óndro
177. up	ópo
178. ripe	lépi
179. year	jári

Segmental unit phonemes are *p t tj k; b d dj g; f s sj; m n nj ng; w j* (semivowels); *r* ([r] and [l], though both are written, are nondistinctive, but said to differ stylistically); *i u, e o, a. tj* and *dj* are palatal affricates; *sj* is a hushing sibilant. In Sranan, the velar nasal *ng* is lenis (so that SM *lánga* and SN *lánga* are not homophonous), the sound of SM *ng*, rarely heard in Sranan, being shown as *ngg* in the latter language. Relevant stress is shown by the acute accent, vocalic nasalization as in Saramaccan by *Vn* or *Vm*. All words end in a vowel, oral or nasal; but initial and medial consonant clusters are common, though they arise from the elision of a vowel that is usually restored in songs and verse.

Negro Dutch: St. Thomas and St. John, Virgin Islands

1. I	mi
2. thou	ju
3. we	õs
4. this	di, dida
5. that	de, dat
6. who?	(a)wi
7. what?	(a)wa
8. not	no, na
9. all	alga
10. many	feel, musji, wee
11. one	een
12. two	twee
13. big	grooto
14. long	lang
15. small	kleen
16. woman	frou/fru
17. man	man
18. person	mẽs; folk
19. fish	fis/fes
20. bird	?
21. dog	hon
22. louse	lus
23. tree	boom
24. seed	saat
25. leaf	blaa
26. root	woltə
27. bark	bark
28. skin	houtu

29.	flesh	fleis/flees
30.	bone	blut
31.	bone	been
32.	fat	fet
33.	egg	eiu
34.	horn	tutú
35.	tail	stet
36.	feather	flim
37.	hair	haa
38.	head	kop
39.	ear	hoo
40.	eye	hogo
41.	nose	nes/nees
42.	mouth	mon/mun
43.	tooth	tan
44.	tongue	tong
45.	claw	?
46.	foot	futu
47.	knee	kini
48.	hand	han
49.	belly	bik
50.	neck	nek
51.	breast	bos
52.	heart	haat
53.	liver	?
54.	drink	dring
55.	eat	jet/jit
56.	bite	bit
57.	see	kii
58.	hear	hoo, horə
59.	know	weet
60.	sleep	sleep
61.	die	doot
62.	kill	máta
63.	swim	zwem
64.	fly	flig
65.	walk	loo, lu
66.	come	koo
67.	lie	lei
68.	sit	set/sit
69.	stand	tan
70.	give	gii
71.	say	see
72.	sun	zon
73.	moon	maan
74.	star	steeree
75.	water	watə/watu
76.	rain	regn/rign
77.	stone	stin
78.	sand	san
79.	earth	gron
80.	cloud	wolk

81. smoke	smook
82. fire	fii
83. ashes	asjisji
84. burn	bran
85. path	pat
86. mountain	bergi
87. red	roo; jaja
88. green	grun
89. yellow	geel
90. white	wit
91. black	swat
92. night	dungku
93. hot	heet
94. cold	kout
95. full	ful
96. new	niw
97. good	fraaj
98. round	ron/run
99. dry	drook
100. name	naam

Compiled from divers unphonemicized sources, the above spellings cannot hope to be more than very broadly phonetic. Geminate vowels are close in the case of *ii, ee*, and *oo*, fully open in that of *aa*, but do not necessarily indicate greater length than lower-mid *e* and *o*, lax *i*, and back *a*. The velar nasal is indicated by *ng*. Romance influence, seen here only in *máta* 'kill' (62), is also evident in ND *keer* 'love' (cf. Ptg. *querer*), *kurí* 'run', *mangké* 'want', *parí* 'give birth'.

Papiamentu (list A): Curaçao

1. I	amí, mi
2. thou	abó, bo
3. we	nos
4. this	e . . . akí
5. that	e . . . ajá/ej
6. who?	k'énde; keng
7. what?	kíko, ki-
8. not	no
9. all	tur
10. many	hópi
11. one	ung
12. two	dos
13. big	grándi
14. long	lárgu
15. small	tjikítu
16. woman	muhé
17. man	hómbər
18. person	hénde
19. fish	piská
20. bird	pára
21. dog	katjó

22.	louse	piću̱w
23.	tree	pálu
24.	seed	simíja
25.	leaf	fója/blátji
26.	root	raís
27.	bark	káska
28.	skin	kwéru
29.	flesh	kárni
30.	blood	sánggər
31.	bone	wésu
32.	fat	gordúra; sébu
33.	egg	wébu
34.	horn	kátju
35.	tail	rábu
36.	feather	plúma
37.	hair	kabɛ́j
38.	head	kabés
39.	ear	oréa
40.	eye	wówo
41.	nose	nanísji
42.	mouth	bóka
43.	tooth	djénte
44.	tongue	léngga
45.	claw	péntji
46.	foot	pía
47.	knee	rudía
48.	hand	mang
49.	belly	baríka
50.	neck	gargánta
51.	breast	pétju
52.	heart	korasóng
53.	liver	hígra
54.	drink	bêbe
55.	eat	kômé
56.	bite	môrde
57.	see	mîre
58.	hear	tênde
59.	know	sábi
60.	sleep	drûmi
61.	die	mûri
62.	kill	mâta
63.	swim	lânda
64.	fly	bûla
65.	walk	kâmna
66.	come	bîni
67.	lie	bûta
68.	sit	sînta
69.	stand	pâra
70.	give	dûna
71.	say	bisá; di
72.	sun	sólo
73.	moon	lúna

74.	star	stréa
75.	water	áwa
76.	rain	awaséru
77.	stone	piédra
78.	sand	sántu
79.	earth	téra
80.	cloud	núbia
81.	smoke	húma
82.	fire	kandéla
83.	ashes	sjinísji
84.	burn	kîma
85.	path	kamín(d)a
86.	mountain	séru
87.	red	kɔrá
88.	green	bɛ́rde
89.	yellow	hel
90.	white	blángku
91.	black	prétu
92.	night	nótji
93.	hot	kajénte
94.	cold	fríu
95.	full	jeng
96.	new	nóbo
97.	good	bong
98.	round	rondó
99.	dry	séku
100.	name	nómbər

Segmental unit phonemes are *p t tj k; b d dj g; f s sj; v z zj; m n nj ng; l r; w j* (semivowels); *h; i u, e o*, lower-mid *ɛ* and *ɔ, a, ə. tj* and *dj* are palatal affricates; *sj* and *zj* are hushing sibilants; *nj* and *ng* are, respectively, palatal and velar nasals ([ŋg] is written *ngg*). The acute accent shows stress; the circumflex, a long, falling tone.

Sãotomense

1.	I	amí; m ~ n ~ ŋ
2.	thou	bo
3.	we	nõ
4.	this	sɛ ~ se
5.	that	salá ~ sala
6.	who?	ke ŋe
7.	what?	ke kwa; ka (AB)
8.	not	na . . . fa
9.	all	túdu
10.	many	mũtu; mõtji
11.	one	úa
12.	two	dósu
13.	big	glãdji; tamɛ̃
14.	long	lũgu
15.	small	pikina
16.	woman	mwála

17. man   ómɛ
18. person   ŋe (cf. 6); nĩŋgé
19. fish   piši
20. bird   bísu
21. dog   kasó
22. louse   iólu
23. tree   pó; álou
24. seed   semĕti ~ semĕtji
25. leaf   fya
26. root   léži
27. bark   káška
28. skin   péli
29. flesh   káni
30. blood   sǎgi
31. bone   ósɔ
32. fat   gódo; gludúla
33. egg   óvu
34. horn   šífli
35. tail   lábu
36. feather   péna
37. hair   kabelu
38. head   kabésa
39. ear   ołá
40. eye   wé
41. nose   líši
42. mouth   bóka
43. tooth   dítji
44. tongue   lígwa
45. claw   íñɛ
46. foot   ɔpé
47. knee   zǔta
48. hand   mõ
49. belly   bɛ́ga
50. neck   tláši klónko; tláši kabésa
51. breast   pétu
52. heart   klosõ
53. liver   ———
54. drink   bebé
55. eat   kumɛ́
56. bite   modé
57. see   bé; piá
58. hear   tĕdé
59. know   sébe
60. sleep   dumíni
61. die   molé ~ molí
62. kill   matá
63. swim   lãdá
64. fly   vwa
65. walk   nda
66. come   bí
67. lie   detá
68. sit   tasǒ

69.	stand	mundjádu
70.	give	dá
71.	say	flá
72.	sun	sólɔ
73.	moon	nwa
74.	star	stléla
75.	water	áwa
76.	rain	súba
77.	stone	búda
78.	sand	aliyá
79.	earth	téla
80.	cloud	nóvi
81.	smoke	fűmu
82.	fire	fóga
83.	ashes	šíža
84.	burn	kema
85.	path	(š)tláda
86.	mountain	oké
87.	red	vlémi/blémi
88.	green	v(l)éde
89.	yellow	malélo
90.	white	blăku
91.	black	plétu
92.	night	nótji
93.	hot	kĕtji
94.	cold	fíyu
95.	full	šá (? = /siá/)
96.	new	nóvu
97.	good	dõ
98.	round	lõndóndɔ
99.	dry	séku; súgu
100.	name	nómi

I should like to thank Dr. Marius Valkhoff (Witwatersrand) and Dr. J. Morais Barbosa (Lisbon) for their help in compiling this list before the complete phonemicization of Sãotomense. Thus, it seems likely, despite some counter examples (see 24, 69, 83, 95), that the voiced and voiceless hushing sibilants [ž] and [š] should be variants (palatalized before a high front vowel or an occlusive consonant) of their hissing counterparts [z] and [s], employed elsewhere. So *šíža* (83) from Ptg. *cinza*, but *bísu* (20), *kasó* (21), and *zũta* (47) from Ptg. *bicho, cachorro*, and *junta* (the second hushing sibilant of *šíža* could be explained as assimilation). And likewise, the voiced and voiceless palatal affricates [ǧ] and [č] (here written *dj* and *tj*) appear to be variants of the voiced and voiceless stops *d* and *t*, occurring before the high front vowel *i*. Dr. Barbosa informs me, however, that *dj* and *z* are often interchangeable in the same word, as in [ǧélu] ~ [žélu] 'money' (*dinheiro*).

On the other hand, the distinctive character of some other features shown in the above list seems to be beyond doubt: *po* 'be able' (*poder*)

≠ *pɔ* 'tree' (*pau*)' ≠ *põ* 'bread' (pão); *nótji* 'night' (*noite*) ≠ *nɔ́tji* 'north' (*norte*); *pétu* 'breast' (*peito*) ≠ *pέtu* '(roasting) spit' (*espeto*); *be* 'see' (ver) = *bε* 'go' (*vai*); *séši* 'six' (*seis*) but *déši* 'ten' (*dez*); *sã* 'lady, Mrs.' (*senhora*) ≠ *sa* 'be' (*ser, estar*); *vĕde* 'shop' (*vender* 'sell') ≠ *véde* 'green'; *vĩ* 'wine' (*vinho*) ≠ *bi* 'come' (*vir*); etc.

It is not clear whether palatalized *ñ* and *ł* (*nh* and *lh* of Portuguese orthography) are or are not phonemes of Sãotomense. Each occurs only once in the above list (45 and 39). Dr. Barbosa says that the latter is sometimes lost (as in *ía* 'island', Ptg. *ilha*) and at others retained, as in *ɔ́ła* 'look' (Ptg. *ólha*). The latter seems not only to be in opposition with ST *ɔ́la* 'hour; time' (Ptg. *hora*), but to form with *ołá* 'ear' (Ptg. *orelha*) a nearly minimal pair based on stress difference.

Lesser Antillean (*list A*): Dominica

1. I	mwĕ
2. thou	u ~ -w
3. we	nu
4. this	sa
5. that	= 4
6. who?	ki mun
7. what?	ki sa (LA-G ka)
8. not	pa
9. all	tut ~ tu
10. many	otã; ã pil
11. one	yõn (pn.), yŏ (adj.)
12. two	de
13. big	ghwã
14. long	lõng
15. small	piti, ti-
16. woman	fãm
17. man	nõm
18. person	mun
19. fish	pwesŏ
20. bird	zwezo, zibye
21. dog	sjiĕ
22. louse	pu
23. tree	pye bwa
24. seed	ghwĕn
25. leaf	fêy
26. root	hwasin
27. bark	lapo bwa
28. skin	lapo
29. flesh	(la)sjê; vyãn
30. blood	sã
31. bone	zo
32. fat	(la)ghwes
33. egg	ze
34. horn	kôn
35. tail	lace

36.	feather	plim
37.	hair	sjive; (pwel)
38.	head	tet
39.	ear	zohwêy
40.	eye	zye
41.	nose	nẽ
42.	mouth	busj
43.	tooth	dã
44.	tongue	lãng
45.	claw	zõng; ghwif
46.	foot	pye
47.	knee	junu
48.	hand	lamẽ
49.	belly	budẽ; vãt
50.	neck	ku
51.	breast	tete
52.	heart	cê
53.	liver	fwa; fwisi di
54.	drink	bwê
55.	eat	mãje
56.	bite	môde
57.	see	(v)wê
58.	hear	tãn
59.	know	sav (cf. *sa* 'can/may')
60.	sleep	dômi
61.	die	mô; muri (arch.)
62.	kill	cue ~ cwe
63.	swim	naje
64.	fly	vole
65.	walk	masje
66.	come	vini
67.	lie	kusje
68.	sit	asid/asiz
69.	stand	dubut
70.	give	bay ~ ba
71.	say	di
72.	sun	solêy
73.	moon	lalin
74.	star	zetwel
75.	water	dlo/glo
76.	rain	lapli
77.	stone	hwosj; (pyê)
78.	sand	sab
79.	earth	tê (substance), latê (world)
80.	cloud	niaj/nwaj
81.	smoke	lafime
82.	fire	dife
83.	ashes	sãn
84.	burn	b(hw)ule/bhwile
85.	path	sjimẽ
86.	mountain	môn; mõtãy
87.	red	hwuj

88.	green	vê; (bwa) vêt
89.	yellow	jõn
90.	white	blã
91.	black	nwê
92.	night	nwit (n.), lãnwit (adv.)
93.	hot	sjo
94.	cold	fwet
95.	full	plẽ
96.	new	nuvo ('another'), nef ('unused')
97.	good	bõ
98.	round	hwõ
99.	dry	sjes
100.	name	nõ

Lesser Antillean (list B): Dominica

101.	ye	zot
102.	he	i ~ -y
103.	they	yo
104.	how?	kumã
105.	when?	ki tã; ki lê
106.	where?	ki kote; o-la
107.	here	esit/isi
108.	there	la
109.	other	lot, dot, lezot
110.	three	twa
111.	four	kat
112.	five	sẽk
113.	sky	syel
114.	day	ju
115.	wind	vã
116.	flow	kule
117.	river	layvyê
118.	wet	muye
119.	wash	lave
120.	snake	tet-sjiẽ, sêpã
121.	worm	vê (tê)
122.	back	do
123.	arm	bwa
124.	wing	zel
125.	navel	lõbwi
126.	guts	thwip
127.	saliva	khwasja
128.	fruit	fwitaj; ghwẽn bwa
129.	flower	flê
130.	grass	zeb
131.	with	epi; êvê(k)
132.	in	adã; ã (LA-S na)
133.	at	ã; (a-)
134.	if	si
135.	mother	mãmã
136.	father	papa

137.	husband	mahwi
138.	salt	sel
139.	child	zãfã
140.	dark	sõm
141.	cut	kupe
142.	narrow	etwet
143.	far	lwẽ
144.	near	pwe
145.	thick	epe
146.	thin	fin
147.	short	kut
148.	heavy	lu
149.	sharp	file
150.	dirty	sal
151.	bad	move
152.	rotten	puhwi
153.	smooth	lis
154.	straight	dwet
155.	correct	kôrek
156.	old	vye
157.	rub	fwote
158.	throw	voye; jete ('discard')
159.	hit	bay ku; fute; fwape
160.	split	fãn
161.	pierce	pêse; coke ('stab')
162.	dig	fuye, khweze
163.	tie	mahwe
164.	sew	kud
165.	fall	tõbe
166.	swell	ãfle
167.	think	sjõje; kalcile
168.	sing	sjãte
169.	smell	sãti
170.	puke	vomi
171.	suck	suse
172.	blow	sufle
173.	fear	pê, khwẽn
174.	squeeze	pije
175.	hold	cẽn; cẽbe
176.	down	ã ba
177.	up	ã ho
178.	ripe	mi
179.	year	lãne, -ã

Segmental unit phonemes are *p t c k; b d dj g; f s sj; v z j; m n (ny) ng; l r; w (hw) y* (semivowels); *h; i (i) u, e o,* lower mid *ê ô, a (â), ẽ õ ã* (nasalized vowels). *c* and *dj* are palatal affricates; *sj* and *j* are hushing sibilants; *ny* and *ng* are respectively palatal and velar nasals; *hw* is a velarized labial semivowel; *i* a high central unrounded vowel. Phonemes in parentheses do not belong to all varieties of this creole: with many speakers, *ny* is replaced by nasalization of contiguous vowels; *hw* falls together with *w* (velarized or not); *i* is replaced by *wi*, *u*, or *i;* back *â* falls together with front *a;* and the oppositions of *e/ê* and *o/ô* are neutralized in checked syllables.

Haitian (*list A*)

1.	I	mwĕ ~ m
2.	thou	u
3.	we	nu
4.	this	sa
5.	that	sila
6.	who?	ki mun
7.	what?	ki sa
8.	not	pa ~ p
9.	all	tut ~ tu
10.	many	ã pil
11.	one	yŏn
12.	two	de
13.	big	grã
14.	long	lŏ(g)
15.	small	piti
16.	woman	fãm
17.	man	nŏm
18.	person	mun
19.	fish	pwesŏ/pwasŏ
20.	bird	zwezo/zwazo
21.	dog	sje
22.	louse	pu
23.	tree	pie bwa
24.	seed	grĕn
25.	leaf	fêy
26.	root	rasin
27.	bark	lapo bwa
28.	skin	lapo
29.	flesh	sjê
30.	blood	sã
31.	bone	zo
32.	fat	grês
33.	egg	ze
34.	horn	kôn
35.	tail	ke/tye
36.	feather	plim
37.	hair	sjive
38.	head	têt
39.	ear	zorêy
40.	eye	je
41.	nose	nĕ
42.	mouth	busj
43.	tooth	dã
44.	tongue	lãg
45.	claw	grif
46.	foot	pie

47. knee   jenu
48. hand   mẽ
49. belly   vãt
50. neck   kolêt; ku; gagãn
51. breast   tete
52. heart   kê/tsjê
53. liver   fwa
54. drink   bwê
55. eat   mãje
56. bite   môde
57. see   wê
58. hear   tãde
59. know   kõnẽ ~ kõn
60. sleep   dômi
61. die   muri
62. kill   tuye
63. swim   naje
64. fly   vole
65. walk   masje
66. come   viin
67. lie   kusje
68. sit   sĩta/sjĩta/sita/sjita
69. stand   kãpe (cf. SM tànapê)
70. give   bay ~ ba
71. say   di
72. sun   solêy
73. moon   lalin
74. star   zetwal
75. water   dlo/dlyo
76. rain   (la)pli
77. stone   piê, rosj
78. sand   sab
79. earth   (la)tê
80. cloud   nwaj
81. smoke   lafimẽ
82. fire   dife
83. ashes   sãn
84. burn   bule
85. path   sjemẽ
86. mountain môn
87. red   ruj
88. green   vêt
89. yellow   jôn
90. white   blãsj
91. black   nwa
92. night   (la)nwit
93. hot   sjo
94. cold   fwêt
95. full   plẽ
96. new   nuvo; nef
97. good   bõ
98. round   rõ

99.	dry	sjesj
100.	name	nõ

Haitian (*list B*)

101.	ye	= 3
102.	he	li
103.	they	yo
104.	how?	kũmã/kõmã
105.	when?	kã
106.	where?	ki kote
107.	here	isit
108.	there	la
109.	other	lôt, zôt
110.	three	twa
111.	four	kat
112.	five	sẽk
113.	sky	lesiêl
114.	day	ju
115.	wind	vã
116.	flow	kule
117.	river	lariviê
118.	wet	muye
119.	wash	lave
120.	snake	sêpã
121.	worm	vê
122.	back	do
123.	arm	bra
124.	wing	zêl
125.	navel	lõbwi
126.	guts	trip
127.	saliva	krasja
128.	fruit	fwi
129.	flower	flê
130.	grass	zêb
131.	with	ak-; avê(k)
132.	in	nã/lã
133.	at	a-
134.	if	si
135.	mother	mãmã
136.	father	papa
137.	husband	mari
138.	salt	sêl
139.	child	pitit
140.	dark	sõm
141.	cut	kupe
142.	narrow	etwat
143.	far	lwẽ
144.	near	pre
145.	thick	epe
146.	thin	mẽs
147.	short	kut

148.	heavy	lu
149.	sharp	file
150.	dirty	sal
151.	bad	move
152.	rotten	puri
153.	smooth	egal; poli
154.	straight	dwat
155.	correct	korêk
156.	old	vie
157.	rub	frote
158.	throw	voye
159.	hit	bay ku; frape
160.	split	fãn
161.	pierce	pêse; tsjoke ('stab')
162.	dig	fuye
163.	tie	mare
164.	sew	kud
165.	fall	tõbe
166.	swell	gõfle
167.	think	pãse; sjõje
168.	sing	sjãte
169.	smell	sãti
170.	puke	vomi
171.	suck	suse
172.	blow	sufle
173.	fear	pê
174.	squeeze	sere
175.	hold	kẽbe
176.	down	ba, ã-ba
177.	up	ã-ro; ã-lê
178.	ripe	mi; rêk
179.	year	ane, ã

Segmental unit phonemes are *p t k; b d g; f s sj; v z j; m n ny; w r y* (semivowels); *l; i u, e o,* lower mid *ê ô; a;* nasalized *ĩ ũ ẽ õ ã.* Haitian Creole has no apical trill or flap, and its *r* represents much the same sound as does LA *hw* (though with a lesser tendency to fall together with *w*). *sj* and *j* represent, as in Lesser Antillean, voiceless and voiced hushing sibilants, respectively. Voiceless and voiced palatal affricates appear to be nondistinctive in Haitian and are therefore represented by *tsj* (/t/ .. /sj/) and *dj* (/d/ .. /j/), which are to be regarded as consonant clusters.

Cayenne Creole: French Guiana

1.	I	mo ~ m
2.	thou	to; u
3.	we	nu
4.	this	sa
5.	that	= 4
6.	who?	ki mun
7.	what?	ki sa
8.	not	pa

9. all	tu ~ tut
10. many	ta
11. one	un ~ wun
12. two	de
13. big	grã; gro
14. long	lõng; lõg (f.)
15. small	piti ~ ti-
16. woman	fãm
17. man	wõm
18. person	mun
19. fish	posõ
20. bird	zozo
21. dog	sjiě
22. louse	pu
23. tree	pye bwa
24. seed	grěn
25. leaf	fêy
26. root	rasin
27. bark	lekôrs
28. skin	lapo
29. flesh	lasjê
30. blood	disã
31. bone	zo
32. fat	gra
33. egg	dize
34. horn	kôrn
35. tail	laco
36. feather	plim
37. hair	sjive
38. head	tet
39. ear	zorêy; zorê (f.)
40. eye	wêy
41. nose	nê
42. mouth	busj
43. tooth	dã
44. tongue	lãng; lãg (f.)
45. claw	zõng; zõg (f.)
46. foot	pye
47. knee	junu
48. hand	lãmě
49. belly	vãt; budě
50. neck	ku
51. breast	?
52. heart	cô
53. liver	fwa
54. drink	bwê
55. eat	mâje
56. bite	môde
57. see	wê
58. hear	tâde
59. know	save
60. sleep	drômi

61. die	muri
62. kill	cué
63. swim	naje
64. fly	vôlô; vole
65. walk	masje
66. come	vini ~ vin
67. lie	kusje
68. sit	asi
69. stand	dibut
70. give	bay ~ ba
71. say	di
72. sun	solêy, soley
73. moon	lalin
74. star	zetwal
75. water	dilo; dlo
76. rain	lapli
77. stone	rosj
78. sand	sab
79. earth	latê ~ tê
80. cloud	nuaj
81. smoke	lafimẽ
82. fire	dife
83. ashes	sãn; sãd (f.)
84. burn	brule
85. path	sjimẽ
86. mountain	mõtãny
87. red	ruj
88. green	vet
89. yellow	jõn
90. white	blã
91. black	nwê
92. night	lãnwit ~ nwit
93. hot	sjo
94. cold	fre
95. full	plẽ
96. new	nov; nuvo
97. good	bõ
98. round	rõ
99. dry	?
100. name	nõ

For the sake of comparison with other French-based creoles, the same orthography as was used in their case is employed here (see wordlist for Lesser Antillean above), except that dorsal or uvular /r/ here replaces /hw/ of Lesser Antillean, and that the aspirate (as in ẽhẽ 'yes') seems to be nondistinctive in this creole.

I should like to thank Mme. Fauquenoy for filling some fifteen lacunae in my own record of this creole and to apologize for preferring my own to her record in a few cases (nos. 14, 39, 44, 45, and 83 above). Both may well be "right." Mme. Fauquenoy says that the oppositions of ã/a, ẽ/e, and õ/o (as in *tãde* 'to hear' but *tade* 'to delay') are neutralized before an immediately following nasal consonant; but I found them to subsist in this position for those dialects of Cayenne Creole (and they are not uncommon) which, lacking an /r/ in preconsonantal position, nevertheless distinguish *kò(r)n* 'horn' and *konèt* 'know', *pè(r)mi* 'permis (permit)' and *pẽ-mi* 'kind of bread' (and see what is said about the same problem in Mauritian Creole under the wordlist for that language, below).

Mauritian Creole: Mauritius

1.	I	mo; mua
2.	thou	to; tua ~ ta
3.	we	nu
4.	this	sa
5.	that	= 4
6.	who?	ki sen nã
7.	what?	ki sisa
8.	not	pa; napa
9.	all	tu
10.	many	buku
11.	one	en
12.	two	de
13.	big	grã
14.	long	lõng
15.	small	piti, ti
16.	woman	fãm
17.	man	zõm
18.	person	dimun
19.	fish	posõ/puasõ
20.	bird	zozo/zwazo
21.	dog	lisiĕ
22.	louse	lipu
23.	tree	pie dibua
24.	seed	semãs
25.	leaf	fej
26.	root	rasin
27.	bark	lekors
28.	skin	lapo
29.	flesh	laser
30.	blood	disã
31.	bone	lezo
32.	fat	lagres
33.	egg	dizef
34.	horn	korn
35.	tail	lake
36.	feather	plim
37.	hair	seve
38.	head	latet
39.	ear	zorej
40.	eye	lizie
41.	nose	nene

42.	mouth	labus
43.	tooth	ledã
44.	tongue	lalãng
45.	claw	grif; zõng
46.	foot	lipie
47.	knee	zunu/zenu
48.	hand	lamẽ
49.	belly	vãt
50.	neck	liku
51.	breast	tete
52.	heart	leker
53.	liver	lifua
54.	drink	buar
55.	eat	mãze ~ mãz
56.	bite	mord ~ morde
57.	see	gete ~ get; truve ~ truv
58.	hear	tãde ~ tãn
59.	know	kõne ~ kõn
60.	sleep	dormi
61.	die	mor
62.	kill	tuje ~ tuj
63.	swim	naze
64.	fly	ãvole
65.	walk	marse
66.	come	vini ~ vin
67.	lie	tale
68.	sit	asize ~ asiz
69.	stand	dibute ~ dibut
70.	give	dõne ~ dõn
71.	say	dir
72.	sun	solej
73.	moon	lalin
74.	star	zetwal
75.	water	dilo
76.	rain	lapli
77.	stone	ros
78.	sand	disab
79.	earth	later
80.	cloud	niaz
81.	smoke	lafime
82.	fire	dife
83.	ashes	lasãn
84.	burn	brile
85.	path	simẽ
86.	mountain	mõtañ
87.	red	ruz
88.	green	ver
89.	yellow	zon
90.	white	blã
91.	black	nwar
92.	night	lanuit
93.	hot	so

94.	cold	fre
95.	full	plẽ
96.	new	nuvel
97.	good	bõ
98.	round	rõ
99.	dry	sek
100.	name	nõ

Dr. Chris Corne (1969, 1970, and 1971) sets up the following segmental unit phonemes: *m n ɲ* (here written *ñ*) *ŋ* (here written *ng*); *p t k; b d g; f s; v z; l r; j; i e a o u*, and three nasalized vowels, here written *ẽ ã õ*. When they are followed by the high front vowel /i/, /t/ and /d/ are strongly palatalized (or even affricated), so that /ti/ = [tji] and /dimun/ = [djimun] (15 and 18). In open syllables /e/ = [e] and /o/ = [o]; in closed syllables /e/ = [ɛ] and /o/ = [ɔ]. In order to justify this interpretation, however, Corne has to regard vocalic lengthening in preconsonantal and word-final positions as an allophone of /r/, which elsewhere "se réalise comme une continuante dorsale ou uvulaire, légèrement articulée et sans friction." Thus [tɔ:či] is phonemicized as /torti/ 'turtle', [lekɔ:s] as /lekors/ (27) and [lasɛ:] as /laser/ (29); while *pur* 'for' (preposition) is distinguished from *pu* (marker of future tense) as in *sa lakaz la a pu pur mua* 'cette maison sera la mienne'. This seems to be a dangerous procedure if, as apparently is the case, this language contains words having lower mid [ɛ] and [ɔ] in open syllables without any lengthening. So Corne himself says: "/get, gete/ se réalise [gɛt, gɛte] 'regarder'"; and adds: "Mais le timbre de /e/ n'est jamais pertinent." Elsewhere he says the same thing of /o/.

Syllable-initial /i/ and /u/ before another vowel are heard as non-syllabic [j] and [w] (see 46, *lipie;* 53, *lifua;* etc.); while /j/ is employed only in word-initial and intervocalic positions (see 39, *zorej;* 62, *tuje;* etc.).

We are also told that the opposition of nasal to oral vowels before a nasal consonant is neutralized in all positions within the word. In the above list I have, however, preferred to show all nasalized vowels as such; for I cannot help suspecting that a nearly minimal pair like [kɔ:n] (34) and [kõn] (59)—/korn/ and /kon/ in Corne's orthography—are distinguished less by the length than by the oral or nasal character of their vowels.

For all the rest, Dr. Corne's orthography has been followed, though the wordlist itself has been compiled from an unpublished M.A. thesis by M. Kiamtia, a native speaker of the language.

REFERENCES

❧

Ahlbrinck, W.
1931   *Encyclopaedie der Karaïben*. Amsterdam: Koninklijke Akademie van Wetenschappen.

Alleyne, M. C.
1961   Language and society in St. Lucia. *Caribbean Studies* 1: 1–11.

Alvarez Nazario, Manuel
1961   *El elemento afronegroide en el español de Puerto Rico*. San Juan: Instituto de Cultura Puertorriqueña.

Anonymous
1882   Arawakisch-Deutsches Wörterbuch; Grammatik der Arawakischen Sprache. In *Bibliothèque linguistique américaine* 8: 69–165, 166–240 Paris: Maisonneuve.

Anonymous
1961   *Glossary of the Suriname vernacular (Woordenlijst van het Sranan-Tongo)*. Paramaribo.

Bailey, Beryl L.
1962   *A language guide to Jamaica*. New York.
1966   *Jamaican Creole syntax: a transformational approach*. Cambridge: Cambridge University Press.
1971   Jamaican Creole: can dialect boundaries be defined? In *Pidginization and creolization of languages*, ed. Dell Hymes, pp. 341–48. Cambridge: Cambridge University Press.

Baker, P.
1969   The language situation in Mauritius. *African Language Review* 8.

Ballantyne, D.
1893   Vincentian Carib. *Journal of the Institute of Jamaica* 1, 7: 295–97.

Barber, Charles L.
1964   *The story of language*. London: Pan Books.

Barbot, John
1732   A description of the coasts of North and South Guinea. In *A collection of voyages and travels*, ed. Awnsham Churchill, vol. 5. London.

Barrena, N.
1957   *Grammatica annobonesa.* Madrid.
Berendt, C. H.
MS   Central American Island-Carib wordlist appended to this author's
          manuscript "Vocabulario comparativo. . . ." Berendt Collection,
          University Museum Library, Philadelphia, c. 1860.
Bernáldez, Andrés
1856   *Historia de los reyes católicos D. Fernando y Dᵃ Isabel.* Granada:
          J. M. Zamora.
Bickerton, D., and Escalante, A.
1970   Palenquero: A Spanish-based creole of northern Colombia.
          Lingua 24: 254–67.
Biet, Antoine
1664   Voyage de la France equinoxiale en l'isle de Cayenne. Paris. In
          Chez François Clouzier, pp. 393–432.
Bouton, Jacques
1640   *Relation de l'establissement des François depuis l'an 1635 en l'isle
          de la Martinique.* Paris: S. Cramoisy.
Breton, Raymond
1665   *Dictionnaire caraïbe-françois.* Auxerre. (Facsimile ed., Leipzig:
          Jules Platzmann, 1892.)
1666   *Dictionnaire françois-caraïbe.* Auxerre. (Facsimile ed., Leipzig:
          Jules Platzmann, 1900.)
1667   *Grammaire caraïbe.* Auxerre. (New ed., Paris: L. Adam & Ch.
          Leclerc, 1877.)
Bright, William
1960   *International Journal of Linguistics* 26: 167–68.
Brown, Roger W., and Gilman, A.
1960   The pronouns of power of solidarity. In *Style in language,* ed.
          T. A. Sebeok, pp. 252–76. Cambridge: MIT Press.
Carvalho, José G. Herculano de
1966 .   *Sobre a natureza de crioulos e sua significaçaopora a linguística
          geral.* Actas do V Colóquio Internacional de Estados Luso-
          Brasileiros, vol. 3. Coimbra.
Casas, Bartolomé de las
1552   *Brevissima relacion de la destruycion de las Indias.* Seville: S.
          Trugillo.
1875–76   *Historia de la Indias.* Madrid: M. Ginesta.
Cassidy, F. G.
1961   *Jamaica talk: three hundred years of the English language in
          Jamaica.* Kingston: Institute of Jamaica.
1971   Tracing the pidgin element in Jamaican Creole. In *Pidginization
          and creolization of languages,* ed. Dell Hymes, pp. 203–21.
          Cambridge: Cambridge University Press.
Cassidy, F. G., and LePage, R. B., eds.
1967   *Dictionary of Jamaican English.* Cambridge: Cambridge University
          Press.

272 REFERENCES

Chevillard, André
1659   *Les desseins de son éminence de Richelieu pour l'Amérique.* Rennes:
        I. Durand. (Reproduction, Guadeloupe: Soc. Hist., 1972.)
Corne, Chris
1969   Les dialectes créoles français de Maurice et des Seychelles. *Te Reo*
        (Auckland, N.Z.) 12: 48–63.
1970   *Essai de grammaire du créole mauricien.* Auckland: Linguistic
        Society of New Zealand.
1971   Le patois créole français de la Guyane (St. Laurent du Maroni):
        esquisse de grammaire. *Te Reo* 14: 81–103.
Cruxent, J., and Rouse, I.
1969   Early man in the West Indies. *Scientific American* 221 (5): 42–52.
DeCamp, David
1968   The field of creole language studies. Unpublished ms.
1971a   Introduction: The study of pidgin and creole languages. In
        Pidginization and creolization of languages, ed. Dell Hymes,
        pp. 13–39. Cambridge: Cambridge University Press.
1971b   Towards a generative analysis of a post-creole speech continuum.
        Ibid., pp. 349–70.
Donicie, Antoon, and Voorhoeve, Jan
1963   *De Saramakaanse woordenschat.* Amsterdam: Bureau voor
        Taalonderzoek in Suriname van de Universiteit van Amsterdam.
Ducoeur-Joly, S. J.
1802   *Manuel des habitans de Saint-Domingue.* Paris: Lenoir.
Dudley, Robert, and Wyatt, Thomas (see Warner 1899, below)
Eersel, Christian
1971   Prestige in choice of language and linguistic form. In *Pidginization
        and creolization of languages,* ed. Dell Hymes, pp. 317–22.
        Cambridge: Cambridge University Press.
Elcock, W. D.
1960   *The romance languages.* London: Faber and Faber.
Entwistle, William James
1936   *The Spanish language together with Portuguese, Catalon, and
        Basque.* London: Faber and Faber.
Fauquenoy, Marguerite Saint Jacques
1972   *Analyse structurale du créole guyanais.* Paris: Klincksieck.
Frake, C. O.
1971   Lexical origins and semantic structure in Philippine creole
        Spanish. In *Pidginization and creolization of languages,* ed. Dell
        Hymes, pp. 223–42. Cambridge: Cambridge University Press.
Freedman, Maurice
1973   *Social and Cultural Anthropology.* UNESCO.
Goeje, C. H. de
1939   Nouvel examen des langues des Antilles. *Journal de la Société
        des Américanistes de Paris,* n.s. 31: 1–120.
1946   *Etudes linguistiques caraïbes.* Vol. 2. Amsterdam: North Holland
        Publishing Co.

Goilo, Enrique R.
1953   *Gramatica Papiamentu.* Curaçao: Hollandsche Boekhandel.
Goodman, Morris F.
1958   On the phonemics of the French Creole of Trinidad. *Word* 14: 208–12.
1964   *A comparative study of Creole French dialects.* The Hague: Mouton.
Hakluyt, Richard
1903–5 *The principal navigations, voyages, traffiques, and discoveries of the English nation.* 12 vols. Glasgow: J. MacLehose.
Hall, Robert A., Jr.
1953   *Haitian Creole: grammar, texts, vocabulary.* American Anthropological Association, memoir 74.
1966   *Pidgin and creole languages.* Ithaca: Cornell University Press.
Hancock, Ian F.
1969   A provisional comparison of the English-based Atlantic creoles. *African Language Review* 8: 7–72.
n.d.   The Malacca Creoles and their language. *Afrasian* 3.
Henderson, Alexander
1872   Grammar and dictionary of the Karif language of Honduras. BAE, Smithsonian Institution, MS 1090.
Herlein, J. D.
1718   *Beschrijvinge van de volk-plantinge Zuriname.* Leeuwarden: Meindert Injema.
Herskovits, Melville
1930/31 On the provenience of the Portuguese in Saramacca Tongo. *De West-Indische Gids* 12: 545–57.
Herskovits, Melville J., and Herskovits, Frances S.
1958   *Dahomean narrative.* Evanston: Northwestern University Press.
Hesseling, Dirk Christiaan
1905   *Het Negerhollands der Deense Antillen.* Leiden: A. W. Sijthoff.
Hildebrandt, Martha
1963   *Diccionario guajiro-español.* Caracas.
Hoff, B. J.
1968   *The Carib language.* The Hague: Martinus Nijhoff.
Holmer, Nils
1949   Goajiro (Arawak), I–IV. *International Journal of American Linguistics* 15: 45–56, 110–20, 145–57, 232–35.
Horth, Auguste
1949   *Le Patois guyanais.* Cayenne.
Hurault, J.
1965   *La vie matérielle des Noirs Réfugiés Boni et des Indiens Wayana du Haut Maroni.* Paris: ORSTOM.
Huttar, George
1972   A comparative word list for Djuka. In *Languages of the Guianas,* ed. Joseph E. Grimes. Norman, Okla.: Summer Institute of Linguistics of the University of Oklahoma.

274 REFERENCES

Hymes, Dell
1971   Introduction to section III. In *Pidginization and creolization of languages*, ed. Dell Hymes, pp. 65–90. Cambridge: Cambridge University Press.
Josselin de Jong, J. P. B. de
1924   *Het Negerhollandsch van St. Thomas en St. Jan.* Amsterdam.
1926   *Het huidige Negerhollands.* Amsterdam.
Jourdain, Elodie
1956   *Du français aux parlers créoles.* Paris: Klincksieck.
Labov, William
1971   The notion of "system" in creole languages. In *Pidginization and creolization of languages*, ed. Dell Hymes, pp. 447–72. Cambridge: Cambridge University Press.
Laet, Joannes de
1625   *Nieuw Wereldt ofte Beschrijvinghe van West-Indien enz.* Leyden: I. Elzevier.
1640   *L'histoire du nouveau monde ou description des Indes Occidentales.* Leyden: B. & A. Elseviers.
Lane, George S.
1935   Notes on Louisiana French, II: Negro French dialect. *Language* 11: 5–16.
Le Page, R. B.
1957/58 General outline of creole English dialects in the British Caribbean. *Orbis* 6: 373–91; 7: 54–64.
1967   Review of R. A. Hall, *Pidgin and creole languages. Journal of African Languages* 6: 83–86
Le Page, R. B., and DeCamp, David
1960   *Jamaican Creole.* Creole Language Studies, I. London: MacMillan.
Lovén, Sven
1933   *Origins of Tainan Culture, West Indies.* 2nd ed. rev. Göteborg: Elanders boktryckeri aktiebolag.
McQuown, N. A.
1955   The indigenous languages of Latin America. *American Anthropologist* 57: 501–70.
Marbot, François
1931   *Les Bambous.* Paris: J. Peyronnet.
Mintz, S. W.
1971   The socio-historical background to pidginization and creolization. In *Pidginization and creolization of languages*, ed. Dell Hymes, pp. 481–96. Cambridge: Cambridge University Press.
Morgan, R.
1959   Structural sketch of St. Martin Creole. *Anthropological Linguistics* 1: 20–24f.
Navarrete, Martin Fernández de
1825–37 *Colección de los viages y descubrimientos que hicieron por mar los Españoles desde fines del siglo XV. Segunda viaje.* Madrid: Imprenta Real.

Noble, Kingsley G.
1965   *Proto-Arawakan and its descendants.* Bloomington: Indiana University.

Ober, Frederick
1877   Wordlists of Dominican and Vincentian (Island) Carib. BAE, Smithsonian Institution, MS 1084.
1879   Ornithological exploration of the Caribbee Islands. *Annual Report of the Smithsonian Institution*, pp. 446–51.
1880   *Camps in the Caribbees.* Boston: Lee and Shepard.
1895   The Aborigines of the West Indies. *Proceedings of the American Antiquarian Society* 9: 270–313.

Osborn, Henry A.
1962   Warao phonology and morphology. Ph.D. dissertation, Indiana University.

Peasgood, Edward T.
1972   Carib phonology. In *Languages of the Guianas*, ed. Joseph E. Grimes, pp. 35–41. Norman, Okla.: Summer Institute of Linguistics of the University of Oklahoma.

Pelleprat, Pierre
1655a   *Introduction a la langue des Galibis.* Paris: S. & G. Cramoisy.
1655b   *Relation des missions des pp. de la Compagnie de Jesus.* Paris: S. & G. Cramoisy.

Raleigh, Sir Walter
1596   *The Discoverie of the large, rich, and bewtiful empyre of Gviana.* Reproduced by the Scolar Press Limited, Leeds, England, 1967.

Rat, J. N.
1898   The Carib language as now spoken in Dominica, West Indies. *Journal of the Anthropological Institute of Great Britain and Ireland* 27: 293–315.

Reisman, Karl
1968   Linguistic values and cultural values in an Antiguan village. Unpublished ms. distributed at 1970 Jamaica Conference on Creole Languages.

Rennard, Joseph
1929   *Les Caraïbes; La Guadeloupe ... d'aprés les relations du R. P. Breton*, Paris: Ficker.

Renselaar, H. C., and Voorhoeve, Jan
1962   Rapport over een ethnologische studiereis naar Mata. *Bijdragen tot de taal-, land- en volkendunde* 118: 328–61.

Robertson, Ian.
1976   A preliminary wordlist of Berbice Dutch [Creole]. Paper read at the August 1976 Conference of the Society for Caribbean Linguistics at the University of Guyana. Mimeographed.

Roth, Walter E.
1915   An inquiry into the animism and folklore of the Guiana Indians. In *30th annual report of the Bureau of American Ethnology, 1908–9*, pp. 103–386. Washington, D.C.

Rouse, Irving
1960   *The entry of man into the West Indies.* Papers in Caribbean Anthropology, no. 6.
1964   Prehistory of the West Indies. *Science* 144: 499–513.

Rowe, C. G., and Horth, A.
1951   Dolos: Creole proverbs of French Guiana. *Journal of American Folklore* 64: 253–64.

Rowlands, Evan Celyn
1969   *Teach yourself Yoruba.* London: English University Press.

Saint Quentin, Alfred et Auguste de
1872   *Introduction à l'histoire de Cayenne . . .* , by Alfred de St. Quentin. *Étude sur le grammaire créole*, by Auguste de St. Quentin. Antibes: J. Marchand.

Schuchardt, Hugo
1914   *Die Sprache der Saramakkaneger in Surinam.* Verhandelingen der Koninklijke Akademie van Wetenschappen te Amsterdam, 14(6). Amsterdam: Johannes Müller.

Schumann, C. L.
1778   Saramaccanisch Deutsches Wörter-Buch: Zuzammen getragen von C. L. Schumann, Bambeij im Jahr 1778. In Hugo Schuchardt, *Die Sprache der Saramakkaneger in Surinam* (q.v.), pp. 46–116.
1783   Neger-Englisches Wörter-Buch. Unpublished ms. Paramaribo.

Sprauve, Gilbert A.
1976   Chronological implications of discontinuity in spoken and written Dutch Creole. Paper read at the August 1976 Conference of the Society for Caribbean Linguistics at the University of Guyana. Mimeographed.

Stewart, William
1962   Creole languages in the Caribbean. In *Study of the role of second languages in Asia, Africa, and Latin America*, ed. Frank L. A. Rice, pp. 34–53. Washington, D.C.: Center for Applied Linguistics.

Swadesh, Morris
1966   *El languaje y la vida humana.* Mexico: Fondo de Cultura Económica.

Sylvain, Suzanne
1936   *Le créole Haitien: morphologie et syntaxe.* Port au Prince.

Taylor, Douglas R.
1947   Phonemes of Caribbean Creole. *Word* 3: 173–79.
1951a   *The Black Carib of British Honduras.* Viking Fund Publications in Anthropology, 17. New York: Wenner-Gren Foundation.
1951b   Structural outline of Caribbean Creole. *Word* 7: 43–59.
1952   Tales and legends of the Dominica Caribs. *Journal of American Folklore* 65: 267–79.
1955   Phonemes of the Hopkins (British Honduras) dialect of Island-Carib (Island-Carib, I). *International Journal of American Linguistics* 21: 233–41.

1956a   Island-Carib, II: word classes, affixes, verbs, nouns. *International Journal of American Linguistics* 22: 1–44.

1956b   Island-Carib, III: locators, particles. *International Journal of American Linguistics* 22: 138–50.

1956c   Language contacts in the West Indies. *Word* 12: 399–414.

1956d   Languages and ghost-languages of the West Indies. *International Journal of American Linguistics* 22: 180–83.

1957   Languages and ghost-languages of the West Indies: a postscript. *International Journal of American Linguistics* 23: 114–16.

1958a   Compounds and comparison. *International Journal of American Linguistics* 24: 77–79.

1958b   Island-Carib, IV: syntactic notes, texts. *International Journal of American Linguistics* 24: 36–60.

1958c   Use and disuse of languages in the West Indies. *Caribbean Quarterly* 5(2): 67–77.

1960a   Compounds and comparison again. *International Journal of American Linguistics* 26: 252–56.

1960b   Some remarks on the spelling and formation of Taino words. *International Journal of American Linguistics* 26: 345–48.

1961a   New languages for old in the West Indies. *Comparative Studies in Society and History* 3: 277–88.

1961b   Some remarks on teknonymy in Arawakan. *International Journal of American Linguistics* 27: 76–80.

1962a   Le créole de la Dominique. In *Encyclopédie de la Pléiade: Language*, pp. 1022–49. Paris: Gallimard.

1962b   Lexical borrowing in Island-Carib. *Romance Philology* 16: 143–52.

1963   The origin of West Indian creole languages: evidence from grammatical categories. *American Anthropologist* 65: 800–814.

1969a   Consonantal correspondence and loss in Northern Arawakan. *Word* 25: 275–88.

1969b   A preliminary view of Arawak phonology. *International Journal of American Linguistics* 35: 234–38.

1970a   Arawak grammatical categories and translation. *International Journal of American Linguistics* 36: 199–204.

1970b   The postpositions of Arawak. *International Journal of American Linguistics* 36: 31–37.

Thomas, J. J.
1869   *The theory and practice of creole grammar.* Port of Spain. (Reprinted ed., London, 1969.)

Thomas, Léon
1953   La Dominique et les derniers Caraïbes insulaires. *Cahiers d'Outre-mer* 6: 37–60.

Thompson, R. W.
1961   A note on some possible affinities between the creole dialects of the Old World and those of the new. In *Creole Language Studies, II*, ed. R. B. Le Page, pp. 107–13. London: MacMillan.

278 REFERENCES

Valkhoff, M. F.
1960   Contributions to the study of creole. *African Studies* 19(2): 77–87.
1966   *Studies in Portuguese and Creole, with special reference to South Africa.* Johannesburg.
Vazquez de Espinosa, Antonio
1948   *Compendio y descripción de las Indias Occidentales*, ed. Charles Upson Clark. Washington: Smithsonian Institution.
Voorhoeve, Jan
1957   The verbal system of Sranan. *Lingua* 6: 374–96.
1959   An orthography for Saramaccan. *Word* 15: 436–45.
1961a   A project for the study of creole language history in Suriname. In *Creole Language Studies, II*, ed. R. B. Le Page, pp. 99–106. London: MacMillan.
1961b   Le ton et la grammaire dans le Saramaccan. *Word* 17: 146–63.
1962   *Sranan Syntax.* Amsterdam: North Holland Publishing Co.
1970   The regularity of sound correspondences in a creole language (Sranan). *Journal of African Languages* 9: 51–69.
1973   Historical and linguistic evidence in favour of the relexification theory in the formation of creoles. *Language in Society* 2: 133–45.
Voorhoeve, Jan and Lichtveld, Ursy, eds., with Eng. trans. by Verney February
1975   *Creole Drum: an anthology.* New Haven: Yale University Press.
Warner, George Frederick, ed.
1899   *The voyage of Robert Dudley . . . to the West Indies, 1594–1595, narrated by Capt. Wyatt, by himself, and by Abram Kendall, master.* London: Hakluyt Society.
Weinreich, Uriel
1953   *Languages in contact.* New York: Linguistic Circle of New York.
1958   On the compatability of genetic relationship and convergent development. *Word* 14: 374–79.
Whinnom, Keith
1956   *Spanish contact vernaculars in the Philippine Islands.* Hong Kong.
Wijk, H. L. A. van
1958   Origenes y evolución del papiamentu. *Neophilologus* 42: 169–82.
Wilbert, Johannes
1965   *Warao Oral Literature.* Caracas: Editorial Sucre.
1970   *Folk literature of the Warao Indians.* Los Angeles: UCLA Latin America Center.
Wilson, James L. et al.
1964   *Introductory Krio language training manual.* Bloomington: Indiana University.
Wilson, William André Auquier
1962   *The Crioulo of Guiné.* Johannesburg: Witwaterstrand University Press.
Young, William
1795   Journal of a voyage undertaken in 1792. In *History of the British West Indies*, ed. Bryan Edwards, 3: 259–301. London.

The Johns Hopkins University Press. *This book was composed in Monotype Times Roman text and display type by William Clowes & Sons Ltd. from a design by Susan Bishop. It was printed on 50-lb. Publishers Eggshell Wove paper and bound in Joanna Arrestox cloth by Universal Lithographers, Inc.*

Library of Congress Cataloging in Publication Data

Taylor, Douglas MacRae.
  Languages of the West Indies.

  (Johns Hopkins studies in Atlantic history and culture)
  Includes bibliographical references and index.
  1. Indians of the West Indies—Languages. 2. Island Carib language.
3. Creole dialects—Caribbean area. I. Title. II. Series.

PM6239.T3   409'.729   76-47382
ISBN 0-8018-1729-3